MISSIONS
IN A NEW
MILLENNIUM

MISSIONS
IN A NEW
MILLENNIUM

Change and Challenges
in World Missions

W. EDWARD GLENNY
and WILLIAM H. SMALLMAN
GENERAL EDITORS

kregel
PUBLICATIONS

Grand Rapids, MI 49501

Missions in a New Millennium: Change and Challenges in World Missions

© 2000 by W. Edward Glenny and William H. Smallman

Published by Kregel Publications, a division of Kregel, Inc., P.O. Box 2607, Grand Rapids, MI 49501. Kregel Publications provides trusted, biblical publications for Christian growth and service. Your comments and suggestions are valued.

For more information about Kregel Publications, visit our web site: www.kregel.com

Coverphotos: © by PhotoDisc, Inc.

ISBN 0-8254-2698-7

Printed in the United States of America

1 2 3 4 5 / 04 03 02 01 00

To C. Raymond Buck

From beginning to end, Christian mission is God's mission. God chooses, equips, sends, and empowers His servants to do His work. C. Raymond Buck is one of God's choice servants, and the imprint of God's hand has been evident at every stage of his life.

Raymond was born in Wichita, Kansas, on September 11, 1924. God gave him spiritual life when he was born again at the age of nine, and God began to call him to ministry during a Sunday morning service when he was a young boy of twelve. This call persisted until, at the age of eighteen, Raymond submitted. After a short stint in the military, Raymond was granted a medical discharge. At the age of eighteen, he was free to enter Ottawa University as a ministerial student. He pastored and ministered intensively while at university, and on September 20, 1944, he was ordained. The following year, on January 28, he married his life's partner, Catherine.

In the next nine years God enabled Raymond to finish three seminary degrees (B.D., M.R.E., Th.M.) and pastor four churches. During this same period God also directed the Bucks to go to French Equitorial Africa (now called the Central African Republic) with Baptist Mid-Missions. The Bucks gave themselves to the training of national leaders in Central Africa from 1955–64, and all four of their children spent part of their lives in that country. After 1964 they were not allowed to return there because of Raymond's illness.

God had other plans. He led Raymond back into the pastorate and a Ph.D. program in education at the University of Kansas. Raymond finished this degree in 1967, and in 1968 he accepted an invitation to join the administration of Baptist Mid-Missions as deputation secretary. He then served as field administrator for Europe and Africa until he was named president of the mission in 1983, a position he held until he retired on December 31, 1989.

Although Raymond retired from the mission, he did not retire from the Lord's work. He and Catherine moved to Minneapolis, Minnesota, where God used him in the classrooms, chapel, and hallways of Central Baptist Seminary to encourage young men and women to serve the Lord of the Harvest. He completed a decade as professor and chairman of the Department of Missions and Evangelism at Central Baptist Seminary.

This collection of essays is dedicated to Dr. C. Raymond Buck. All the writers contributing to this volume have had the distinct privilege of serving with Dr. Buck either in Baptist Mid-Missions (in Africa or Cleveland) or at Central Baptist Seminary. We wish to honor him because we believe he is worthy of honor. And in honoring him, we believe we are honoring the God who chose, equipped, sent, and empowered him.

CONTENTS

SECTION THREE: STRATEGIC STUDIES

PREFACE

There are too many caricatures of "the good old days" in the halcyon days of missions. Dedicated people seemed to get on a boat and sail away for a lifetime of untiring service, to retire on their laurels if they did not die in harness. In reality, life on the mission field was then as complicated as it is now, though there were different chuckholes in the road in colonial times. Missionary service is not more complex; our study of it has become more detailed. From the vantage of three generations of Western missionaries we have analyzed and categorized and theorized and intellectualized the missionary process. At heart, however, it is still the same: Spirit-filled men and women are sent out by their churches to win people, and peoples, to Christ and gather them into churches that perpetuate and propagate the biblical message of the sending church in appropriate cultural dress.

That simple formula plays out with incredible variants in different cultures that receive the impact of the gospel. Many of the theological, exegetical, historical, cultural, and tactical dimensions of missions are spread out before us here in a sampling of issues that must be addressed by today's missionary. Instead of paganism and colonialism, the modern missionary faces pluralism, postmodernism, selfism, boomerism, ecumenism, new ageism, charismatism, humanism, and a host of other "isms that ought to be was'ms," to borrow a phrase. No one person masters all of these issues, so we call on a panel of experts.

You are about to enter an extended conversation with sixteen people who have never all been in the same room at the same time. Many of them have never met each other. The threads that bind them together are fine and strong: All are independent Baptists. All have a passion for missionary work, though many have not been in full-time service as missionaries. All have been colleagues of C. Raymond Buck, Ph.D., either in his years with Baptist Mid-Missions or his years with Central Baptist Theological Seminary, and write these chapters in his honor. You will meet Dr. Buck shortly.

9

This august body of ministry trainers and practitioners is hardly a body. They have not interacted with each other, except as the editors partitioned off territories for treatment. They have not critiqued one another's work, an exercise which would have enriched and complicated the work. Each contributor has been singled out by the editors for his or her friendship with Dr. Buck and capacity to contribute a chapter to a seminary textbook on issues in contemporary missiology. For all that, their oneness of mind is as remarkable as the variety in technical levels and viewpoints on debatable issues.

W. EDWARD GLENNY

CONTRIBUTORS

Leigh E. Adams, B.S.E., Th.M., is president of Fellowship of Missions and the retired vice-president of Baptist Mid-Missions.

Kevin T. Bauder, Th.M., D.Min., is associate professor of Systematic and Historical Theology at Central Baptist Theological Seminary, Plymouth, Minnesota.

Roy E. Beacham, B.A., M.Div., Th.D., is professor of Old Testament Studies and chairman of the Old Testament Department at Central Baptist Theological Seminary, Plymouth, Minnesota.

Daniel Keith Davey, B.S., M.Div., Th.M., Th.D., is senior pastor of Colonial Baptist Church and president of Central Baptist Theological Seminary in Virginia Beach, Virginia.

W. Edward Glenny, B.A., M.A., M.Div., Th.M., Th.D., Ph.D. (candidate), was formerly director of Postgraduate Studies and professor of New Testament at Central Baptist Seminary and is now professor of Biblical Studies and New Testament at Northwestern College, St. Paul, Minnesota.

Michael A. Grisanti, B.A., M.Div., Th.M., Ph.D., was formerly professor of Old Testament at Central Baptist Seminary and now is associate professor of Old Testament at The Master's Seminary, Newhall, California.

Charles A. Hauser Jr., B.B.A., Th.M., Th.D., is dean and professor of Bible Exposition, Central Baptist Theological Seminary, Plymouth, Minnesota.

Clinton W. Kaufield, B.R.E., M.A., Ed.D., was vice president of Academic Affairs at Baptist Bible College of Indianapolis (Indiana) and has served with Baptist Mid-Missions since 1977.

Douglas R. McLachlan, B.A., M.Div., D.D., is the pastor of Fourth Baptist Church, Plymouth, Minnesota, and is president of Central Baptist Seminary in Plymouth.

Robert W. Milliman, B.S., B.A., M.Div., Th.M., Th.D., is assistant to the dean and associate professor of New Testament at Central Baptist Theological Seminary, Plymouth, Minnesota.

David W. Ronan, B.A., M.Div., Ph.D., is adjunct professor at Asian Baptist Theological Seminary and a church planter in Japan.

William H. Smallman, B.S., M.Div., M.A., D.Miss., is first vice president of Baptist Mid-Missions, Cleveland, Ohio, and adjunct professor of Missiology at several Baptist seminaries including Central Baptist Seminary, Plymouth, Minnesota.

John E. Stauffacher, B.A., Th.M., Ph.D., is a church planting missionary with Baptist Mid-Missions and professor of Church History at the French Baptist Pastoral Institute, Algrange, France.

Polly Strong, B.R.E., B.A., M.A., is the author of several books in English, Sango, and French. She has served for twenty-five years with Baptist Mid-Missions in the Central African Republic.

Gerald K. Webber, B.A., M.Div., D.D., is president of Continental Baptist Missions after serving with Baptist Mid-Missions.

Michael H. Windsor, B.A., M.A., M.L.I.S., M.Div., Th.M., Th.D., is professor of Historical Theology and director of Library Services at Central Baptist Theological Seminary of Virginia Beach, Virginia.

MISSIONS
IN A NEW
MILLENNIUM

INTRODUCTION

1

WILLIAM H. SMALLMAN

MISSIONS— PERSONNEL WITH PURPOSE

A Survey of Contemporary Missions Principles

M issionary service comprises not just principles but people, people who have been transformed by the power of the gospel, and who share that inestimably good news with those who might have no other chance to hear it. In the ministry of missions, the church sends out its messengers for the purposeful communication of the gospel, across cultural and geographical boundaries, in order to establish self-reproducing churches among all peoples for the glory of the one and only Savior.

This brief survey of contemporary missiological principles will focus on those involved in missions, whether they be people targeted for evangelism, partners involved in missionary teams, or personnel in training for missionary service. Through missions, the Incarnate One makes Himself known through His new body, the church, embodying and empowering His presence in the lost world.

I. People Groups

Today there are at least 4 billion people who don't consider themselves "Christian," nearly half of whom have never even meaningfully heard of Jesus Christ. They could form a line that would circle the globe at the equator twenty-five times, marching tirelessly toward hell. These unreached peoples are our primary task and target.

There are well over twelve thousand identifiable groups of people in the world today. These may be tribes, minorities within majority populations, or majority populations themselves, subdivided to levels of ethnic origin and consciousness. For example, my great-grandfather was Irish, but I don't live out my Irish cultural identity in a primary social group, so I'm generic WASP instead of "Irish-American." Missions researchers have focused on those groups that have over ten thousand persons, among whom less than 2 percent are evangelical believers in Christ. This narrows the field to 1,739 unreached people groups as the primary target for cross-cultural missionary outreach in the twenty-first century.

A. Worlds for Evangelism

Missions research leader Dr. David Barrett has divided the world's population, with respect to the gospel, using estimated population figures of the year 2000.[1]

World A: The Unevangelized World (25.7 Percent of the World)

These 1.56 billion souls have limited or no access to the gospel and are primarily those listed in the people groups and affinity groups within and beyond the 10/40 Window. The major blocs are Islamic, Hindu, Buddhist, and other Asian faiths, and traditional tribal (animistic) religions. Numerous sects and spin-off groups consider themselves to be a part of these major world religions, though they follow some particular leader or principle not recognized by the rest.

World B: The Evangelized Non-Christian World (41.28 Percent of the World)

These 2.5 billion souls do not call themselves Christians but have access to the gospel since they live in contact with those who identify themselves as Christians. They are the minority and immigrant populations in the Western world that retain their traditional faiths among a majority of professing Christians. For example, most of the world's Jews and non-religious secularists live among professing Christian populations.

World C: The Christian World (33.02 Percent of the World)

These 2 billion souls identify themselves as Christians in one of four major categories: Roman Catholic, Eastern Orthodox, Protestant, and cults or splinter sects that consider themselves Christians, though they remain outside the establishment. Protestants can be further subdivided into ecumenical and evangelical, with further distinctions among evangelicals as fundamentalist evangelicals, conservative evangelicals, neo-evangelicals, and the Pentecostal and charismatic movements (which cross many of the other lines as well). Estimates of the number of truly born-again Christians, inside and beyond evangelical churches, range from 6 percent to 11 percent of the world's population, depending on definitions. Other crossover groups include the conciliar evangelicals (evangelical believers who are members of churches in the World Council of Churches) and evangelical Catholics.

B. 10/40 Window

Luis Bush of Argentina, the CEO of A.D. 2000 and Beyond, has defined and promoted a specific window on the world of the lost.[2] This "window" is the area between 10 and 40 degrees north latitude, from the western tip of Africa to the eastern extreme of Japan. Within that 10/40 Window are found (in 1998)

- 62 nations, in their entirety or in significant parts.
- 3.4 billion people, comprising about 59 percent of the world's population.
- 97 percent of the least evangelized people groups.
- home bases for the majority of Hindus, Buddhists (with Confucionist, Jainist, and other syncretistic Asian faiths), Muslims, and formally non-religious people.
- 81 percent of the most desperately poor people of the world.
- 8 percent of the world's evangelical cross-cultural missionaries.
- 1 percent of missionary expenditure.

C. Affinity Blocs

In order to categorize the 1,739 unreached people groups, the Joshua Project has divided them into thirteen Affinity Blocs.[3] An Affinity Bloc is a broad grouping of people with similar languages, cultures, religions, and politics. Every bloc may also contain widely dissimilar and unrelated linguistic minorities, but often there is one particular culture that is dominant. The current listing of affinity groups identified by the Joshua Project 2000 shows the inherent logic of the categories. They are listed here in alphabetical order:

- **Arab World:** North Africa down to the Sudan, connected to the Middle East across to Iraq, where Arabic is the dominant language

- **Cushitic Horn of Africa:** East Africa under the Arabian Peninsula, with Somali, Afar, and other peoples
- **Eurasian:** Various people groups of the former Yugoslavia, the Caucasus, and Russia
- **Indian South Asian:** Aryan, Dravidian, and tribal peoples of the vast Indian subcontinent, predominantly Hindu
- **Indo-Iranian Southwest Asian:** Kurds, Persians, most Afghans, Pakistanis, and so on. Islam dominates
- **Jewish:** Jewish peoples in Israel and as minority populations in the Diaspora, both religious and nonobservant
- **Malayo-Polynesian:** The Malay peoples of Malaysia, the Philippines, and Indonesia and scattered Polynesian peoples around the Pacific
- **Sahel African:** Wide variety of peoples in Sub-Saharan Africa, including clusters of Hausa, Nubian, and others
- **Sinitic:** Ethnic Chinese in and beyond their mainland home, the Han Chinese majority
- **Tibetan-Himalayan Asian:** Mongolians, Tibetans, Burmese, Koreans, Japanese, and others influenced by Chinese culture
- **Southeast Asian:** Thai/Dai peoples of Southeast Asia, China, and Northeast India, with other Southeast Asian mainland people groups
- **Turkic:** Turkic people groups scattered from Southeast Europe across into China
- **Non-10/40 Window:** This is a special category since twelve of the thirteen Affinity Blocs fall within the 10/40 Window! This category covers the groups of more than ten thousand people, under 2 percent of which are evangelical, located outside the Window, including tribal groups in Central and South America, central and southern Africa, the northern latitude tribal peoples, Papua-New Guinea, and other aborigines.

1. Gateway People Clusters (GPCs)

Certain people groups are similar to one another and form cultural clusters, whether or not they are contiguous geographically. The similarities are based on language, culture, religion, or economic system. Most GPCs embrace at least 1 million persons. Among such clusters are certain people groups that serve as gateways to other related groups and are thus important to mission strategy in those regions.

2. Gateway Cities

Within the 10/40 Window, one hundred cities have been identified as the most likely or practical points of entry into their countries. These have become the targets of concerted prayer efforts seeking to overthrow the spiritual strongholds that have held those populations in bondage to the forces of satanic religion and irreligion.[4]

3. Priority Ranking

The Joshua Project 2000 has a system of quantifying the evangelistic need of a people group by giving weight to five factors:[5]

• Percent of evangelical population	30% weight
• Church status	25%
• Availability of Scripture, radio, etc.	20%
• Mission work among them	15%
• Population size	10%

The people groups with the lowest numbers are given the highest priority for new missionary effort among them.

D. Evangelism Types

Since the 1974 Lausanne Conference on World Evangelization, nomenclature for the relationships between the evangelists and those they evangelize has become common currency in missionary literature and strategy.[6]

- E-0 *Evangelizing those already within gospel-preaching churches.* These include the children of believers raised in the church and professing believers who discover they have never truly repented and trusted in Christ. The evangelist is regarded as an *insider*.
- E-1 *Evangelizing those of one's own culture group.* Homoethnic evangelism is always the most effective type. People will listen to their peers with more sincere attention than they will to foreigners, whether of high or low prestige. Such witnesses are seen as *equals* within the general societal structures.
- E-2 *Evangelizing those of a different but similar culture.* The vast majority of cross-cultural missionaries go into heteroethnic ministry and have to make their way across cultural and

linguistic barriers to effectively minister the gospel. They are always looked upon as *foreigners,* whether their standing is low or high in the host culture.

- E-3 *Evangelizing those of a radically different culture.* E-2 and E-3 are different only in degree; as the gap widens between cultures, there is less language and lifestyle held in common. These messengers are regarded as *strange.*
- E-4 *Evangelizing those of a culture that is hostile to the gospel.* Some people are taught to distrust or hate the messengers of the gospel, so these evangelizers must overcome the perception of being *enemies* to the people or harmful to the culture.

The gap is not between a Western viewpoint and the viewpoint of those being evangelized, but between the evangelist's cultural base and that of the evangelized. So Japanese witnessing to Japanese in São Paulo experience E-1 evangelism, and they experience E-3 evangelism when they turn to their Brazilian neighbors.

II. Partnership Models

Missions is not a solo work but a symphony, demanding the harmonious creativity of many players. This cooperative effort calls for input from people of many nations and several generations.

A. Stages in Mission Development

Every church movement develops through phases as it matures. In an exemplary study, Dr. W. Harold Fuller outlines four typical stages of transition as seen in the Africa Inland Church in Kenya, as it moved from the control of the Africa Inland Mission to self-governance.[7] The study provides an excellent model for tracing similar transitions in other mission work. The basic model fits a village ministry in technologically primitive settings or an urban ministry with well-educated nationals.[8]

1. Pioneer

When the missionaries first arrive on the mission field, they are the full scope of resources for ministry. They take the initiatives, make the decisions, and provide the materials and personnel for all aspects of the ministry. In this stage, the gift of leadership is in demand.

2. Parent

The first converts undergo basic training in Christian life and service under the tutelage of the missionaries. Their immature faith makes them analogous to infants or adolescents in relation to the missionaries who reflect the outcome of generations of Christian influence in their home cultures. The parental missionaries must avoid paternalism as they exercise their gift of teaching.

3. Partner

As the national churches and their leaders become mature and responsible, the missionaries must consciously yield the power for decision making in their churches to them, serving with them as mentors and trainers in a less public way. The change is from a parent-child relationship to an adult-adult relationship.

4. Participant

Once the national churches are in their second and third generation of leaders, they are to control their own churches and the ongoing evangelization of their countries. At this stage, foreign missionaries should be there only at the invitation of the national church leaders, and then only as participants in the work those leaders are directing and designing. Western workers are generally still welcome at this stage, especially for the pioneer work they carry out on the frontiers of evangelized territories and for the resources they bring to the process. They can also prepare to begin the pioneer stage again elsewhere, perhaps in partnership with national missionaries.

B. Supporting National Workers

There is a significant desire among North American churches to direct missionary financing to national workers instead of sending expensive foreign workers. The nationals are seen as more effective, lower in cost, already enculturated, and anxiously awaiting support to accelerate their work of evangelization. Perspective will be gained from a review of the basic principles here.[9]

1. The Richest Churches Can and Must Aid the Poorest

Surely there are ways that the richest churches in the history of the church can help sister churches that struggle with poverty, persecution, and slow development. There are grants to this end among churches in

North America, so the principle of churches helping other more needy churches has already been accepted.

2. Support Must Include Accountability

Blindly tossing money at a problem is destructive. There must be parameters to measure ministry success and cost-effectiveness appropriate to the cultural setting in which church planting and other missionary activities take place. Donors can define the "result" they expect, and seek reports back through the channels that handle the contributions.

We must beware that we do not hold national workers prisoner by supporting them at the lowest socioeconomic level. Churches ask why they should finance costly Americans when they can support national missionaries for fifty dollars per month. That amount, however, covers only subsistence living, with little or nothing for ministry expenses or construction. The incomes and lifestyles of nationals vary, depending on their education, family attributes, and social status expectations. Many tensions can arise between indigenous pastors who struggle along on what their churches can afford and national workers who have their income supplied from outside. There can be further tension between national missionaries in different categories and with different levels of outside support. While it is true that a middle-class Haitian or Indian requires somewhat less than a middle-class American in Haiti or India, expecting nationals to get by on the lowest level of financial support can be a form of ecclesiastical slavery. Nationals who remain loyal to the very people who refuse to pay them at least what they would get from their own compatriots should never be held in this kind of bondage.

Financial support must always include the observance of appropriate social laws. We heard recently of a missionary in South America who generously supported a national worker for about twenty years. When it became necessary to discontinue the support, the national worker turned and sued the mission and the missionary for not paying his social security and retirement all those years! Many countries require employers to pay health insurance and retirement benefits that can equal salary. Such laws should never be ignored by well-meaning Christian organizations.

3. Workers Must Be Identified with Churches of the Same Faith and Order

National workers are to be linked with an established, or nearly established, body of churches that the financial supporters can identify and cooperate with. That is to say, there is little point in supporting autonomous preachers who are not anchored to some fellowship of churches for accountability. A lot of money is thrown away on preachers who will never produce what the contributors expect. Just because we are giving to world evangelization does not mean biblical convictions are to be thrown away. We must never be persuaded to support a ministry "over there" that we would not support at home.

4. Workers Must Not Be Taken Away from the Ministries of Others

The loudest single complaint heard in missions is that often, after years are invested in the training and nurturing of future pastors and missionaries, these same pastors and missionaries are hired away by some other movement. One group does all of the cultivating while another takes the harvest. Yes, "it is all the Lord's work," but that is far easier to say when you get new workers free than when you lose them.

Organizations wishing to support nationals should first train and develop them. One group must not take away the finest of the local workers, removing them from fruitful service, only to deploy them in other ministries. National workers should not be lured away by financial promises since this practice will not increase the effective preaching of the gospel. It merely moves the "market share" about within the various circles of support.

5. Workers Must Have Appropriate Training

Appropriate training is a fluid concept since so much depends on the nature of ministry to be undertaken. It is best for national workers to receive all the training possible within their own church movement, within their own nation, and within their own cultural family of nations before going to a "foreign" environment to be further trained for a particular ministry. Academic levels should be as high as is practical, though there will sometimes be a few nationals who have access to a master's or doctoral level of study outside or within their own countries. Discourage them from training beyond the needs of the ministry, in case they end up in another profession. Under no circumstances is it wise to support those nationals who offer zeal without knowledge, and who are untrained and unequipped for the most arduous of ministries—cross-cultural church planting.

6. Worker Selection Should Be Overseen by Responsible Churches

Foreign missionaries are not always the best judges of character and leadership qualities among members of the society they serve. The leaders of the national churches—and their national missions—should oversee the selection of national missionaries to work in partnership with the foreigners who will be the conduits of support.

7. Support Is Given to or Through National or Foreign Agencies

The best channel for support is a national mission agency or an on-site missionary with a related mission agency to ensure there is equitable distribution. It is important to avoid favoritism, or the autonomy of *prima donna* missionaries. American mission agencies cannot receive and receipt donations designated for personnel who are not their own. They can, however, receive donations for categories of national workers (e.g., "church planters in India," or "scholarships for Brazilian seminary professors") and pass these funds along through established channels for distribution to those who are truly worthy and needy. The information on the outcome of the donations can be passed back along the same web of communication and thereby satisfy the donors that their funds are producing what they intended. Some of those established channels will be the national mission agencies and the nationalized seminaries, now governed by the national churches, that the foreign mission has helped to set up.

8. Foreigners Must Not Allow Money to Weaken Work or Workers

National workers who rely primarily on outside financial support are always in danger of becoming perpetually dependent. A time limit should be set on the financing of church plants, with the expectation that the new church will, at some point, take over responsibility for its own support. We should not support pastors of established churches since that is the duty of the churches themselves. Church plantings can properly be given money during the establishment phase, to help with projects for new church properties, transportation, building, literature, and so on. Dependent ministries, however, will never become indigenous, nor gain the self-identity necessary to persevere in long-term ministry.

If these simple principles are followed, North American support of national workers will produce a far more lasting ministry in the long run. Praise God, there are thousands of worthy national workers to whom funds may be confidently entrusted. There will be mistakes and failures, but the results will be well worth the risks involved.

C. National Mission Agencies

One of the most significant and encouraging trends today is the accelerating emergence of missions founded by churches of the Third World. (The term preferred in such countries is "Two-Thirds World," since this is roughly their population ratio in the world.) A directory of such national missions and missionaries gives hope that their escalating numbers will competently supplement the stagnant number of North American missionaries available.[10]

North American agencies have generally resisted the incorporation of foreign nationals as missionaries to their own countries, or even to other countries. To do so would separate these missionary nationals from the very churches that the process seeks to strengthen. It would inevitably eliminate the best leaders from the national churches, when it is the national churches that the mission intends to build up for long-range continuing ministry. It is preferable, therefore, to encourage the national churches to found and operate their own mission agencies. These agencies then would remain an integral part of the churches and their ministries, with or without the ongoing presence of the missionaries who are the temporary foreign element.

As a prime example, in Brazil the churches that Baptist Mid-Missions associates with in the Brazilian Association of Regular Baptist Churches have established five mission agencies. These are home mission agencies involved in regional church planting in that vast country. At least two of them are already sending Brazilian missionaries across the border or overseas to Uruguay, Colombia, Portugal, Mozambique, and elsewhere. There is more vision than resources for this project just now, but this is the kind of activity the mission seeks to foster.

The most recent reliable statistics and projections on missionaries from the Two-Thirds World indicate dynamic growth:[11]

non-Western missionaries
for 1990: 48,884
for 1995: 89,160
for 2000: 64,230

total missionaries
35.6% of 137,170
45.1% of 197,430
55.5% of 295,952

D. Partnership Models

"Partnership" is more than a contemporary buzzword—it is an integral part of missions in the twenty-first century. It was publicly acknowledged back in 1942 that churches had been established in every nation of the world and that Christianity was the first truly international faith. This was hailed as "the great new fact of our time." A significant number of those receiving churches have come to a sense of their own autonomy, distinct from the governance, and at times convictions, of their founding churches. The Western sending churches are now working in various partnership arrangements with their national counterparts, either during or after the nationalization of the churches.[12]

1. Foreign Missions and National Churches

The classic model for independent mission agencies is one of contact between sending and receiving churches. Missionaries who go to the receiving nations as church planters mediate between the two. The missionaries and the mission leaders are familiar to the national churches, but the sending churches have virtually no direct contact with them beyond an occasional visit to the field. The missions themselves work toward strong national churches based in the receiving nations.

2. Foreign Churches and National Churches

The international denominational model extends the organizational umbrella of the sending churches over the newly formed national churches as daughter churches, and then sister churches, within the denomination. This may also include the extending of benevolence and governance in perpetual foreign control.

A variation on this model is the American megachurch, which functions as its own mission agency, sending its own church personnel as missionaries. The national churches established will have contact with that local church but virtually no others.

3. Foreign Missions and National Missions

A few mission agencies have incorporated national missionaries and administrators into their operations on a par with the Western missionaries, thus internationalizing the mission—but this remains rare. The notable example of this method is New Tribes Mission. The more common, and generally more practical, approach is for the Western foreign mission personnel to help the new national churches organize their own mission agencies to function as an integral part of their own association of churches. The two mission agencies then can share strategy and even resources as sister missions with a common aim. A healthy outgrowth of this model is partnership in church planting, in which a foreign missionary and a national pastor team up to establish a new church, which as soon as possible supports the national worker as its pastor.

4. National Missions and National Missions

Within the nations of the Two-Thirds World, national mission agencies tend to cooperate in partnership far more freely and frequently than did their Western counterparts. They can cooperate across lines of tradition that the founding missionaries would not have crossed, because they are less oriented to those traditions. Their collective mentality and holistic worldview of churches help them to plan missionary service together and execute these plans, even as they build separate families of new churches.

III. Personnel Development

The number of North American missionaries abroad more than doubled in the years from World War II to 1960, but that surge of personnel is now approaching retirement and is not being replaced by a similar surge. From about 1980 the number of North American career missionaries serving overseas remained static, and it is now in slow decline. Much of the slack is being taken up by cross-cultural missionaries sent out by churches of the Two-Thirds World. The Great Commission has not been rescinded, however, and North American churches cannot simply send money, while neglecting to send their men and women.

As churches face the challenges of a new millennium, the problem is not one of sending enough new missionaries but of sending those who are the right kind of people. In this newest phase of missions our priority is not to win souls but to train soul-winners; not to teach people to read doctrine but to encourage them to reflect and write theology out of the heart of their own cultural context; not to plant churches but to develop Christian statesmen who will build their own churches, churches with firm biblical standards and the promise of fruitfulness, churches that will last for generations after the founding missionaries are gone.

A. Missionary Formation

The demands on the missionary of the next millennium are going to be heavier than ever as the world moves into a pluralistic posture, resists the uniqueness of the Christian gospel, stumbles into postmodernity completely unprepared for its chaotic philosophy, and shrugs off its former preference for Western standards. These are not "the good old days" for world missions!

Eight categories of development for new missionary personnel are presented here. They are not in any particular order of priority, and they overlap each other. All of them are vitally important for the missionary of the new millennium.[13]

1. Spiritual Development

The spiritual formation of missionary personnel has been more presumed than demonstrated. No ministry is more demanding or hazardous than that of missionary work. It asks hardy souls to strap a target over their hearts and march into territory long held by the enemy of the Savior. The early Jesuit missionary trainees passed through a rigorous series of Ignatius Loyola's "spiritual exercises" to develop their spiritual sensitivity and theological acuity. After twenty-eight intense days of initiation, divided into five periods of meditation, prayer, and fasting, one could become a novice and suffer two more years of preparatory studies and devotional development.[14] Small wonder that the Society of Jesus rocked the world for the Roman Church. Too much of our present missionary training focuses on the intellectual equipping of future ministers, and too little on the personal, spiritual toughening necessary for the demands of ministry.

Spiritual development must come from within the missionary candidates themselves and include

- personal spiritual discipline in deep fellowship with God,
- victorious living in relation to temptation and obedience,
- pervasive godliness of character and reflection of the inner presence of Christ,
- balanced spiritual warfare and biblical confronting of the occult,
- family life that practices having Christ as head of the home through the husband, and
- personal financial responsibility as a part of spiritual stewardship of all resources for God.

2. Biblical Soundness

There is no substitute for solid training in the knowledge, interpretation, and application of the Scriptures. The Bible is the heart of any missionary ministry. Technical levels of Bible study will vary with the nature of the person's intended ministry. Soundness will include

- basic Bible knowledge—book by book, key verses memorized, key questions answered, biblical history understood;
- theological orientation—Christian doctrine within a system that synthesizes the flow of God's working in the world and in individuals;

- hermeneutics—a system of interpretation in harmony with the theological system that underlies one's basic grasp of the Bible; and
- confidence in the utter perfection of the Bible as God's inerrant Word, and the sufficiency of the Bible as the final resource for ministry to all people.

3. Church Ministry Awareness

Biblical missionary ministry flows from the sending church to the receiving church. The sending church is the foundation and final authority for the missionary on the field. The outcome of missionary ministry should be churches that reproduce, with appropriate cultural variety, the biblical convictions of the sending church. The future missionary will develop an awareness of the local church with regard to

- the local church priority in ministry,
- evangelism as a lifestyle,
- discipleship training and spiritual multiplication, and
- the sending church's denominational distinctives and practices.

4. Cultural Adaptation

Prospective missionaries must comprehend that they are not culturally neutral but are the products of their own culture, with well-defined (if unconscious) ethnic identities, natures, and experiences that will bias them against other cultural values and practices. An awareness of the dimensions of culture in general, including language and religion, will greatly aid appreciation of and adaptation to the host culture. Preparation for such adaptation should include the study of

- cultural anthropology and sociology—the study of peoples and of people, offering categories for understanding the structure and flow of societal life;
- language-learning methodology, articulatory phonetics, becoming bicultural;
- cross-cultural communications and evangelism of people who are different; and
- penetration of a community for God and development of an incarnational attitude.

5. Worldview Interaction

The genius of the cross-cultural missionary is his or her ability to communicate the gospel clearly across the cultural divide. The essential orientation of different peoples can vary widely. It involves their sense of reality, of God, and of self. This basic, internalized set of philosophical presuppositions common to a populace is called its *worldview*. Worldview drives the values of a people, which in turn govern the organizational structures of its social order. If missionaries do not comprehend the worldview of their hosts or, worse yet, do not comprehend that their own worldview colors their message, vital connection and communication will not take place.

Missionaries must be trained to be sensitive to the worldviews of other peoples and to develop the mental agility necessary for comprehending systems of thought with which they do not essentially agree. It is not enough to have our worldview shaped by the Bible if that orientation produces a narrowness incapable of comprehending those who are not so oriented. Some specific studies are prescribed for future missionaries:

- Cross-cultural communications equips one to clarify the message in a new idiom.
- Linguistics and language training are obvious necessities for communication.
- Religious movements and worldview studies in general aid in comprehension of worldview for the targeted field and region, and articulation of the uniqueness of Christ in a pluralistic context.
- Apologetics helps define and defend the gospel before other worldviews.

6. Interpersonal Finesse

The conflicts among missionaries are legendary. But there is an essential closeness and interrelatedness of missionaries who are involved in one another's ministries that home church pastors would not tolerate. The closeness of missionaries to and interdependence on one another is the focus of ministry. This demands training in sensitivity as well as in methodology for cooperation. Helpful preparations include

- interpersonal communications with cross-cultural dimensions,
- interethnic experience in being around those different from oneself,

- Christian diplomacy and conflict resolution, and
- orientation to followership and servanthood.

7. Communications Skills

The essence of ministry is communication, which in turn is based on commonality. Basic skills and attitudes can be developed to empower communicators:

- understanding and analyzing a message in order to express it clearly to others;
- teaching skills, organization of material, presentation for facilitation of learning;
- mastery of pedagogical and andragogical principles, whether or not one is a "teacher"; and
- pulpit presentation of Scripture and one's ministry, whether or not one is a pastor.

8. Managerial Skills

Virtually all missionaries, though followers, are leaders of other people. Fundamental skills in management will prove helpful in churches and institutions as well as within the mission's own structures. Missionaries who have training in key management areas can also help the receiving churches take a proactive stance for the future:

- management skills—leading and directing people in ministry tasks;
- computer skills—using technology within reasonable boundaries;
- teamwork skills—identifying and balancing strengths and weaknesses for team effectiveness; and
- strategic planning and project management for creating the future rather than finding it.

B. Categories of Missionary Personnel Today
1. Traditional Missionaries

In the time since William Carey established conventional missionary service more than two hundred years ago, its patterns have slowly evolved. Full-time personnel are supported financially by churches. The churches send out missionaries through mission agencies, which are either denominational or independent, to plant like-minded churches and to support ministries that accompany and enhance that basic objective.

A full missionary career typically involves thirty to forty years of active service.

2. Nonresidential Missionaries (NRMs)

A nonresidential missionary is a career foreign missionary who is matched up with a single unevangelized population segment for the purpose of initiating and coordinating pioneer evangelization and who lives outside the targeted population centers because legal residence for a missionary is either prohibited or highly restricted.[15]

From the nonresidential base, the NRM networks with all other concerned Christians and organizations to facilitate the establishment of ministry there. Activities include steps to

1. research and survey the situation of that population,
2. become fluent in the population's main language,
3. draw up and implement a range of options and resources for evangelism,
4. report regularly to a home office that monitors progress and sends help as needed,
5. report data to missionary research data networks, and
6. relate as a part of a global team to other NRMs, each of whom is assigned to a different population segment.

3. Tentmaker Missionaries

Tentmaker missionaries, (nonstipendary or self-stipendary missionaries), provide their own financial support through employment in commerce, industry, education, military, or diplomatic service on their fields of service. They follow the model of the apostle Paul, who worked in leather, making tents, pouches, and sandals when there was a lack of support from churches (Acts 18:3; 20:34; 1 Cor. 9:6, 12; 2 Cor. 11:7–9).[16]

The concept of the self-supporting missionary is not new. The definition of such CWOs (or Christians Working Overseas) must include the concept of believers who are working outside their own countries specifically to offer Christian evangelistic witness and who are commissioned for such ministry by their sending churches, whether or not significant financial support is involved.

The general idea is that otherwise closed countries can be targeted for CWO entry, because all nations have doors open for employment. Tentmakers find their own way into the country through their work and then initiate or participate in low-profile outreach ministries with national believers (or missionaries).

Tentmaking, by its very nature, bypasses the conventional mission agency. The workers, for good reasons, do not want to be identified as "missionaries."

1. Advantages for self-stipendiary missionaries:
   a. freedom to enter countries closed to titled missionaries;
   b. non-ministry identity, which sometimes adds credibility to Christian witness. Not being a "paid" representative of the church lends freedom to enter the culture as a friend rather than as an agent;
   c. access to sectors of the society, especially through professional contacts, often closed to "missionaries";
   d. independence from the missionary system and freedom to vary approaches with the opportunities.

2. Disadvantages for self-stipendiary missionaries:
   a. most of one's time and energy going to the employer, not to the ministry;
   b. lack of a network of supportive fellow Christians—a sense of being alone, detached from the missionary community even where there is one nearby;
   c. lack of recognition as missionaries by American churches, who then fail to pray for them;
   d. lack of the systems for language training and cultural orientation;
   e. working in a hostile religious setting and corrosive moral environment; and
   f. loss of tax advantages enjoyed by recognized religious workers.

In 1990 there were an estimated 150,000 tentmakers active around the world, with that number expected to double to 300,000 by the year 2000. Ted Yamamori is still campaigning for 600,000 Christian American tentmakers, whom he calls "God's Special Envoys."[17]

4. Double-Identity Missionaries or Bivocational Witnesses

In countries that do not admit persons identified as "missionaries," or agents of religion under similar titles, Christian witnesses can enter with a different passport identity. Their skills in other professions are in demand within those nations, so they enter to work under a different professional identity and there witness for Christ. They may be physicians, engineers, professors in various fields in universities or other levels of schools, teachers of English, or executives and managers in industry and commerce. This category overlaps with tentmakers in that these workers may also be associated with a missionary organization that presents itself as an agency for services other than religious ones to benefit the populace, and workers may be supported as "missionaries" by the churches that send them.

Many mission agencies have established parallel corporations specifically to create such non-missionary identities. This is not a matter of deceit or duplicity but of taking necessary steps to enter countries otherwise closed to missionaries. It is wise for such parallel corporations to identify themselves openly as Christian in their defining documents to prevent any subsequent "discovery" of their "real" nature and purpose. Governments generally are aware of that double purpose and appreciate not being pressured to react to the religious dimensions of the personnel involved.

C. The New Breed

The missionaries that Western churches seek today are not so much pioneers as partners and participants. Western churches possess the experience and resources to send mentors and trainers who will work to develop national workers and then work through them, with them, and for them before moving on to repeat the process. The new missionaries will derive a sense of success in ministry from the accomplishments of those whom they have trained for ministry rather than from statistics of their own that they send home to results-oriented supporters.

Paul's mission teams rarely stayed more than a few months at any one place although, in the case of the troubled church at Corinth, he stayed as much as two or three years. The apostolic investment of time was remarkably brief compared to the years that modern missionaries spend in one church. Today, the new breed of church planter will, from the beginning, work in partnership with a national copastor who is being groomed to head up the work. The expatriate missionary can quickly switch roles and serve as associate pastor, mentoring the national pastor from behind the scenes.

Missionary service is the most demanding and dynamic enterprise in Christian ministry today. It begins with people being sent out, people reaching people, and people developing people for ministry. The ministry phases can be summarized as "move in, win over, build up, hand over, move on!" Every phase of the model depends on people with the self-emptying attitude of Jesus Christ working through them. When Jesus proclaimed, "I will build my church," He could foresee the key personnel who would carry out that promise, prophecy, and program.

Study Questions

1. Explain the basis of the principle that, when God has a job to do in this world, He uses people to do it.
2. Describe how the identification of Affinity Blocs and Gateway Cities can be useful in the development of missionary strategy.
3. What are two or three basic principles that can be applied when decisions must be made about the support of national workers?
4. Describe how recent decades have seen a deepening of cross-cultural preparation for missionaries. Is this necessary? Do missionaries sent out from churches in the Two-Thirds World also need such cultural orientation? Why or why not?
5. What essential mindset is needed in the new missionaries being sent out from North America in this decade?

Chapter Notes

1. David B. Barrett and Todd M. Johnson, "Annual Statistical Table on Global Mission: 2000," *International Bulletin of Missionary Research* 24, no. 1 (January 2000): 24–25. The designations of World A, B, C were introduced in this series of annual statistical tables in 1991. The characteristics were more fully developed by the same authors in *Our Globe and How to Reach It* (Birmingham Ala.: New Hope, 1990) and in many missions publications since then.
2. Patrick Johnstone, John Hanna, and Marti Smith, eds., *The Unreached Peoples* (Seattle: YWAM, 1996), 14–15, 19. The 10/40 Window is now expounded in most treatments of contemporary missions, for example, Gailyn VanRheenen, *Missions: Biblical Foundations and Contemporary Strategies* (Grand Rapids: Zondervan, 1996), 209–14.
3. Patrick Johnstone, "Affinity Blocs and the Unreached Peoples," in Johnstone, Hanna, and Smith, *Unreached Peoples,* 22–23. That chapter lists only eleven Affinity Blocs, but the website for Joshua Project 2000 has modified the designations somewhat and expanded the listing to the thirteen categories shown here as of 7 April 2000. See www.ad2000.org/peoples/index.htm.

4. A general map is in Johnstone et al., *The Unreached Peoples,* 19. A more detailed map is visible at www.gmi.org/products/pttwiii2.htm.
5. From www.ad2000.org/peoples/prio1.htm.
6. Ralph D. Winter, "The Highest Priority: Cross-Cultural Evangelism," in J. D. Douglas, ed., *Let the Earth Hear His Voice* (Minneapolis: World Wide Publications, 1975), 213–25. This paper presents only E-1, -2, and -3, while he introduces E-0 in the next paper, pp. 230–31, not as sharply defined as in this present chapter. The E-4 category was added later by other missiologists.
7. W. Harold Fuller, *Mission-Church Dynamics* (Pasadena, Calif.: William Carey Library, 1980), appendix G, 272. The diagram effectively summarizes the thrust of this exemplary book.
8. Details of principles and procedures for the nationalization process are developed in this author's forthcoming book *Able to Teach Others Also: Nationalizing Global Ministry Training* (Pasadena, Calif.: William Carey Library, 2000).
9. Additional treatment will be found in Daniel Rickett and Dotsey Welliver, eds., *Supporting Indigenous Ministries,* (Wheaton, Ill.: BGC Monographs, 1997).
10. The most recently published research in this field is listed and summarized in *From Every People,* by Larry D. Pate (MARC, 1989) with directories and very useful analysis.
11. Lawrence E. Keyes and Larry D. Pate, "Two-thirds World Missions: The Next 100 Years," *Missiology* 21, no. 2 (April 1993): 187–206. This data is from p. 190.
12. The four models noted here were partially listed, but richly illustrated, in James H. Kraakevik and Dotsey Welliver eds., *Partners in the Gospel,* (Wheaton, Ill.: BGC Monographs, 1993), xvii–xix. The principles of expatriate-national partnerships are further expounded in two other useful works, William D. Taylor, ed., *Kingdom Partnerships for Synergy in Missions* (Pasadena, Calif.: William Carey Library and WEF Missions Commission, 1994); and Luis Bush and Lorry Lutz, *Partnering in Ministry* (Downers Grove, Ill.: InterVarsity, 1990).
13. This author prepared an earlier version of this listing for discussion at an InterFace consultation for independent Baptist mission agency executives and missions professors at Harrisburg, Pennsylvania, in April 1997.
14. The rigorous spiritual exercises, designed to examine the soul and prepare a novice for the demands of missionary service are described in general terms in John W. O'Malley, *The First Jesuits* (Cambridge, Mass.: Harvard Univ. Press, 1993) and may still be found in some bookstores of the Society

of Jesus. A more accessible summary is found in Alfred Henry Newman, *A Manual of Church History* (Philadelphia: American Baptist Publication Society, 1931), vol. 2, 369–72.

15. Adapted from V. David Garrison, *The Nonresidential Missionary* (Monrovia, Calif.: MARC, 1990), 13.

16. In Acts 18:5 the MT and TR have Paul "burdened," "fully surrounded," or "deeply involved" *[suneixeto]* "in spirit" while the UBS and N-A have "in the word" as the object of that focused concern. This latter would suggest that the arrival of Silas and Timothy with an offering from Philippi allowed Paul to quit his secular occupation for the time being and concentrate his energies on, or "be claimed, totally controlled" by, the ministry of the Word (so reads Gerhard Kittel, *Theological Dictionary of the New Testament* [Grand Rapids: Eerdmans, 1970], vol. 7, 838). The preferred reading here *[en pneumati]* is a commentary on the missionaries' spiritual, not economic, circumstances.

17. Tetsunao Yamamori, *Penetrating Missions' Final Frontier* (Downers Grove, Ill.: InterVarsity, 1993). This book does not report on how many have gone out since his prior book in 1987. He develops the principles for tentmaker ministry, enlarging on the classic work of J. Christy Wilson, *Today's Tentmakers* (Wheaton, Ill.: Tyndale, 1979).

SECTION ONE
BIBLICAL STUDIES

2

MICHAEL A. GRISANTI

THE MISSING MANDATE

Missions in the Old Testament

Is the Old Testament concerned only with lifeless ritual and tedious historical narratives? Does it simply focus on life and culture in the distant past or describe coming eschatological events? Do the first thirty-nine books of the Bible contribute at all to the New Testament emphasis on carrying the gospel to the nation-groups of the world? Most important to this essay, does God ever give His chosen nation, Israel, a mandate to carry out missions?

Volumes have been written dealing with the Old Testament's presentation of a missionary mandate (or the lack of it). Various scholars have described Israel's role and mission with regard to the world as either centripetal (inward moving) or centrifugal (outward moving).[1] Centripetal movement is found in biblical texts that attribute to Israel the role of being a sign and witness, of attracting others. The attracted nations come to the "center"—to Israel (Zion, Jerusalem)—to receive instruction and revelation (Ps. 87; Isa. 2:2–3; 25:6ff.; 55:3b–5; Mic. 4:1–2 et al.). Centrifugal movement describes Israel's active involvement in bringing God's redemptive message to the world. Due to space constraints, this essay cannot provide an overview of that debate.[2]

Both the beginning and end of Scripture emphasize a concern for people of "every nation and tribe and tongue and people" (Rev. 14:6 NASB), forming a grand envelope structure that frames the entire story of Scripture. Genesis 1–11 provides an overview of the origins and prehistory of all humankind, and Revelation ends the canon with a book in which God's purposes are equally related to the whole created order.[3]

This essay focuses on four Old Testament passages (Gen. 1:26–27; 12:1–3; Ex. 19:4–6; Isa. 40–55) that provide a glimpse of God's intentions for the world. Although the Old Testament (in consonance with the New Testament) manifests a worldwide perspective, all of these Old Testament passages demonstrate that the basic appeal was "come" and not "go." Non-Jews were invited to come and see what God was doing with His servant nation, Israel. In the Old Testament there was no widespread sending of God's people out to share the Lord's salvation with all peoples.

Ultimately, mission does not originate with human sources but is rooted in the nature of God.[4] God initiates reconciliation between Himself and His fallen creation. Missions begins in the heart of God. Since Genesis 1:1 opens the Bible with the statement, "In the beginning God . . . ," and since God is the spring from which mission flows, the Old Testament's contribution to this significant endeavor demands attention. The present essay contends that the Old Testament begins the biblical development of mission.[5]

Genesis 1:26–28

God's plan for His creation spans both Testaments and is bracketed by two creations. The Scriptures begin with the creation of the universe (Gen. 1–2) and end with a description of a more glorious creation, that of the new heaven and earth (Rev. 21–22). Yahweh's creation of the universe and all it contains was not for the sake of His handiwork, but for His own purposes. As the apostle Paul writes concerning Christ, "For by him all things were created . . . all things were created by him and *for him*" (Col. 1:16 NIV, emphasis added).

God's Intention to Extend His Rule Throughout the World

A motif that begins in Genesis 1 and continues throughout the Bible is God's intention to extend His rule over all creation. God made man, the crowning jewel of His creation, to function as His image. The statement that the Godhead created man "in our image, in our likeness" (Gen. 1:26) delineates man's function (what he is to be and do) and not merely his essence (what he is like).[6] God created man to serve as His agent for establishing God's sovereign will and sway over the universe.[7] As the image of God, man is to represent God Himself as the sovereign over all creation. Man is to carry out this mediatorial/representative role by means of exercising lordship over all creation (Gen. 1:28–29).[8] Unfortunately, Adam's sin disrupted the accomplishment of Yahweh's intentions for His creation. Adam and Eve's sin marred God's perfect order and initiated the human tendency to rebel against God's rule. No longer would the earth and animal world willingly submit to His direction. Adam's sin disrupted the harmony of all human relationships (with God, with other human beings, with creation). After casting Adam and Eve out of the garden, Yahweh initiated the provision of reconciliation for fallen humankind. It is the salvation provided by this reconciliation that enabled Adam (and humankind) to return to his role as God's vice-regent.

Man's Rebellion and God's Response

This penchant to rebel against God's sovereignty (whether direct or mediated through His representatives) manifests itself in the abhorrent human conduct leading up to the Flood and the rebellion at Babel. God's response to both rebellions was severe judgment (universal flood, worldwide dispersal). In each case one could ask, Does this judgment mean the end of God's redemptive dealings with mankind? Yahweh resolves that tension by raising up other mediators (Noah, Abram) to carry out His purposes for mankind after each judgment. In fact, the textual interwovenness of the narratives describing these rebellions and God's response, with the genealogies in Genesis 5 and 11, carefully delineates the significant role played by these mediatorial figures. These genealogical notices (Gen. 5:32; 11:10–26) link Adam, Noah, and Abram, who were each ten generations apart. This literary pattern identifies these individuals "as single representatives and bearers of the potential for blessing of human life in history."[9]

Genesis 1:26–28 details God's original intention to extend His rule through humankind over all of His creation and His plan to use humankind to function as His vice-regents. Adam and Eve's fall into sin disrupted (but did not prevent) the accomplishment of those intentions and created the need for reconciliation. Among many other things, the rest of the Bible delineates the means by which God will provide that reconciliation and demonstrates the manner in which He will transmit that message of reconciliation to the sinful world.

Genesis 12:1–3

The narrative that immediately precedes Yahweh's call of Abram out of Ur (Gen. 11:27–12:3) delineates God's judgment against His rebellious creatures at Babel (11:1–9). The historical stage onto which

Abram enters appears to be characterized by chaos and rebellion. Once again, Yahweh raises up a special individual to function as His vice-regent and to begin the long-term process of restoring equity and order to the world. More than that, in His choice of Abraham, God singles out a people to carry out that representative role. Genesis 12:1–3 enjoys a strategic location in the immediate context, introducing the subsequent patriarchal accounts and setting them in relation to the record of God's dealings with the whole of humanity in Genesis 1–11. Moberly suggests that this passage provides the worldwide context for the subsequent delineation of Yahweh's purposes for Israel, "whose existence is to be related to YHWH's purposes for the whole world."[10] According to Wright, "God's commitment to Israel is predicated on his commitment to humanity as a whole. The universality of the Bible's mission to the nations is not a NT 'extra,' but integral from the very beginning of God's historical action"[11] (cf. Pss. 22:27; 72:17; Jer. 4:1–2).

The Worldwide Implications of Yahweh's Election of Abraham

God's call for Abram to leave his home in Ur and set out for a land of God's choosing constitutes Yahweh's election of Abraham to father a special people for Himself. In Genesis 12:1–3 (the initial expression of the Abrahamic covenant, restated and developed in subsequent chapters [Gen. 15, 17]), Yahweh delineates His intentions for Abraham and the means by which He will accomplish His purposes for the world.[12] There is both a particularism and a universalism that pervades this covenantal arrangement. As was clear since the creation of mankind, God's intentions encompass the entire world. He will one day establish His rule over all His creation (Gen. 1:26–28). In Genesis 12:1–3 the Lord not only reveals what He will do for Abraham, but He begins to demonstrate the means by which He will address His universal purposes. God will cause Abraham to father a great nation, not for his (or its) sake, but because Abraham (and the nation) will be the means through which Yahweh blesses all nations.

Even the structure of Yahweh's promise to Abraham places emphasis on the worldwide impact of His intentions. Following Yahweh's command that Abraham "leave," four subordinate cohortatives (each prefixed with a conjunction) delineate the intended impact of that command: "I will make you into a great nation and I will bless you; I will make your name great, . . . I will bless those who bless you."[13] The final clause of 12:3, "and all peoples on earth will be blessed through you," interrupts this chain of intent cohortatives. This perfect verb (וְנִבְרְכוּ—prefixed with a *waw* consecutive) sets off the final clause from the preceding chain of cohortatives as the consequence or real result of the departure of Abraham (12:1).[14]

The Meaning of the Verb, "They Will Be Blessed/Bless Themselves"

The *crux interpretum* in this passage concerns the semantic nuance of the *Niphal* perfect verb, וְנִבְרְכוּ. The diversity of the verbal forms of בָּרַךְ in the five statements/restatements of the Abrahamic covenant in Genesis occasion this debate. Each of these statements promises that the nations will experience blessing. Three instances employ a *Niphal* perfect form of the verb (Gen. 12:3; 18:18; 28:14) and two passages utilize a *Hithpael* perfect of בָּרַךְ (Gen. 22:18; 26:4). Scholars wonder why the writer uses a *Niphal* (which is generally passive, but sometimes reflexive) on three occasions and a *Hithpael* (which is usually reflexive) in two other instances.[15] Consequently, various scholars discuss whether the promised experience of blessing by the nations has a passive,[16] reflexive,[17] or receptive[18] nuance.

Reflexive Meaning. The reflexive meaning ("all nations will bless themselves") signifies that God's chosen people will be so blessed by Him that all will wish for a like blessing, and will invoke it upon themselves.[19] The nations will point to Abraham as their ideal. As Martin-Achard writes, "In the eyes of mankind the Patriarch will be the representative of God's human creation crowned with blessing by his God; there is something proverbial about his prosperity."[20] Abraham's name will become a formula of benediction or a proverbial expression of a desire for abundant divine blessing (cf. Gen. 48:20).

Van Groningen prefers the reflexive nuance because he believes that the text "places an obligation or responsibility upon the nations, namely, to respect Abraham and to receive his service."[21] Ross contends that in light of the immediately preceding cohortative ("I will bless those who bless you"), all the families of the earth will bless themselves depending on how they treat Abraham and his seed.[22]

Receptive Meaning. Those who favor the receptive (middle) sense translate the *Niphal* verb "acquire blessing (for) himself, procure himself blessing"[23] or "win for themselves a blessing," "find for themselves a blessing."[24] Emphasis is placed on the nations' procurement of blessings by means of some connection with Abraham.[25] In support of their view, proponents point out that since the *Pual* or *Qal* passive participle is usually employed for the passive of בָּרַךְ, a middle sense is more likely here. Dumbrell posits that the *Niphal* is a medio-passive stem that emphasizes the participants in the action.[26] Dumbrell also argues that the reflexive meaning is "decidedly anti-climactic" in the present context.[27] In Genesis 12:2b Abraham is already held up as an example and particularly as an offset to the tower builders who had sought personal benefit in their own way. It would be natural for the passage to move from Abraham, as an example of blessing to Abraham, as "the focus of blessing, the mediator through whom blessing will reach the world, since in him, as the narrative has made clear, the Babel consequences are to be reversed."[28] Wenham asserts that a receptive understanding of the *Niphal* verb "brings the passage to a triumphant and universal conclusion."[29] Finally, this emphasis on the nations' participation is consonant with the general Old Testament depiction of the nations "as seekers, coming to a reconstituted Israel."[30]

Passive Meaning. Those who identify a passive nuance in all five statements affirm that Genesis 12:1–3 presents Abraham (and his descendants) as God's chosen instrument of blessing the nations. Von Rad asserts that "Abraham is assigned the role of a mediator of blessing in God's saving plan, for 'all the families of the earth.'"[31]

Dumbrell's suggestion that the flow of argument in Genesis 12:1–3 anticipates a movement from Abraham *as an example* to Abraham *as a mediator* supports the passive view as well. In response to those who seek to understand the *Niphal* constructions in light of the normally reflexive *Hithpael,* Waltke and O'Connor cite Genesis 12:3 and 22:18 as examples of the *Niphal* stem mixed with *Hithpael:* "Since the *Hithpael* historically tends to take on the passive function of the *Niphal . . .* it is not surprising that the stems are occasionally confounded."[32] Qumranic Hebrew also, at times, employs the *Hithpael* as a passive (as in Mishnaic Hebrew and Aramaic).[33] Waltke and O'Connor go on to conclude that the "passive import of both verbs is clear from the context: it is God who blesses (Gen. 12:3a; 22:17), that is, who fills the potency for life, albeit through an agent."[34] Finally, in contrast to those who refer to the middle or reflexive notion as the most common significance of the *Niphal,* Waltke and O'Connor affirm that although the *Niphal* does have obvious middle and reflexive categories of meaning, the passive sense is the most common.[35] They delineate the differences between the middle and passive categories, especially significant to the present passage. Waltke and O'Connor suggest that the middle is more "process" oriented and non-agent oriented, while the passive is more "state" oriented and agent oriented.[36]

Sailhamer suggests a unique alternative, contending that the three *Niphal* and two *Hithpael* constructions of בָּרַךְ in Genesis are distinct and are not to be understood identically.[37] He views the *Hithpael* occurrences as iterative in nuance,[38] envisioning the promise with respect to the future "seed," and as signifying that "the blessing will continue (iterative) to be offered to the nations through the seed of Abraham."[39] Although intriguing, Sailhamer's suggestion faces two obstacles. First, these five instances of בָּרַךְ are each found in statements/ restatements of covenantal promises to Abraham and/or his descendants as they relate to the nations. Rather than indicating something unique, the reference to "offspring" simply states the obvious. It is not only through Abraham as an individual but through his descendants that the nations will be blessed. Second, the references to "offspring" (22:18; 26:4; 28:14) all occur after there were Abrahamic descendants.[40] No distinction between the *Niphal* and *Hithpael* constructions naturally arises from the text. Consequently, they should all be translated in the same fashion.

The Theological Significance of Yahweh's Election of Abraham

Some question the significance of this debate. After all, the important point is that Yahweh promises divine blessings to the nations. God's program has worldwide implications and is not limited to Israel. The passage reveals, however, more than the worldwide extent of Yahweh's purposes for His creation.[41] The passive nuance is preferred over the middle, primarily because of its clear stress on instrumentality. It is God's intention to use Abraham to bless the nations—not the nations' procurement of blessing—that stands most prominent in Genesis 12:1–3. This passage delineates God's choice of an instrument through whom He will bless the world. As Hamilton suggests, Genesis 12:3 "clearly articulates the final goal in a divine plan for universal salvation, and Abram is the divinely chosen instrument in the implementation of that plan."[42]

There is a clear linkage between God's first statement of His purpose for humankind (to rule the earth—Gen. 1:26–28) and His election of Abraham as a mediatorial figure. As Merrill concludes, the programmatic statement of the Abrahamic covenant (Gen. 12:1–3) affirms

> in every respect the covenant mandate of Genesis 1:26–28, with the special proviso that Abraham and his descendants were to serve as models of, as well as witnesses to, the implementation on earth. That is, the Abrahamic nation would become a microcosm of the

kingdom of God and would function in that capacity as an agency by which God would reconcile the whole creation to Himself.[43]

Paul's successful ministry among the Gentiles/nations raised the urgent question: "How can Gentile nations be part of the people of God, if membership of that people is defined by circumcision, the Mosaic covenant, and keeping the law?" Paul was forced to justify his mission strategy from the Scriptures and his answer fundamentally was, "Consider Abraham!" (Gal. 3:6–8, 14:26–29; cf. Rom. 4:16–17). As Wright points out, from the very beginning, "It had been God's purpose to bring the nations into the sphere of blessing as part of his people. . . . Therefore, the Gentile mission was a *fulfillment,* not a contradiction of the Scriptures. The Abrahamic covenant is the fount and origin of biblical mission in its redemptive sense."[44]

Exodus 19:4–6

In Exodus 19:4–6, Yahweh presents the people of Israel with a unique and sobering challenge (before revealing to them the Law, i.e., the Mosaic covenant). Doubtless, their conformity to the Law would have caused them to be a distinct nation among the pagan nations of the world. That distinctiveness was not, however, an end in itself. From the very outset, this divinely intended distinctiveness carried with it worldwide implications. By conducting their lives in conformity with the demands of the Law, the nation of Israel would have been able to function as God's servant nation, representing God and His character before the surrounding nations of the world.

The Literary and Theological Context of Exodus 19:4–6

Exodus 19 serves as a hinge between the Exodus event and the giving of the Law (Mosaic covenant). Wright argues that it "defines the identity and agenda God has for Israel and sets both in the context of God's own action and intention."[45] Elliot summarizes the significance of this passage by describing it as "one of the most dominant expressions of Israel's theology and faith in the entire Old Testament."[46] The present treatment of Exodus 19 focuses on the three expressions that explicate Israel's role as Yahweh's servant nation.[47]

The two similar clauses in 19:3c and 6c ("This is what you are to say to the house of Jacob and what you are to tell the people of Israel," and "These are the words you are to speak to the Israelites") form an envelope structure around Yahweh's statement concerning Israel's role as His servant nation.[48]

Exodus 19 stands at the beginning of Moses' presentation of the Mosaic/Israelite covenant. In this covenant, Yahweh promises to be a special God to His people and His subjects promise to live as His redeemed children. The summary of the Mosaic covenant, which Exodus 19:3b–8 provides, includes both of those aspects.[49] The focus of the present work is on those three divine promises (and intentions).

What is unique in this address of Israel is not the obligation to obey the covenant (cf. Gen. 17:9–10; 22:18; 26:5) but Yahweh's commission that Israel be (1) a special possession from among all nations, (2) a kingdom of priests, and (3) a holy nation. These three expressions provide a twofold perspective. They appear to be both *benefits* for Israel and Yahweh's *ideal* for His chosen people. They are the consequence of faithful conformity to the covenant and summarize Yahweh's intentions for Israel.

Exodus 19:4: Yahweh's Care for Israel

Exodus 19:4 recapitulates Yahweh's care for Israel, demonstrated in His delivering her from Egyptian bondage and bringing her safely ("on eagles' wings") to Sinai. This depiction of Yahweh's care for His chosen nation with the metaphor of an eagle's care for its young emphasizes His protection and guidance of Israel (cf. Deut. 32:10–12). It is as Israel's compassionate Sovereign that He gives His people a unique responsibility. This presentation of Yahweh links the present passage with Israel's experience of the Exodus from Egypt. Yahweh's liberation of Israel forms the foundation for the subsequent function statements.

Exodus 19:5–6: Yahweh's Intentions for Israel

The Structure of 19:5–6. Exodus 19:5–6 is cast in the form of a conditional sentence, having a protasis followed by a twofold apodosis. The protasis delineates Yahweh's expectations of His chosen nation: "Now if you obey me fully and keep my covenant" (19:5a NIV).[50] A form of the verb הָיָה and לְ introduces the two primary elements of the apodosis: (1) "you will be my treasured possession"; (2) "you will be for me a kingdom of priests and a holy nation." The second element of the apodosis has two parts, which are mutually interpretive ("kingdom of priests" and "holy nation").[51] In all, these three expressions delineate Israel's unique position as God's chosen people. The first expression depicts Israel as Yahweh's special possession by means of divine election. The second and third expressions outline the manner in which Israel is to function as Yahweh's סְגֻלָּה.[52]

Exodus 19:5b: Yahweh's Treasured Possession. First, Yahweh promises that if Israel lives in conformity to His expectations, "out of all nations you will be my treasured possession" (סְגֻלָּה) (19:5b NIV). Although the older lexical sources associate סְגֻלָּה with the Akkadian cognate *sugullu*,[53] it is better linked with the Akkadian *sikiltu* and the Ugaritic *sglt*.[54] Based on that cognate, Greenberg concludes that סְגֻלָּה "comes to mean a dear personal possession, a 'treasure' only in the sense of that which is treasured or cherished."[55] It denoted valuable property to which a person has exclusive possession rights.[56] This Akkadian term occurs in the sphere of suzerain-vassal relationships.[57] Consequently, סְגֻלָּה functions as a covenant term employed to represent a relationship of the suzerain/sovereign with one of His especially privileged vassals.[58] Five of the seven other Old Testament occurrences of סְגֻלָּה connote Israel's special position or privileged status before Yahweh (like the present passage—cf. Deut. 7:6; 14:2; 26:18; Ps. 135:4; Mal. 3:17). On two occasions it signifies royal wealth, i.e., the special treasure acquired by kings (1 Chron. 29:3; Eccl. 2:8). As God's סְגֻלָּה, Israel is considered to be Yahweh's special possession.[59] As the exclusive Sovereign of the entire world, Yahweh regards Israel above all the nations of the world as His priceless treasure.[60] This special relationship between Yahweh and His chosen nation is both an ideal that Yahweh holds before Israel as well as the beneficial result of their conformity to His covenantal expectations.

God's election of Abraham in Genesis 12 constitutes His choice of Israel to function as a special *people* before Him. It is to His chosen *nation* that Yahweh speaks in Exodus 19. Israel's exodus from Egypt is the event that marks her transition from a people to a nation. Yahweh's liberation of Israel from Egyptian bondage (on "eagles' wings," 19:4) also emphasizes Yahweh's exclusive ownership of Israel. Israel is no longer slave to the Egyptian Pharaoh, because, Yahweh asserts, I "brought you to myself" (19:4 NIV).

The clause that concludes 19:5, כִּי-לִי כָּל-הָאָרֶץ, does not function as an apologetic parenthesis or as a justification for Yahweh's election of Israel, but provides a conclusion for the argument of 19:4–5, conveying the purpose for which Israel has been chosen.[61] The clause "because the whole earth is mine" (19:5d, paraphrase), signifies that Yahweh commissions Israel to be His people *on behalf of* the earth which belongs to God.[62]

Exodus 19:6a: "Kingdom of Priests." The second expression, כֹּהֲנִים

מַמְלָכָה, has occasioned the most discussion and is capable of at least four grammatical categories of translation. The semantic range of מַמְלָכָה provides one of the complicating factors. This noun can either signify the exercise of rulership (1 Sam. 13:14; 24:20; Jer. 27:1) or connote the sphere over which that authority is exercised (Num. 32:33; Deut. 3:4, 10, 13).[63]

The first two alternatives treat the two elements independently (that is, not part of a construct relationship). First, Bauer contends that the two nouns stand in apposition to each other, "kings, that is, priests," signifying priestlike kings whose royalty is an extension of Yahweh's kingship.[64] Second, Briggs and Kaiser regard the two elements as a compound noun, "kings and priests."[65] Kaiser explains that the "kings and priests" of Israel "were to be mediators of the gospel as missionaries to the nations . . . and they were to be partakers in the present aspects and coming reality of the 'kingdom of God.'"[66]

The next two translations understand the two elements as components of a construct relationship. Several scholars separate the first designation from the next one ("holy nation") and interpret מַמְלֶכֶת כֹּהֲנִים as a "royalty of priests" who lead the worship of Yahweh's "holy nation" (גּוֹי קָדוֹשׁ).[67] Other scholars translate the phrase as a normal construct relationship where the dependent (absolute) element *(nomen rectum)* modifies the construct element *(nomen regens),* that is, "a kingdom of priests."[68]

The translation "kingdom of priests" most naturally expresses the construct relationship. The juxtaposition of "kingdom of priests" and "holy nation" and the clear correspondence between the political terms ("kingdom" and "nation") and the characterizing adjectives ("priestly" and "holy") argue for the synonymity of the last two expressions. As a kingdom of priests Israel will enjoy a mediatorial role (as a witness and as a vehicle of blessing for the world) in the accomplishment of Yahweh's intentions for the varied peoples of His creation.[69] Dumbrell asserts that Israel's function as "priests"

> does not refer to a structured cultic priesthood, since that will be brought into being by legislation flowing from the Sinai arrangement. The use of the word here appears to be wider than merely cultic and be associated with the blessings conferred on Israel by virtue of her Abrahamic connection, to which the "covenant" of v. 5 seems to refer.[70]

As a nation Israel is to be devoted to this mediatorial role between Yahweh and the pagan nations. As Noth suggests, "Israel is to have the role of the priestly member in the number of earthly states" to draw near to God and do service for the world (cf. Isa. 61:5–6).[71] Wright contends that "as the people of Yahweh they would have the historical task of bringing the knowledge of God to the nations, and bringing the nations to the means of atonement with God."[72]

This ideal is never fulfilled in the Old Testament and becomes an object of expectation for the messianic times.[73] Vanhoye correctly points out, however, that "what is emphasized is not the equality of all the Israelites among themselves, but the privileged position of Israel with respect to the other peoples."[74]

Exodus 19:6b: "Holy Nation." The final designation for Israel, קָדוֹשׁ גּוֹי, is almost synonymous to the preceding designation. As a "holy nation" Israel is to function as "a people set apart, not simply *from* other peoples/nations, but *for* a specific purpose. Israel is to embody God's purposes in the world."[75] The political term גּוֹי is rarely used for Israel in the Old Testament.[76] Its application to Israel in both Genesis 12:2 and Exodus 19:6, however, carries special significance. The Mosaic covenant clearly builds on the foundation laid in the Abrahamic covenant, continuing its provision with more specificity. The Mosaic covenant particularizes the promises of the Abrahamic covenant to operate through Israel. As Dumbrell points out, "Israel's national distinctiveness, and thus her national role, is also in mind. No longer does she belong merely to a general community of peoples from whom she can only with difficulty be differentiated. She has now been elevated into a distinct entity and endowed with special privileges."[77] It was only as a "holy nation" that Israel could carry out her function of being Yahweh's priesthood in the midst of the nations. This involved her being "recognizably, visibly and substantively different, as the people belonging uniquely to Yahweh and therefore representing His character and ways to the nations who did not yet know him as God."[78] Israel had to be a different kind of nation because Yahweh was a different kind of God.

The Theological Significance of Exodus 19:4–6

As a "kingdom of priests and a holy nation" Israel functions as "a societary model for the world. She will provide, under the direct divine rule which the covenant contemplates, the paradigm of the theocratic rule which is to be the biblical aim for the whole world."[79]

As with the Abrahamic covenant, the conditionality/unconditionality of this utterance demands consideration. Is Israel's status as Yahweh's "treasured possession" entirely tied to covenantal obedience, or is it unconditional in some sense? Wright contends that as "God's peculiar possession, Israel had imposed upon her an obligation, which to keep is life but to violate is disaster. Her election was not unalterable; it could be annulled by her own acts."[80] McClain, who relates the second phrase ("kingdom of priests") to the mediatorial kingdom, asserts that this "kingdom-covenant" was conditional, unlike the Abrahamic covenant.[81] Bright adds that

> Israel could never properly take her status as a chosen people for granted; it was morally conditioned. . . . Hers was a cosmic God who in a historical act had chosen her, and whom she in a free, moral act had chosen. The covenant bond between them was thus neither mechanical nor eternal.[82]

On the other hand, Moberly emphasizes the unconditional character of these designations for Israel:

> In Ex. 19:5 . . . the relationship between obeying God's voice and being his possession is not that between an action and a subsequent result. The protasis is a definition of the requirements of the position or vocation designated by the titles of the apodosis; it explains what being God's people means. To break the requirements of the protasis (obeying God's voice and keeping his covenant) would not mean subsequently ceasing to be God's people. Rather the act of unfaithfulness itself would be a denial of their position as God's people. But such a denial of their status need not entail the abrogation of that status.[83]

Unlike the Abrahamic covenant (an unconditional royal grant covenant), the Mosaic covenant is analogous to the conditional suzerain-vassal covenant, an agreement more conditional in nature. Nevertheless, Israel's status as God's chosen people (rooted in the Abrahamic covenant) is unchanging. God establishes the Mosaic covenant with Israel as the instrument whereby this servant people can bring to pass God's intentions for them and to enable them to serve as His vehicle of providing redemptive blessings for the nations (Gen. 12:3). In the Mosaic covenant (and Ex. 19:5–6) Yahweh offers His chosen nation the opportunity to be, according to Merrill, "a people who could model among the kingdoms of the earth what it meant to be the dominion of the Lord, and who could serve as a channel by which His salvation could be mediated to them."[84] Yahweh sets before Israel the potential for a twofold function: model and mediator.

Although the Mosaic covenant is a suzerain-vassal type and is technically conditional, Yahweh, the unchanging God, established it. His election of Israel to be His servant nation is without precondition. As Israel conforms to Yahweh's covenantal expectations, she functions in that capacity. Whenever she fails in this regard, however, God promises to terminate that special function. As Merrill explains, "It was only the acceptance of servanthood with all its blessings that was conditional."[85] Israel's actual function as Yahweh's servant nation depended on her obedience to the terms of servanthood delineated in the Mosaic covenant.

Consequently, Yahweh's designation of Israel as His "treasured possession . . . a kingdom of priests and a holy nation" is both a promise and an ideal. As a promise, these designations will only apply to that generation of God's people who faithfully serve and actually function as His servant nation. As an ideal, however, these designations are part of her everlasting status as God's chosen people. As with the Abrahamic covenant, the enjoyment of the benefits of this arrangement is the only conditional element. This role of Yahweh's "treasured possession" is a state or position, not based on morality.[86] According to Merrill, Israel's status as God's elect people is "a matter of unqualified divine initiative; that Israel was to function in a special way as the people of God would now rest in Israel's free choice."[87] Only her effective fulfillment of His intentions is decided by her obedience. The way to function as God's redeemed people before the world is to keep the covenant.[88] It is because of her special position before God (סְגֻלָּה) that Israel can even carry out this God-given mediatorial function (cf. Deut. 7:6; 14:2; 26:18).

Isaiah 40–55

According to the prophet Isaiah, God's original intention to make Israel a great nation (Gen. 12:1–3) and to use her as His servant nation (Gen. 12:3; Ex. 19:6) still applied in his day. The prophet delivers to exiled Israel the promise of God to liberate His chosen people from banishment and to restore them to great power and glory in their home-land. Yahweh certifies the credibility of His promises by highlighting His absolute uniqueness. He is the only true God and He is able to carry out all of His promises. His absolute supremacy is indicated especially in comparison to the nothingness of the pagan gods and the subordina-tion of the Gentiles' destiny to His sovereignty. Although Yahweh will bring destruction upon the intransigent Gentiles, He will also provide submissive Gentiles with the opportunity to participate in His redemptive benefits. Those Gentiles who are spared from destruction will expedite the return of God's children from their worldwide exile to their home-land and will hold a subject position with regard to Israel (an economic, rather than an ontological, distinction).

The prophet underscores Israel's role in providing a witness to the nations. According to Martens, "Her mission is to the peoples of the world, not in the New Testament sense of going forth to them with the message about Yahweh, but in the sense of being a people of God whose life shall draw nations to inquire after Yahweh (cf. Isa. 2:1–4)."[89] Even if one grants that mission and witness in the Old Testament is centripetal (the na-tions are drawn to Israel—"Come") and, by contrast, mission and witness in the New Testament is centrifugal (the church is commanded to bring the gospel message to the nations of the world—"Go"), in both the Old and New Testaments, God's concern extends to the nations.

In Isaiah's day, however, the nation of Israel was unfit to function as God's servant nation. Her rebellious conduct occasioned her present exilic circumstances. Through the prophet, however, God offers to restore His elect nation. Yahweh raises up His servant to enable His chosen nation to fulfill her divine calling, that is, to function as His servant nation, His means of blessing all the nations of the earth. The servant's ministry to Israel provides the foundation for the servant's worldwide impact. Not only does the servant restore Israel to her role as God's servant nation, but he functions as the mediator of divine blessings for all peoples.[90]

What About the Old Testament and a Missions Mandate?

In His covenant with Abraham, God affirms that Abraham and his descendants will be His vehicle for blessing the nations. He further speci-fies Israel's function as His servant nation (a mediatorial/representative role) by commissioning her to be a "treasured possession, . . . a kingdom of priests, and a holy nation" (Ex. 19:5–6 NIV). In the second half of Isaiah (chaps. 40–55) the prophet promises that Yahweh will soon restore His chosen nation to great power and glory in her homeland. Nations from around the world will expedite this restoration. Gentiles will help the Jews, scattered throughout their regions, in their trek home. They will serve God's children as a nursing mother or as a foster father who cares for a child in her or his charge. Yahweh will invite the Gentiles to enjoy His salvation and will, by means of His servant, establish justice and equity throughout the land. In Romans 11, the apostle Paul demonstrates that Gentile Christians enjoy redemption by partaking of covenantal privileges originally provided for God's chosen nation.

From the very beginning, Yahweh's purposes had worldwide implications. The general parameters have been in place since God's choice of Abraham. God intends to bless the world by means of His servant nation. His intention to establish His rule over the entire world through His image-bearers will be accomplished in part by the spread of His redemption. Both Israel in the Old Testament (Isa. 43:10–12) and the church in the New Testament (Luke 24:48; Acts 1:8) received the divine exhortation, "You are My witnesses." They both were similarly entrusted with the task of confirming to the nations the identity of Yahweh as the true God and source of salvation. Although there are clear differences between the Old and New Testament's presentation of the idea of mission (Old Testament—Israel as a passive witness; New Testament—the church as both a passive and active witness), the idea of missions is a fundamental part of biblical theology. Participation in missions is nonnegotiable, is not merely the task of "missionaries," but rather, is part of the *raison d'être* for the whole people of God.[91] Although both testaments share a divine mandate for God's people to function as divine witnesses/representatives, the Old and New Testaments differ to some degree in the way that the respective peoples of God (Israel and the church) carried out that divine mandate.

Ultimately, God's rule will encompass His entire creation. All nations will submit to His rule, whether by their destruction or their willing worship of the incomparable Sovereign of the universe.

Study Questions

1. What is the difference between the centripetal and centrifugal views of Israel's role and mission with regard to the world?
2. Where does mission ultimately begin? Explain.
3. What was God's original intention for creating man in His image (Gen. 1:26–28)?
4. Explain how in Genesis 12:1–3 God begins to reveal the means by which He will address His universal purpose.

5. Summarize the three descriptions of Israel in Exodus 19:5b–6 and what these descriptions teach concerning Israel's purpose and mission.
6. What does Isaiah 40–55 contribute to the Old Testament teaching on missions?
7. In question 1 you defined the centripetal and the centrifugal views of Israel's role and mission with regard to the world. Which view is appropriate for Israel, and which is appropriate for the church?

Chapter Notes

1. For example, Walter Vogels, "Covenant and Universalism: Guide for a Missionary Reading of the Old Testament," *Zeitschrift für Missionswissenschaft und Religionswissenschaft* 57 (1973): 31. For a fuller explanation of his approach to this issue, see his *God's Universal Covenant: A Biblical Study* (Ottawa: Univ. of Ottawa Press, 1979).
2. For an overview of that debate, especially as it relates to Isaiah 40–55, see the present author's article, "Israel and the Nations in Isaiah 40–55: An Update," *The Master's Seminary Journal* 9, no. 1 (spring 1998): 39–61.
3. Charles H. H. Scobie, "Israel and the Nations," *Tyndale Bulletin* 43 (1992): 285.
4. Gailyn Van Rheenen, *Missions: Biblical Foundations and Contemporary Strategies* (Grand Rapids: Zondervan, 1996), 14.
5. It is seldom recognized that the mission of Jesus Himself, as well as the mission He entrusted to His followers, was shaped and programmed by the Scriptures we call the Old Testament (Chris Wright, "The Old Testament and Mission," *Evangel* 14 [1996]: 37).
6. Eugene H. Merrill, "A Theology of the Pentateuch," in Roy Zuck, ed., *A Biblical Theology of the Old Testament* (Chicago: Moody, 1991), 14.
7. Eugene H. Merrill, "Covenant and the Kingdom: Genesis 1–3 as Foundation for Biblical Theology," *Criswell Theological Review* 1 (1987): 298.
8. Merrill ("Covenant and the Kingdom," 298) points out that by means of this creation mandate, God (the Sovereign) outlines to man (His vassal) the meaning of the vassal's existence and the role he is to play in the Sovereign's eternal plans for His creation. For numerous indications of royal overtones, see William J. Dumbrell, *The End of the Beginning: Revelation 21–22 and the Old Testament* (Grand Rapids: Baker, 1985), 176.
9. R. Bryan Widbin, "Salvation for People Outside Israel's Covenant?" in W. Crockett and J. Sigountos, eds., *Through No Fault of Their Own? The Fate of Those Who Have Never Heard* (Grand Rapids: Baker, 1991), 78 n. 9;

cf. Michael Fishbane, *Text and Texture: Close Readings of Selected Biblical Texts* (New York: Schocken Books, 1979), 30–31.

10. R. W. L. Moberly, *The Old Testament of the Old Testament: Patriarchal Narratives and Mosaic Yahwism,* Overtures to Biblical Theology (Minneapolis: Fortress, 1992), 141.

11. Wright, "The Old Testament and Mission," 39.

12. This covenant arrangement is unconditional in that it exists regardless of the behavior of the recipient. It is only the enjoyment of the covenant benefits that is conditional upon the obedience of the subordinate covenant partners (cf. Merrill, "A Theology of the Pentateuch," 26; and Walter C. Kaiser Jr., *Toward an Old Testament Theology* [Grand Rapids: Zondervan, 1978], 93–94).

13. Although the third and fourth cohortatives are the only ones clearly identifiable by their form, the first two evidently function as cohortatives as well. Patrick D. Miller Jr. ("Syntax and Theology in Genesis XII 3a," *Vetus Testamentum* 34 [1984]: 475–76 n. 2) provides substantial grammatical support for the categorization of the first two verbal forms as "cohortatives."

14. Hans Walter Wolff, "The Kerygma of the Yahwist," *Interpretation* 20 (1966): 138. Cf. Bruce K. Waltke and M. O'Connor, *An Introduction to Biblical Hebrew Syntax* (Winona Lake, Ind.: Eisenbrauns, 1990), 529–30, #32.2.2. Walter Vogels (*God's Universal Covenant: A Biblical Study* [Ottawa: Univ. of Ottawa Press, 1979], 40) provides a diagrammatic analysis of the threefold development in Genesis 12:1–3 which can only be summarized here: (1) "Go" (12:1); (2) "Thus" (4 cohortatives—12:2–3b), (3) "so then, all the families of the earth . . ." (12:3c).

15. Grammarians and scholars are not agreed on the major semantic categories of the *Niphal* verbal stem. On the one hand, Vogels (*God's Universal Covenant,* 42) asserts that the *Niphal* is not normally passive and Lambdin (*Introduction to Biblical Hebrew* [New York: Charles Scribner's Sons, 1971], 175–77) concludes that the *Niphal* is more accurately designated a medio-passive (no agency). Waltke and O'Connor (*Introduction to Biblical Hebrew Syntax,* 382, #23.2.2) counter that the passive sense is the most common use of the *Niphal* stem (cf. Gesenius's *Hebrew Grammar,* ed. E. Kautzsch, tr. A. E. Cowley, 138, #51f., which states that the *Niphal* "in many cases" represents the passive). The present work makes no attempt to provide a final answer to this question. It does assume that a passive nuance is a legitimate and common option for the *Niphal* stem.

16. Eduard König, *Die Genesis eingeleitet, übersetzt und erklärt,* 3d ed. (Gütersloh: C. Bertelsmann, 1925), 457–58; Oswald T. Allis, "The Blessing

of Abraham," *Princeton Theological Review* 25 (1927): 297–98; U. Cassuto, *A Commentary on the Book of Genesis,* trans. I. Abrahams (Jerusalem: Magnes, 1964), 2:315; B. Jacob, *Genesis,* ed. and trans. E. Jacob and W. Jacob (New York: Ktav Publishing, 1974), 86–87; Philip B. Payne, "A Critical Note on Ecclesiasticus 44:21's Commentary on the Abrahamic Covenant," *Journal of the Evangelical Theological Society* 15 (1972): 186–87; Kaiser, *Toward an Old Testament Theology,* 13–14; G. Charles Aalders, *Genesis,* trans. W. Heynen, Bible Student's Commentary (Grand Rapids: Zondervan, 1981), 1:269–70; Nahum M. Sarna, *Genesis,* JPS Torch Commentary (Philadelphia: Jewish Publication Society, 1989), 89, 358; Victor P. Hamilton, *The Book of Genesis Chapters 1–17,* New International Commentary on the Old Testament (Grand Rapids: Eerdmans, 1990), 374–75; John H. Sailhamer, "Genesis," in *The Expositor's Bible Commentary,* ed. F. Gaebelein (Grand Rapids: Zondervan, 1990), 2:114; and Merrill, "A Theology of the Pentateuch," 27.

17. A. Dillmann, *Genesis: Critically and Exegetically Expounded,* trans. W. Stevenson (Edinburgh: T & T Clark, 1897), 2:11–12; Hermann Gunkel, *Genesis,* 6th ed. (Göttingen: Vandenhoeck & Ruprecht, 1964), 165; J. Skinner, *A Critical and Exegetical Commentary on Genesis,* The International Critical Commentary (Edinburgh: T & T Clark, 1912), 244–45; H. H. Rowley, *The Missionary Message of the Old Testament* (London: Carey, 1944), 26–27; H. Junker, "Segen im Alten Testament als Heilsgeschichtliches Motivwort," in *Sacra Pagina,* ed. J. Coppens, A. Descamps, and É. Massaux, Bibliotheca Ephemeridum Theologicarum Lovaniensium, no. 12–13 (Paris: J. Gabalda et Cie, 1959), 1:553–55; Robert Martin Achard, *A Light to the Nations: A Study of the Old Testament Conception of Israel's Mission to the World,* trans. J. Smith (London: Oliver and Boyd, 1962), 33–35; E. A. Speiser, *Genesis,* The Anchor Bible (Garden City, N.Y.: Doubleday, 1964), 86; Bertil Albrektson, *History and the Gods,* Coniectanea Biblica, Old Testament Series, no. 1 (Lund: CWK Gleerup, 1967), 79–80; Walther Somali, *1 Mose 12–25: Abraham,* Zürcher Bibelkommentare (Zürich: Theologischer Verlag, 1976), 21 n. 4; William Yarchin, "Imperative and Promise in Genesis 12:1–3," *Studia Biblica et Theologica* 10 (1980): 177 n. 36; Claus Westermann, *Genesis 12–36: A Commentary,* trans. J. Scullion (Minneapolis: Augsburg, 1985), 151–52; and Allen P. Ross, *Creation and Blessing: A Guide to the Study and Exposition of the Book of Genesis* (Grand Rapids: Baker, 1988), 264. Gerard Van Groningen (*Messianic Revelation in the Old Testament* [Grand Rapids: Baker, 1990], 134 n. 19) prefers the reflexive translation but retains Abraham's (and Israel's) mediatorial function with regard to God's blessing

the nations (cf. James Muilenburg, "Abraham and the Nations," *Interpretation* 19 [1965]: 392–93).

18. Joseph Schreiner, "Segen für die Völker in der Verheissung an die Väter," *Biblische Zeitschrift* 6 (1962): 6–7; *Theologisches Handwörterbuch zum Alten Testament,* s.v. "ברך," 1:364; A. De Groot, *The Bible on the Salvation of Nations,* trans. F. Vander Heijden (De Pere, Wis.: St. Norbert Abbey Press, 1966), 25–27; Wolff, "The Kerygma of the Yahwist," 137–43; Hans-Peter Müller, "Imperativ und Verheissung im Alten Testament," *Evangelische Theologie* 28 (1968): 561; Gerhard Wehmeier, *Der Segen im Alten Testament* (Basel: Friedrich Reinhardt Kommissionsverlag, 1970), 178–79; Vogels, *God's Universal Covenant,* 42–43; R. E. Clements, *Abraham and David: Genesis XV and Its Meaning for Israelite Tradition,* Studies in Biblical Theology, no. 5 (Naperville, Ill.: Alec R. Allenson, Inc., 1967), 15; William J. Dumbrell, *Covenant and Creation: A Theology of Old Testament Covenants* (Nashville: Nelson, 1984), 70–71; Thomas Edward McComiskey, *The Covenants of Promise: A Theology of the Old Testament Covenants* (Grand Rapids: Baker, 1985), 56–57; and Gordon J. Wenham, *Genesis 1–15,* WBC (Waco, Tex.: Word, 1987), 277–78.

19. Scharbert suggests that if a passive was intended, a *Pual* would have been used (*Theological Dictionary of the Old Testament,* s.v. "בָּרַךְ," 2:297).

20. Martin-Achard, *Light to the Nations,* 34.

21. Van Groningen, *Messianic Revelation in the Old Testament,* 134.

22. Ross, *Creation and Blessing,* 264. Ross suggests that the original meaning of 12:3c may have been broad ("bless themselves") which later revelation further specified (through Abraham's seed, that is, the Messiah).

23. Schreiner, "Segen für die Völker in der Verheissung an die Väter," 7 (All translation from foreign language works are the responsibility of the present author). Wolff ("The Kerygma of the Yahwist," 137 n. 31) translates 12:3b, "all the families of the earth can gain a blessing in you," emphasizing the mediatorial function of Israel (". . . in the people of Abraham all humanity can gain blessing," ibid., 140).

24. Dumbrell, *Covenant and Creation,* 71.

25. Proponents of the receptive nuance vary in the significance given to Abraham's instrumentality in the provision of that blessing. For example, J. Scharbert suggests that the passive, reflexive, and receptive nuance is compatible with the motif of universal salvation/blessing because each alternative "denotes a declaration of solidarity with So-and-so, and on this basis the nations can depend on the blessing of Yahweh" (*Theological Dictionary of the Old Testament,* s.v. "בָּרַךְ," 2:297). Others lay stress on Abraham's (and Israel's) integral part in that bestowal of blessing (cf. Gerhard

von Rad, *Genesis,* trans. J. Marks, Old Testament Library [Philadelphia: Westminster, 1972], 160; Muilenburg, "Abraham and the Nations," 392–93).

26. Dumbrell, *Covenant and Creation,* 70.

27. Ibid., 70.

28. Ibid.

29. Wenham, *Genesis 1–15,* 278. Wenham suggests a fourfold progression: (1) Abraham alone is blessed; (2) Abraham's name is used as a blessing; (3) Abraham's blessers are blessed; (4) all families find blessing in Abraham. Wenham concludes that whether receptive or reflexive, both lead to a passive nuance. If those who bless Abraham are blessed, and all families bless Abraham, then it follows that all families will be blessed/find blessing in him.

30. Dumbrell, *Covenant and Creation,* 71.

31. Von Rad, *Genesis,* 160.

32. Waltke and O'Connor, *Introduction to Biblical Hebrew Syntax,* 395. Allis ("The Blessing of Abraham," 281–82) cites twenty-five passages where the *Hithpael* could have a passive sense. Hamilton (*The Book of Genesis Chapters 1–17,* 375 n. 19) adds "three" more to that list (Prov. 31:30; Eccl. 8:10; Ps. 72:17). Hamilton incorrectly refers to Proverbs 31:30 as an example not considered by Allis (cf. Allis, "The Blessing of Abraham," 281).

33. E. Qimron, *The Hebrew of the Dead Sea Scrolls,* Harvard Semitic Studies, no. 29 (Atlanta: Scholars Press, 1986), 48–49.

34. Waltke and O'Connor, *Introduction to Biblical Hebrew Syntax,* 395.

35. Ibid., 382.

36. Ibid., 383.

37. Sailhamer, "Genesis," 2:114. Sailhamer observes that the three *Niphal* occurrences are immediately followed by the preposition בְּ and a pronominal suffix (12:3; 18:18; 28:14). The preposition בְּ and זַרְעֶךָ ("offspring") immediately follow the two *Hithpael* instances (22:18; 26:4).

38. Cf. R. Williams, *Hebrew Syntax: An Outline* (Toronto: Univ. of Toronto Press, 1967), 28–31.

39. Sailhamer, "Genesis," 2:114.

40. Ibid. Sailhamer correctly observes that זַרְעֶךָ occurs in 28:14, where a *Niphal* form is found, but misunderstands its significance. He emphasizes that the *Niphal* form is "added to the end of the clause" in order to maintain his clear-cut distinction between the *Niphal* and *Hithpael* occurrences. However, the two instrumental expressions ("through you . . . through your descendants") encompass the objects of this covenantal blessing ("all the families of the earth"). It is likely a rhetorical (chiastic?) tool to emphasize both the instrumentality and the extent of these covenantal

provisions. It may also be that Jacob is addressed ("through you") because in him Abraham's descendants are finally delimited ethnically. If there is any distinction between these statements/restatements of blessing for the nations, the first two occurrences of בָּרַךְ focus attention on Abraham, who is not only the mediator of these blessings but the source/foundation of this mediatorial arrangement. The other patriarchs enjoy this position derivatively.

41. Speiser (*Genesis,* 86) recognizes that the "distinction may be slight on the surface, yet it is of great consequence."
42. Hamilton, *The Book of Genesis Chapters 1–17,* 374.
43. Merrill, "A Theology of the Pentateuch," 27; cf. 86–87.
44. Wright, "The Old Testament and Mission," 39.
45. Ibid., 40.
46. John Hall Elliott, *The Elect and the Holy,* Supplements to Novum Testamentum, no. 12 (Leiden: E. J. Brill, 1966), 59.
47. A recent and thorough examination of this passage and its contribution to Israel's role as Yahweh's servant nation is Robert Ray Ellis, "An Examination of the Covenant Promises of Exodus 19:5–6 and Their Theological Significance for Israel" (Ph.D. diss., Southwestern Baptist Theological Seminary, 1988).
48. Wilfred G. E. Watson, *Classical Hebrew Poetry: A Guide to Its Technique,* JSOT Supplement Series, no. 26 (Sheffield: JSOT Press, 1984), 282–83.
49. Exodus 19:4 relates the basis for the covenant (Yahweh's intervention on Israel's behalf). Exodus 19:5–6 delineates the responsibilities dictated by the proposed covenant (the three expressions describing Israel's role/function) and 19:7–8 provides the record of the peoples' agreement to live in accordance with this covenant.
50. This not only serves as the statement of regulations for Israel to follow, but refers to the already established relationship between Yahweh and His people.
51. The structure of this conditional sentence suggests that the two expressions in the second element of the apodosis are not to be interpreted apart from one another. According to this view, the two elements of the apodosis are introduced by apodosis *waws* (which introduce "a consequential independent clause [apodosis] after a conditional dependent clause [protasis]," Waltke, and O'Connor, *Introduction to Biblical Hebrew Syntax,* 521, cf. 526). The conjunction joining the second and third expression is a simple sequential or relative *waw* (ibid., 526–27). The significance of that structure manifests itself in the ensuing interpretation of the last two expressions (19:6). However, someone who desires to keep the last two expressions

distinct from one another can argue that there is simply an ellipsis of the הָיָה plus לְ or that the second *waw* is also an apodosis *waw*.

52. Merrill ("Theology of the Pentateuch," 33) affirms that "Israel's value as God's possession lay precisely in her function as a holy kingdom of priests."

53. *Brown-Driver-Briggs Lexicon,* s.v. "סְגֻלָּה," 688; Lexicon in Veteris Testamenti Libros, s.v. "סְגֻלָּה," 649.

54. With Hebrew words that occur seldom in the Old Testament (leaving interpreters few contexts to examine for help in understanding a given word's meaning), scholars appeal to related words in other similar (cognate) languages (e.g., Aramaic, Ugaritic, Akkadian, etc.). The Ugaritic word *sglt* (this term has no vowels because Ugaritic texts contain few vowel indicators) and the Akkadian term *sikiltu* appear to be semantic parallels of the Hebrew noun sĕgullā (סְגֻלָּה) in their respective languages. Although S. Kaufman (*The Akkadian Influences on Aramaic, Assyriological Studies,* no. 19 [Chicago: Univ. of Chicago Press, 1974], 93) questions the legitimacy of this association of סְגֻלָּה with *sikiltu,* the evidence for a cognate relationship appears to be overwhelming. Cf. Moshe Greenberg, "Hebrew *sĕgullā:* Akkadian *sikiltu," Journal of the American Oriental Society* 71 (1951): 172–74; *Theological Lexicon of the Old Testament,* s.v. "סְגֻלָּה," 2:791; *Hebrew and Aramaic Lexicon of the Old Testament* (s.v. "סְגֻלָּה," 3:742 cites both *sug/kullu* or *sikiltu* as possible Akkadian cognates). *Theologisches Wörterbuch zum Alten Testament* (s.v. "סְגֻלָּה," 5:749–50) compares סְגֻלָּה only to *sikiltu. The Assyrian Dictionary* (s.v. *"sikiltu,"* 15:244–45) gives "possession, acquisition" as a general meaning for *sikiltu.* The more specific meaning of "private possessions" (as opposed to illegally acquired goods) serves as the meaning comparable to סְגֻלָּה. Speiser ("Nuzi Marginalia," *Orientalia* 25 [1956]: 1–4) and Gordon (*Ugaritic Textbook,* Analecta Orientalia, no. 38 [Rome: Pontifical Biblical Institute, 1965], 448, #1735) point out potential Hurrian and Ugaritic cognates (respectively) as well. Weinfeld (*Deuteronomy 1–11,* AB [New York: Doubleday, 1991], 368) points out that *sikiltu(m)/sugiltu(m)* occurs in the Akkadian sources of the second millennium B.C. (e.g., a royal seal of Abban of Alalakh) as an epithet for a true believer in his god.

55. Greenberg, "Hebrew *sĕgullā:* Akkadian *sikiltu,"* 174.

56. Sarna, *Genesis,* 104.

57. Elisabeth Schüssler Fiorenza (*Priester für Gott* [Münster: Verlag Aschendorff, 1972], 140) points out that the Ugaritic term occurs in correspondence between a Hittite king and a Canaanite vassal king of the city-state of Ugarit; cf. Weinfeld, 368. The suzerain (Hittite king) describes his vassal (Ugaritic king) as his *sglt* (Dietrich, Lorete, and Sanmartin,

eds., *Die Keilalphabetischen Texte aus Ugarit* [Neukirchen-Vluyn: Neu-kirchener Verlag, 1976] 2.39:7, 12).

58. Weinfeld, *Deuteronomy 1–11,* 368.

59. The fact that Israel is Yahweh's "treasured possession . . . kingdom of priests and a holy nation" is emphasized by the repeated לִ. It is before and in relation to Yahweh that Israel possesses these functions/roles.

60. The placement of a reference to Yahweh's universal sovereignty before and after סְגֻלָּה emphasizes the intensity of Yahweh's relationship with His chosen people. The מִן of the first phrase (מִכָּל־הָעַמִּים) is best taken com-paratively to emphasize the deliberate nature of Yahweh's choice of Israel. He elected the nation of Israel rather than any other nation of the world, all of which are under His absolute control.

61. Dumbrell, *Covenant and Creation,* 89.

62. Terrence E. Freitheim, *Exodus,* Interpretation (Louisville: John Knox, 1991), 212. Dumbrell (*Covenant and Creation,* 89) delineates a threefold parallel between God's choice of Abraham and Israel in Genesis 12:1–3 and Exodus 19:4–5 respectively. He writes, "Both are chosen outside of the land of promise, the choice of both is meant to serve the wider pur-poses of divine intention expressed through the initial act of creation, and both Israel and Abraham are the points of contact through whom this wider scope of divine purpose will be achieved." Wright ("The Old Testa-ment and Mission," 40) also observes a similar balance of particularity and universality in this account and the Abrahamic covenant when he writes, "God's very special place for Israel, their identity and task, is here set in the context of his universality as God in relation to the nations of the earth."

63. Brown-Driver-Briggs Lexicon, s.v. "מַמְלָכָה," 575.

64. J. B. Bauer, "Könige und Priester, ein heiliges Volk (Ex 19,6)," *Biblische Zeitschrift* 2 (1958): 283–86.

65. Charles A. Briggs, *Messianic Prophecy* (New York: Charles Scribner's Sons, 1889), 102–3; Kaiser, *Toward an Old Testament Theology,* 107–10.

66. Walter C. Kaiser Jr., "Exodus," in *The Expositor's Bible Commentary,* ed. F. Gaebelein (Grand Rapids: Zondervan, 1990), 2:417.

67. Wilhelm Caspari, "Das priesterliche Königreich," *Theologische Blätter* 8 (1929): 105–10; William L. Moran, "A Kingdom of Priests," in *The Bible in Current Catholic Thought,* ed. J. McKenzie (New York: Herder and Herder, 1962), 11–20; Georg Fohrer, "'Priesterliche Königtum,' Ex. 19,6," *Theologische Zeitschrift* 19 (1963): 359–62; and R. Vande Walle, "An Administrative Body of Priests and a Consecrated People," *Indian Journal*

of Theology 14 (1985): 57–72. This view obviously places emphasis on Israel's internal constitution rather than on her worldwide function.

68. R. B. Y. Scott, "A Kingdom of Priests (Exodus XIX 6)," in *Oudtestamentische Studien,* no. 8, ed. P. de Boer (Leiden: E. J. Brill, 1950), 216–19; U. Cassuto, *A Commentary on the Book of Exodus,* trans. I. Abrahams (Jerusalem: Magnes, 1967), 227; Brevard S. Childs, *The Book of Exodus,* Old Testament Library (Philadelphia: Westminster, 1974), 367; Dumbrell, *Covenant and Creation,* 84–90; McComiskey, *Covenants of Promise,* 68–69; Ernest W. Nicholson, *God and His People: Covenant and Theology in the Old Testament* (Oxford: Clarendon, 1986), 172–73; Willem A. VanGemeren, *The Progress of Redemption: The Story of Salvation from Creation to the New Jerusalem* (Grand Rapids: Baker, 1988), 148; and Merrill, "A Theology of the Pentateuch," 32–33; Seock-Tae Sohn, *The Divine Election of Israel* (Grand Rapids: Eerdmans, 1991), 196. Scott ("A Kingdom of Priests [Exodus XIX 6]," 219) renders the designation, "a kingdom set apart like a priesthood," and posits that this expression "simply designates Israel as worshipers of Yahweh." Fiorenza (*Priester für Gott,* 150; cf. 148–49) argues that Exodus 19:6 presents an ideal of democratic theocracy in implicit opposition to the institutional monarchy and priesthood: "In this manner Israel stands in complete immediacy to her God. This immediacy and nearness of Israel to Yahweh . . . requires no mediating institutions, whether royal or priestly."

69. Ellis ("Examination of the Covenant Promises of Exodus 19:5–6," 142–48) contends that Exodus 19:4–6 does not clearly present a mediatorial function for Israel. That truth does not become explicit until Isaiah 40–55. However, one's interpretation of Genesis 12:1–3 may provide the foundation for that mediatorial role. Ellis recognizes that possibility in Genesis 12:3 but rejects it. Instead, he suggests that Exodus 19:4–6 simply presents Israel as a servant nation and that subsequent Scripture provides further specifics.

70. Dumbrell, *Covenant and Creation,* 86.

71. Martin Noth, *Exodus,* trans. J. Bowden, Old Testament Library (Philadelphia: Westminster, 1962), 157.

72. Wright, "The Old Testament and Mission," 40.

73. Ibid., 152–54.

74. Albert Vanhoye, *Old Testament Priests and the New Priest According to the New Testament,* trans. J. Orchard (Petersham, Mass.: St. Bede's Publications, 1986), 247.

75. Freitheim, *Exodus,* 212–13.

76. Alfred Cody, "When Is the Chosen People Called a Goy?" *Vetus Testamentum* 14 (1964): 1–6.

77. Dumbrell, *Covenant and Creation,* 87.

78. Wright, "The Old Testament and Mission," 41.

79. Ibid.

80. G. Ernest Wright, *The Old Testament Against Its Environment,* Studies in Biblical Theology, no. 2 (London: SCM, 1950), 54.

81. Alva J. McClain, *The Greatness of the Kingdom* (Winona Lake, Ind.: BMH Books, 1974), 62–63.

82. John Bright, *The Kingdom of God: The Biblical Concept and Its Meaning for the Church* (Nashville: Abingdon, 1953), 29.

83. R. W. L. Moberly, *At the Mountain of God: Story and Theology in Exodus 32–34,* Journal for the Study of Old Testament—Supplement Series, no. 22 (Sheffield: JSOT Press, 1983), 226–27 n. 4.

84. Merrill, "A Theology of the Pentateuch," 167–68.

85. Ibid., 87.

86. Contra Durham (*Exodus,* Word Biblical Commentary [Waco, Tex.: Word, 1987], 262) who suggests that fulfilling these conditions will transform God's elect people from "the sons of Israel" to "Israel," a community of faith transcending biological descendancy."

87. Merrill, "A Theology of the Pentateuch," 32.

88. Freitheim, *Exodus,* 213.

89. Elmer A. Martens, *God's Design: A Focus on Old Testament Theology,* 2d ed. (Grand Rapids: Baker, 1994), 238.

90. For a more detailed examination of how Isaiah 40–55 contributes to the concept of missions, see the present author's article, "Israel's Mission to the Nations in Isaiah 40–55: An Update," *The Master's Seminary Journal* 9, no. 1 (spring 1998): 39–61.

91. Wright, "The Old Testament and Mission," 39.

3

ROY E. BEACHAM

MISSIONS THROUGH MODELING

A Call to Holiness

There is an inherent danger in committing oneself to the unknown. Thus, it is uncommon for people to assume serious obligations based solely on hearsay. Mere verbal assurances are rarely enough when making major, life-altering decisions. We all tend to be "show me" people; we want to "see," "hear," "taste," and "feel" what we are getting into before we pledge ourselves. We like to see objective, visible realities.

Evangelism and missions are often conceptualized as tasks that are chiefly verbal. It is certainly true that the verbal communication of the gospel is *essential* to the fulfillment of the Great Commission, and all believers are clearly *commanded* to engage in verbal witness. Yet it seems extraordinary to expect people around the globe to accept the gospel account and make major, life-altering decisions based solely on the verbal communication of that message. Further complicating matters, the message of the gospel is often delivered by persons quite unknown and strangely foreign to the listener. As glorious as the message of the Cross is to the believer, it is "foolishness" to those who are perishing.

It is noteworthy that in the Scriptures God does not reveal Himself to humankind solely through verbal means. God's *general* revelation of Himself, for example, is quite objective (see Ps. 19:1–6). "The heavens are telling of the glory of God; and their expanse is declaring the work of His hands" (v. 1 NASB), and that revelation itself is enough to render man "without excuse" (Rom. 1:20 NASB).[1] God's *special* revelation was often—

though not exclusively—given in verbal form. The acts of God in history, His signs and His wonders, His theanthropic appearances, and a multitude of other experiential phenomena all served to make God known to man through means other than speech. In fact, the greatest of all revelations of God was objective. Though "no man has ever seen God," Jesus Christ was sent by the Father in order to "make [God] evident" (John 1:18).[2] Christ "dwelt [tabernacled] among us, and we saw His glory" (v. 14 NASB).

In the Old Testament, the "tabernacle" or "temple" was, perhaps, the single, most important "objectifier" of the otherwise invisible God; and the single, most important characteristic of the tabernacle/temple was "holiness."[3] Paul, in his epistles to the Corinthians, frequently appealed to the Old Testament temple as an "objective" form of divine revelation that bore great significance for New Testament believers. The Old Testament temple, to Paul, was intricately tied to divine revelation—objective divine revelation—and revealing God to the world both verbally *and* visually was, to Paul, a major responsibility of the church. The Corinthians had much to learn from this edifice, truths that would greatly affect their lives and ministries. The church today could benefit from these lessons as well. If the message of the gospel is to be effectively communicated from our lips, it must also be modeled in our lives. Clarity in the verbalization of the gospel is inexorably linked to purity in the visualization of the gospel. For the world, seeing the truth is often crucial to believing the truth. To Paul, the Old Testament temple was a chief example of subjectivity finding expression in objectivity.

Why did Paul engage in temple imagery? What are some of the lessons that the Old Testament temple might teach us today? What bearing does this ancient object lesson have on modern evangelism and missions? To discover the answers, we must first examine the tabernacle and temple in the Old Testament. Then we will turn to Paul in the New Testament and analyze his engagements of temple imagery in the epistles to the Corinthians.

The Function of the Temple in the Theocratic Era

The concept of an earthly tabernacle or temple as it related to God found concrete expression only after the exodus from Egypt. Initially, God chose to meet with Moses on a mountain top, Mount Sinai (Ex. 3:4, 12; 19:1–3, 9–13). Though the text is not explicit, it seems that the idea of Moses meeting with God and mediating between God and the people at a "tent" began at Moses' own tent (Ex. 18:7, 12–16).[4] Later, it appears that a special tent, one other than Moses' own residence, was set up at some distance from the encampment for the purpose of meeting with God and seeking the Lord (Ex. 33:7). Eventually God gave Moses explicit instructions concerning the fabrication of a unique tent, the "tabernacle" (Ex. 25–31), which would be at the very center of Israelite life and worship (Numbers 2). Later, after the conquest of Canaan and settlement of the tribes and after the more turbulent years of Saul and David, Solomon constructed the temple, a structure similar to the tabernacle but larger and more permanent (1 Kings 5).

What was the function of the tabernacle and temple? What did God intend by instructing Israel to build such places? There is no doubt that God had many intended purposes for the tabernacle and temple in the theocratic era. Two important functions, however, seem to relate most closely to the temple imagery that Paul engages in his letters to the Corinthians. First, the tabernacle/temple in the Old Testament functioned as a residence of God. Second, the tabernacle/temple in the Old Testament functioned as a reflector of God.

The Old Testament Temple as a Residence of God

Perhaps the most obvious purpose for the tabernacle/temple in the Old Testament era was as a temporary dwelling place for Yahweh, the God of Israel. Just as man lived in a tent or house, so God chose that such a place should be constructed for Himself, once Israel had become a nation and the theocracy was established.[5] The tabernacle/temple served as the earthly habitation of God, a place for Yahweh, the theocratic King, to reside among His chosen people.

The Temple and Divine Residency

God, in His introductory instruction to Moses concerning the building of the tabernacle, explicitly stated that its function was to be that of a divine residence: "Let them construct a sanctuary for Me, that I may dwell among them" (Ex. 25:8 NASB). When the tabernacle was completed, God manifestly took up residence in this tent as "the glory of the LORD filled the tabernacle" (Ex. 40:34–35 NASB; cf. Ps. 114:1–2). Likewise, when Solomon completed the construction and furnishing of the temple, the "glory of the LORD filled the house of the LORD . . ." and took its place between the cherubim above the ark of the covenant (1 Kings 8:6–11 NASB). On that occasion, Solomon reaffirmed the residential function of this glorious edifice: "The LORD has said that He would dwell in the thick cloud. I have surely built You a lofty house, a place for Your dwelling forever" (1 Kings 8:12–13 NASB).

The Temple and Personal Communion

As the residence of God, the temple/tabernacle became the place where God would meet with man and man could commune with God.[6] The temporary precursor to the tabernacle, the initial "tent of meeting," served this communal function. "Everyone who sought the LORD would go out to the tent of meeting which was outside the camp. And it came about, . . . whenever Moses entered the tent, the pillar of cloud would descend and stand at the entrance of the tent; and the LORD would speak with Moses. . . . Thus the LORD used to speak to Moses face to face, just as a man speaks to his friend" (Ex. 33:7–11 NASB). Upon the completion of the divinely prescribed tabernacle, God met with the mediator from His seat above the ark of the covenant, for "when Moses went into the tent of meeting to speak with Him, he heard the voice speaking to him from above the mercy seat that was on the ark of the testimony, from between the two cherubim, so He spoke to him" (Num. 7:89 NASB; see also Ex. 25:22). As the residence of Yahweh God—the Theocrat of national Israel—the temple/tabernacle served as the place where God would meet with man and man could commune with God.

The Temple and Resident Holiness

It is quite stupendous to consider the fact that Yahweh, the one and only true God, the Creator of the universe, the Sovereign of all ages, would take up residence among created men. For Israel to serve as the nation among whom God Himself dwelt was an unfathomable privilege. Such high privilege, however, carried with it grave responsibility, for this tabernacle of God was a "sanctuary" (מִקְדָּשׁ—Ex. 25:8) which was "consecrated" (נִקְדַּשׁ—Ex. 29:43) by God's manifest glory. Thus, by the mandate of God, holiness (קֹדֶשׁ) was an essential component of the tabernacle/temple. In its function as the dwelling place of God, God intended His house to possess what might be called a resident holiness. Resident holiness was an intrinsic sanctity, an immanent holiness that judicially enveloped the edifice itself by virtue of the residency of the holy God within it.[7]

The responsibility of collective holiness. By virtue of the resident holiness of God in its association with the tabernacle/temple, certain obligations fell upon the community of Israel as a whole. First, the congregation was responsible collectively for building the tabernacle (Ex. 25:1–8; 35:1–29). Since it was a residence for God, they were to build it in precise accord with God's pattern—there was no room for personal innovation (Ex. 25:9, 40; 39:42–43; cf. 1 Chron. 28:11–12, 19). Second, the congregation was collectively responsible for maintaining the residence of God in precise accordance with God's instructions (Num. 1–7; 9:15–23; 28:1–29:40).[8] In this responsibility as well, there was no place for personal innovation or careless negligence.[9] These collective responsibilities, which were based upon the resident holiness of the tabernacle/temple, had a unifying effect upon the community. The tabernacle/temple was the only place on earth where God had chosen to dwell, and it was to be the only locus of legitimate, sacrificial worship. Because God lived in this edifice, the preservation of its sanctity was under the care of the community as a whole. The people collectively were responsible for upholding the purity of God's exclusive habitation, both in its initial construction and in its continued upkeep. Because of God's residency among them, the people of God were bound to practice a unified holiness that was to be preserved if God was to continue to abide and work among them.

The responsibility of personal holiness. The resident holiness of God not only called for responsibility on the part of the community, it also invoked a degree of individual responsibility as well. Because God dwelt in the tabernacle/temple, each individual was responsible for maintaining personal holiness if he or she was to access God's presence individually. Everything evil (רֶשַׁע) and wicked (רַע) was antithetic to residency with the God who inhabited this house (Ps. 5:4). The eyesight of the "Holy One" was too "pure" to behold evil (רַע) or "wrongdoing" (עָמָל) (Hab. 1:13). Those persons who desired to "seek protection as a sojourner" (גּוּר) in God's "tent" (אֹהֶל) or who cared to "dwell as a resident" (שָׁכַן) on God's "holy hill" (הַר קָדֹשׁ) had to themselves live in strict accordance with the letter and the spirit of God's holy instruction (Ps. 15). Therefore, intricate laws of sacrifice (Lev. 1–7) and purification (Lev. 11–15) were issued by God in order that naturally sinful people might be able to approach and commune with God personally. The people of God were bound to practice a personal holiness if God was to continue to abide and work among them.

Particular Features of Resident Holiness

At least three corollaries derive from the concept of the resident holiness of the tabernacle/temple. First, resident holiness was *centripetal.* This was a purity routed inward; it was directed *toward* the presence of God. The closer the proximity to God, the higher the demand for sanctity. One obvious factor that supports this assertion is that the most pristine locus of purity in the tabernacle/temple was the inner sanctum, the "most holy place," the "holy of holies." The very heart of the tabernacle/temple was the seat between the cherubim above the ark of the covenant where Yahweh God actually dwelt. In this place and only once a year could the high priest approach God, and even then only with great sacrificial ceremony, in order to atone for the sins of the people and to expurgate all defilement (Lev. 16).

Second, resident holiness was *theological*. This purity served the interest of God and was important to Him. Everything that God selected for use in temple service had to possess a holiness obvious to Him. For this reason, God demanded that the implements of the tabernacle/temple and all of its service personnel be sanctified in His sight (Ex. 29:42–44; Lev. 8–9). Likewise, every communicant who wished to approach God had to be cleansed. Only by strictly following the laws of sacrifice and purity could common men have access to this divine residence. Every consecrated appurtenance and every sacred personage was reserved for God's exclusive use.

Finally, resident holiness was *relational*. This purity was essential to continued fellowship between God and man; it was a holiness upon which the very essence of the theocracy was founded. If national Israel, the beneficiaries of God's residence, failed to maintain the holiness that was essential to His presence, they would be deprived of the benefit. The Theocrat would depart from His residence. Israel was explicitly apprised of this relational arrangement (Jer. 7:1–15; 1 Kings 9:6–9). Eventually the nation sinned so consistently and so grievously against the resident holiness of God that the glory-cloud did depart from the temple (Ezek. 8–11).[10]

Summary

The most obvious purpose of the temple in the Old Testament was its function as a residence for God. Here God could dwell among humankind and humankind could commune with God. Holiness—resident holiness, an internal purity—was essential to this function. The temple precincts had to be kept holy, entirely pure, inviolably sacrosanct, without any vestige of defilement before its chief resident, Yahweh, the God of gods. This holiness was centripetal—directed in toward the presence of God. It was theological—important to God. It was also relational—requisite in God's sight if He were to remain in His sanctuary and work in and through His people Israel.

The Old Testament Temple as the Reflector of God

Perhaps a less obvious purpose of the Old Testament tabernacle/ temple was its function as a reflector; the edifice served as a means of revealing the otherwise unobservable essence and character of God to the world at large. God's abode, in reality, far transcended the realm of the earth, and God Himself was an invisible, spirit being. Yet God caused His glory to shine in an earthly residence and in an observable form. The tabernacle/temple, then, served to reflect the light of God's ineffable glory on the earth, much as the moon reflects the brilliant light of the sun. The tabernacle/temple was a reflector of God's character in that He had chosen this facility as a repository of both His "name" and His "testimony." For this reason, the temple served not only as a place where God dwelt among His people but also as a place where God revealed Himself to them.

The Temple as a Repository of God's Name

Before the establishment of a permanent, central place of worship in the Land of Promise, sacrifice and worship were associated with those locations where God had manifested His presence: "You shall make an altar of earth for Me, and you shall sacrifice on it your burnt offerings and your peace offerings, your sheep and your oxen; in every place where I cause My name to be remembered, I will come to you and bless you" (Ex. 20:24 NASB). Once Israel had entered the land, worship and sacrifice were limited to the permanent, central altar. Unlike the foreign "nations" who "serve(d) their gods on the high mountains and on the hills and under every green tree," Israel was instructed to "seek the LORD at the place which the LORD your God will choose from all your tribes, to establish His name there for His dwelling" (Deut. 12:1–14 NASB). Important to the terminology that God used to describe the appointed, central locus of worship was the term *name* (שֵׁם). The temple was persistently described as the place where God chose to manifest "His name" (Deut. 12:5, 11, 21; 14:23; 16:2, 6, 11; 26:2).

Name terminology is significant to the temple because of the importance of the "name" in Old Testament and ancient Near Eastern thought. In these cultures, "names were considered a substantial part of the existence of the one named" so much so that "a name might come to represent all that the person was."[11] The name of God, then, was so inextricably related to the essence of God that invoking the "name of the LORD" often constituted an assertion of His actual presence (Ex. 23:20–21; Isa. 30:27).[12] Frequently in the Old Testament "the name of God signified the whole self-disclosure of God. . . ."[13] The phrase, "the name of the LORD," often was engaged to connote all of the fullness of the revealed nature of Yahweh God.[14] God's decision to associate His name with the temple signified, therefore, a divine choice to reveal His character, His person, and His nature in and through that place.

In his dedicatory address for the newly constructed temple (1 Kings 8), Solomon evidenced his awareness of the revelatory nature of the "name of the LORD" in its association with this edifice. Solomon knew God to be an unseen spirit being, an unparalleled essence who could neither be physically observed nor geographically contained. The king recognized that God's actual abode was subjective and otherworldly: "Will God indeed dwell on the earth? Behold, heaven and the highest heaven cannot contain You, how much less this house which I have built!" (1 Kings 8:27 NASB). Solomon also knew, however, that God had chosen this building, the temple, as the locus of His name, as the place where He would manifest His character and nature on earth. Though God's permanent abode was subjective, heavenly, and otherworldly, God's temporary abode was objective, earthly, and this-worldly: "Now the LORD has fulfilled His word which He spoke; for I . . . have built th[is] house for the name of the LORD, the God of Israel" (1 Kings 8:20). The temple, then, was the place where the otherwise subjective, unobservable, and seemingly incomprehensible God made Himself objective, observable, and comprehensible. As a revelatory vehicle to a godless humanity, the temple reflected the nature and essence of God in this world.

A Revelatory Reflector for Israel

The temple was the place where God's people, Israel, could seek the Lord in order to find Him, turn to the Lord in order to enjoin Him, and learn of the Lord in order to fear Him (1 Kings 8:28–40). This was the place, the only place in the Mosaic era, where God had chosen to manifest His essence permanently. The temple was the site where local Israelites could come to know the essential qualities of their great God and to worship Him (Ps. 5:3–7). The temple was the edifice to which the exiled Jews could turn to worship the awesome nature of their Lord and beseech His mercy (Dan. 6:10–11; 9:1–19). This building was the avenue of approach to God, even for the recalcitrant and rebellious person who had discounted God's instruction and enjoined his own will (Jonah 2:1–9).[15] The temple in Jerusalem came to be the place where Israel could specially observe and specifically learn the qualities, character, and nature of the otherwise invisible and incomprehensible Deity, for this was the exclusive place of the manifestation of their high and holy God (Isa. 6:1–4).

A Revelatory Reflector for the Nations

It is noteworthy that the function of the temple as the exclusive locus of God's manifest character was not limited only to Israel. Solomon also understood the temple to be the locus of the manifestation of God's character to *all of the world* in that era. First Kings 8:41–43 records this concept: "Also concerning the foreigner who is not of Your people Israel, when he comes from a far country for Your name's sake (for they will hear of Your great name and Your mighty hand, and of Your outstretched arm); when he comes and prays toward this house, hear in heaven Your dwelling place, and do according to all for which the foreigner calls to You, in order that all the peoples of the earth may know Your name, to fear You, as do Your people Israel, and that they may know that this house which I have built is called by Your name" (NASB). Even the foreigner, the Gentile who lived apart from God, might come to approach God there. Indeed, by looking to the temple, the place where God had chosen to manifest His character, "all the peoples of the earth may know that the LORD is God; there is no one else" (1 Kings 8:60 NASB).

The Temple as a Repository of God's Testimony

Not only was the tabernacle/temple the repository of God's *name,* the place where God chose to manifest His essence on earth, it was also the repository of God's *testimony.* When Moses descended from Mount Sinai, he carried with him two tablets of stone on which were inscribed the representative commandments of God (Ex. 24:12).These tablets were called the "tablets of testimony" (Ex. 31:18; 32:15; 34:29). Moses was commanded to place these tablets inside of the ark upon which the glory-cloud would reside, and so the ark was called the "ark of the testimony" (Ex. 25:16, 21; 40:20–21). Because these tablets were kept in the tabernacle, the tent itself became known as the "tent of the testimony" (Num. 1:50, 53; 9:15; 17:7). The tablets were still in the ark when Solomon dedicated the first temple (1 Kings 8:9).

As the residence of God, the tabernacle was a "tent of meeting." As the reflector of God, the tabernacle was a "tent of testimony."[16] Important to the comprehension of this function of the tabernacle is the term *testimony* or *witness* (עֵדוּת). The word *testimony* in the Old Testament derives from a stem that in Semitic languages "has the sense of repetition and permanence."[17] Only in Hebrew does the root take on the meaning of "witness" or "testimony."[18] The development of the word semantically seems to suggest that a "witness" who bears "testimony" is one who reiterates or affirms something original.[19] So the "tablets of testimony" were, in a sense, a "reiteration, affirmation," or "replication" of God.[20] They reflected in writing the essence of God. The character and nature of God could be known by examining these documents, and that revelation—in conjunction with the revelation of His name—was reposit in the tabernacle/temple.

It is notable that national Israel was also assigned the responsibility of bearing both the name (Isa. 43:1–7) and the testimony (Isa. 43:8–13; cf. 44:6–8) of their God. As the tablets of testimony reflected the nature of God in written form, so the nation of Israel was to reflect the nature of God in human form, "For the LORD has redeemed Jacob and in Israel He shows forth His glory" (Isa. 44:23 NASB).[21] This is why Israel was required to be holy like her God (Lev. 11:44–45; 19:2). This is why Israel was not to follow the practices of Egypt or the surrounding nations (Lev. 18:3–5, 24–30). This is why God's people were to be "set apart from the peoples" of the earth (Lev. 20:7–8, 26). This is why the nation was to be separate, distinct, different from the world around her (Deut. 7:1–6). The name of God and the testimony of God resided among them (Ex. 19:5–6) and as a theocratic people, Israel was to be solely responsible for the care of the tabernacle/temple of God. To associate with and to live like the nations around them was to "profane [God's] holy name." Rather, they were to "sanctify" the name of the God who had "sanctified" them (Lev. 22:32). Israel was to be holy like her God, which essentially meant that Israel had to look, think, behave, and in every way function in a manner different from all of the nations around her. Through the tabernacle/temple, this nation was the repository of God's name and God's testimony.

The Temple and Radiant Holiness

God's name—the quality of His character—was made manifest to the entire world through the tabernacle/temple in the theocratic era. God's testimony—the written revelation of God—was reposit in this place. The attention of both Jew and Gentile, indeed of all of humankind, was to be drawn to this locus, for the tabernacle/temple served as a reflection of God's essence in the world. Just as holiness was crucial to the function of the temple as the residence of God, so holiness was essential to the function of the temple as the reflector of God, for Yahweh God was holy, unique, completely different from the imaginary gods of the nations, and distinct from all of created humankind. This holiness, the holiness associated with the temple as a reflector of God's character, might be called a *radiant* holiness. *Radiant* holiness certainly derived from the *resident* holiness of God. Yet radiant holiness was functionally distinct. Whereas the *resident* quality of God's holiness had primary reference to the immanence of God's person within the temple, the *radiant* quality of His holiness had primary reference to the emanation of God's person out from the temple. The temple was not only to *house* the glory of God, it was to *reveal* it. God's holiness was to emanate from the temple as a testimony to His character and His distinctiveness, outshining all of the false and impotent gods of the nations. For this reason, the temple had to be holy, set apart, uniquely distinct from the world round about it.

Particular Features of Radiant Holiness

As with resident holiness, at least three corollaries derive from the concept of the radiant aspect of God's holiness. First, radiant holiness was *centrifugal*.[22] It was a purity that was externally routed, radiating out from the presence of God.[23] The farther humanity was from God, the more necessary the revelation of this holiness. Since the darkness of human sin had penetrated to the farthest reaches of the created order, the ineffable brilliance of God's holiness was required to drive it away. In the Mosaic era, the tabernacle/temple served as an objective source of this ineffable brilliance.[24]

Second, radiant holiness was *anthropological*. Radiance was directed toward mankind; it was a holiness that was important to humanity. Just as there had to be a holiness obvious to God if the temple was to function as His divine residence, so there had to be a holiness obvious to man if the temple was to function as a reflector of God. Man had to be able to "see" God, that is, know about God intellectually, if man was going to be drawn to "experience" God, that is, know God personally. The temple provided explicit evidence as to who God was and what He was like, and the temple provided irrefutable proof that man could have access to God and know Him personally.

Finally, radiant holiness was *revelatory*. Radiance was essential to perpetuate the knowledge of God. It was a holiness upon which the hope of humanity rested. Man could know nothing of God apart from God's self-revelation, and the most direct of all revelations of God in the theocratic era was God's self-revelation in the temple. In this place, during this time, the very essence of God resided. How might the Philistines view for themselves the "great name, and [the] mighty hand, and [the] outstretched arm" of Yahweh, God of Israel (1 Kings 8:42)? How were the Phoenicians and Sidonians to "know [His] name," that is, comprehend the essence of His nature (1 Kings 8:43a)? How might the Ammonites, the Moabites, and the Edomites come to "fear [Yahweh] as [did His] people Israel" (1 Kings 8:43b)? The essential revelatory truths about God could be discovered by looking to the temple, the place that God had selected as the earthly repository of His name and testimony. If the manifest holiness of God, which emanated from the temple, was hidden from the nations, or if the nations failed to look to this objective repository of the holiness of God, they would be denied the very ingredient necessary for knowledge of Him: divine revelation. The radiant quality of God's holiness was revelatory in function. It was designed to perpetuate the knowledge of God.

Summary

Less distinct, but no less important than the function of the tabernacle/temple as God's residence in the Old Testament, was the function of the tabernacle/temple as a reflector of God's character. Here God displayed His glory to humankind and humankind could discover the nature and characteristics of God. Holiness, of course, was essential to the reflective function of the tabernacle/temple. This was a radiant holiness, an emanating purity. The temple gave evidence to the uniqueness of God, who was unlike any created being or any created object. God alone was worthy of worship, and the temple—so long as its sanctity was preserved—provided objective testimony as to the uniqueness and holiness of the person, the nature, and the work of this singular God. The radiant quality of God's holiness was centrifugal. It emanated out from the presence of God. The radiant quality of God's holiness was anthropological. It was a holiness important to humanity, one that had to be obvious to man. The radiant quality of God's holiness was revelatory. It was a purity that was requisite in man's sight if man was to know God and access God's grace. In the tabernacle/temple, God had deigned to make Himself known to man, and man was directed to know his God.

The Function of the Temple in the Era of the Church

Since the Day of Pentecost, God has determined to accomplish His purpose on earth through the work of the local church. In this current era, God no longer inhabits a *building* by taking the form of a glory-cloud. Rather, during the stewardship of the church, God has chosen to inhabit *people* by means of the person of the Holy Spirit. Through Spirit baptism, all believers are joined to the body of Christ (1 Cor. 12:13). Commensurate with this baptism, God indwells the body of each individual believer in the person of the Holy Spirit, who serves as the alter ego of the risen and ascended Christ (John 14:15–26). In this age, then, by virtue of this exchange of divine habitat, the temple is no longer structural, it is personal.

The apostle Paul used this personal temple imagery repeatedly in his letters to the Corinthians.[25] In writing to the Corinthians, Paul addressed a congregation that was struggling with numerous, serious difficulties: false teachers, rival parties, sexual sins, disorderly conduct, and even doctrinal wavering. In both of his extant epistles to this church, Paul invoked temple imagery to call believers back to biblical truth and biblical living (1 Cor. 3:16–17; 6:19–20; 2 Cor. 6:16). His basis of argument appears to rest on the dual function of the Old Testament temple. The temple was a residence of God and a reflector of God. Paul argued that the church at Corinth, specifically the believers who comprised that local body, had to comprehend their function as God's residence and as God-reflectors if they were to function as God intended His church to function in the present age. A brief sketch of the epistles to the Corinthians will serve to probe Paul's use of temple imagery in his letters to this church.

The New Testament Church as the Residence of God

In his first epistle to the Corinthians, Paul twice engaged temple imagery (3:16–17; 6:19–20). In both, Paul emphasized the *resident* aspect of God's holiness. God resided within these believers. In 1 Corinthians chapters 1–4 Paul emphasized the *communal* aspect of God's resident holiness—that is, God dwelt within the church *corporately.* On this basis, Paul called the people to abandon their mindless division. In chapters 5–6 the apostle emphasized the *personal* nature of God's resident holiness—that is, God dwelt within the church *individually.* On this basis, Paul confronted the problem of moral disorder in the church. In both cases, Paul argued from temple imagery that the residency of the Spirit of God in the body of Christ, the church, was wholly antithetical to such division and disorder.

The Problem: Mindless Divisions in the Church

In 1 Corinthians chapters 1–4, Paul spoke firmly to the Corinthian church about factionalism.[26] Paul asserted from the very beginning of his letter that these divisions were mindless; they were grounded in wrong thinking (1:10). Just as quickly, the apostle disassociated his own ministry from such worldly wisdom (v. 17). The church, Paul reminded them, was founded upon the gospel of Christ, not the clever machinations of man, and Christ's gospel was "foolishness" to man (vv. 18–25). Yet the simplicity of the gospel had within it an equalizing and unifying effect, for no true believer, no member of the church, could rightfully elevate himself, but only Christ (vv. 26–31). Paul's original ministry to them was conducted in the weakness of Paul's humanity so that it might manifest the power of God's Spirit (2:1–5), for only the Spirit of God could reveal the true wisdom of God (vv. 6–16). This Holy Spirit, Paul said, is the One who was promised to dwell in them. "Now we have received, not the spirit of the world, but the Spirit who is from God, so that we may know the things freely given to us by God" (v. 12 NASB).

Unfortunately, the Corinthians were no longer subjecting themselves to the indwelling Spirit nor attending to His instructions for the church; rather, they had turned to their own fleshly thinking (3:1). They had left off following the mind of the Spirit and were following after men (vv. 1–4). They had lost sight of the fact that men were only servants in the building and maintenance of the church; the church was actually God's "field" and God's "building" (vv. 5–9). A building designed by God as His residence must employ the precise materials and follow the exact pattern of the master builder; no substitute methodology would suffice, for God would judge the authenticity of each man's building efforts (vv. 10–16).

The climax of Paul's argument against mindless factionalism and self-aggrandizing division is found in the next two verses, where Paul employs temple imagery (vv. 17–18). The Corinthians must remember that they, corporately and individually—as the church of God and the body of Christ—are the "temple of God and that the Spirit of God dwells in [them]" (v. 16 NASB). God no longer dwells in physical structures; He lives in physical beings—a truth more amazing than the fact that the great God of the universe, at one time in history, lived in a shelter on the earth. Now He inhabits human beings themselves, members of the church. With such great truth comes grave responsibility, for this bodily temple is the residence of deity, and everything about this temple must be holy. It must be specifically built in accordance with exact, divine specifications. It must be singularly maintained according to the precise instructions of God. For "if any man destroys the temple of God, God will destroy him, for the temple of God is holy, and that [temple] is what you are" (v. 17 NASB).[27] The wisest of men cannot improve upon God's pattern and procedure (vv. 1–21). The only requirement for temple building and temple maintenance is "faithfulness" to the pattern and procedures of God (4:1–2), and God alone will judge those efforts (vv. 3–5).

The Solution: Resident Holiness Expressed Communally

In confronting the Corinthians' mindless division, Paul made it clear that the problem was divided thinking (1:10) and worldly wisdom (v. 20). Their arrogance was expressed by their advancing of self (4:6; cf. 18–21). Paul was calling them to corporate unity, and the chief motivation for such unity was the indwelling Spirit of Christ. Paul's argument, grounded in temple imagery, seems to proceed as follows. The body of each believer is the temple of the Holy Spirit,[28] therefore, the body of each local church corporately can also be called the habitation of God.[29] Because the temple is the singular place of God's residence—the dwelling place of God—it must preserve a resident holiness. The preservation of resident holiness is a communal responsibility. The community as a whole is to build the temple precisely and exclusively according to God's specifications. Members of that community are not to interject their own schemes. The community as a whole is to maintain the temple in exact accord to God's designs, not man's.

The Corinthian church had failed in this regard. It had allowed the clever machinations of some to draw it away from the simple designs of God, and the more it followed after the designs of men, the further it drew away from the pattern of God. Instead of being united through the person, work, and mind of the indwelling Spirit, it had interjected the thinking of man; and to interject human devices into the building and/or maintenance of God's temple was to interject defilement. Such defilement only served to destroy the sanctity of the temple, and God would bring reciprocal destruction on any who would so desecrate the sanctity of His habitation. Resident holiness demanded communal purity. And communal purity was maintained only through corporate obedience to the indwelling presence of God. If Christ is in us all, and Christ is not divided, then there is no room for selfish innovation and schismatic divisions among us. The church must express the resident holiness of God communally if God is to abide and work within and through it.

The Problem: Moral Disorder in the Church

In the next chapters, 1 Corinthians 5–6, Paul turned to the topic of moral disorder. Sexual immorality was openly known among the church's membership (5:1), and such tolerance of sin in the church was unacceptable and had to be purged (vv. 2–13). Paul then touched on the matter of public litigation. The self-centeredness that had surfaced in the church corporately through its factionalism (chaps. 1–5), had also manifested itself individually as brothers in Christ disputed with each other in secular courts of law (6:1). Such disorderly conduct was unacceptable. Disputes were either to be handled within the church itself or abandoned altogether (vv. 2–8). Paul concluded this section by listing all manner of immoral conduct (vv. 9–10) and reminding the Corinthian believers that regeneration had delivered them from such behavior (v. 11). Their bodies were no longer personal property; they belonged to Christ and should not be prostituted (vv. 12–18).

The climax of his argument against moral disorder was based again upon temple imagery: the bodies of these Corinthian believers were the temple of the Holy Spirit (vv. 19–20). The resident Holy Spirit within them was a gift of God (v. 19b). Furthermore, His residency indicated ownership, and ownership meant authoritative control (v. 19c). Paul then interjected another metaphor, referring to their redemption as from the slave market (v. 20a). In any case, their responsibility was to "glorify God in [their] body" (v. 20b).

The Solution: Resident Holiness Expressed Personally

In confronting the moral disorder of the Corinthians, Paul made it clear that the problem was human lust (5:1) and worldly living (6:9–10). Their arrogance was expressed in the way they ignored sin (5:2). Paul was calling them to personal purity, and the chief motivation for purity was the indwelling Spirit of Christ. Resident holiness demanded not only corporate unity but also personal purity. Paul's argument followed the same line as that which he forwarded against their mindless divisions, only here the application was individual rather than congregational. The Spirit of God inhabits each believer in the church. Holiness, then, is requisite for each individual. The temple is not to be used to gratify human lusts. In fact, all such impurities must be expurgated from the habitation of God. The temple is a place to glorify God, to honor Him through sacrifice, worship, fellowship, and praise. Resident holiness demands personal purity, and personal purity is maintained only through personal obedience to the indwelling presence of God. If Christ is in each one of us, and if He is undefiled, then there is no room for personal vice or immoral disorder within us. The church must express the resident holiness of God personally if God is to abide and work within and through it.

Summary

In his first epistle to the Corinthians, the apostle Paul engaged temple imagery twice in order to correct some of the flagrant errors that had crept into this church. In both cases, his argument was based upon the resident quality of God's holiness in the temple, a holiness that placed demands on the community as a whole as well as on each individual. Communally, resident holiness demanded that the membership of the church be diligent in abstaining from fleshly thinking. Since God dwelt in each of them individually, then He also dwelt in all of them corporately. Thus, the continued edification (building) of His residency and the daily ministrations (maintenance) of His residency were to be be carried out by the community in accordance with His pattern and requisites, not in accordance with human plans and devices. God expects to see holiness manifest in the church as a community, a holiness that gives thorough attention to His revelation, honors His headship, subordinates self, and renounces factionalism. Such communal holiness will manifest itself in corporate unity. On the other hand, with regard to each individual, resident holiness demands that every member of the church individually be diligent in abstaining from fleshly living. God Himself inhabits personally each member's body. Thus, no moral impurities or defiling practices are to be tolerated. God expects to see holiness manifest in church members individually, a holiness that abstains from fleshly lust and promptly seeks cleansing from every defilement. Such individual holiness will manifest itself in personal purity.

As in the Old Testament temple, resident holiness in the church, both communally and individually, is first *centripetal*. It primarily looks inward into the inner workings of the temple, the body itself. Corporately, resident holiness demands that the body as a whole examine itself to see if it has been infected with human thinking. Individually, resident holiness demands that individual members examine themselves to see if they have been infected with human lust. Second, resident holiness is also *theological*. It addresses the concerns of God; it gives great attention to that which matters to Him. Communally, the body as a whole must attend to the wisdom of God, His holy Word; and individually each member must attend to godly living, for godly thinking and godly living matter to God. Finally, resident holiness is *relational*. This is a holiness that is essential to continued fellowship, a holiness upon which the community itself is founded. Inner holiness is imperative if the church is to maintain fellowship with God and if its constituents are to maintain fellowship with each other. "You are a temple of God" (3:16 NASB); "your body is a temple of the Holy Spirit" (6:19 NASB).

The New Testament Church as the Reflection of God

In his second epistle to the Corinthians, Paul's use of temple imagery seems to draw more heavily on the *radiant* aspect of God's holiness over against the *resident* aspect, which supported Paul's argument in his first epistle. Just as in the Old Testament, it is assumed that the radiant holiness of God derives from His resident holiness. Holiness cannot emanate from an impure source. Radiant holiness is as important to the function of the temple, however, as is resident holiness. Radiant holiness focuses on the outworking of sanctity that derives from its inworking. Radiant holiness reveals God to the world by distinguishing God from the world. Paul, in writing again to the church at Corinth, addressed the congregation's need to display its holy relationship to God by guarding its associations with the world. The name of God and the testimony of God were at stake in these external relationships. Paul called the church body, then, to be distinct from the world around it so that the light of God's character might clearly shine through it.

The Problem: Association with the World

In 2 Corinthians Paul takes up various themes, one of which is his instruction regarding separation from unbelievers (6:14–18). It is debated as to why the apostle interjected this theme at this juncture in the book, but there is little doubt as to Paul's meaning.[30] Perhaps Paul was building upon the fact that his own ministry before the Corinthians and before the world was conducted "in holiness and godly sincerity, not in fleshly wisdom but in the grace of God" (1:12 NASB). Such a "holy" or "unique" kind of ministry was important to Paul, because he recognized that God had chosen to manifest "through [His servants] the sweet aroma of the knowledge of Him in every place" (2:14 NASB). Because of this great responsibility to manifest God to the world, Paul had "renounced the things hidden because of shame, not walking in craftiness or adulterating the word of God, but by the manifestation of truth" Paul commended himself "to every man's conscience in the sight of God" (4:2 NASB). Paul affirmed that "If anyone is in Christ, he is a new creature," and having been given the "ministry of reconciliation" as an ambassador for Christ, that newness had to be evident to the world if the world was to see Christ through His ambassadors (5:17–20). Paul called the Corinthians to bear witness that his ministry among them was fashioned after the character of God and not the philosophies and practices that characterized the world system. It should not be surprising, then, to find Paul calling the Corinthians themselves to examine their own behavior and associations, to see whether they should find themselves more in conformity to the unbelievers around them or to the Christ who redeemed them.

The Solution: Radiant Holiness Expressed Consistently

In reaction to his fear that the Corinthians had compromised their uniqueness by associating with unbelievers, Paul called them to separation from unbelievers and, presumably, from the corresponding principles and practices of such unbelief (2 Cor. 6:14–18). This plea for separation, in Paul's address to the Corinthians, is based on the fact that all church-age saints "are the temple of the living God" (v. 16b NASB). Such believers have no legitimate partnership with unbelievers, for the two are wholly antithetical (vv. 14–16a). The basis of true fellowship among church-age believers is grounded in an exclusive relationship with God (vv. 16c–18). They are the very "temple of the living God," and if the world is to see the living God in the temple, the temple of God must be radically distinct from the world. " 'Come out from their midst and be separate,' says the Lord; 'and do not touch what is unclean'" (v. 17 NASB). World-likeness only serves to intersect the believers' relationship with their Father and certainly makes them look like something other than true "sons and daughters" (v. 18 NASB). Paul seems to be arguing quite clearly, based upon Old Testament temple imagery, that if the world is in the church, Christ will never be seen by the world.

Paul's desire was that the Corinthians, like Israel of old, refrain from joining with the world to the extent that they become like them. God's name should not be profaned, His testimony should not be defiled. But the unthinkable can happen if the bearers of God's name and testimony choose to associate themselves with the world system and begin to take on the qualities of that system. To the extent that such compromise should happen, the radiant quality of God's holiness is dimmed. As with Israel, should the bearers of God's holiness become so like the world that the expression of God's radiant glory is extinguished, then God must bring condemnation on the failed light bearers. God desires that His holiness be seen by the world, and clear reflections require pure reflectors. "Therefore, having these promises, beloved, let us cleanse ourselves from all defilement of flesh and spirit, perfecting holiness in the fear of God" (7:1 NASB).[31]

Summary

In the second epistle to the Corinthians, the apostle Paul engaged temple imagery in order to call the church to responsible and obedient ministry in the world. The basis of Paul's argument was the radiant quality of God's holiness as it related to the temple, a holiness that was to reflect God's name and His testimony in the world. In this church age, God has chosen to objectify Himself not in a building but in the bodies of church-age believers. Their maintenance of a radiant holiness is essential. How are our unregenerate neighbors, fellow workers, loved ones, friends, classmates, and other associates going to "see" God? How will they know who God is and what He is like? How will they envision God-like living? The character, essence, and distinctiveness of God is made evident in this age by looking to God's temple—His saints; and this distinctiveness is apparent only if these saints remain distinct from the world. God's children must be holy, as God is holy, or the unique message of the gospel is hidden from those who perish. God's children must not take on partnership with the world. It is essential that His people be separate. It is vital that God's temple not be defiled with uncleanness, for if the holiness of God does not radiate from God's temple—His children in this age—only darkness can follow.

Radiant holiness in the church is *centrifugal.* It primarily emanates outward from the temple, which is our bodies. It demands that no obstruction or defilement be allowed to diffuse or darken the brilliant holiness of God's character and testimony, which resides within in pristine purity. Radiant holiness is *anthropological.* It addresses the needs of man; it gives great attention to that which matters to humanity. Without a perfect likeness of God, without an objective picture of His nature and His truth, there is little chance—humanly speaking—that the world will seek Him, much less find Him. Finally, radiant holiness is *revelatory.* This is a holiness that is imperative to human witness; it is a holiness through which the truth of the gospel itself is objectively manifest. It is a living revelation of truth in this age. If the gospel is hidden by our lives, it is not likely that it will be received from our lips. The church must remain distinct from the world.

Conclusion

Paul's engagements of temple imagery in his epistles to the Corinthian church are powerful reminders of our obligations as God's messengers today. God has given His church the mandate to spread the message of the gospel to every creature, and this mandate requires us all to be verbal harbingers of the truth. But we have not completed the assignment if we stop there. In fact, we leave the world to believe something the world may have little objective reason to accept as reality, other than our *ipse dixit.* Certainly God could expect this kind of nonevidential response from man. We know, however, that God *has* chosen to make the message of the gospel "alive" in our day. In fact, He fully expects the message of the gospel not only to be "audible" but also to be "visible." He expects the reality of His saving grace to be objectified in the church: our bodies, the temple of the living God.

This expectation from God places great responsibility upon us all. The world must not look at the church, the temple of God in our dispensation, and see corporate infighting, discord, and schism (1 Corinthians 1–4). To the degree that our churches are focused on themselves and are unable to spiritually discipline themselves, to that degree the temple will be polluted, and the reality of oneness in Christ will be lost in the sight of the unregenerate, despite our verbiage. Further, the world must not look at the church and see personal immorality, fraudulent behavior, and a host of other fleshly practices (1 Corinthians 5–6). Insofar as the flesh rules the body, the temple has been defiled; and the cleansing, life-giving nature of the gospel will mean nothing to the lost person who looks at the child of God and sees, regardless of what we say, the works of the Devil. Finally, the world must not look at the church and see a reflection of itself (2 Corinthians 6). If the church takes on partnership with the world system, it will inevitably mimic the world system; and if the church looks more and more like the world, the world will see less and less of God, no matter what our verbal confessions seem to affirm.

Does mission work mean announcing the good news of the gospel to the lost? Yes! And speak we must! But should we expect the lost to believe words that have no fruition in objective reality? Not if we have God's mind. He would have the lost "see" the truth as well as "believe" it. Africans, Latins, Asians, Caucasians—all the peoples of the world— must not only "hear" the message of the gospel, they must "see" the reality of that message in the lives of its messengers: in households, in schools, in marketplaces, in workplaces, and in play places all around the world. God-likeness must reside in and must radiate from our local churches corporately and from our individual bodies personally if the message is truly to impact all nations. Thus, these resident and revelatory instruments of God must be kept holy, pure, and distinct from the world. Such is our responsibility as children of God. We are temples of the Holy Spirit.

Study Questions

1. Most believers are familiar with the concept of presenting the gospel verbally through personal testimony or printed material. Summarize, in a few sentences, what it means to "model" the gospel and the truth of Scripture through holy living.
2. In what ways does "modeling" the gospel complement the "verbal" witness of biblical truth? Is one more important than the other? Why or why not? Why might "modeling" be more difficult?
3. If believers truly "model" holiness, what effect does this behavior have on God? How does "modeling" holiness affect the lives of the believers themselves? How does it affect unsaved people?
4. From the content of this chapter, list the three particular features of "resident holiness" and summarize the practical effect that these features should have on the New Testament church as the "residence" of God.
5. From the content of this chapter, list the three particular features of "radiant holiness" and summarize the practical effect that these features should have on the New Testament church as the "reflector" of God.
6. Can you think of instances in the life and ministry of Jesus where He either practiced or commanded the concept of "living" rather than just "speaking" the message of Scripture? Cite some specific references.
7. Besides those listed in this chapter, think of passages in the book of Acts and/or the Epistles where "modeling" the truth is either asserted or commanded. Cite some specific references.
8. Explain how the principle of "modeling" the truth of Scripture transcends cultural boundaries and compels the missionary to truly "Christianize" indigenous peoples over against simply "Americanizing" them.

Chapter Notes

1. All quotations of Scripture in this article are taken from the *New American Standard Bible* unless otherwise noted.
2. This author's translation.
3. The term "holiness," throughout this article, should not be understood either exclusively or chiefly in its ethical sense: that is, "apart from sin." The term "holiness" in the Old Testament is primarily *relational,* referring broadly to anything which "belongs to deity." Relationally the term connotes that which is "apart" or "distinct" from everything that is common,

profane, created, and creaturelike. "Holiness" speaks essentially of "transcendence, separateness, uniqueness, and distinctiveness." For an excellent theological discussion of this concept see A. B. Davidson, *The Theology of the Old Testament* (Edinburgh: T & T Clark, 1904), 144–60, 252–59.

4. It appears that Jethro, Moses' father-in-law, met with Moses at Moses' own tent (Ex. 18:7) where they offered sacrifices and, along with Aaron and the elders, ate a meal "before God" (v. 12). It also appears that this was the place where the people came to Moses in order to "inquire of God" (v. 15).

5. The theocratic, mediatorial kingdom of God in history began with the giving of the covenant on Mount Sinai and continued in its purest form until the time of the Babylonian exile. After the Exile the framework of the kingdom was reestablished, but the glory-cloud never again took up residence in the temple. This functional, post-exilic kingdom continued until the destruction of Jerusalem by the Romans in A.D. 70. (For an overview of the theocratic, mediatorial kingdom concept see the *Dictionary of Premillennial Theology,* ed. Mal Couch [Grand Rapids: Kregel, 1996], s.v. "Kingdoms, Universal and Mediatorial," by Roy E. Beacham, 235–37).

6. Under the Old Testament theocratic structure, this personal interaction with God at the tabernacle/temple was conducted through God's appointed mediators. Moses first facilitated this communion, then the priesthood.

7. The suggestion that the holiness which enveloped the temple precincts was "judicial" in nature is meant to assert that this holiness was not some kind of dynamic force that possessed a life of its own. Rather, this was an assigned holiness that, in conformity with the innate, holy character of God Himself, was legally required by God to adhere, as it were, to everything that was to be closely associated with God.

8. "Maintenance" of the tabernacle included supporting the facility and its personnel through tithes and offerings and enforcing as well as obeying its rituals and codes. Ryrie suggests that there are fifty chapters in the Bible that give instruction concerning the tabernacle (Charles Caldwell Ryrie, *Ryrie Study Bible: Expanded Edition, New American Standard Bible,* 1995 Update [Chicago: Moody, 1995], 129, note at Exodus 25:1).

9. That Israel as a nation failed to uphold prescribed temple procedures both practically and financially is most evident in the word of the Lord through the prophets. See, for example, Malachi's condemnation of the nation's derelict worship (1:7ff.) and negligent giving (3:8ff.).

10. Alva J. McClain best summarizes the historical setting and the theological significance of the departure of the "glory" from the temple in chapter 11 of his work *The Greatness of the Kingdom* (Winona Lake, Ind.: BMH Books, 1974), 120–29.

11. *New International Dictionary of Old Testament Theology,* s.v. שֵׁם, by Allen P. Ross, 4:149.

12. *Theological Word Book of the Old Testament,* s.v. שֵׁם, by Walter C. Kaiser, 2:934.

13. Ibid.

14. *New International Dictionary of Old Testament Theology,* s.v. שֵׁם, by Ross, 4:149.

15. Even in the stomach of the great fish, where actual direction was impossible to determine, Jonah directed his prayer "toward (the) holy temple" (Jonah 2:4, 7).

16. J. H. Kurtz points out the significance of the tabernacle as the "tent of witness" (or "testimony") in *Sacrificial Worship of the Old Testament,* trans. James Martin, (Edinburgh, T & T Clark, 1863; reprint, Minneapolis: Klock and Klock, 1980), 42.

17. *Theological Word Book of the Old Testament,* s.v. עוּד, by Carl Shultz, 2:648.

18. E. Jenni and C. Westermann, eds. *Theologisches Handbuch zum Alten Testament,* 2 vols., (Munich, 1971, 1976) s.v. עוּד, by G. Gerleman, 2:210.

19. *Theological Word Book of the Old Testament,* s.v. עוּד, by Shultz, 2:648.

20. "The law of God is his testimony because it is his own affirmation relative to his very person and purpose" (ibid., 650).

21. See chapter 2 by Michael A. Grisanti, "The Missing Mandate: Missions in the Old Testament," in this volume.

22. Conceptualizing God's holiness as something centrifugal is not to imply that Israel had some form of mandate that required them actively to take the message of God to all of the nations of the world. See, again, the article by Michael A. Grisanti in this volume.

23. The radiant aspect of God's holiness, like God's resident holiness, should not be understood as something dynamistic, that is, as a materialistic "force" with an essence and power of its own. Just as resident holiness could be attached to or associated with sacred precincts, personnel, and property in a *judicial* sense, so radiant holiness emanated from the temple as a juridical concept, not as a magical power. Much like Isaiah "saw the LORD" through his mind's eye, albeit prophetic in his case (Isa. 6), so Israel and the nations were to look to the temple in their minds eye in order to see, conceptually, what God was like. (That some in Israel actually did conceptualize about God and their relationship to Him in His holy residence see, for example, Pss. 15; 24; 27:4–8; 61:4; Isa. 33:14–22). The temple served as an agent of special revelation in a way not unlike, though not wholly parallel to, the more general revelation of creation

itself. If the heavens could declare the glory of God (Ps. 19:1), and if the world was held accountable enough to be condemned for their lack of knowing God through the revelation of creation (Rom. 1:18–20), so the temple could manifest God's glory throughout all of the earth and men could be held responsible for that recognition. (See also the note below.)

24. Certainly there was a *de jure* sense in which the radiant glory of the sovereign God already permeated all of the earth (Isa. 6:3). Ultimately, however, only in the eschaton will God's glory be evident *de facto* throughout all of the earth, much like it was evident in Egypt at the time of the Exodus (Num. 14:20–22a). In that future day "the earth will be filled with the knowledge of the glory of the LORD, as the waters cover the sea" (Hab. 2:14).

25. Paul also engaged temple imagery in Ephesians 2:21–22.

26. Gordon D. Fee's outline of 1 Corinthians 1–6 is helpful in overviewing the content of these chapters. See *The First Epistle to the Corinthians,* New International Commentary on the New Testament (Grand Rapids: Eerdmans, 1987), 21–22.

27. For the translation "that [temple] is what you are," where the relative pronoun refers back to the antecedent "temple," see ibid., 149 n. 21.

28. See the discussion of 1 Corinthians 6:19–20 below where the referents are singular.

29. The referents in 1 Corinthians 3:16–17 are clearly plural.

30. Some commentators go so far as to suggest that this passage is non-Pauline. For an overview of the issues regarding both the authenticity of this pericope and its relationship to the context, see Ralph P. Martin, *2 Corinthians,* Word Biblical Commentary (Waco, Tex.: Word, 1986), 190–95, who accepts a somewhat modified view. See also Philip E. Hughes, *The Second Epistle to the Corinthians,* New International Commentary on the New Testament (Grand Rapids: Eerdmans, 1962), 241–44, who espouses a more traditional view.

31. The separation of 2 Corinthians 7:1 from the preceding pericope (6:14–18) by a chapter division in many of the versions is quite unfortunate.

4

W. EDWARD GLENNY

THE GREAT COMMISSION

A Multidimensional Perspective

It is arguable that there are no passages in the Bible more important for defining the church's mission than Jesus' post-resurrection commissions to His disciples. Since these passages are proclaimed regularly in most churches, one might question whether a book addressing topics in missions should devote space to them. Because of their foundational nature and theological content, however, we feel a book addressing topics in missions would be incomplete without doing so.

The purpose of this chapter is to study Jesus' post-resurrection commissions to His disciples found in Matthew, Luke-Acts, and John.[1] The works of these three authors will be considered independently, allowing each author to speak in his own literary context and to develop his own unique emphases and categories. Furthermore, it is at this first stage of study that the historical context and role in redemptive history of the various events and words in these passages will be emphasized.[2] Since the theology of the individual biblical authors is complementary, and the ultimate goal of the study of Scripture is to develop a systematic theology, at the conclusion of this chapter I will attempt to systematize the theology in the Lord Jesus' post-resurrection commissions to His disciples.[3]

Matthew 28:16–20

The post-resurrection commission that Jesus gives to His disciples in Matthew is generally known as the Great Commission. He gave it to

them on "the mountain" in Galilee, a place which He had previously
designated (28:16; cf., 26:32; 28:7, 10). It is unclear how many disciples
were present on the mountain with Jesus, but if there were more than the
Eleven, as some suggest, it might explain why some worshiped and some
doubted when they saw Jesus (28:17).[4] After the resurrected Jesus came
to the group of disciples on the mountain, He gave to them their commission. The theological basis for this commission, and in that regard
the most important verse in the passage, is verse 18. It is expedient that
we do not pass over this verse too quickly.

The Basis of the Commission

Two observations are foundational to the discussion of Matthew
20:18. First, it is important to recognize that Jesus is talking about being
given authority and not power. As a member of the Godhead, Jesus has
always had power *(dynamis)*. Such inherent power is an essential part of
the divine nature. Power is not the same thing, however, as the right to
exercise power; that is authority *(exousia)*. Authority is freedom; it is
power that is free to decide and to act. To illustrate these concepts, it
might help to envision a tremendously talented employee who has the
ability and power to make the company for which she works a great
success. For one reason or another, however, she is not given authority
to implement her ideas, and the company never profits from her ability
(i.e., power). To make matters worse for our make-believe company, and
to further illustrate the difference between these two concepts, we could
posit that the CEO of this company, who somehow possesses all the
authority to make decisions and to act for the company, has very limited
ability and does not delegate authority to others in the company. The
point is that power and authority are two different things. Although Jesus
has always had inherent power as the Son of God, that does not mean He
has always had the authority to exercise the power that is essential to His
nature.[5] This point is often missed by interpreters of Matthew 28, and
yet it is an important element in understanding the reason Jesus gives
the Great Commission to His disciples.[6]

The second initial observation concerning Jesus' announcement of
His authority in verse 18 is that He now has a new, greater dimension of
authority than He previously possessed. This new authority is seen in
His statement that it "has been given to me" and in the degree of the
authority that He now possesses, i.e., "all authority in heaven and on
earth." The only one who could give such absolute authority to Jesus is
the Father (Matt. 11:27). Although it is true, as Carson cautions, that the

coming of Jesus "to kingly authority cannot be reduced to a single moment in redemptive history,"[7] it is at the same time true that He possesses absolute authority and lordship by virtue of His death and resurrection from the dead (Rom. 1:3–4; esp. Phil. 2:5–11).[8] Ephesians 1:20–23 clearly states that the time when Jesus was given absolute authority was at His resurrection/exaltation/ascension. In fact, in Romans 14:9 Paul states that Christ's resurrection gave Him the ability to extend His authority over the dead, and 1 Peter 3:18–22 teaches that, at the time of His resurrection, Jesus' authority extended to include the most remote outposts of the spiritual realm (cf. esp. v. 22 and 1 Cor. 15:45).[9]

Since the universal authority of Christ cannot conflict with the Father's sovereign authority, it is necessary to explain as precisely as possible how the two relate. Christ's authority, which was given to Him by the Father and which He will freely give back to the Father (1 Cor. 15:28), does not include authority over the Father (1 Cor. 15:27).[10] In this age, the Father and the Son function as a coregency, in which Christ functions as vice-regent and is given all authority by the Father to administer the universe. The work of God is now administered by Jesus Christ. That explains, for example, why the gift of the Holy Spirit can be called the promise of the Father (Luke 24:49; Acts 1:4; 2:33), and yet Jesus administers this promise (Luke 24:49; Acts 2:33). In fact John 14:16 and 26 clarify that the Spirit comes from the Father, the Father sends the Spirit in Jesus' name, and the Father sends the Spirit when Jesus asks.[11]

D. R. de Lacey summarizes what Christ's lordship means for the Trinity: "The Father, by bestowing lordship on the Son, shares with him his status and functions; the Son, by remaining in submission to the Father and ultimately restoring to him all lordship and dominion, never usurps his authority."[12] Several passages in the New Testament, including 1 Corinthians 15, Ephesians 1:9–10 and 4:10, and especially Colossians 1:19–20, indicate that the Father's purpose in giving universal authority to Jesus Christ is finally to reconcile to Himself all things in the universe through the incarnate Son.[13] This last fact ties in again with Matthew 28:16–20 and gives a clue as to why Christ's universal authority is given as the basis for the Great Commission. The beginning of the new creation (2 Cor. 5:17), which God is in the process of accomplishing in this world, is the reconciliation of individuals to Himself in Christ (2 Cor. 5:18–19; Col. 1:19–23). Jesus, the provider of universal salvation, has authority to pour out that salvation and its benefits, without any national or racial barriers, to all who come to God in His name.

That Jesus has authority over everything on earth and in the heavens has several implications. First, all creatures are required to worship and submit to Him. Second, since He is Lord, all must come to God through Him, or in His name. He is the one who administers God's redemptive program in this age. Third, His words and teachings have absolute authority and should be obeyed by all. Fourth, His representatives also go with great authority, since they represent the Lord of all. This means that even when they meet resistance, the representatives of Christ must do His will and proclaim His message, since His authority is greater than any other. Fifth, since He is sovereign over all, whatever situation His representatives encounter, they must accept it as His will. In this regard, His purposes are often accomplished through the suffering of His people, which He as sovereign wills and determines that they endure. The Father's purposes were accomplished through Christ's own suffering. Sixth, since He has all authority, Christ is also able to protect and prosper His servants as He wills. Seventh, people who place themselves under Christ's authority have the ability to do what He commands them. His authority becomes theirs.

The preceding implications lead naturally to the Great Commission.[14]

The Content of the Commission—Matthew 28:19

The content of the commission has been developed in many fine works, and, therefore, I will not attempt to develop it further here.[15] It is important, however, that we understand the main ideas in this passage. As is generally known, "make disciples" is the only finite verb in verses 19–20a. The verbal structure is participle+imperative+participle+participle.[16] The three participles, "go," "baptizing," and "teaching," are all syntactically subordinate to the main verb, indicating that there are three activities that constitute disciple making. Although some suggest that the participle "go" simply enlivens the narrative, and does not have the force of an imperative,[17] the grammatical structure indicates that the participle is more likely an attendant circumstance participle with imperatival force.[18] This imperatival force is implied, even if one does not accept the grammatical arguments for it; how can Jesus' followers make disciples of all nations if they do not go to them? In addition, not only does the grammatical construction match that of an attendant circumstance participle with imperatival force and the context support an imperatival force for the participle, "go," but also the imperatival force of the commission "to go" is preserved in several other complementary passages (cf., esp. Luke 24:45–49; John 20:21; Rom. 10:10–15).[19] Therefore, it is best to understand the participle "go" as having the force of an imperative, while at the same time the structure of the passage clearly places the main emphasis on the verb "make disciples."[20]

The verb "make disciples" *(matheteuo)* in Matthew 28:19 occurs only three other times in the New Testament, two of them in Matthew (13:52; 27:57; Acts 14:21).[21] This emphasis, or mission task, "differs considerably from that assigned in the other synoptics, where the emphasis is on the proclamation of the gospel (cf. Mark 16:15; Luke 24:47)." The occurrence of this verb in the New Testament that gives the most insight into its meaning is Matthew 13:52. In that context Jesus teaches

> . . . that "every scribe that has become a disciple of the kingdom" has a special responsibility: to "bring forth" (that is, teach) "his treasure." For Matthew, the focus of the disciples' mission is less one of public proclamation than one of intensive instruction. This perspective, of course, is in accord with Matthew's portrait of Jesus as a teacher who repeatedly instructs his disciples at length and in depth. Such intensive instruction would be viewed by Matthew's Jewish readers as natural for any disciple, but especially necessary for Gentiles coming into the church.[22]

The contexts in which this verb is found in the New Testament emphasize that "being instructed as a disciple is a mark of a true disciple."[23] This emphasis is consistent with the meaning of other discipleship words in Matthew.[24] It is important to remember that the process of disciple making involves more than teaching—as important as that may be—especially in the gospel of Matthew.[25] A study of the concept of discipleship in Matthew indicates that discipleship involves identifying with a person who is superior in knowledge and authority, placing ourselves under that person's authority, learning from that person, understanding and then obeying his teaching, following his leadership, and then seeking to disciple others.[26] If I am making disciples, I am already a disciple. I am attempting to lead, influence, and help others to become what I already am. Thus, all true disciples of Jesus are in the business of making disciples, because Jesus has commanded His disciples to do so.[27]

The objects of this discipling, that is "all nations" *(panta ta ethne),* have been understood to be either the Gentiles, that is all nations except Israel, or all people, including Israel.[28] The first option was certainly not the interpretation of the early church, which understood that the gospel was to go to the Jews first (Acts 3:26; 18:6; Rom. 1:16), nor does the use of *ethnos* in Matthew always mean Gentiles and exclude Jews (21:43).[29] Furthermore, in support of the latter position, one can make a strong case that the full expression, *panta ta ethne,* which Matthew uses four times (24:9, 14; 25:32; 28:19), refers to "'tribes,' 'nations,' or 'peoples' and means 'all peoples [without distinction]' or 'all nations [without distinction],' thereby including Jews."[30] Finally, the phrase *panta ta ethne* is found twice in the Septuagint (Gen. 18:18; 22:18), both times in the reaffirmation of the promise to Abraham that through him all the nations of the earth will be blessed (Gen. 12:3). Matthew's point is that God is fulfilling this promise in this age through Jesus the Messiah, the descendent of Abraham (1:1), and this promise will be fulfilled as the church obeys the Messiah's command and makes people from all nations His disciples. Therefore, it is wrong to exclude Israel from the "all nations" of the Great Commission.[31]

Some make much of the fact that the "nations," or *ethne,* in verse 19 are people groups or ethnic groups.[32] They emphasize that the task of the church in this age is to reach every people group, and therefore leaders should plan their mission strategy accordingly. As a result, sometimes the focus is not to reach as many people as possible but rather to reach as many different people groups as possible. This focus would be evidenced by not expanding work within one people group when other groups still need to be reached. The emphasis on people groups helps expand the range of the gospel; because the gospel is penetrating one area or country does not mean that all people groups in that geographical area or country have been reached with the gospel, or that the whole area has heard the gospel.[33] The people group emphasis has gone too far, however, if the commission is understood as commanding simply the introduction of the gospel in each people group so that at least someone is a Christian or one church is established. Plural collectives, such as "nations," "may have all-embracing force,"[34] thus referring to all people included in the collective group. With this interpretation in mind and considering the early church's desire to spread the gospel message within people groups, it is best to understand Jesus' commission as a command to go everywhere to all people. This means Jesus commands His disciples to make disciples of all people in each people group, not to reach at least some in each people group.

I have already explained that the two participles, "baptizing" and "teaching," are not attendant circumstance participles, and thus they do not have the same imperatival force as the first participle, "go," in the

Great Commission. If, however, they are, as many suggest, participles of means, that is, giving the means by which the command to make disciples is to be accomplished, then they carry at least a tinge of imperatival force.[35] For how can one obey the command to "make disciples" without obeying the means by which this is to be accomplished, especially when those means are clearly explained? What needs to be emphasized, perhaps, is that other important activities, which are not specified but are a part of all the things Jesus commanded (v. 20), are also part of the means of making disciples. One of the most obvious is preaching the gospel and evangelizing the lost (Luke 24:47).

Baptism is, as Gundry suggests, "the rite of initiation" for all who enter the school of Christ.[36] Christ's baptism differs from John's because John's was into *(eis)* repentance and Christ's is into *(eis)* "the name of the Father, and of the Son, and of the Holy Spirit." Zerwick states, "The use of *eis* seems to suggest the end and effect of baptism, a special relation to the Holy Trinity assumed by the person baptized."[37] Although the Great Commission teaches Jesus' disciples to use a Trinitarian baptismal formula, the only evidence of actual Christian baptisms in Scripture indicates the early church baptized in Jesus' name (Acts 2:38; 8:16; 10:48; 19:5; note also Rom. 6:3). The early church did not, however, always use a single set formula, and furthermore, when one was baptized in Jesus' name, acknowledging Him as Savior and Lord, that person was in essence acknowledging the Trinity.[38] I have argued above that to call Jesus "Lord," in the correct sense of that term, is to acknowledge the Trinity.[39] The Trinitarian formula declares that Jesus is divine and equal in essence to the Father and to the Spirit, and this is at least part of what one confesses when one confesses Jesus as Lord.

Not only is He equal in essence to the Father and to the Spirit, but beyond that, from this point on His words have ultimate authority. His disciples are commanded to teach the following generations of disciples not only to know but also to do and to obey everything He commanded until the end of the age. This statement is especially noteworthy in light of the authority of the Old Testament Scriptures and their importance to Jesus and His followers. His words, not the Old Testament Scriptures, now have ultimate authority. He has fulfilled the Scriptures (Matt. 5:17–18); He has not perpetuated or annulled those Scriptures, but He has fulfilled them. Now He has the authority to command obedience to "everything He has commanded," as Yahweh did in the Old Testament (Ex. 29:35; Deut. 1:3, 41; 7:11; 12:11, 14).[40]

The Power to Complete the Commission

The Great Commission concludes with a promise. Jesus will be with His disciples until the end of the age. The divine presence is what has distinguished God's people in every age, and it is the divine presence in the church that makes it different from every other religious group and gives it authority to speak for God. The presence of Jesus with His people in this age authenticates them as God's people, as the presence of Yahweh did in Israel (Num. 33:12–16; 34:8–9). Also, the presence of God assures protection for His people as they do His will, just as it did for God's people in the Old Testament.[41]

The basis of the Great Commission is the fact that Jesus now possesses "all authority" in the universe. Because He possesses this authority He has the right to command His disciples to "go and make disciples of all nations." He also has the authority to command all nations "to obey all that He has commanded." And finally He has the authority to promise that His divine presence will accompany His disciples as they carry out this task "all the days even unto the end of this age."[42] The new commission that Jesus gives the church is based on His new position of authority in this age.

Luke 24:44–49; Acts 1:8

The post-resurrection commission of Jesus in Luke-Acts, is implied in His instructions to the Eleven in Luke 24:44–49 and is clearly stated in Acts 1.[43] Since Acts 1:8 is linked with the commission in Luke 24 by common themes, and Acts 1:1–8 appears to further describe the commission that Luke begins in the last chapter of his gospel, both passages will be included in this section.[44] Jesus' instructions in Luke 24:44–49 apparently occurred on Easter evening, and the historical context of the events in this passage is parallel to those in John 20:19–23, which also occurred on Easter night in Jerusalem.[45]

When we apply these passages from Luke and John to the church, an important issue is the determination of the recipients of these commissions in their original context. Luke 24:33 suggests that those present in that context were the Eleven and some others with them. The mention of the Eleven, however, is earlier in the evening than the time when Jesus appeared to the disciples, and in John it is stated that Thomas was not present when Jesus appeared to the disciples (20:24). Therefore, apparently Thomas left the gathering before Jesus arrived.[46] And if Thomas left, it is very likely that others left also. Furthermore, that Thomas is singled out as being absent, though many other more loosely connected disciples were doubtless also absent, suggests that the "disciples" who are referred to in John 20:19 and present in Luke 24:36–49 are the Ten ("the Twelve, less Judas and Thomas").[47] Having said this, it does not require that the application of the commission in Luke be limited to the Eleven or Twelve any more than it means that Thomas was to be excluded from it because he was not present. The instructions in Luke 24:47 and 49—that this message is to be proclaimed to all nations beginning from Jerusalem and that the disciples will be empowered for this task by the Holy Spirit—indicate that the commission is to be obeyed by all of Jesus' disciples.[48] The circumstances of John 20:24 does, however, give a special authority to the Eleven, who had private instruction with the risen Lord. This insures the reliability of their accounts of the events of Jesus' life and of Jesus' interpretation of those events, which He gave directly to them.

Luke 24 is an account of the discovery of the empty tomb (24:1–12), the meeting of the resurrected Jesus with the two disciples on the road to Emmaus (24:13–35), the resurrection appearance of Jesus to the disciples in Jerusalem and His instructions to them (24:36–49), and Jesus' ascension (24:50–53).[49] In Luke's account these instructions to the disciples in Jerusalem complement Jesus' words to the two disciples on the road to Emmaus (esp. 24:25–27; cf. 24:31). He rebukes the two disciples for their lack of understanding of all that the prophets had spoken concerning the Christ, and then He explains to them "the things concerning Himself in all the Scriptures" (NASB). In 24:44–47 He gives to the disciples more details about His fulfillment of the Scriptures, and He opens their minds so that they might understand the things in the Scriptures concerning Him.[50]

The Fulfillment of Jesus' Words and the Old Testament

In verse 44 Jesus connects to the Scriptures the things He had taught the disciples when He was with them.[51] The things He had taught them were the things written about Him in the three sections of the Old Testament—the Law, the Prophets, and the Psalms (cf. the emphasis on "all" the Scripture in 24:25, 27)—and now these things were being fulfilled in His death and resurrection.[52] The language that Jesus uses indicates that all the Scriptures teach these things and that the fulfillment of the Scriptures in Him is a comprehensive fulfillment (cf. Matt. 5:17–18). Furthermore, Jesus had taught them while He was with them during His earthly ministry that it was necessary *(dei)* that the things in the Scriptures concerning Him must be fulfilled (cf. 24:7, 26).[53] This "divine necessity" is a key theme in Luke, which complements the author's emphasis on the stage-by-stage outworking of God's plan, the fulfillment of Old Testament promise in Jesus, and the continuity and design of God's plan of salvation.[54] All of these themes are seen in Luke 24. Of course, Luke's main point was that God's plan was centered around Jesus and that He was the one who fulfilled and made sense of the Jewish Scriptures. The early church believed that it had the Old Testament Scriptures right, and the Jews (and others who did not see Jesus as the fulfillment of those Scriptures) were not interpreting them correctly.

That Jesus is the fulfillment of the Scriptures is not, however, easily grasped. In verse 45 Jesus opens the minds of the disciples to grasp this fact, and His hermeneutical method guides the church from this point in its interpretation of the Old Testament. Several factors are involved in this new insight that the disciples are given into the Scriptures. First, the disciples are now able to read the text after the initiation of its fulfillment. Jesus has been vindicated by His resurrection from the dead, and now His sufferings and resurrection, about which He taught them earlier, make sense. Second, Luke's language in 24:44–45b indicates that the disciples now are beginning to see the Scriptures as a whole (cf. 24:27). Jesus takes them through all the Scriptures, and He shows them "all the things written" there concerning Himself. This was no atomistic approach to the text but rather a holistic reading of the Old Testament that must have helped to open their minds to the complementary nature of the many prophecies concerning Him there.[55] Third, we dare not miss the point, emphasized in Luke 24, that these disciples understood the text of Scripture correctly because Jesus gave them insight (vv. 27, 32, 45).[56]

Three Components of Scriptural Fulfillment

Luke employs three infinitives in verses 46–47 to designate three basic elements of scriptural fulfillment. The Scriptures say that the Christ (Messiah) should suffer, should rise from the dead, and that repentance should be preached in His name to the Gentiles.[57] The suffering of Christ is prophesied in Psalms 22; 31; 69; 118; and Isaiah 53. His resurrection from the dead is prophesied in Psalms 16:10; 110:1; and 2 Samuel 7:13.[58] These prophecies would not have been commonly understood by the Jews of Jesus' time, as Luke 24 indicates. The concept of a suffering Messiah was not a part of first-century Jewish understanding of Scripture. The New Testament clarifies the fact, however, that these two events—the suffering and the resurrection of the Messiah—are central to God's plan for the ages and constitute the heart of the gospel message (1 Cor. 15:3–8).[59]

The third infinitive, "to preach," moves beyond the historical events of Christ's life to the next step in God's plan. With this infinitive and the phrases that follow it, Jesus teaches the disciples that the Old Testament also prophesies that the message of repentance for the forgiveness of sins should be preached in His name to the nations and that this preaching should begin at Jerusalem. There is no single verse in the Old Testament that prophesies all of this, and it is helpful to compare passages like Romans 10:11–21 and especially Romans 15:7–13 to see how Paul combines Old Testament passages to support his Gentile mission.[60] Here it seems best to understand Jesus' statement in verse 47 concerning Old Testament prophecies of a mission to the Gentiles to be a deduction from several passages in the Old Testament, similar to Paul's pattern in Romans 10 and 15.

That verse 47 gives more details about the message to be preached than Matthew does is important for the purposes of this chapter.[61] The content of the message is "repentance for the forgiveness of sins." This "repentance" involves a change of mind, but it is not only a change of mind. As Bock explains, "Repentance involves turning to and embracing God in faith. Forgiveness of sins comes to those who stretch out a needy hand to Jesus, clinging to him alone and recognizing that without him there is no hope."[62] Forgiveness of sins removes the barriers between a person and God and allows a person to come into a right relationship with God. It involves an "opening of eyes so that one may turn from darkness to light and from the authority (or dominion) of Satan to God" (Acts 26:18).

The authority for this preaching is Jesus' name.[63] As Matthew 28:18–20 teaches, the resurrected Jesus has all authority in heaven and earth, and it is only through His name that any one has authority to proclaim forgiveness of sins and the benefits that accompany forgiveness. Jesus has conquered sin, death, and hell, and He has freed the human race from the curse of the Law (1 Cor. 15:53–56; Gal. 3:13–14).[64] The Jewish Messiah is universal Lord and resurrected Savior.

The scope of the proclamation of this message is "to all the nations," the exact phrase that is also found in Matthew 28:19 and was discussed above *(panta ta ethne)*. Luke differs from Matthew's commission in that here the mission to "all nations" is fulfillment of Old Testament Scripture, the same as Jesus' death and resurrection (Acts 10:42–43; 26:22–23). Also, Luke clarifies that the mission to all nations is to begin from Jerusalem (Acts 1:8).[65] The disciples understood that the preaching was to begin in Jerusalem, which may be why they missed the full intent of Jesus' instructions to preach "to all the nations."[66] On the basis of the accounts in Acts 1–15, it appears that the disciples interpreted Jesus' instructions to mean that they were to preach the message of repentance to Jews in "all the nations." This would have been a natural Jewish interpretation of Jesus' instructions and "a logical conclusion from the international Jewish audience in Acts 2."[67] In fact it took the disciples nearly a decade to understand that when Jesus instructed them to go "to the nations" He meant that they were to go to all of the people in all nations (Acts 10:34–48).[68]

Key to the message that is to be preached, according to Luke 24, is that it is contained in the Scriptures (cf. Luke 16:31). Not only is the message contained in the Scriptures, so are the instructions that it is to be preached to all nations, and the accomplishment of all of this fulfills the promise and prophecy of the Scriptures. Luke emphasizes that the message and mission of the church is based on Old Testament Scripture and that there is continuity with that Scripture because the church's message and mission fulfills the Old Testament.[69]

The Mission of the Disciples

In verse 48, Jesus announces that the disciples are witnesses of these things. The most important word in this verse is "witnesses," which will become a major theme in Acts.[70] In Acts this word often designates a "witness" of the resurrection (1:22; 2:32; 3:15; 5:32; 10:41; 13:31; 22:15; 26:16), and in at least two instances seems to signify a "witness" of Christ's sending of the Spirit to demonstrate His exaltation (5:32; 10; 39). The disciples whom Jesus addresses in Luke 24 on Easter night and whom He sends forth in Acts 1:8 are a special group of "witnesses." They have seen with their own eyes the fulfillment of the Scriptures in the events of Jesus' life, and they have heard Him explain and interpret those Scriptures. An important concept, which is integral to this context in Luke 24 and to the book of Acts and is foundational to Christianity, is the truth that Christianity is much more than a theology or a set of ethical principles. Christianity is the story of Christ and of God's actions in history in and through Christ. These first disciples were official "witnesses" of God's fulfillment of His promised scriptural plan in Christ, and this guaranteed the accuracy of the foundation that they laid for the church.

Next, Jesus promises the empowerment for this witnessing (24:49). This empowerment is "the promise of My Father," which in this context is to be "clothed with power from on high" (NASB),[71] but in Acts is clearly the outpouring of the Spirit at Pentecost.[72] Jesus now mediates the Father's promise, and He will empower the disciples to continue the work, that He has begun and to fulfill the Old Testament prophecies concerning the preaching of the gospel message to all the nations. Since this preaching must begin from Jerusalem, they are to remain in Jerusalem until they receive empowering by the Spirit.[73]

At the time of His ascension, as recorded in Acts 1:8, Jesus reiterates the instructions He gave to the disciples on Easter night (Luke 24:44–49). In the Acts context Jesus commands them to be His witnesses, and He gives to them more detailed instructions about their mission of preaching to all nations beginning from Jerusalem.[74] Their preaching is to reach all nations as the disciples progress from Jerusalem to "the end of the earth." The book of Acts demonstrates the progression of the message of Christ to "the end of the earth," which for Luke is Rome, the center of the Roman Empire. The "all nations" of Luke 24:47, however, do not receive the preaching of the gospel in the book of Acts, and this dimension of Old Testament promise is still not completely fulfilled today. That the fulfillment of this command is promised in the Old Testament should give the church confidence and urgency as it moves forward to accomplish the task. This command comes out of the heart of God and is based on His eternal plan; He must bring it to fruition.

John 20:19–23

The historical context of Jesus' post-resurrection commission in John 20 is the same as that of Luke 24:44–49, discussed above.[75] The commission, as recorded in John, is important because it gives more details of Jesus' words to His disciples on that first Easter night. In his gospel, John places the commission following the visits of Mary (20:1–2) and Peter and John (20:3–10) to the empty tomb and Jesus' appearance to Mary outside the tomb (20:11–18). Following Jesus' commission, John tells of Jesus' appearance to Thomas and the disciples one week later (20:24–29) and discloses the purpose of the gospel (20:30–31). In the commissioning account in John 20:19–23, Jesus takes great care to comfort the disciples before He commissions them.

Jesus Comforts the Disciples

For John it is important that his readers know the ten disciples (minus Judas and Thomas) are gathered together in a room with the doors locked for fear of the Jews (v. 19). The locked doors indicate the great fear felt by the disciples at this time (cf. the same situation eight days later, 20:26); they also give Jesus the opportunity to teach the disciples a lesson about

Himself and His victory over all who have opposed Him. Jesus, in His resurrected, spiritual body, passes through the closed doors and, standing in the midst of the disciples, shows them His hands and side. Jesus' ability to pass through the locked doors, here and also the following week, as described in verse 26, emphasizes His power over the laws of nature, and His hands and side prove that "the risen Lord is none other than the crucified sacrifice."[76] Others who had been crucified could have shown the wounds on their hands and feet, but only Jesus could show the scar on His side. Twice on this occasion Jesus comforts the disciples with the greeting, "Peace be with you" (vv. 19, 21 NASB; cf. also v. 26). The repetition of this greeting would remind them of Jesus' previous promise to give them His peace and of His instructions to them at that time not to be afraid but instead to have courage (14:27; 16:33). The full meaning of the peace that Jesus bequeaths to the disciples is difficult to understand, but it certainly includes "the peace of reconciliation and life from God," and it is the complement of Jesus' "'It is finished' on the cross."[77]

The appearance of Jesus to the disciples must have assured them that His enemies had not conquered Him; the apparent overpowering of Jesus by civil and religious authorities, which they had witnessed in the last few days, was not the last word. Jesus has now entered into a new realm of existence, and He possesses power over death and the grave. Furthermore, He assures them that they are at peace with God. In fulfillment of Jesus' promise in His farewell discourse (14:18; 16:22), the disciples are overjoyed when they grasp that it is Jesus, alive from the dead.

The Commission of Jesus to the Disciples

Before commissioning the disciples, and apparently on the basis of their recognition of Him ("therefore," v. 21), Jesus again bequeaths His peace to them. If nothing else, this greeting would have given the disciples assurance that they were in a right relationship with God and that, even though what Jesus was going to say may involve difficulty in this world, their God has authority over everything in this world, and they are at peace with Him (cf. 14:27; 16:33).

Jesus' commission in verse 21 echoes His words in 17:18: "As you sent Me into the world, I also have sent them into the world" (NASB). In chapter 20 He addresses the disciples directly and says, "As the Father has sent me, so I send you." The key words here and the great contribution of John in his form of the commission are the words, "As . . . so. . . ." Whatever else these statements mean, they certainly indicate that the mission of

Jesus is a model for the mission of His followers. As we shall attempt to demonstrate, however, Jesus' mission is more than simply a model for the mission of His disciples.

To understand this commission, several false ideas that have been based on it must be addressed. First, it has been suggested that because there are two different words for "send" in verse 21 *(apostello* and *pempo),* they have different meanings in this context.[78] Andreas J. Kostenberger refutes this suggestion in his recently published dissertation *The Mission of Jesus and the Disciples According to the Fourth Gospel.*[79] Kostenberger concludes that they should "be viewed as virtual synonyms" with "no semantic difference."[80] Other interpretations of Jesus' commission to the disciples in John 20:21 suggest that it means the followers of Jesus are to perform the same miracles and works of ministry that He performed. Another option is that, since the context speaks of forgiveness of sins and we cannot do the very same things that Jesus did, this commission has no application to our ministry to the poor and needy.[81] Both interpretations are faulty and can be challenged by analyzing what Jesus means when He says that He is sending His followers, as the Father sent Him.

Jesus' commission in John 20:21 must be read in light of His similar words in 17:18. In the previous context He emphasizes that He and the disciples are sent into the world; the passage under consideration here "focuses more on Jesus' investing of his disciples with authority and legitimation."[82]

Since Jesus sends the disciples as the Father sent Him, it is important to understand Jesus' mission. Kostenberger identifies four characteristics of the sent one in Jesus' mission. He summarizes these characteristics as

> (1) bringing glory and honor to the sender; (2) doing the sender's will, working his works, and speaking his words; (3) witnessing to the sender and representing him accurately; and (4) knowing the sender intimately, living in close relationship with the sender, and following his example. All of these aspects of what one sent is required to be and do, are applicable to the disciples as they are sent by Jesus.[83]

According to Carson, the correct context to determine the mission of Jesus that is being referred to in John 20:21—and therefore our mission as well—is in the sending passages in John. When this theme is studied in John's gospel, "it is the perfect obedience of the Son that is especially emphasized (e.g., 5:19–30; 8:29), an obedience that has already been made a paradigm for the relation of the believers to Jesus (15:9–10)."[84]

It is necessary at this point to make an important distinction. Some may infer from Jesus' words in John 20:21 that His followers are to begin a new mission that is patterned after His mission. That is not, however, what He said. Jesus used the perfect tense when He said, "As the Father has sent me . . . " thereby indicating that His sending did not end when He ascended.[85] The Son's sending by the Father is still continuing in the Son's sending of His followers. The disciples were not to begin a new work but rather were to carry on what Christ began. The "as" in Jesus' commission indicates that "the Father's sending of the Son serves both as the model and the ground for the Son's sending of the disciples."[86] The work that the Father sent the Son to do continues on in the followers of Jesus, who make up His body in this age (Eph. 1:23).[87] Now, instead of the Father, Jesus is the divine sender, who has all authority to administer the divine work of salvation (Matt. 28:18).[88] As the Father sealed and sanctified the Son and poured out the Spirit on the Son without measure (1:32; 3:34; 4:34; 5:19; 6:27; 10:36; 17:4), so also Jesus' disciples will be sanctified by the Spirit, who has been promised to them (John 14–16; 21:22), and by God's Word (17:17).[89] Kostenberger summarizes that "the Spirit provides a crucial element of continuity between the ministry of Jesus in the flesh and the work of the exalted Jesus through his disciples."[90] With the assistance of the Spirit, the disciples now share in Jesus' mission.[91] Before He died, Jesus had promised the Spirit to the disciples to enable them to witness in the world (15:25–27; 16:7–11). Jesus' gift of the Spirit in John 20:22 must also be understood in the same manner, especially in light of His commission in 20:21.

The disciples will need the Spirit's enablement to obey this daunting commission, which involves "perfect obedience to the Son, modeled on Jesus' perfect obedience" to the Father.[92]

The commission is overwhelming.

> The disciples are to bring glory and honor to *Jesus* (as well as to the Father; cf. 15:8, 16). They are to do *Jesus'* will, perform *Jesus'* works, and speak *Jesus'* words. The disciples are to witness to *Jesus* and to represent *him* accurately. And they are to know *Jesus* intimately, live in close relationship with *him,* and follow *his* example.

In a word, *their* relationship to *their* sender, Jesus, is to reflect *Jesus'* relationship with *his* sender, the Father.[93]

As the church defines its mission by modeling and following Jesus, it must remember that which was at the center of His mission:

> He came as the Father's gift so that those who believe in him might not perish but have eternal life (3:16), experiencing new life as the children of God (1:12–13) and freedom from the slavery of sin because they have been set free by the Son of God (8:34–36) . . .[94]

Two Final Problems

Two major issues in John 20:22–23 relate to Jesus' commission in verse 21: (1) What does Jesus mean when He says, "Receive the Holy Spirit" (v. 22 NASB)? And (2) what is the forgiveness and retention of sins of which Jesus speaks (v. 23)? The statement in verse 22a "And when He had said this . . ." connects the bestowal of the Spirit (v. 22b) with the commission in verse 21. Although some think Jesus actually imparted the Holy Spirit to the disciples on this occasion, the simplest and most consistent explanation of this passage is that it points forward to Pentecost, a future event for the disciples, but a well-known past event for John's readers.[95] Several facts lead to this conclusion.

First, the disciples give little if any evidence of enablement by the Spirit in the days between Easter and Pentecost; in fact, they are still behind locked doors eight days later when Jesus appears to them again (20:26), and later they return to their fishing (21:1–14). Second, since in John the promise of the Spirit is dependent on Jesus' return to the Father and His glorification (7:37–39), "a two-fold coming of the Spirit somehow suggests that Jesus returned twice."[96] Third, at other times in the gospel of John, Jesus indicates that His hour has already arrived, or He is now being glorified in the presence of the Father, all of which points to events that are still in the future when Jesus speaks of them (12:23, 31; 13:31; 17:1, 5).[97] In a similar manner the bestowal of the Spirit, spoken of in John 20:22, points forward to and anticipates the events of Pentecost. And fourth, since the text (20:22a) connects the gift of the Spirit in 20:22 with the commission in 20:21, it is most natural to understand all of the context as pointing forward to Pentecost. The Spirit is given to accomplish the commission in this context, and the Spirit comes when that commission work begins.[98]

Therefore, it is most consistent to understand John 20:22 as a symbolic anticipation of the endowment of the Spirit, which is poured out on the church beginning at Pentecost. In typical Johannine fashion, Jesus' statement points forward to the realization of His previous promises of the Spirit in John 14–16. Perhaps John was trying to communicate, by his inclusion of these words, that in His glorified, resurrected state Jesus has the authority to administer the promised gift of the Spirit (7:39).[99]

The fact that Jesus breathes further emphasizes that He is the one who now administers the Spirit.[100] The verb *breathed (emphysao)* occurs only this one time in the New Testament. Although most English versions translate the verb as "he breathed on them," the text simply states "he breathed" or "he exhaled."[101] What then is the purpose of this action, other than perhaps to emphasize that Jesus is the one giving the Spirit? This unusual verb harks back to its use in Genesis 2:7 and Ezekiel 37:9 in the Septuagint.[102] In the first context, God breathes into Adam the breath of life at creation, and in the second, at God's command, the prophet calls on the wind to breathe the breath of life into dried-up bones so that they may live. The dried-up bones represent Israel, given new life and returned to her own land by the power of the Spirit. Jesus' action of breathing on the disciples indicates the beginning of the new creation, which has now been accomplished by Him, and the resurrection life, of which all people who are "in Christ" partake by the presence of the life-giving Spirit in their lives (2 Cor. 5:17).[103] This new life is not only for the Twelve but is for all who are "in Christ," the same people who are sent forth by Jesus to continue the mission He began (John 20:21). The enduement of this new life will come at Pentecost, when Jesus' ascension, exaltation, and glorification are complete (John 7:37–39; Acts 2:33).

The final problem to be considered in this context is the meaning and application of verse 23. The words are reminiscent of Matthew 16:19 and 18:18.[104] The perfect passive verbs "they are forgiven" and "they are not forgiven" have God as their subject, and the aspect of the perfect tense verbs suggests the idea that "they stand forgiven" or "they do not stand forgiven." Thus, the verse gives authority to the disciples of Jesus to forgive and to retain sins.[105] Since God is the only one who effectively or ultimately is able to forgive sins, this verse must refer to the authority of those who are sent by Jesus to mediate God's forgiveness through the message that they proclaim. As they are sent forth by Jesus to continue His work (v. 21), they are empowered by the Spirit (v. 22) to bring salvation or judgment, as He also did (cf. John 3:16–18; 9:39; 12:31).[106] Jesus' followers have the great responsibility of proclaiming in Jesus' name that anyone who believes that Jesus is the Christ has life through His name (20:31) and that anyone who rejects Jesus is condemned (3:18). In this regard Jesus' followers continue His work and do even greater works than He did (14:12–14).[107]

Barrett explains well the importance of this passage for the definition of the Church's mission:

> As Jesus in his ministry was entirely dependent upon and obedient to God the Father, who sealed and sanctified him (4.34; 5.19; 10.37; 17.4, and other passages: 6.27; 10.36), and acted in the power of the Spirit who rested upon him (1.32), so the church is the apostolic church, commissioned by Christ, only in virtue of the fact that Jesus sanctified it (17.19) and breathed the Spirit into it (v.22), and only so far as it maintains an attitude of perfect obedience to Jesus (it is here, of course, that the parallelism between the relation of Jesus to the Father and the relation of the church to Jesus breaks down). The life and mission of the church are meaningless if they are detached from this historical and theological context.[108]

Conclusion

In this article I have attempted to demonstrate that the post-resurrection commissions of Jesus to His disciples have direct application to the church. The commissions involve the proclamation of the gospel message to all nations until the end of the age. They require that the church go out into the world to continue the work that Christ began, ministering by the power of the indwelling Spirit of God.

Foundational to the commission that Jesus gives to the church is that its mission is the work of God. When the church goes forth in Jesus' name to preach the gospel message and make disciples of all peoples, it is fulfilling the Old Testament, continuing the work of Christ, and obeying the command of the Lord Jesus. Thus, in the work of the church there is continuity with the Old Testament Scriptures and with God's work in Christ.

But there is also discontinuity, since in this age Jesus is central. He is now administering God's salvation program. He is sovereign over the mission and He sends forth the witnesses. His witnesses go with His authority, power, and presence in the person of the Holy Spirit. He is the model and the ground of their mission. He is their message since He is the promised Old Testament salvation, and His teachings are now the content of their instruction. All salvation is in His name, and His followers identify with Him by baptism in the name of the triune God, of whom He is the second person. He forgives the sins of all who repent and believe in Him through the preaching of His followers, and all who do not repent are judged for not submitting to Him.

The church has the great responsibility and privilege of continuing the work of God in reaching the nations and bringing the universe into a right relationship with Him through Jesus, who is Lord and Christ.

Study Questions

1. Why is Jesus' universal authority foundational to the commission He gives in Matthew 28:19–20?
2. What does one do to disciple another person in Christ? What characterizes a disciple of Christ?
3. What verses in the Old Testament teach that Christ must die and be raised from the dead? What verses in the Old Testament teach that repentance and forgiveness of sins must be preached to all nations beginning at Jerusalem?
4. What does the New Testament mean when it says that we are to preach and baptize "in Jesus' name"?
5. In what ways are Christians sent as Jesus was sent?
6. Are Jesus' post-resurrection commissions the responsibility of the church, or are they limited to the apostles? Explain your reasons for answering as you do.
7. In light of the three passages studied in this chapter, who is ultimately responsible for the fulfillment of Jesus' post-resurrection commissions? What attitudes and mind-sets should Christians have toward their participation in these commissions?

Chapter Notes

1. I will address these passages in the order in which they were apparently written rather than in the order that the events in them occurred. Luke–Acts will be considered to be one work for the purposes of this essay, since Luke wrote both books, and since Acts is clearly designated to be a sequel to the gospel of Luke (Acts 1:1). The commission that is recorded in Mark 16:15–16 will not be developed in this essay because it is similar to the commission in Matthew 28 and adds little to the discussion, and

also because the textual support for its authenticity is not strong. The most unique elements in the Markan commission are the mention of the "gospel" and "belief," both of which concepts are included in the other commissions. For a summary of the textual issues involved in Mark 16, see James R. White, *The King James Only Controversy* (Minneapolis, Minn.: Bethany House, 1995), 255–57; and Bruce M. Metzger, *A Textual Commentary on the Greek New Testament,* 2d ed. (New York: American Bible Society, 1994), 102–7.

2. This first stage is an attempt to develop the biblical theology of these separate passages. See D. A. Carson, "Current Issues in Biblical Theology: A New Testament Perspective," *Bulletin for Biblical Research* 5 (1995): 17–41 for a helpful introduction to biblical theology.

3. For an introduction to the relationship between biblical and systematic theology see D. A. Carson, "Unity and Diversity in the New Testament: The Possibility of New Testament Theology," in *Scripture and Truth,* ed. D. A. Carson and John D. Woodbridge (Grand Rapids: Zondervan, 1983), 61–95.

4. The disciples, who had previously seen the resurrected Jesus (some had seen Him several times), would have probably not been afraid but would have worshiped Jesus; the others, who had not yet seen Jesus since His resurrection, would have probably been afraid. For support that two groups are in view, see Robert H. Gundry, *Matthew: A Commentary on His Literary and Theological Art* (Grand Rapids: Eerdmans, 1982), 594; and D. A. Carson, "Matthew," in *The Expositor's Bible Commentary,* vol. 8, ed. Frank E. Gaebelein (Grand Rapids: Zondervan, 1984), 592–94. Gundry points out the construction in 26:67, which seems to refer to two groups and is parallel to 28:17. It is possible that Matthew 28:16–20 is the occasion when Jesus appeared to more than five hundred brethren at once (1 Cor. 15:6). Robert Duncan Culver, *A Greater Commission: A Theology for World Missions* (Chicago: Moody, 1984), 148–49 discusses this last possibility and favors it. For another discussion of Matt. 28:18–20, see ch. 13.

5. For a helpful discussion of the concept of authority in the New Testament, on which the above discussion is based, see *Theological Dictionary of the New Testament,* s.v. *"exousia,"* by Werner Foerster, 566–75; and *New International Dictionary of New Testament Theology,* s.v. "might," by Otto Betz, 606–11. The administrative structure of the Trinity is described in passages like 1 Corinthians 11:3; John 14:26; 16:7, 13–14; 17:2.

6. For example, Culver (*A Greater Commission,* 149) writes, "What is the extent of the 'all authority' (v. 18) given to Christ? Jesus' assertion of 'all power' seems to refer to the power of deity assumed by Him at His resurrection and ascension and has regard to the human nature only, since as

regards His divine nature 'all power' had been His always. On the other hand it may have been a personal assertion of His eternal power and Godhead as the Son of Man." It is interesting that Culver distinguishes between the two concepts, and yet he substitutes one for the other. On the other hand some, as William L. Banks, *In Search of the Great Commission: What Did Jesus Really Say?* (Chicago: Moody, 1991), 69–97, do not even address verse 18, which is the basis for what follows, but instead only consider verses 19–20.

7. Carson, "Matthew," 595. During Jesus' earthly ministry He teaches the Scriptures with authority (Matt. 7:29), has authority on earth to forgive sins (Matt. 9:6, 8), gives authority to the Twelve to cast out unclean spirits and heal every kind of disease and sickness (Matt. 10:1–8) and to cleanse the Temple and teach the people there (Matt. 21:12–27).

8. One could argue that Philippians 2:9–11 primarily means that Jesus, by virtue of His resurrection and exaltation, is shown to be God and thus worthy of worship. With this interpretation, Jesus' being given "the name" in Philippians 2:9 means that He "bears the name of the one Lord, Yahweh." For this interpretation see Moises Silva, *Philippians,* in The Wycliffe Exegetical Commentary, ed. Kenneth Barker (Chicago: Moody, 1988), 128–31; and J. B. Lightfoot, *St. Paul's Epistle to the Philippians* (Grand Rapids: Zondervan, 1953), 113. This understanding of Philippians 2:9–11 does not seem likely, however, when it is compared with other New Testament passages that speak of Christ's lordship. The point of Peter's sermon in Acts 2 is that God has made Jesus, whom the Jews crucified, both Lord and Christ (v. 36). This new position is evidenced by something new that takes place on that day; that new thing is the pouring forth of the Spirit, which Jesus now administers (v. 33). Now Peter preaches that people are to call on Jesus' name for salvation and be baptized in Jesus' name (vv. 21, 38), and if they do that they will receive the promised Holy Spirit, which Jesus now pours forth (v. 33). The point of this sermon is not that Jesus has been given the name of Yahweh, but rather that Jesus now has the authority to pour forth the Spirit, a function of Yahweh in the Joel prophecy, which Peter quotes (Joel 2:28–32 in Acts 2:16–21). In 1 Corinthians 8:6, Paul says that there is "one Lord." The point of this verse is that there is not any area of authority that is excluded from His lordship. But, at the same time, Paul says that there is "one God the Father" (1 Cor. 8:6), "who is over all" (Eph. 4:6). The apparent contradiction between these passages is eased by Paul in 1 Corinthians 15:24–28, where he explains that God the Father, who has authority over the Son (1 Cor. 11:3), has given to Jesus authority to reign until all of His enemies are brought under His

dominion (v. 26), and then Christ will give all authority back to the Father (v. 28). First Corinthians 15:27 states that the only thing not under Jesus' authority is the Father Himself, because He put all things under Jesus' authority. It is the Father's plan to bring all things to completion through the Son, and then the Father Himself will reassume the rule of the universe (Eph. 1:9–10). In this present age, Jesus, who has had all things put under His authority by the Father, is the Head of the church, which He is filling with His character and ruling over. In the coming age His rule will extend to the whole universe (Eph. 1:20–23; cf. 1 Cor. 15:25). Ephesians 1:20–23 clearly teaches that the time when all authority was given to Christ was at the time of His resurrection/ascension/glorification. For the view that "the name" that is given to Christ in Philippians 2:9 is Lord and that the main idea of the verse is His exaltation to a place of rulership, see Ralph P. Martin, *Carmen Christi,* rev. ed. (Grand Rapids: Eerdmans, 1983), 229–48; and Gerald F. Hawthorne, *Philippians,* Word Biblical Commentary (Dallas: Word, 1983), 90–96.

9. For an interpretation of 1 Peter 3:18–22 which relates this whole passage to Christ's universal lordship described in verse 22, see J. Ramsey Michaels, *1 Peter,* Word Biblical Commentary (Waco, Tex.: Word, 1988), 194–222.

10. The contrasts between Adam and Christ in 1 Corinthians 15 are evident (esp. vv. 20–27 and 45–49). The quotation from Psalm 8:6 in verse 27 emphasizes the fact that Christ is the one who will accomplish the subjection of all things, which Adam did not accomplish.

11. Jesus' statements in John 14:16 and 26 give insight into the meaning and function of Yahweh in the Old Testament. Since it is Yahweh who promises the Spirit in the Old Testament, it seems that Jesus now mediates the salvific benefits that Yahweh mediated under the Old Covenant arrangement and promised in connection with the New Covenant.

12. D. R. de Lacey, "'One Lord' in Pauline Christology," in *Christ the Lord,* ed. Harold H. Rowdon (Downers Grove, Ill.: InterVarsity, 1982), 201. In light of the New Testament's teaching on the lordship of Christ, and following de Lacey's development, that Jesus is called Lord means that He is God—He is sovereign over the universe—and yet in light of the fact that He is not God the Father, who is over all, it means that Jesus is a member of the Godhead (the Trinity), and His sovereign authority has been given to Him by the Father. As Paul so clearly teaches in Philippians 2:5ff., Jesus does not usurp the Father's authority, nor does He even demand His own prerogatives, as Deity, but instead the Father bestows all authority in the universe upon Him after He humbles Himself and obediently

accomplishes the Father's will. Therefore, to call Jesus Lord, in the correct sense of the term, is a confession of the Trinity. Jesus has all authority in the universe, and He administers the universe as the Father's co-regent, being so designated by the "one God and Father" (1 Cor. 8:6). It should also be noted that, because Jesus is the one who fulfills many of the Old Testament prophecies concerning Yahweh (i.e., Joel 2:28–32 in Acts 2:16–21, Isa. 8:12–14 in 1 Peter 2:8 and 3:14–15; Ps. 102:25 in Heb. 1:10), this does not mean that the Lord Jesus Christ is exactly the same person as Yahweh in the Old Testament. The ineffable name of Yahweh is used in the Old Testament at times to refer to the Father and at other times it refers to the Son. In Genesis 19:24, Yahweh apparently refers to these two different members of the Trinity. Also, the Old Testament speaks of the Spirit of Yahweh. Thus, the name has a plenary sense in the Old Testament. Yahweh is the covenant-making God of the Old Testament and is best understood to refer to the Godhead, as it is administered by the Father, who has supreme authority in the Godhead (1 Cor. 11:3; 1 Cor. 15:27–28). Yet the members of the Godhead can individually be referred to as Yahweh or the Spirit of Yahweh. The Lord Jesus Christ, the God-man, was given all authority to function as Lord and co-regent with the Father after His resurrection until He has brought all things under His dominion and restored creation to God's original design. The fact that He was given this authority (Matt. 28:18) and that, in order to accomplish God's purpose for man and creation, He had to be the God-man before He received this authority, means that the Lord Jesus is not exactly identical to Yahweh. The name Yahweh refers to the Godhead, as administered by the Father, before the Son became a man. The reason that Old Testament references to Yahweh can now be applied to Jesus Christ is that He is a member of the Trinity, and in this age Jesus functions as Yahweh functioned in the Old Testament. Jesus is now the mediator of new covenant blessings (Heb. 8:1–6), and in this age people come to God through Jesus' name (Acts 2:36–38; Rom. 10:13, etc.). Jesus is Lord, and He administers the work of the Godhead in this age, as Yahweh did in the previous dispensation. Lars Hartman, *Into the Name of the Lord Jesus: Baptism in the Early Church* (Edinburgh: T & T Clark, 1997), 47–50 and 150–51, has a helpful discussion of the relationship of Jesus to the Trinity in the baptismal formulas in the New Testament. See also F. F. Bruce, "Paul's Presentation of Jesus," in *Promise and Fulfillment,* ed. F. F. Bruce (Edinburgh: T & T Clark, 1963), 49–50, for a helpful discussion of the fact that Paul puts Jesus "on a par with Yahweh" and does not hesitate to give to the Lord Jesus Yahweh's name.

13. See also 2 Corinthians 5:18. It was important in God's sovereign plan that Jesus finish His work on this earth and be established as the resurrected and glorified God-man when He received the universal authority He now possesses. This was necessary so that He might, through His sufferings, bring many sons into glory by His work of reconciliation (Heb. 2:10, 16–18) and so that He might restore man to the place of dominion over creation, which was lost when Adam sinned (Heb. 2:5–8). Man realizes this dominion or authority over creation when he shares in the dominion and authority of Christ that will be fully exercised in the future millennial kingdom (cf. Gen. 1:26–27; Ps. 8:4–6; Heb. 2:5–8; 1 Cor. 15:24–28).

14. It is surprising, since all authority has been committed to the risen Christ, that He commissions His disciples to do His work for Him, and that He does not instead accomplish His will by exercising His own universal authority. The obvious lesson is that in this age God has chosen to accomplish His will in reconciling the world to Himself and thus bring glory to Himself through the obedience and cooperation of people. In the age to come, Christ will fully exercise His authority and bring all things into conformity with His moral will. In this age, Christ is exercising His authority in this world through His body, the church, as the church carries out its ministry of reconciling people to God through Christ. Hartman (*Into the Name of the Lord Jesus,* 149), while acknowledging the influence of Daniel 7:13–14 on Matthew 28:18–20, asserts that making disciples is a typically different way of exerting power from that encountered in Daniel 7:14. He continues, "making people disciples involves respect for their own free will, a feature which hardly is to be imagined behind Daniel 7."

15. See, for example, Carson, "Matthew," 594–99; Robert Duncan Culver, *A Greater Commission,* 148–54; John D. Harvey, "Mission in Matthew," in *Mission in the New Testament: An Evangelical Approach,* ed. William A. Larkin Jr. and Joel F. Williams, American Society of Missiology Series, no. 27 (Maryknoll, N.Y.: Orbis Books, 1998), 119–36, esp. 128–34; and Shawn L. Buice, "The Great Commission Passages," *Mid-America Theological Journal* 22 (1998): 81–96. For more popular treatments see David M. Howard, *The Great Commission for Today* (Downers Grove, Ill.: InterVarsity, 1976), 52–74; and William L. Banks, *In Search of the Great Commission* (Chicago: Moody, 1991), 69–98.

16. A helpful study of the structure of the commission is found in Bruce J. Malina, "The Literary Structure and Form of Matt. XXVIII. 16–20," *New Testament Studies* 17 (1970): 87–103.

17. Culver, *A Greater Commission,* 150–51, following William F. Arndt and F. Wilbur Gingrich, trans. and eds., *A Greek-English Lexicon of the New*

Testament, 2d rev. ed. (Chicago: Univ. of Chicago Press, 1958), 692, although Arndt and Gingrich do not cite Matthew 28:19 as an example of this use of the participle. Culver also develops this idea in "What Is the Church's Commission?" *Bibliotheca Sacra* 125 (1968): 243–53.

18. This position is explained and defended in Daniel B. Wallace, *Greek Grammar Beyond the Basics* (Grand Rapids: Zondervan, 1996): 642, 645 and Cleon Rogers, "The Great Commission," *Bibliotheca Sacra* 130 (1973): 258–67. On p. 642 Wallace lists five features of an attendant circumstance participle: (1) The tense of the participle is usually aorist; (2) the tense of the main verb is usually aorist; (3) the mood of the main verb is usually imperative or indicative; (4) the participle will precede the main verb—both in word order and time of event (though there is a very close proximity); and (5) these participles occur frequently in narrative literature and elsewhere. These features match the structural pattern in Matthew 28:19 with the first participle "go" and the imperative "make disciples." In fact, Wallace notes that in the New Testament "virtually all aorist participle+aorist *imperative* constructions involve attendant circumstance participles" (642 n. 71). The other two participles in the commission ("baptizing" and "teaching") do not follow this pattern, since both are present participles following the aorist imperative. The attendant circumstance participle is dependent on the main verb semantically, since it cannot exist without it. In other words, the going that Jesus speaks of here is a going to make disciples. But at the same time, the action ("going") is coordinate with the finite verb and translated like the verb (i.e., with the same mood as the main verb), and it is connected to the main verb by "and." (See p. 640 for a more complete definition.) Blomberg correctly cautions that "too much and too little often have been made of this observation [that the main command in the Great Commission is to make disciples]." Too much is made of it when the disciples' "going" is overly subordinated, so that Jesus' charge is to proselytize merely where one is. Matthew frequently uses "go" as an introductory circumstantial participle that is rightly translated coordinate to the main verb—here "go and make" (cf. 2:8; 9:13; 11:4; 17:27; 28:7). Too little is made of it when all attention is centered on the command to "go," as in countless appeals for missionary candidates so that foreign missions are elevated to a higher status of Christian service than other forms of spiritual activity. Craig Blomberg, *Matthew,* in New American Commentary, ed. David S. Dockery (Nashville: Broadman, 1992), 431.

19. See Carson, "Matthew," 595.

20. Harvey, "Mission in Matthew," 131.

21. An excellent resource for understanding the words and concepts related to discipleship in the Bible is Michael J. Wilkins, *Discipleship in the Ancient World and Matthew's Gospel,* 2d ed. (Grand Rapids: Baker Books, 1995). The verb *matheteuo* is intransitive in Matthew 13:52 and 27:57 and transitive in its other two occurrences in the New Testament.

22. Harvey, "Mission in Matthew," 131–32. For a helpful discussion of the probable Jewish heritage of the recipients of Matthew, see Raymond E. Brown, *An Introduction to the New Testament* (New York: Doubleday, 1997), 212–13.

23. Wilkins, *Discipleship in the Ancient World and Matthew's Gospel,* 163. He discusses the meaning of this word in the New Testament on pages 160–63.

24. Ibid., 126–72.

25. Teaching is a very important part of disciplemaking. Oscar S. Brooks (*Matthew xxviii 16–20 and the Design of the First Gospel,* JSNT Supplement Series 10 [1981]: 2–18) traces the theme of teaching through Matthew, and argues that the gospel is designed in such a way that the two themes of authority and teaching are consistently emphasized in each section of the gospel to support the controlling thesis found in 28:16–20 and to prepare the reader for the final paragraph. On the importance of teaching in Matthew, see also Wilkins, *Discipleship in the Ancient World and Matthew's Gospel,* 171–72.

26. See especially Matthew 11:29; 12:46–50; 10:24–25 and the thorough discussion in Wilkins, *Discipleship in the Ancient World and Matthew's Gospel,* 126–72. On the connection between authority and teaching in Matthew, see Brooks, "The Design of the First Gospel."

27. Carson, "Matthew," 596, seems to be right in saying that "The injunction is given to the Eleven, but to the Eleven in their role as disciples (v. 16). Therefore, they are paradigms for all disciples." Those who argue that the Great Commission is not directly applicable to believers in the present age, because it was given before Pentecost, have several problems: (1) Why does Jesus assure the disciples that He will be with them "until the end of the age" as they carry out this commission? It is hard to believe that the Great Commission is only directly applicable to the disciples for a few days until Pentecost and the beginning of the church age, since Jesus commands His disciples to teach the next generation of disciples "to observe all things He has commanded," and He assures them of His presence long beyond Pentecost. (2) Why does Matthew include this commission at the conclusion of his gospel, which he was writing in the middle of the first century, if it does not apply to his recipients? Interpreters of the Gospels must remember that they have a twofold historical context.

They are not only dealing with the time when the events took place but also with the fact that the events were written after Pentecost for believers in this age. (3)Verses like Matthew 26:13 also indicate that the contents of the gospel were intended for believers in this age. (4) It is very likely, especially in view of the importance of the Great Commission at the conclusion of Matthew, that Matthew is "at least in part a manual on discipleship," and was constructed to "equip the disciples in the making of disciples" (Wilkins, *Discipleship in the Ancient World and Matthew's Gospel,* 172). Whether this last point is true or not, it is most likely that the textbook that the first recipients of Matthew used to carry out Jesus' Commission to "teach [others] all things whatsoever I have commanded you" was the gospel itself. It is unlikely that they possessed any other text or manual.

28. My discussion of this phrase follows closely the development in Carson, "Matthew," 596. The Great Commission differs from Jesus' commission to the Twelve during His earthly ministry (Matt. 10:5–6). Before His resurrection His ministry was focused on Israel (cf. 15:24–26).

29. As Carson ("Matthew," 596) argues, "Would he [Matthew] say that any Jewish Christians in any church known to him should not be baptized and taught?"

30. Carson, "Matthew," 596. Charles Ryrie, who understands Matthew 25:32 to refer to the Gentile nations, believes that "surviving Jews will also be judged at this same time (Ezek. 20:33–38)," *Ryrie Study Bible* (Chicago: Moody, 1978).

31. For further support of this understanding of "all nations" see Harvey, "Mission in Matthew," 133–34; and Buice, "The Great Commission Passages," 85.

32. See H. C. Goerner, *All Nation's in God's Purpose* (Nashville: Broadman, 1979); Donald A. McGavran, *Understanding Church Growth,* rev. ed. (Grand Rapids: Eerdmans, 1980); and John Piper, *Let the Nations Be Glad* (Grand Rapids: Baker, 1993).

33. See the helpful discussion in Buice, "The Great Commission Passages," 85.

34. Carson, "Matthew," 596, where he gives further grammatical support for this.

35. Wallace (*Greek Grammar Beyond the Basics,* 645) argues that the participles are participles of means. Carson's ("Matthew," 597) arguments to the contrary are not convincing, although I think he is right that there is a bit of imperatival force in the two participles. Culver (*A Greater Commission,* 151) argues that the two participles, "baptizing" and "teaching," are not coordinate. Instead, because there is no conjunction joining them, the first participle, "baptizing," is to be understood as having imperatival force,

and the second, "teaching," modifies the first. Culver not only misses the force of the participle "go," to which he does not give imperatival force, but he then wrongly understands "baptizing" as meaning to "convey an imperative idea." Furthermore, his theory that "teaching" modifies "baptizing" is not convincing. The absence of a coordinating conjunction between the two participles does not require that the second modify the first.

36. Gundry, *Matthew,* 596.

37. Maximilian Zerwick, *Biblical Greek* (Rome: Scripta Pontificii Instituti Biblici, 1963), 35. Zerwick bases this statement on the fact that Matthew avoids the confusion of *en* and *eis,* which is common in Hellenistic Greek. Carson ("Matthew," 597) understands Christian baptism to be "a sign both of entrance into the Messiah's covenant community and of pledged submission to his lordship." S. McKnight, "Gospel of Matthew," in *Dictionary of Jesus and the Gospels,* ed. Joel B. Green, Scot McKnight, and I. Howard Marshall (Downers Grove, Ill.: InterVarsity, 1992), 539.

38. See Carson's helpful discussion on the issue of a baptismal formula in the early church ("Matthew," 598). Especially helpful here is Hartman, *Into the Name of the Lord Jesus,* esp. 37–50, 147–53. On pp. 150–52 he discusses possible reasons why only Matthew employs a Trinitarian baptismal formula in the New Testament.

39. See n. 12 and the discussion in that context. McKnight correctly concludes, "The distinction between Jesus as 'Savior' and Jesus as 'Lord' is a modern one and wholly foreign to the message of Jesus and the Gospels."

40. Wolfgang Trilling, *Das wahre Israel: Studien zur Theologie des Matthäus-Evangeliums* (Munchen: Kosel, 1964), 37, and the discussion in Carson, "Matthew," 598. This authority that Christ now assumes confirms the discussion earlier in this essay. Jesus now has all authority because He now functions in the capacity in which Yahweh previously functioned.

41. See the helpful discussion in Gundry, *Matthew,* 597. He lists several Old Testament passages supporting this point: Genesis 26:24; 28:15; Exodus 3:12; Joshua 1:5, 9; Judges 6:12, 16; 2 Samuel 7:3; Isaiah 41:10; 43:5; Haggai 1:3; cf. Matthew 28:10. Once again, the fact that Jesus now functions as Yahweh did in the Old Testament, both in His presence with and in protection of His people, supports the point made above that He has now been given the authority to mediate God's rule on this earth, just as it was mediated by Yahweh in the Old Testament.

42. For a more complete development of the four uses of "all" or *pas* in the Great Commission, see chapter 13 in this volume by Daniel Davey.

43. Senior states concerning Luke 24:44–49 that "its net effect is to instruct the community on the nature and scope of its mission." Donald Senior

and Carroll Stuhlmueller, *The Biblical Foundations for Mission* (Maryknoll, N. Y.: Orbis, 1983), 256.

44. On the connection of these two passages see, for example, Walter L. Liefeld, *Luke,* vol. 8 of The Expositor's Bible Commentary, ed. Frank E. Gaebelein (Grand Rapids: Zondervan, 1984), 1057.

45. The account in Luke 24:36–49 apparently is a parallel to the account in John 20:19–23. See the discussion in Grant R. Osborne, *The Resurrection Narratives: A Redaction Study* (Grand Rapids: Baker, 1984), 246–51. John 20:19–23 is the topic of the next section of this essay.

46. John 20:24 states that Thomas, one of the Twelve, was not with them when Jesus arrived. Thus, the possibility is left open and is perhaps implied that he had been with them earlier that evening.

47. D. A. Carson, *The Gospel According to John* (Grand Rapids: Eerdmans, 1991), 646. Carson gives further support for this interpretation.

48. The outpouring of the Spirit in Acts, which initiated the proclamation described in Luke 24:44–49, was given to more than the Twelve (Acts 1:15; 2:1–21).

49. There is some debate concerning the context of Jesus' instructions in 24:44–49. According to Culver (*A Greater Commission,* 145) verses 48–49 belong to an occasion later than verses 44–47. He also suggests that verses 44–47 may be a summary of what Jesus told His disciples during His resurrection appearances. In this last idea he follows I. Howard Marshall, *The Gospel of Luke: A Commentary on the Greek Text* (Grand Rapids: Eerdmans, 1978), 904. Since, though, the common particle *de* in verse 44 does not indicate a special transition, "the event [in vv. 44–49] seems to follow directly after the meal" and is best understood to be a continuation of the meeting of the disciples with Jesus described in verses 36–43. So Darrell L. Bock, *Luke,* 2 vols., Baker Exegetical Commentary on the New Testament (Grand Rapids: Baker, 1996), 2:1935.

50. For an excellent discussion of the topic of mission in Luke and Acts, see William J. Larkin Jr., "Mission in Luke" and "Mission in Acts," in *Mission in the New Testament,* 152–69 and 170–86. For more popular treatments of Jesus' commission in Luke 24, see Howard, *Great Commission for Today,* 14–29; and Banks, *In Search of the Great Commission,* 99–110.

51. By the "Scriptures" I am referring to what Christians call the Old Testament.

52. See Bock, *Luke,* 1938–39, for a helpful discussion of some of the texts Jesus could have used from the Old Testament. According to the New Testament, Jesus is the topic of the Old Testament Scriptures when they are interpreted correctly (Luke 24:25; Acts 13:29; John 5:39; 20:9).

53. Of the ninety-nine times *dei* (it is necessary) occurs in the New Testament, forty are in Luke–Acts.

54. For a helpful discussion of these important themes in Luke-Acts see Darrell L. Bock, "A Theology of Luke-Acts," in *A Biblical Theology of the New Testament,* ed. Roy B. Zuck (Chicago: Moody, 1994), 87–117; and D. C. Allison Jr., "Eschatology," in *Dictionary of Jesus and the Gospels,* 208–9.

55. See n. 47. To make Jesus the topic and the hermeneutical key to the Old Testament would have been a new approach. It must have given new insight into the text.

56. Note the parallel passages in 1 Corinthians 1:21–25 and 2 Corinthians 3:12–18. It seems that Luke may be contrasting the experience of the disciples in Luke 24 with the promise of the serpent in Genesis 3:5 and 7 that the eyes of Adam and Eve would be opened if they ate of the tree of the knowledge of good and evil. In Genesis 3:6 and 8 the Septuagint uses the same phrase found in Luke 24:31 ("the[ir] eyes were opened"), with only a change of verb tense in verse 6. This Greek verb is repeated in Genesis 3:6, 8 (LXX) and Luke 24:31–32, and 45. Whereas in Genesis 3 the eyes of the first couple were opened to know and experience sin, guilt, shame, and all the consequences of sin, in Luke 24 Jesus overcomes the curse and opens the minds of the disciples to know and experience (v. 32) true fellowship with God in the Scriptures through the Son, who is the main subject of the Scriptures. This passage strongly implies that the spiritual insight and understanding, which the regenerate enjoy (1 Cor. 2:10–14; 2 Cor. 4:4), is the ability to see in the text of Scripture the fulfillment of God's promises in Jesus.

57. The article with *Christos* in verse 46 indicates that it is a title: "the Christ."

58. These are not meant to be comprehensive lists of prophecies of these events but rather representative texts, so that the reader has an idea of the types of texts to which Jesus is referring. Most of the prophecies of Christ, even of His death and resurrection, are not propositional statements clearly declaring that such and such will happen to the Christ. Instead, the great majority of the prophecies concerning Christ are what are called typological prophecies. Many, such as the prophecies concerning Him in Psalms 22 and 69, are the experiences of David, which are designed by God to foreshadow and be prophetic of the experiences of Christ, David's greater Son. This is one reason a holistic approach to the Old Testament is necessary in order to understand and correctly interpret the prophecies concerning Christ. See the discussion above. The fact that Jesus would

rise from the dead on the third day (Luke 24:46; 1 Cor. 15:4) is generally implied in verses like Psalm 16:10. Here, a quick resurrection is suggested, rather than a resurrection on the last day, which was the usual Jewish hope. Other verses sometimes cited as Old Testament prophecies of Jesus' resurrection on the third day are Hosea 6:2 and Jonah 2:1.

59. First Corinthians 15:3–8 states, as does Luke 24, that an essential part of the gospel message is that these things happened "according to the Scriptures." Luke seldom develops the substitutionary nature of Christ's death; the Luke 24 context is an example of that (but cf. Acts 20:28). It is likely that Jesus included in what He said things that were written in the Scriptures "concerning me" (v. 44)—not only on His death and resurrection but also on preaching to all nations (vv. 46–47). The disciples certainly defended their ministry to the Gentiles on the basis of its being an extension and continuation of Jesus' ministry (i.e., the use of Isaiah 49:6 in Acts 13:47). The continuation of Jesus' ministry by His followers is explicit in the gospel of John.

60. Other Old Testament passages that might be used to support Jesus' statement in Luke 24:47 are Isaiah 42:6; 49:6; and 60:3. Note the use of Isaiah 49:6 in Acts 13:47 to support Paul's ministry to the Gentiles. In this last passage Paul sees his ministry to the Gentiles as an extension of the ministry of Christ, the messianic servant of Isaiah 49:6.

61. Buice, "The Great Commission Passages," 88.

62. Bock, *Luke,* 2:1940. Bock notes that the Old Testament connection and basis for this statement demand that repentance be more than a change of mind. In the Old Testament, repentance "involves 'turning' not just 'agreeing'" (1939).

63. Luke employs the preposition *epi* in Luke 24:47 (also in Acts 2:38) in the phrase normally translated "in Jesus' name." Perhaps a more precise translation is "because of Jesus' name," (Hartman, *Into the Name of the Lord Jesus,* 37). Arndt and Gingrich suggest "in connection with" or "by the use of" for a translation of *epi* in this phrase (*Greek-English Lexicon,* 288).

64. The authority for the ministry of the church inherent in Jesus' name (Acts 2:38; 3:6; 4:7; 8:16; 9:15–16; 10:43, 48; 15:14).

65. On the Gentile mission in Luke-Acts, see Senior and Stuhlmueller, *The Biblical Foundations for Missions,* 260–61, 272. Senior states (p. 272) on the basis of Paul's speeches in Acts 14:15–17 and 17:23–31 that the offer of salvation to the Gentiles is "part of God's saving care for all peoples already expressed in creation"(272). Along this same line, J. H. Bavinck believes that Genesis 1:1 is the basis of the Great Commission as it is given in the Gospels (*An Introduction to the Science of Missions* [Grand

Rapids: Baker, 1960], 12). The Gentile mission in Luke-Acts is also grounded in the fact that now Jesus is Lord of all (Acts 2:36–39; 10:34–36).

66. On the importance of Jerusalem in Luke-Acts, note the journey of Jesus to Jerusalem to die in Luke 9:51–19:44; esp. 13:31–35; and, of course, Acts 1:8.

67. Bock, *Luke,* 2:1940.

68. This length of delay is based on the assumption that the Cornelius events in Acts 10 took place about A.D. 40–41. The Gentiles were not received on an official basis until the Jerusalem Council in A.D. 49.

69. It is easy for modern Christians to forget that the first Christians preached Christ from the Old Testament, and they sought to convince the Jews that their interpretation of their own Scriptures was wrong by using those very same Scriptures (Acts 17:2–3; 26:22–23).

70. Acts 1:8, 22; 2:32; 3:15; 5:32; 10:39, 41; 13:31; 22:15, 20; 26:16.

71. Note the similar image in 1 Chronicles 12:18.

72. On "the promise of the Father," see Acts 1:4; 2:33, 39. This is the Old Testament promise that is poured out by Christ in Acts 2 and found in Old Testament passages like Joel 2:28–32 (quoted in Acts 2:16–21); Isaiah 32:15; 44:3; and Ezekiel 39:29. The fact that Jesus now promises the Spirit and pours out the Father's promise demonstrates His administration of the work of God in this age. In His position as Lord He functions as the Mediator of salvation and its benefits and promises. The designation of this promise as "the promise of my Father" further supports the point made in this chapter that Yahweh, the covenant-keeping God of the Old Testament, is the Godhead administered by the Father, who is the head of Christ (1 Cor. 11:3). This understanding of Yahweh is necessary since Yahweh's promise of the Spirit in Joel 2 is now called "the promise of my Father."

73. The identification of the Spirit as "power from on high" is consistent, since "power is what the Spirit supplies" (Bock, *Luke,* 2:1943). Bock has a helpful discussion on Luke's use of the word "power."

74. The future tense of the verb "you shall be" in Acts 1:8 could be understood to have imperatival force. Wallace (*Greek Grammar Beyond the Basics,* 568) classifies this verb as a predictive future but notes that it may have imperatival force. There is compelling evidence, however, that this future-tense verb is better understood as a prediction than as a command. First, the parallel future tense at the beginning of the verse ("But you shall receive power . . .") is a prediction (or promise). Second, Luke 24:47 says that it is written in the Old Testament that the gospel must be preached to all nations beginning from Jerusalem, and Acts 1:8 seems to be a further development of Jesus' teaching in Luke 24:47. Culver (*A Greater Commission,* 136) calls Acts 1:8 "a statement of fact, not a command or

commission at all." The preaching of the followers of Jesus, as it is described in Acts, seems to be more the natural outworking of the internal work of the Spirit than the obedience of a command (esp. Acts 4:20). Larkin ("Mission in Acts," 186) summarizes the teaching of mission in Acts: "One theme particularly stands out: the theocentric nature of the mission in its commissioning, agency, and results. Luke would remind us when our attention is so focused on human stratagems for what we are going to do for God in mission, that, first to last, Christian mission is the mission of God. God calls and sends His servants on mission. He, himself is on mission, opening individual hearts and the door of faith to various ethnic groups."

75. Martin Erdmann, "Mission in John's Gospel and Letters," in *Mission in the New Testament,* 207–26, is a helpful introduction to the topic of mission in these New Testament books. Banks, *In Search of the Great Commission,* 19–30; and Howard, *Great Commission for Today,* 32–51, are popular treatments of the commission of Jesus in John 20.

76. Carson, *The Gospel According to John,* 647.

77. George R. Beasley-Murray, *John,* vol. 36 of Word Biblical Commentary (Dallas: Word, 1987), 379.

78. The same word *(apostello)* is used twice in 17:18. See Banks *(In Search of the Great Commission,* 23–30) who argues for a distinction in meaning between *apostello* and *pempo* in John.

79. Andreas J. Kostenberger, *The Mission of Jesus and the Disciples According to the Fourth Gospel* (Grand Rapids: Eerdmans, 1998).

80. Ibid., 102. See his discussion of this issue on pages 97–106.

81. Carson *(The Gospel According to John,* 648–49) deals with both of these faulty interpretations.

82. Kostenberger, *Mission of Jesus and the Disciples,* 190.

83. Ibid., 191. See his full development of this idea on pages 45–140. He carefully distinguishes Jesus' mission from ours with regard to the Incarnation, that is, His "coming into the world," which "is never in the Fourth Gospel presented as the model for the mission of the disciples or believers in general" (191 n. 180).

84. Carson, *The Gospel According to John,* 648.

85. The perfect tense indicates a present state of affairs resulting from past action. See Wallace, *Greek Grammar Beyond the Basics,* 572–82, for a thorough discussion of the perfect tense.

86. Raymond E. Brown, *The Gospel According to John,* vols. 29 and 29A of *The Anchor Bible* (Garden City, N.Y.: Doubleday, 1970), 2:1036. For further support for this view, see Carson, *The Gospel According to John,* 648–49;

Beasley-Murray, *John,* 379–80; Kostenberger, *Mission of Jesus and the Disciples,* 191–92; and B. F. Westcott, *The Gospel According to St. John* (1881; reprint, Grand Rapids: Eerdmans, 1973), 294. Note John 13:20 on the continuity of Jesus' mission in His followers.

87. Several other passages in John parallel the ideas in 20:21. See especially 13:16, 20; 14:12–14; and 17:18.

88. On Jesus' present position of authority, see the discussion above on Matthew 28:18.

89. See the helpful discussion in Carson, *The Gospel According to John,* 648–49.

90. Kostenberger, *Mission of Jesus and the Disciples,* 192.

91. Beasley-Murray (*John,* 380) comments concerning John 14:12–14 that "the disciples go forth to their mission and seek the Lord's aid therein, and in response to their prayers *he* will do through them 'greater things' than in the days of his flesh, 'that the Father may be glorified in the Son'— in the powerful mission that *he* continues!"

92. Carson, *The Gospel According to John,* 649. Carson notes that the commission in John to perfectly obey the Son is as challenging as teaching people to obey all that Jesus has commanded. I would add that the commission is as challenging as the command to go to all nations and is certainly related to it.

93. Kostenberger, *Mission of Jesus and the Disciples,* 190–92.

94. Carson, *The Gospel According to John,* 649.

95. See Carson, *The Gospel According to John,* 649–55, for a helpful discussion of this issue. Carson's conclusion is the same as this author's. Some think that the absence of an article in John 20:22 indicates that Jesus bequeaths some spiritual power or anointing and not the Holy Spirit, Himself. The absence of the article, however, with other references to the Holy Spirit, supports the interpretation that in John 20:22 "Holy Spirit" *(pneuma hagion)* refers to the person of the Holy Spirit (John 1:33; Acts 2:4; 8:7, 15).

96. Carson, *The Gospel According to John,* 650.

97. See Carson, *The Gospel According to John,* for a fuller discussion of this concept (653). On p. 655, Carson notes the analogous situation in John 13:8, when in the Upper Room Jesus tells the disciples, "Unless I wash you, you have no part with me." He notes that those words can be read as simply referring to footwashing, or they can more correctly be understood to point forward to the spiritual washing, which Jesus, the Lamb of God, is going to provide.

98. The view that John 20:22 refers to a "theocratic anointing" of the apostles to enable them to lay the foundation of the church is presented in Larry D. Pettegrew, *New Covenant Ministry of the Holy Spirit* (Lanham, Md.:

Univ. Press of America, 1993), 71–73. Although Pettegrew does not deal with the connection of verse 22 with verse 21, he does lean heavily on verse 23, arguing that the authority to "forgive" and to "retain" sins is a special authority given to the apostles alone. Pettegrew discusses this "theocratic anointing" on pp. 8–10 and identifies Jesus' anointing at His baptism as a theocratic anointing such as, he argues, the apostles receive in John 20:22. The problem with his interpretation is that the anointing that Jesus receives at His baptism is described elsewhere in Scripture as the basis for the anointing that is poured out on Jews at Pentecost and on Gentiles in Acts 10–11 (compare Matt. 3:11; Luke 3:16; Acts 1:5; 2:33; 11:15–17). Jesus' anointing is not described as the basis of a special anointing of the apostles. Another interpretation of John 20:22 is that of Gary M. Burge, *The Anointed Community* (Grand Rapids: Eerdmans, 1987), esp. 114–49. In his detailed study, Burge concludes that John 20:22 fulfills the expectation of the Spirit so fully developed in John 14–16. If Acts 2 is also a fulfillment of the expectation of the Spirit in John 14–16, then, for him, this suggests the alignment of John 20:22 and Acts 2 (149). He is willing to overlook some of the historical discrepancies between Acts 2 and John 20:22 in order to reconcile them theologically. This same openness to accommodate chronology to theology is seen in the commentary of Beasley-Murray, *John,* 380–82.

99. In the words of Acts 2:33, being "exalted to the right hand of God, and having received from the Father the promise of the Holy Spirit, He has poured forth this which you now see and hear."

100. The Father had given the spirit to Jesus (1:33; 3:34), and now, after His glorification, Jesus has authority to give the Spirit to His followers (7:37–39).

101. Carson, *The Gospel According to John,* 651. Carson explains, "The lexica give as the meaning of the verb *(emphysao)* 'he breathed in' or 'he breathed upon' but actual usage outside the New Testament (this is the only place it occurs in the New Testament) does not encourage the view that the preposition 'in ' or 'upon' was part of the meaning of the verb itself. In its dozen or so uses in the LXX, for instance, there is always some additional syntactical structure to carry this prepositional force wherever it is needed." The NIV and the NASB translate the verb "he breathed on them." The KJV puts "them" in italics, indicating it was supplied.

102. The verb recurs eleven times in the Septuagint. See the discussion on this word in Beasley-Murray, *John,* 380–81; Carson, *The Gospel According to John,* 651–52; and Burge, *Anointed Community,* 125.

103. The concept of new creation or regeneration is important in John, cf. 3:1–8.

104. The saying in John 20:23, however, is clearly independent and not John's reformulation of the passages in Matthew. See the discussion in Carson, *The Gospel According to John,* 655; and Beasley-Murray, *John,* 382–83. It is clear that the context in Matthew 16 and 18 is one of church discipline. The context in John 20, however, is different; John 20:23 is clearly found in a context addressing the mission of Jesus' disciples and their empowerment by the Spirit (vv. 21–22). In the gospel of John, the ministry of Jesus is to the world (1:29; 3:16; 12:31–32; esp. 17:18), and the work of the Spirit is to convict the world (16:7–11). If the disciples of Jesus are to continue His work by the power of the Spirit, it is not consistent to limit their work to the church. See Kostenberger, *Mission of Jesus and the Disciples,* 193–94.

105. Although some would limit this authority to the Twelve, as the founders of the church, it does not seem necessary. The same arguments used above, applying Luke 24:44–49 to the church at large, apply here since this is the very same historical situation. Furthermore, if verses 21 and 22 are for the church, then verse 23 must be also.

106. The result of the ministry of Jesus (John 9:35–41) and the Holy Spirit (John 16:7–11) is also the forgiveness or the retention of sins.

107. The disciples do not replace Jesus, nor are they identical with Him. Their identity with Jesus, as they continue His work, lies in the fact that they, like Jesus, have been sent into the world with the same purpose (e.g., to give life, 20:21, 31) and empowerment (20:22). See Kostenberger, *Mission of Jesus and the Disciples,* pp. 194–97, for a more complete development of these ideas.

108. C. K. Barrett, *The Gospel According to St. John,* 2d ed. (Philadelphia: Westminster, 1978), 569.

SECTION TWO

THEOLOGICAL STUDIES

5

CHARLES A. HAUSER JR.

HELL

Motivation for Missions?

How lost are the lost? This has become an issue among evangelicals. In the current theological scene, some question the literalness of hell and the concept of eternal punishment. While liberalism has long rejected any teaching of eternal judgment, it is only in the last twenty years that serious questions about hell have appeared in writings by evangelicals. These questions have been addressed in two books, both with the same title, written fourteen years apart. The first was written by Jon E. Braun in 1979[1] and the second by John Blanchard in 1993.[2] Both books reflect the growing tendency among evangelicals to discount or at least soften teaching concerning eternal punishment and its application in preaching to the unbeliever. In this chapter we will conduct a brief historical survey of the church's attitude concerning hell from the Reformation to the middle of the twentieth century, then outline the main current theories on the subject, and finally conclude with a section on the biblical teaching on hell with an application to missionary work.

Historical Survey

Three areas reflect and measure the church's attitude concerning hell: hymnology, preaching, and literature on mission theory.

Hymnology

Early hymn books have sections that are notably absent in the hymnals of the middle to late twentieth century. In hymnals of the last half of the nineteenth century and the first forty years of the twentieth century particularly, the concepts of lostness and judgment are prominent. There are hymns warning of spiritual death, the coming judgment of those rejecting Christ, the wrath of God, and the danger of being lost for eternity. These teachings were used both as a caution to unbelievers and as a motivator for believers to be faithful witnesses to a lost world. "The Great Judgment Morning" was copyrighted in 1894, and songs like "Why Will Ye Die?" and "The Great Day Coming" are found in a hymnal published in 1902. A few songs written during this time period—"Rescue the Perishing" (1898) and "Almost Persuaded" (1902)—are still sung today by many congregations. Most of the others, however, are no longer found in modern hymnals because the subject matter is no longer in vogue. Most modern hymnals have no section at all on judgment or the wrath of God.

Preaching

Preachers from the Reformation forward had much to say about judgment and eternal punishment. Perhaps in America the most famous preacher to emphasize these points was Jonathan Edwards, who lived from 1703 to 1758. As one author put it, "His most powerful Sermons appeal[ed] to the conscience by the terrors of condemnation awaiting the unregenerate."[3] Even his sermon titles, such as "Wrath upon the Wicked to the Uttermost," were calculated to drive the point home. Edwards was not unique, however, in his emphasis. Robert Hall, a Baptist preacher, and George Whitefield, a Methodist revivalist, both taught the same in their sermons. Whitefield, in a sermon titled "The Method of Grace," stated "that the least deviation from the moral law . . . deserves eternal death at the hand of God."[4] Charles Spurgeon, in his sermon "Woe to Come," pled with his hearers "to flee from the wrath to come! Who can tell the terrors of the day of judgment? . . . Yet certain it is that after the woe of judgment there comes the woe of hell."[5] B. H. Carroll, another Baptist, echoed the same theme in a revival message entitled "The Wages of Sin." In it he stated,

> The second death is after the resurrection of the body, the body made immortal and the Death, then, means . . . the eternal banishment from God after the resurrection and judgment. . . . There is no reformation in hell. There is no means provided. There is no gospel preached. There is no altar of prayer. There is no offer of compromise.[6]

It did not matter which theological viewpoint one held—from Reformed to Wesleyan, from Baptist to interdenominational—the message was essentially the same. Preachers on judgment and eternal punishment included William G. T. Shedd, Charles Hodge, H. A. Ironside, Ralph W. Neighbour, A. W. Tozer, and John R. Rice. They taught that, unless their listeners accepted Jesus Christ as Savior, they faced eternal punishment and eternal separation from God.

After World War II, however, the subject of hell became less frequent in the public ministry of the church. This was so noticeable by 1974 that one writer stated,

> Too many evangelicals have opted for a "pop gospel" in their evangelistic approach. In plain and simple language this means that "sensitive" concepts, such as the serious consequences of sin and hell, though believed in, are astutely avoided in any initial evangelistic presentation. . . . The problem with the approach of many contemporary evangelicals is that for public image reasons hell is deliberately concealed. It is removed to a safe innocuous place to insure that the evangelistic presentation remains culturally acceptable.[7]

Missionary Theology

There is not an abundance of literature examining the missionary enterprise from a theological perspective. At the beginning of the twentieth century, however, some writings were produced that considered missions from a more theological viewpoint. One of the earliest, published in 1907, was written by Arthur J. Brown.[8] In his book he develops three primary motives for the missionary enterprise, one being the world's evident need of Christ. He states that humanity has, above all,

> a relation to Jesus Christ that not only lends a new dignity to this earthly life but that saves his soul and prepares him for eternal companionship with God. "Neither is there salvation in any other." . . . We do not hear as much as our fathers heard of the motive of salvation of the heathen. Our age prefers to dwell upon the blessings of faith rather than upon the consequences of unbelief.

And yet if we believe that Christ is our "life," it is impossible to avoid the conclusion that to be without Christ
is death. Reason as well as revelation tells us that man
has sinned, that "the wages of sin is death" and that this
truth is as applicable to Asia and Africa as to Europe
and America.[9]

This quotation suggests that, as early as 1907, emphasis had begun
to shift from the judgment of God to the salvation of the individual.
Nevertheless, the concept of judgment was still present in the message.
By 1912 a struggle over the motive for missions was becoming evident.
One side stressed humanitarian service and the other salvation from sin
and death. Edward Pfeiffer saw the problem clearly. Other causes, he
wrote, should not "obscure or belittle the more tremendous and enduring
issues that hinge upon the reality of death and a judgment to come"[10] Sin
and the consequences of sin "are realities which no sophistry or philosophy
will ever dispose of."[11] The tendency of many to substitute a social or
humanitarian reason for missions was the result of a retreat from the
"vital and fundamental truths of the Gospel."[12] This tendency continued
to play a major role in groups strongly influenced by liberal theology.
Edward Soper, writing in 1943, rejects eternal punishment and hell as
motives for missions. To him, this motivation makes a monster out of God:

Can we justifiably claim that a man is hopelessly consigned to eternal punishment, no matter how earnestly
he has striven to be a good man, for the one reason he
has not . . . accepted Jesus Christ? Immediately everything noble and just and Christian in one's breast rises
in repudiation of such a declaration. . . . What kind of
monster does it make of God who would be party to the
condemnation of a person who admittedly could not have
known of the offer of salvation. . . . God is just; God is
love; he cannot be unjust, and he cannot be unloving.[13]

For Soper, salvation does not come only through Christ. "The man
who has not heard of him; he is saved by his attitude [faith] towards the
best he knows."[14] This means, of course, that there is more than one way to
salvation, and the uniqueness of Christ and the Christian message is laid
aside. While the uniquenss of Christ was always affirmed in evangelical

circles, these new ideas did help foster the idea that hell was a subject only to be hinted at, not one that people ought to be confronted with publicly. And the avoidance of the subject of hell eventually led to a rethinking of it. Thus, we have those today who claim to be evangelicals but who completely reject the concept of eternal punishment. One evangelical stated, "If the doctrine of eternal punishment was clearly and unmistakably taught in every leaf of the Bible, and on every leaf of all the Bibles of all the world, I could not believe a word of it."[15] C. S. Lewis also was bothered by the concept of hell. His feeling was, "There is no doctrine which I would more willingly remove from Christianity than this, . . . I would pay any price to be able to say truthfully, 'All will be saved.'"[16] As a result, there are various approaches to the interpretation of hell among evangelicals. These interpretations comprise the next section of our study.

Present Theories on Hell

It is impossible in a short chapter to give a detailed account of the many current views on hell. Only the views that have influence within evangelical thought will be mentioned.

Universalism

Universalists believe that all will be saved and that a God of love would never put an individual in a place of everlasting torment. Even if there were a short period of judgment, God in His mercy eventually would cause all human beings to come to Him. Some proponents of universalism follow Origen, who said all judgment is remedial. Toon suggests three bases for the theory: universalism as decreed by God (taught by F. D. E. Schleiermacher); universalism as an optimistic hope (held by C. W. Emmer); and universalism as the election of all people to salvation (proposed by Karl Barth).[17] In its various forms, this idea became more accepted, at least in the major denominations, as the nineteenth century ended, and in the twentieth century it became a respected position. It especially gained support through the work of Karl Barth, although Barth's own position was not always clear. The theory is usually based on the love of God and the belief that people could never be truly happy in heaven knowing family members and friends were undergoing torment in hell. Most frequently, universalism is found in circles influenced by liberal theology rather than among conservatives.

Annihilation

Some who hold to the theory of annihilation prefer the name conditional immortality. However it is named, annihilation teaches that, sooner or later, the unbeliever will longer exist. Annihilation either takes place at death or after a period of judgment for sin. Evangelicals who hold this view react strongly against the idea that God would eternally punish anyone. Although his view is filled with emotionalism and a strong Arminian bias, Pinnock, an annihilationist, argues his objection to the traditional view of hell as well as anyone. He states that

> . . . we are asked to believe that God endlessly tortures sinners by the million, sinners who perish because the Father has decided not to elect them to salvation . . . and whose torments are supposed to gladden the hearts of believers in heaven. . . . The traditional view of the nature of hell has been a stumbling block for believers and an effective weapon in the hands of skeptics for use against the faith.[18]

He uses several lines of reasoning to support his position. First, he believes that the biblical passages dealing with future punishment should be interpreted as meaning complete destruction of the unbeliever. Second, he thinks that the moral character of God demands that He destroy the wicked rather than punish them forever. Third, he believes that the traditional view is based upon the false teaching of the immortality of the soul, which he believes is a Hellenistic belief derived from Plato not the Bible. He says the Bible teaches that immortality comes as a gift of God when one believes in the gospel.[19] He asks the question, "What lifestyle, what set of actions, would deserve the ultimate of penalties—everlasting conscious punishment?"[20] Instead of eternal punishment, which to him is unreasonable, annihilation is a logical and easy belief:

> It is easy to accept that annihilation might be deserved by those whose lives turned in a definite NO to God, but it is hard to accept hell as everlasting conscious torment with no hope of escape or remittance as a just punishment for anything. . . . It is too heavy a sentence and cannot be successfully defended as a just action on God's part.[21]

For Pinnock, to believe in eternal punishment would deny God's boundless mercy and moral goodness. Pinnock declares, however, that "God is morally justified in destroying the wicked because he respects their human choices."[22] Proponents of annihilationism believe that after a period of punishment in hell, God in His mercy makes those who have rejected Him cease to exist.

Purgatory

Purgatory, as a view of the afterlife, is usually connected with Roman Catholic theology. Certain non-Catholics, however, have expressed similar views, so it is valid to consider it.[23] In reality, very few go to hell, because most individuals are eventually made pure enough to enter heaven. As Hayes points out, "For some Christians hell is clearly a fact, while for others it is a possibility, and for yet others, it is a situation that will eventually be overcome."[24] To define what is meant by purgatory, Hayes explains that

> [Purgatory] is commonly understood to refer to the state, place, or condition in the next world between heaven and hell, a state of purifying suffering for those who have died and are still in need of such purification. This purifying condition comes to an end for the individual when that person's guilt has been expiated.[25]

This view of the afterlife is based on certain theological suppositions that derive more from reason than from an exegesis of Scripture. It is held that, while God is infinite, human beings are finite and limited. They are sinners, guilty before God. Since most people die as imperfect lovers of God, and since heaven is the perfection of love, most are not ready for heaven. In order for the masses of mediocre Christians to escape hell, a place in the next life is needed for the cleansing necessary to enter into heaven. The rationale is that "not everyone seems 'bad enough' to be consigned to eternal hell. And most do not seem 'good enough' to be candidates for heaven. Therefore, something has to happen 'in between.'"[26] It is in the Roman Church's evolving teaching concerning the sacraments of the Eucharist and penance that the concept of purgatory has its roots.[27]

Hell as a Metaphor

This approach to the subject of hell concedes that the Bible clearly teaches everlasting punishment for those who do not believe in Jesus Christ as Savior. Hell is a real place of frightful judgment, but it is not a place of literal fire and brimstone. These descriptions of hell are metaphors to illustrate, in vivid terms, the terrible judgment that awaits those who reject God. As William Crockett puts it, "The Scriptures do teach about a real hell, a place of frightful judgment. But precisely what it will be like, we do not know."[28] Those who espouse hell as metaphor do not do so in order to make the subject more acceptable to the culture of the day. Submitting to the culture of the day would undermine the authority of Scripture. Rather, they appeal to Jewish literature to demonstrate that fire was used in a nonliteral sense and also that the description of heaven found in the Bible is not literal in every detail. They believe that the descriptions of heaven found in the Bible are related to the way great cities were pictured in biblical times and are not the way we would picture heaven today. Crockett ends his discussion by asking the question, "Does God communicate truth to people in ways they can understand at their particular time in history?"[29] He points out the symbolism in the book of Revelation with regard to heaven and then applies the same approach to hell. He concludes that hell is a real place of judgment but one that is described by symbolic language. He also believes that the language used of hell is contradictory if taken in a literal sense. How can there be literal fire and complete darkness at the same time? How can bodies decay and never be destroyed? How can spirit bodies be affected by physical fire? These contradictions lead him to conclude that, while the punishment will be great, the words found in Scripture are not to be taken literally. At the same time, he affirms "that the wicked will be forever banished from the presence of God is somber indeed. Whatever their punishment, wherever they are sent, the final judgment cannot be anything but laden with sorrow."[30]

Hell as Literal

This view simply states that the words of Scripture must be accepted at face value. The Bible says what it means and means what it says. It not only projects a terrible judgment for the wicked but also a judgment that continues throughout eternity. A literal hell is considered by most to be the traditional view of the church. The proponents of this view believe that the overly graphic picture of hell given in the past should not bring about a rejection of clear biblical teaching on the subject. Appeal is made to the teaching about hell by Jesus Himself, who talked more about hell than He did about heaven. As Walvoord states, "All the references to *gehenna,* except James 3:6, are from the lips of Christ Himself, and there is an obvious emphasis on the punishment for the wicked after death as being everlasting."[31] The emphasis is on judgment unending. If the words concerning the duration of the wicked's judgment are taken in context, their meaning suggests a judgment that does not end. "While the term 'forever' may sometimes be curtailed in duration by its context, such termination is never mentioned once in either the Old or New Testament as relating to the punishment of the wicked."[32] The word used in the Greek for "everlasting" lends support to the literal view of hell.

> The strongest evidence that the word *aionios* is meant to teach the endlessness of the punishment of the wicked is in the fact that the same word is used to describe the blessed life of the godly. In a number of passages the two uses of the word lie side by side. Only a violent twisting of meaning can lead to any other conclusion than this: if *aionion* describes life which is endless, so must *aionion* describe endless punishment. Here the doctrine of heaven and the doctrine of hell stand or fall together. W. R. Inge says, "No sound Greek scholar can pretend that *aionios* means anything less than eternal."[33]

Also, Scripture indicates that the punishment in hell does not destroy those who experience it, as is demonstrated by the throwing into hell of the beast and false prophet in Revelation 19:20. Over a thousand years later, when Satan is thrown into hell as well, these two individuals are still there (Rev. 20:10).

Biblical Teaching

Two presuppositions are foundational in the examination of scriptural teaching on hell. The first is that Scripture is the authoritative Word of God in everything that it teaches. Buis is correct when he states that there is a connection between the doctrine of hell and belief in the inspiration of Scripture. He believes the two stand or fall together. "The only way to escape the doctrine of eternal punishment is to deny the infallibility of Scripture, and to deny that it is the one rule of faith and practice."[34] The question is not whether or not our culture likes the doctrine or that somehow we can make it culturally acceptable to the modern mind. The question is: Does the Bible teach it? The second presupposition is that there is only one way of salvation. Peter was correct when he stated, "There is salvation in no one else; for there is no other name under heaven that has been given among men, by which we must be saved" (Acts 4:12 NASB). Any other approach denies the uniqueness of the God-man, Jesus Christ. This is the foundation upon which a correct understanding of the biblical doctrine of hell can be constucted. Because of space limitations, our study will limit itself to the teaching of Jesus and the New Testament in general.

One problem in coming to an understanding of the doctrine of hell is the translation of the word *hades* in the King James Version. Hades is different from hell and yet ten times it is translated "hell" in the King James version. Hades sometimes is a reference to the grave, but it is also a place of the departed spirits of the lost. It is connected closely with death in the New Testament but is always distinct from death. This is seen, for example, in passages such as Revelation 1:18; 6:8; and 20:13–14. Hell is the final abode of the lost and originally was created for Satan and the angelic beings who fell with him (Matt. 25:41).

Teaching of Jesus

It is noteworthy that Jesus, often presented as the paragon of love who would never approach a subject negatively, is the one in Scripture who says the most about hell. Love and hell are not mutually exclusive subjects. One can teach both without being inconsistent. The gospel of Matthew contains many of Christ's teachings concerning hell. As one author put it, in commenting on Matthew 23:15, "The contemporary Christian portrayal of Jesus as meek and mild is shattered by Jesus' next usage of the term *gehenna* in Matthew's gospel. Jesus had obviously not read the latest edition of 'How to Win Friends and Influence Jewish Leaders.'"[35]

Certain terms need to be defined for a proper understanding of specific passages. A first group of words deals with the places to which the unrighteous are sent. The term *hades*, as stated earlier, is used in the New Testament to describe the place of retribution for the unrighteous, and it is used in this way at least ten times in the New Testament. A key passage demonstrating this is Luke 16:22–26. It does not matter if this passage is taken literally or as a story told by Christ to teach a truth. The evident meaning is that there is a place where the unrighteous undergo judgment after death. A second word is *gehenna*. It is used twelve times in the New Testament, eleven of these by Christ. This word has an interesting history. In the Old Testament, *gehenna* was the place where

Israelites sacrificed their children to pagan gods. As a result, Josiah, a righteous king, had it made into a garbage dump, a dump that still existed for the city of Jerusalem at the time of Christ. From the second century on, the word was used in Jewish apocalyptic literature as representing the hell of the last judgment, and this is also the meaning of the word in the New Testament.[36]

The second group of words deals with time. Only two related words will be considered. The first one is *aion.* In order to escape the concept of eternality in the teaching of Scripture, some interpreters attempt to make *aion* refer to the quality of time rather than to its duration. As stated previously, this is not a valid understanding of the word, and it is not supported by New Testament lexicons. Bauer lists the meaning of *aion* as "eternity," "eternally" and "in perpetuity."[37] The second and related word is *aionios,* an adjective form. Again, the lexicon gives the meaning of "eternal" or "without end." Bauer states it is used "very often of God's judgment" and "of eternal life."[38] No support is given to the argument that quality of time is a meaning for *aionios* in the context of judgment. Instead, the idea of duration is shown to be what writers of Scripture had in mind when they used the word. As one author concluded, "In every single instance where it refers to a future time [it] designates an endless period, a completely unlimited duration."[39] This understanding is crucial for the proper interpretation of New Testament passages on the judgment of the unrighteous. It is confirmed by what Jesus said when He referred to the final judgment. He called it the eternal fire in Matthew 18:9. In Mark 9:48, Jesus describes hell as a place where the "worm does not die" nor is "the fire quenched." The verbs used are significant as they mean "to come to an end" and to be "extinguished."[40] Thus the judgment experienced in hell does not come to an end, nor is the fire of judgment ever put out.

Summarizing the teaching of Jesus, it is clear that He believed in a future resurrection of judgment (John 5:29), that there was no escape from it (Matt. 23:33), that originally it was prepared for Satan and his angels (Matt. 25:41), that judgment begins right after death (Luke 16:24), that the final judgment is the fire of hell (Matt. 13:42, 45; 25:41), and that the punishment is eternal (Matt. 25:46). The only way this testimony can be nullified is to redefine the words of Christ, to say that the words are really not the words of Christ, or to say that Christ accommodated Himself to the views of His day and did not actually believe what He said. All of these redefinitions are not acceptable to those who hold to the deity of Christ and to the verbal inspiration of Scripture.

The words in the Gospels used by annihilationists to prove their doctrine do not teach what annihilationists say they do. The Hebrew verb "to cut off" can refer to death, but it does not mean annihilation, as is demonstrated by its use when referring to the Messiah in Daniel 9:26.[41] Neither does the Old Testament word for "destroy" help the annihilationists' position. While it can mean "to perish" in the sense of "to die," it does not have the connotation of annihilation. It also is used of those who are taken captive as well as of lost property.[42] Annihilationists are no better off when they come to words used in the New Testament. The verb "to ruin" or "to destroy" is certainly used in the sense of killing. But once again there is no concept of ceasing to exist in the word.[43] It is used of the attempt of the Jewish leaders to silence Jesus in Matthew 2:13; 12:14; and 27:20, but it is clear that their desire was to kill Him and not to annihilate Him. In Luke 15 verses 4, 8, and 24, Jesus uses the word in the sense of something that is lost.

Other New Testament Teaching

The rest of the New Testament is in agreement with the teaching of Christ. Paul held to a resurrection of the unrighteous (Acts 24:15). The unrighteous are storing up wrath for themselves that they will experience in the day of wrath and the revelation of the righteous judgment of God (Rom. 2:5). They cannot escape this judgment (1 Thess. 5:3), and this judgment is to be experienced both negatively and positively. The unrighteous will *not* share in the inheritance of the righteous (1 Cor. 6:9), but they *will* experience the retribution of God (2 Thess. 1:8). They will pay the penalty of eternal destruction or ruin, which will involve a separation from the presence of Christ (2 Thess. 1:9). Peter talks about the fallen angels who are kept under punishment while they wait for the day of judgment (2 Peter 2:8). They are already in hell where they are reserved for the coming judgment. (2 Peter 2:4). John, in the book of Revelation, sees the unrighteous as undergoing eternal torment that involves the lack of rest day and night (Rev. 9:11). The term John uses for hell is the "lake of fire." Into this place God throws the beast and false prophet (Rev. 19:20), Satan (Rev. 20.10), and all the unrighteous after their final judgment (Rev. 20:15). Being cast in the lake of fire is called the second death.

By death, Scripture never means the end of existence. Instead, it is a separation of some kind. For example, Paul states that being absent from his physical body would mean being in the presence of the Lord. Death was a positive experience to which he looked forward with joyful anticipation (Phil. 1:21–23). Physical death, then, is the separation of the material and immaterial of a human being. Spiritual death is the separation of a human being from God. Thus, Scripture can call living human beings spiritually dead (Eph. 2:1). The second death, then, is an eternal separation of the unrighteous from the presence of God and an experience of continual torment. The casting of the unrighteous into hell, as the result of the Great White Throne Judgment, is called the second death (Rev. 20:14). The conclusion of New Testament teaching is clear, if one is willing to accept it. The fact of judgment is found along with the eternal nature of it. The use of the same term "eternal" of the new life given to the believer and of the judgment given to the unbeliever is also supportive of the doctrine of hell. What the one is, the other must be as well. As one author concludes,

> These passages from the Epistles and Revelation give evidence that the apostles follow their Master in teaching the serious alternatives of life. They teach clearly the fact of judgment, resulting in eternal life or eternal death, which is not a cessation of existence, but rather an existence in which the lost experience the terrible results of their sins. The New Testament is very reserved in its descriptions of this state of punishment, especially in comparison to some other literature on the subject such as the non-canonical apocalyptic literature and also some later commentators. Nevertheless, the New Testament leaves the inescapable impression that this state is very real and highly undesirable.[44]

Immortality of the Soul

One other question needs to be considered—the immortality of the soul. Those who believe in annihilation argue that this concept comes into Christianity from Greek philosophy and is not the teaching of Scripture. According to their position, only the believer has an immortal soul, and this is a gift given by God at the time of salvation. It is true that God is the only one who has inherent immortality, but this does mean that human beings are not immortal. The human soul's immortality is derived rather than inherent. Those who hold to the lack of an immortal soul in human beings are sometimes confusing immortality with eternal life. While eternal life is a gift that the unbeliever does not possess, it does not mean that the unbeliever ceases to exist. As previously stated, death in Scripture always means a separation of some kind and never the end of existence. As one theologian puts it, concerning the soul's immortality, "Revelation does not give minute details upon these subjects, yet the principle features are strongly drawn, and salient."[45] He then goes on to say, "Belief in the immortality of the soul, and its separate existence from the body after death, was characteristic of the Old economy, as well as the New."[46] He then looks at the Old Testament passages that demonstrate this truth. If the soul of an unbeliever ceases to exist, it could be viewed as a blessing rather than a punishment. It would mean the release of that individual from God's punishment, and certainly release is preferred to a continuing judgment by God. The continued existence of the immaterial part of man was a common belief of the church up to the nineteenth century.[47] This belief was so common that one author wrote "I believe it is correct, therefore, to say in modern English that evangelical Christians believe that all men are personally immortal."[48] *Personally* is perhaps not the most accurate form, since Scripture uses the term *person* only of the physical body. This point is noticed by both Chafer and Blanchard.[49] In scriptural usage the word "person" is not related to the immaterial part of man but to his material being. Whatever terminology is used, the idea of a continual existence of the immaterial part of man underlines the teaching of Scripture. As Shedd succinctly states, "This doctrine like that of the divine existence, is nowhere formally demonstrated, because it is everywhere assumed."[50]

Character of God

Another common objection to the idea of eternal punishment is that a loving God could never be so unkind as to consign a human being to such a state. This would violate the very character of God. What is overlooked in this argument, however, is that God is more than love. He is also holy and righteous, and one attribute of God cannot cancel out the others. Ignoring the holy character of God is a result of trivializing sin. We ignore the strong statements in Scripture of God's hatred of sin and how it is an offense against Him. The words "hate" and "abhor" are used of the unrighteous. In Habakkuk 1:13 it is stated that God cannot look on wickedness with favor, and in Hebrews 1:9 it is said of Christ that He loved righteousness and hated lawlessness. It must be remembered also that the unrighteous have rejected God's infinite sacrifice for sin when they reject Christ. The penalty must bare some relationship to what is rejected:

> An infinite atonement was necessary because man's sin,
> being against the most holy God, is an infinite offense.
> The enormity of that offense is demonstrated by the fact
> that it deserves eternal punishment. . . . If we lose sight
> of the fact that the wicked deserve punishment, the re-
> demption is utterly pointless and nonexistent.[51]

In spite of a culture that tries to deny the negative in life and wants
only to think of good things, we must, if we are to be faithful to Scripture, affirm that the Bible teaches the future eternal punishment of those
who do not accept Christ as their Savior. Scholarship cannot successfully explain away the clear teaching of Scripture on this subject. Every
unbeliever is under the judgment of God and, at the point of physical
death, the judgment becomes a permanent condition. No amount of linguistic gymnastics can change the facts. Here is one of the unchanging
truths of Scripture that needs to be affirmed in our relativistic age. Contrary to current thought, human beings are basically not good, as Paul
proves in Romans 1–3 and summarizes in Romans 3:10–18. They are
sinners separated from God and God's truth. Punishment, as it is presented in the Bible, is not always corrective or educational. Society does
not like to think in biblical terms, but in the area of judgment and punishment, as in many other areas, we cannot afford to conform to the
spirit of the age. There is future punishment, and it is eternal.

> The issue of the duration of punishment for the unrigh-
> teous is *the* issue for professing Christians in the late
> twentieth century. . . . There is a growing number who
> are insisting that, contrary to the obvious teaching of
> the historic church, the Bible teaches only a temporary
> period of punishment. Hiding under the guise of schol-
> arship, too many theologians and biblical researchers
> have applied newly invented linguistic hardware to
> "prove" that the words forever and eternal do not mean
> "endless."[52]

"Whatever one is at the end of life will continue for all eternity.
There is no basis for expecting change for the better."[53]

Application to Missions

What is the application of this doctrine in the area of missions? What difference does it make if there is a real hell, and the punishment of those that go there is eternal? In the final analysis, it makes a great deal of difference.

First, the doctrine of hell and eternity reveals the seriousness of sin. In a Christian world where sin often is depreciated and many times ignored, this doctrine calls the believer to an awareness that God cannot tolerate sin. That many today find this teaching difficult to accept reveals how far we have strayed from the biblical concept of sin. One writer concludes that if we find this hard to accept, "we need to go back to the Scriptures and get a fresh sense of the seriousness of sin."[54]

Second, the doctrine of hell and eternity is a teaching of Scripture that needs to be communicated to believers along with the other doctrines of the Bible, such as the gospel. Like Paul, we must give the "whole counsel" of God to the members of the church.

Third, the relativistic philosophy of the day needs to be challenged. There is such a thing as absolute truth, and part of this truth is the reality of everlasting punishment. Instead of surrendering to relativism, we need to oppose it.

> The mood of relativism has influenced the evangelical movement too. Evangelicals are often apologetic about the biblical view of retribution. . . . Many Christians today are apologizing for God rather than contending for his truth. Their hearers may praise them for their broadmindedness and say that they are not like other evangelicals. But they remain critical of God. This is like a lawyer who saves his reputation at the cost of having his client convicted.[55]

Fourth, the doctrine of hell and eternity demonstrates, even to good people, that they face a decision in which their eternal destiny is at stake. When emphasis is placed solely on what one gets out of salvation, without a doctrine of punishment, the gospel does not appeal to as many people. In their view, they are good enough and have no need for anything that the church has to offer. It is only when the biblical concepts of sin, the righteousness of God, and eternal judgment are presented that they become aware of their need of the Savior.

Many today feel that our generation is too sophisticated
to endure talk of hell. So we preach mainly on what
Christ will give people and how those are the things
that they are looking for. But many self-sufficient people
feel that they are not in need of anything from the church.
They reject Christianity, saying it is for weak people,
not for "self-made people" like themselves. They need
to be confronted with the prospect of judgment.[56]

Another writer puts it this way: "The purpose of this shocking doctrine of eternal damnation is to warn against unbelief and carnal security
and thus to save from eternal damnation."[57]

Fifth, judgment emphasizes the responsibility of the believer. Believers must recognize the basic problem of sin. We know the solution to
that problem is Jesus Christ and the salvation that comes from a faith in
His substitutionary death on the cross. We must communicate these truths
to a world that is looking desperately for answers. How can the lack of
faithfully proclaiming this truth be justified? Fear or timidity are not
justifiable reasons for remaining silent. The apathy that is apparent in
failing to proclaim the truth demonstrates that there is no longer a vital
belief concerning this clear doctrine of Scripture. Can the danger of eternal
damnation be known and yet no warning given?

If a doctor fails to warn his patient of a growing cancer,
and the patient dies due to the lack of appropriate treatment, the doctor is likely to be held responsible. . . . If a
doctor used fear to persuade some who were resisting his
advise to break a potentially dangerous habit, and by doing so saved them from sure death, few would find fault
with him. But that is not the way many people respond to
preaching about hell. . . . They are not eager to repent of
their independence from God. That involves giving up
things they enjoy. Satan will use this distaste for repentance to keep them blinded and resistant to repentance.[58]

Finally, and related to the previous application, is the motivation
this doctrine should provide for missionary endeavor. If you observed
an accident, would you not stop to help those involved? If you came
across a burning building, would you not attempt to rescue those inside?

Yet the church today seems to be content to ignore the plight of the lost. Its people have become complacent in the enjoyment of the church's nice buildings and their own middle-class incomes. They are interested more in their young people earning above-average incomes and having acceptable vocations than in challenging them to a life of self-sacrifice for the Lord. Spiritual lethargy is the order of the day. When a church reaches the goal of giving 10 percent of its annual budget to missions, it considers itself outstandingly missions-minded. In actuality, it should be ashamed of its lack of support for missions. Such a church illustrates self-centeredness, and its vision for others is deficient. Ninety percent of its budget is still going to meet its own needs. History demonstrates that the Lord honors churches that have a vision for others and that designate significant funds to carry out that vision. The doctrine of hell might shake the church out of its lethargy and into concrete action. "It gives a sense of urgency to the task. Jude, urging Christians to evangelism among those who have been mislead by false teachers, says 'Snatch others from the fire [of judgment] and save them'" (v. 23 NASB).[59] Perhaps this urgency has been lost because the church no longer teaches or preaches about hell, even though the idea still might be found in our doctrinal statements.

> The vision of lostness was a strong motivating force in the lives of some of the heroes of Christian history. The seventeenth-century Scottish preacher Samuel Rutherford once told a person, "I would lay my dearest joys in the gap between you and eternal destruction." Hudson Taylor said, "I would have never thought of going to China had I not believed that the Chinese were lost and needed Christ." D. L. Moody told an audience in London, "If I believed there was no hell, I am sure I would be off tomorrow for America." . . . William Booth said he would wish that his Salvation Army workers could spend one night in hell in order to see the urgency of their evangelistic task.[60]

The doctrine of hell has had a positive effect in the missionary endeavor of the church. If there were no eternal judgment, there would be no need to spend time or energy in preaching the gospel to the ends of the earth. But since there is such a judgment, the church needs to get busy and carry out the missionary task that her Lord has entrusted to her.

The doctine of hell makes a difference. It needs to preached, though the world would prefer to hear otherwise. The subject has never been popular. Even preachers famous for speaking on it did so with tears in their eyes.

Like a doctor who tells a patient he has a disease that must be treated, so the believer must tell the unbeliever there is something wrong in his life that needs to be remedied. Eternal consequences are at stake.

Study Questions

1. What hymns or gospel songs do you know that mention hell or eternal judgment?
2. What is universalism?
3. What is annihilation, and what arguments does Pinnock use to support it?
4. Explain the purgatorial and metaphorical views of afterlife.
5. What two presuppositions does this chapter suggest are foundational to a discussion of the biblical teaching on hell?
6. What individual in the Scriptures says the most about hell? Summarize that person's teachings on the topic.
7. Summarize in a few sentences what you feel is the importance of the doctrine of hell for your personal involvement in Christian mission.

Chapter Notes

1. Jon E. Braun, *Whatever Happened to Hell?* (Nashville: Nelson, 1979).
2. John Blanchard, *Whatever Happened to Hell?* (Durham, England: Evangelical Press, 1993).
3. Jesse L. Hurlbut, *Sunday Half Hours with Great Preachers* (W. E. Scull, 1907), 159.
4. Ibid., 184.
5. Charles H. Spurgeon, *Spurgeon's Sermons,* vol. 13 (Grand Rapids: Zondervan, n.d.), 95.
6. J. B. Cranfall, ed., *Revival Messages* (Nashville: Broadman, 1941), 172,176.
7. Braun, *Whatever Happened to Hell?* 94.
8. Arthur J. Brown, *The Foreign Missionary* (New York: Revell, 1907).
9. Ibid., 14–15.
10. Edward Pfeiffer, *Mission Studies: Historical Survey and Outlines of Missionary Principles and Practice* (Columbus, Ohio: Lutheran Book Concern, 1912), 220.
11. Ibid.

12. Ibid., 229.

13. Edward Soper, *The Philosophy of the Christian World Mission* (New York: Abingdon-Cokesbury, 1943), 142–43.

14. Ibid., 144.

15. Clark Pinnock, "The Destruction of the Finally Impenitent," *Criswell Theological Review* 4, no. 2 (1990): 253.

16. C. S. Lewis, *The Problem of Pain* (New York: Macmillan, 1947), 108–9.

17. Peter Toon, *Heaven and Hell* (Nashville: Nelson, 1986), 187–93.

18. Clark Pinnock, "The Conditional View," in *Four Views on Hell,* ed. William Crockett (Grand Rapids: Zondervan, 1996), 136.

19. Ibid., 148.

20. Ibid., 152.

21. Ibid.

22. Ibid., 151.

23. C. S. Lewis seems to allow for some sort of purification after death. Cf. *Letters to Malcolm: Chiefly on Prayer* (San Diego: Harcourt, Brace, Jovanovich, 1973), 108–9.

24. Zachary Hayes, "The Purgatorial View," in *Four Views on Hell,* 92.

25. Ibid., 93.

26. Ibid., 99.

27. Ibid., 108.

28. William Crockett, "The Metaphorical View," in *Four Views on Hell,* 49.

29. Ibid., 56.

30. Ibid., 61.

31. John Walvoord, "The Literal View," in *Four Views on Hell,* 20.

32. Ibid., 18.

33. Harry Buis, *The Doctrine of Eternal Punishment* (Grand Rapids: Baker, 1957), 49–50.

34. Ibid., 51.

35. Larry Dixon, *The Other Side of the Good News* (Wheaton: Victor, 1992), 126.

36. Walter Bauer, *A Greek-English Lexicon of the New Testament,* 2d ed. rev., ed. Wilbur Gingrich and Frederick Danker (Chicago: Univ. of Chicago Press, 1979), 152.

37. Ibid., 27.

38. Ibid., 28.

39. Braun, *Hell,* 161.

40. Bauer, *Greek-English Lexicon of the New Testament,* 745, 810.

41. Francis Brown, S. R. Driver, and Charles Briggs, *A Hebrew and English Lexicon of the Old Testament* (Oxford: Clarendon, 1972), 504.

42. Ibid.
43. Bauer, *Greek-English Lexicon of the New Testament,* 95.
44. Buis, *Doctrine of Eternal Punishment,* 48.
45. William Shedd, *Dogmatic Theology,* vol. 2 (Grand Rapids: Zondervan, 1971), 592.
46. Ibid., 612.
47. Toon, *Heaven and Hell,* 111.
48. James O. Buswell, *A Systematic Theology of the Christian Religion,* vol. 2 (Grand Rapids: Zondervan, 1963), 302.
49. L. S. Chafer, *Systematic Theology,* vol. 7 (Dallas: Dallas Seminary Press, 1948), 191; Blanchard, *Whatever Happen to Hell?* 217.
50. W. G. T. Shedd, *The Doctrine of Endless Punishment* (reprint; Minneapolis: Klock and Klock, n.d.), 59.
51. Braun, *Hell,* 25.
52. Ibid., 158.
53. Millard Erickson, *Christian Theology,* vol. 3 (Grand Rapids: Baker, 1985), 1235.
54. Ajith Fernando, *Crucial Questions About Hell* (Wheaton: Crossway, 1994), 131.
55. Ibid., 133–34.
56. Ibid., 130.
57. Franz Pieper, *Christian Dogmatics,* vol. 3 (St. Louis: Concordia, 1953), 540.
58. Fernando, *Crucial Questions About Hell,* 135–36.
59. Ibid., 143.
60. Ibid., 144–45.

6

MICHAEL H. WINDSOR

SOLUS CHRISTUS

Is There Another Savior?

Salvation is a momentous concept. William James observed, "To be converted, to be regenerated, to receive grace, to experience religion, to gain an assurance, are so many phrases which denoted the process, gradual or sudden, by which a self hitherto divided, and consciously wrong, inferior and unhappy, becomes unified and consciously right, superior and happy."[1] The apostle Paul put the matter more simply: "If anyone is in Christ, he is a new creation; old things have passed away; behold, all things have become new" (2 Cor. 5:17 NKJV).

The biblical concept of salvation takes into account the nature of God, the nature of man, and the nature of sin. All man-made doctrines of salvation can be distilled into a theology of works. Each teaches that if a person will only engage in his cult's assigned works, then God will be pleased with that person's efforts. These cultic works may be detailed, prescribed rituals, or they may be as simple and generic as living a "good life." Theologies of salvation by works, however, do not take into account the divine revelation that God has given in the Bible.

In contrast to man-made religions, the Bible presents a divine offer of salvation. This offer of salvation takes into account the nature of God: He is holy. It takes into account the fallen, defiled, and sinful nature of man. Because of man's sin, there is an alienation between God and man. The reconciliation of sinful mankind to a holy God is accomplished in the person and work of the Lord Jesus Christ.

The theology of the Reformers of the sixteenth century can be condensed into three phrases: *sola Scriptura, sola fide,* and *sola gratia.* The person of Jesus Christ is essential in order to understand the meaning of each of these phrases. He is the Savior revealed in Scripture. He is the Savior in whom sinners need to put their faith. His substitutionary work for sinners is the ground for God's gracious forgiveness of sinners. Underlying the Reformation theology was the person of Jesus Christ.

The person and work of Jesus Christ have been watershed issues throughout the history of Christianity. In their era, the Reformers reclaimed and set forth biblical truth in their theology of salvation. Each generation of Christians must appropriate and set forth the truth of divine revelation for itself. Perhaps we need to add a fourth phrase—*solus Christus*—to our theological storehouse in this generation. As revealed in Scripture *(sola Scriptura)* and applied by grace *(sola gratia)* through faith *(sola fide),* Christ Jesus is the only Savior and the only means of salvation *(solus Christus).*

Some contemporary Christian theologians have moved from a biblical and historical teaching concerning salvation to a denial of the uniqueness of the work of salvation revealed in the Bible. That is, they deny that salvation is accomplished through the substitutionary work of Jesus Christ for sinners.

People can respond to the Christian gospel in various ways. One response is an outright rejection of the message. Akin to rejection is a postponement of acceptance, which amounts to a rejection of the message for the present time. Like Felix, the Roman governor, this type of person procrastinates and decides to wait for a more "convenient time" (Acts 24:25).

But even among those who profess to embrace the message of the Christian gospel, variations exist concerning their understanding of the nature of the gospel message. Some clearly embrace the gospel message with the biblical and theological limitations intact. Such a person gathers from the Scripture that there is but one means of salvation. That one means of salvation is faith in the person and work of the Lord Jesus Christ. A person with such views is often described as an "exclusivist" (Jesus Christ is the exclusive means of salvation). Exclusivism was once the only seriously considered viewpoint among orthodox Christians. Ronald Nash observed, "Once upon a time Christians were identifiable by an unqualified commitment to Jesus Christ as the one and only Savior of the world. But the unity of Christians on this fundamental issue has disappeared."[2] Nash referred to this doctrine as a "fundamental issue."[3]

A century ago the fundamentalist/modernist controversy was forming. One of the major issues underlying the controversy was the modernist view of the person and work of Jesus Christ. The modernist view of Christ negated the deity of Jesus and the necessity of understanding His work at Calvary as a vicarious atonement. In the course of time, lines of demarcation were drawn. Now some within the realm of orthodoxy, would blur the clearly enunciated soteriology of fundamentalists.

One such blurring of the gospel is pluralism. Pluralism teaches that Christ is one of many means of access to God. This is a denial of the exclusivity of the gospel message. This denial may be in the form of some sort of universalism, that is, that everyone will be redeemed (e.g., classic theological liberalism). A missionary observed concerning his own experience, "I learned that there is truly only one God in this entire world but that this one God is known by hundreds—yes, thousands—of different names in different languages."[4] The implication of the multiplicity of names for God is that God is not approached through only one Savior.

When a person rejects the exclusivity of the gospel message, it generally follows that such a person also rejects other key doctrines of the Bible. Often doctrines concerning the identity of the person and work of Christ (Christology), the nature of man and sin (Christian anthropology and hamartiology), and the nature of the Bible (bibliology) are altered to accommodate such a theological worldview.

Another contemporary theological blurring of the gospel message is inclusivism. This view suggests that the work of Jesus Christ is the basis for forgiveness of sin but that the application of that salvific work to sinners goes beyond the historic Christian perspective. Historically, Christians have believed that only those who put their faith in Christ are redeemed. An inclusivist believes that Christ is the basis of salvation, but the application of salvation might extend to (1) all humankind (universalism), or (2) all good people, or (3) all people of faith (no matter the object of their faith).[5] Ronald Nash observed that some form of inclusivism pervades half of the Bible faculties among so-called evangelical institutions, and the rate would be even higher among the Southern Baptist schools (the largest evangelical group).[6] Only slightly less deviant in doctrine would be the students at evangelical schools. According to Hunter, one-third of the students in such schools are open to the possibility that sinners may be saved by means other than personal faith in the Lord Jesus Christ.[7]

Clark H. Pinnock champions evangelical inclusivism on the basis of God's "salvific will and feelings welling up from within [himself] that God is not one to cast off millions who through no fault of their own lacked an opportunity." Pinnock further suggests that God includes all men and women in salvation who have an adequate "level of faith."[8] In another work Pinnock observes that, "According to the Bible, people are saved by faith, not by the content of their theology."[9] Again he suggests, "It is possible to appreciate positive elements in other faiths recognizing that God has been at work among them. . . . If people in Ghana speak of the transcendent God as the shining one, as unchangeable as a rock, as all-wise and all-loving, how can anyone conclude otherwise than that they intend to acknowledge the true God as we do?"[10] Another evangelical inclusivist suggests that "repentance" and "genuine faith" are adequate for salvation, but he makes the concepts of repentance and of faith so vague and so broad as to empty them of biblical content.[11]

This chapter will investigate and present the biblical evidence for the uniqueness of Christ's person and work and will argue for the uniqueness of the gospel message and the absolute necessity for hearing and believing the gospel of Christ in order to receive eternal life. Issues addressed will be: (1) the uniqueness of Jesus Christ; (2) the content of the gospel message; and (3) the identification of those who are the redeemed.

Christ's Uniqueness Presented in the Bible

That the uniqueness of the person and work of Jesus Christ is asserted in the Bible does not settle the issue for everyone.[12] Responses to the Bible include outright rejection of its claims and subtle deflection of its assertions. Some deny the inspiration of Scripture, the deity of Christ, and the salvific teachings of the Bible concerning man's need and Christ's accomplishments. Others have rejected the overt teaching of the Scripture by means of reinterpretation. This reinterpretation is often grounded in cultural changes from the biblical era to today. That the Bible clearly presents a particular view of Christ and His work does not deter these philosophers from deviating from biblical teaching.[13]

The uniqueness of Christ can be seen throughout the New Testament. His uniqueness is to be seen in the various passages that describe Him as "the only begotten Son of God." His uniqueness is seen in the claims of divinity made by Jesus Christ. His claims of being the sole avenue through which humankind might approach God is a third line of textual evidence concerning the uniqueness of Christ.

The Only Begotten

The phrase "only begotten" is a translation of the Greek word μονογενη." The translation of this word as "only begotten" is in accord with its etymology, but such a translation fails to capture the significance of the word. Nearly four hundred years ago the translators of King James Version translated the word according to its etymology rather than its significance. Certainly in the first century the word could be used of an only child. Such is the case with the son of the widow of Nain (Luke 7:11), the nobleman's daughter (Luke 8:42), or Jephthah's daughter (Judg. 11:34, LXX).

While μονογενης can mean an only child (and Jesus Christ is the only incarnation of God), the emphasis of the word μονογενης is the uniqueness of what it describes. Many contemporary translators recognize this significance and translate the word as "only" rather than as "only begotten."[14] Thus Greek lexicons suggest translation possibilities of "only" or "unique (in kind)."[15] "The expression indicates Jesus' unique personality, relation to the Father, and mission."[16] D. R. Bauer noted, "He is Son of God in a sense not true of anyone else. . . . John calls attention to this uniqueness by designating Jesus the 'only *(monogenēs)* Son.'"[17]

This concept of uniqueness is well illustrated in Hebrews 11:17, which informs us that Abraham, by faith, was prepared to sacrifice his "only begotten son," Isaac, as an offering. Isaac was not the only son born to Abraham, nor even Abraham's firstborn son. Other sons would include Ishmael and the children of Keturah. But Isaac was the unique son of Abraham, for Isaac was the fulfillment of God's promises to Abraham.

In similar fashion, the person of Jesus Christ is unique. His life and ministry accomplished a unique work. And thus He is a unique Savior. The natural theological implication of this uniqueness is that no other person can accomplish what the Lord Jesus accomplished in the provision of salvation for sinners.

Christ's Claims to Deity

It might be observed that Jesus of Nazareth was the "disguised God." That is to say, during His earthly ministry His purpose was found primarily in the fulfillment of His incarnational agenda—to fulfill doxologically the divine will by providing atonement for sin. Ultimately, that incarnational agenda could be fulfilled only by one who was God. The Savior must be both divine and human.

Jesus of Nazareth lived for thirty-plus years and demonstrated His moral perfection as a man. He lived a life of moral perfection and submission to God's will. Such a life was what God intended for Adam and all his descendants. As the theological Second Adam, Jesus fulfilled all that was expected of a man. Having proved Himself humanly sufficient, He voluntarily became our substitute in experiencing divine wrath against sin. This work of substitution required that He be God, for a mere man, even if perfect, would be inadequate to accomplish the work of redemption. Thus, it was necessary for Jesus to be divine as well as human.

In more than one biblical passage Jesus Christ is specifically identified as God. Under the imagery of the Logos, John reminds us that Christ was "in the beginning," that He was not only with God, but that He Himself is God (John 1:1).[18] When confronted with the resurrected Christ Jesus, the formerly doubting disciple, Thomas, clearly declares Jesus to be both his Master and God (John 20:28).

In Titus 2:13 Jesus Christ is plainly identified as "our great God and Savior."[19] The writer of Hebrews speaks of Jesus as God when he applies Psalm 45:6–7 to Christ. "But to the Son He says: 'Your throne, O God, is forever and ever'" (Heb. 1:8 NKJV). The thought that the mythological gods of the Greco-Roman pantheon might take form and appear among humanity was not a foreign thought to the world of the first century. More foreign to their worldview was the concept that God Himself should truly and permanently become man. Thus, the first century Christian writers found it necessary to stress the true humanity of Christ rather than His deity; but His deity is asserted when appropriate to the line of argumentation.

There are both direct and indirect assertions of Christ's deity in the New Testament. New Testament writers often cite Old Testament situations in which it is prophesied that Yahweh will accomplish something, and they identify a fulfillment of this in the person and work of Jesus Christ, thus identifying Christ as God incarnate. For example, Malachi 3:3 and Isaiah 40:3 refer to the preparation of a way for the Lord. This is fulfilled in John the Baptist's preparatory ministry for Jesus, thus identifying Jesus as the Lord of the Old Testament (Luke 3:4–6). Similarly, Paul quotes Joel 2 when he writes, "Whoever calls upon the name of the Lord shall be saved" (Rom. 10:13 NKJV), hence identifying Jesus the Savior as Yahweh the Savior.

Repeatedly throughout the New Testament we find circumstances where Jesus of Nazareth demonstrated that behind the veil of His humanity existed God. He demonstrated the attributes of God. Thus, He not only lives, but is the life-giving God (John 1:4, 14:6). As well as having been born, He is eternal (John 1:1). The examples of Scripture that identify Jesus as God could be multiplied.[20]

As God in the flesh, He is worthy of worship. Beginning in Bethlehem we see angels praising Him and shepherds and magi worshiping Him.

At the conclusion of His earthly ministry His disciples worship Him (e.g., Matt. 28:9, John 20:28).

Christ as the Door to the Father

The uniqueness of the Lord Jesus Christ is again evidenced by His claim to be the only way humankind might come into fellowship with the Father. Some argue that Jesus Christ is simply one among many, that "all roads lead to Rome." Jesus, however, used the metaphor of a door (John 10:7, 9) to describe Himself as the means of access to our Creator and the joys of heaven (John 3:18, 36; 1 John 5:12).

On the last night He spent with His disciples prior to His crucifixion, Jesus unambiguously declared His uniqueness as the Savior. He asserted, "I am the way, the truth, and the life. No man comes to the Father except through Me" (John 14:6 NKJV). Jesus' statement sets forth a universal principle: There are no other means by which a sinner can receive eternal life than the provision offered by Jesus Christ. In our ecumenical age of "political correctness," such a perspective is often held to be hard-hearted, narrow-minded, or provincial, but such a principle is only as narrow as New Testament theology. Clark Pinnock grounds his objections to this New Testament perspective on biblical generalities. He argues that God's mercy, the fact that "God loves everyone," and Luke's "generous and inclusive attitude to outsiders" in the theology of Acts are indicative of God's inclusivistic love for all humankind.[21] It is true that God is abundant in mercy and that He has a universal love for humankind, but that mercy and love are exhibited in giving a Savior, Jesus Christ our Lord. This is John's theological application in John 3:16—because God loved all humankind He sent His Son so that everyone who puts their faith in the salvific work of Christ is granted eternal life.

Jesus' apostles understood and communicated Jesus' uniqueness as the mediator between God and mankind. Peter reminded the crowds in Jerusalem, "Nor is there salvation in any other, for there is no other name under heaven given among men by which we must be saved" (Acts 4:12 NKJV).[22] Paul explained that the content of his gospel was the death, burial, and resurrection of Jesus Christ as foretold in the Hebrew Scriptures (1 Cor. 15:1–5). John Sanders argues that the theological implication of Acts 4:12 is that all who come to God through Christ will be saved, but that does not imply one cannot come by some other avenue.[23] But such an assertion runs contrary to the apostolic statement that "neither is there salvation in any other."

Paul had very harsh words for the person who altered the gospel message: "Let him be accursed" (Gal. 1:8–9 NKJV). Anyone who altered the gospel message concerning God's gracious offer of salvation through Jesus Christ insulted God by changing God's revealed Word and plan of salvation and harmed others by robbing them of the only message that brought forgiveness of sin and the promise of eternal life. Clearly, New Testament theology, as expressed through the words of the Lord Jesus Christ or through the words of His apostles, conveys the message that outside of faith in Jesus Christ men and women are condemned, lost, and hopeless.

Christ's Uniqueness in Biblical Theology

When a reader grasps the uniqueness of the person of Jesus Christ, it is easy to comprehend the concept that Christ alone is the Savior offered by God to humankind. No other person was born of a virgin. No other person led a sinless life. No other person confirmed the meaning of His death by resurrection from the dead. These apostolic claims recorded for us in the New Testament are stupendous. They illustrate for us that Jesus of Nazareth was a unique person. His uniqueness is observable in His life from birth to death. Tertullian, in the third century, observed the implications of the uniqueness of Jesus Christ: "The Son of God died; it is by all means to be believed, because it is absurd. And he was buried and rose again; the fact is certain because it is impossible."[24] Tertullian apprehended that the apostolic claims for Jesus Christ were so outlandish as to require them to be true. No sensible people (and the apostles were sensible men) would make such incredible claims unless they were convinced that these incredible claims were truly accomplished by Jesus Christ.

The theology of the New Testament demands that we acknowledge the uniqueness of Jesus Christ. He is the focal point of all true ministry. "The supremacy of God in missions is affirmed biblically by New Testament truth that since the incarnation of the Son of God all saving faith must henceforth fix on him."[25]

The Virgin Birth

The Virgin Birth of Christ was a theological necessity. On more than one occasion Jesus made assertions that His enemies clearly understood were claims of deity. He claimed eternality and divinity ("Before Abraham was, I am," John 8:58 NKJV), and they prepared to stone Him. He claimed a unique and divine union with God ("I and My Father are one," John 10:30 NKJV), and they wanted to stone Him for blasphemy "because You, being a Man, make Yourself God" (John 10:33 NKJV). It was Jesus' claim that he fulfilled the divine role of eternal judge and messianic king that sealed His fate before the court of Jewish authorities (Matt. 26:64–65).

Looking at Jesus of Nazareth, the Pharisees and Sadducees saw only a fellow human being. Indeed, He *was* a fellow human being. The eternal Creator had embraced humanity by becoming human. This is the whole meaning of the Incarnation; as a consequence of His Incarnation through Mary, God became human. Using incarnational language, the angel Gabriel explained to Mary that she would have a child, not through a normal sexual relationship with a man, but rather "the Holy Spirit will come upon you, and the power of the Most High will overshadow you; therefore, the child to be born will be called holy, the Son of God" (Luke 1:35 RSV). The purpose of the Virgin Birth is to introduce infinite God into human history as the God-man. Only an infinite God could adequately and eternally deal with the consequences of human sin. But only a man would be an appropriate sin-bearer, because only a man could die and atone for "the wages of sin" (Rom. 6:23 NKJV). The writer of Hebrews unites these ideas in his argument for the supremacy (and uniqueness) of Jesus Christ. To complete the work of eternal salvation a greater sacrifice than the animal sacrifices prescribed in Old Testament ritual was needed (Heb. 9:11–14). Therefore God sent His own Son in a body (incarnation) to be that sacrifice (Heb. 10:5–10).

His Sinless Life

The impeccability of Jesus was also a theological requirement for Him to qualify as Savior. His sinlessness at conception is reflected in Gabriel's words when the angel announced the coming child as "that Holy One" (Luke 1:35 NKJV). His sinlessness in life is seen as He entered His ministry. In the wilderness temptations Jesus chose to suffer want, obscurity, or pain *in the will of God* rather than satisfy Himself in any realm outside the will of God (Matt. 4:1–11). In the midst of His ministry, Jesus challenged His detractors, "Which of you convicts Me of sin?" (John 8:46 NKJV). Not one of His opponents could step forward and identify a lie that had been told, a dishonesty that had been perpetrated, or a moral point at which He had failed. Even after Jesus had been arrested, the Sanhedrin could not find two legitimate witnesses to accuse Jesus. In the end, Caiaphas had to settle for charges of blasphemy and sent Jesus off to stand accused before Pilate (Matt. 26:57–66).

The sinless character and life of Jesus was a theological necessity. If

He was to serve as the sin-bearer for sinful humanity, then it would be mandatory that He have no sin of His own. In every way, His life demonstrated His sinlessness. As a sinless man He was an acceptable sin offering for His fellow humans. The apostle Paul makes this point when he states that God "made Him who knew no sin to be sin for us, that we might become the righteousness of God in Him" (2 Cor. 5:21 NKJV). Peter uses Christ's impeccable character as an example to challenge his readers to respond in a godly fashion when persecuted. Jesus "committed not sin, nor was deceit found in His mouth" (1 Peter 2:22, paraphrase).

Being accountable for no sin of His own, He became an adequate volunteer (John 10:17–18) to suffer the consequence of sin (death) for humanity (substitutionary atonement). Being infinite God, He could provide an eternal salvation (vicarious atonement). No other person qualified. All the rest of humankind has sinful disqualifications. Jesus of Nazareth, and Jesus alone among all people, is qualified to be the Savior by virtue of His sinless life.

His Death and Resurrection

When I was a teenager, my pastor asserted that the resurrection of Jesus Christ was the divine guarantee of the completion of His work of salvation. That was more theology than I could comprehend as a teenager, but it is truth. At the edge of death on that Roman cross, Jesus gave a final shout, *"Tetelestai,"* and then He died. Frequently this single Greek word is translated, "It is finished." In the first century it was scribbled on bills when they were fully paid.[26] The implication is that the debt of sin had been fully paid by Jesus Christ on the cross.

The theological connections are as follows. Sin brought death. God had warned Adam that sin would bring death (Gen. 2:16–17; Rom. 5:12). The whole typology of Old Testament ritual sacrifice portrays the fact that sin results in judgment and death. The prophet Ezekiel reminded Israel that "the soul who sins shall die" (18:4 NKJV). Paul wrote, "The wages of sin is death" (Rom. 6:23 NKJV). In a divinely orchestrated circumstance involving God's activity and man's activity, Jesus was crucified ("Yet it pleased the Lord to bruise Him; He has put Him to grief," Isa. 53:10 NKJV; Jesus, "being delivered by the determined counsel and foreknowledge of God, you have taken by lawless hands, have crucified, and put to death," Acts 2:23 NKJV). Jesus, as humanity's substitute and sin-bearer, needed to die. This He did on the cross at Calvary.

If Jesus had taken upon Himself the consequence of human sin and had not fully pay the debt, He would have remained dead. He was the substitutionary sin-bearer, and "the wages of sin is death" (Rom. 6:23 NKJV). If he had remained dead, the sinner would have no assurance that the debt of his sin had been paid (we have no guaranteed redemption). But, His resurrection demonstrated the completeness of His atonement. His resurrection declared that His sacrifice for sin was effective. Paul asserted that the divine nature of Christ is demonstrated by His completed work of salvation, in that He rose from the dead (Rom. 1:4). Earth's history has known many bold warriors, noble martyrs, and provocative philosophers, but only one man claimed to be giving His life in a salvific sacrifice and then demonstrated the effectiveness of His atoning work by rising from the dead. Christ Jesus of Nazareth is unique.

The uniqueness and adequacy of Jesus Christ as Savior is but one side of the theological equation of salvation. There is a Savior; His name is Jesus of Nazareth. How, then, does one get saved? Like the Philippian jailer, we ask, "What must I do to be saved?" (Acts 16:30 NKJV).

The Application of Jesus' Salvific Work

The classic biblical text that expresses the gospel of Christ is John 3:16. This verse informs us of the love of God for a godless world: "For God so loved the world" (NKJV). But the verse also informs us that God expressed His love through two channels. First, the love of God is expressed through the sacrificial giving of God in which He sent His Son into the world to be a substitutionary, atoning sacrifice: "He gave His only begotten (unique) Son" (NKJV). This is the Son who was "lifted up" (crucified), thus fulfilling the typological imagery of the brazen serpent (John 3:14) and of the sacrificial Lamb (cf. John 1:29). Jesus Christ was the sacrifice for sin, and the cross was the altar upon which He died.

But this atoning work of Jesus Christ is efficacious only to those who "believe" (3:15–16). The purpose of John's gospel is to convince his readers to "believe that Jesus is the Christ, the Son of God, and that believing you may have life in His name" (John 20:31 NKJV). Thus, when John writes, "Whoever believes in Him should not perish but have everlasting life," the implication is that whoever does not believe does not have everlasting life. John clearly affirms that eternal life is only for those who have put their faith in Jesus Christ as their atoning sacrifice and their savior from the penalty of sin.

Invariably faith has content. It is not enough to have "faith in faith" or simply to be sincere in what one believes. A person who believes (has faith) believes something. That something is the content—or object—of his or her faith. One is not saved by sincere faith in a false savior. "Faith of itself cannot save, but it is the instrument by which Christ and His salvation are received. It does not take a great faith to make one a Christian, but faith in a great Saviour."[27]

Yet some contemporary theologians state that sincere faith is sufficient to meet God's requirements, no matter what the content (or object) of that faith. Pinnock wrote,

> Faith in God is what saves, not possessing certain minimum information. A person is saved by faith, even if the content of faith is deficient (and whose is not?). The Bible does not teach that one must confess the name of Jesus to be saved. One does not have be conscious of the work of Christ done on one's behalf in order to benefit from that work. The issue God cares about is the direction of the heart, not the content of theology.[28]

Such inclusivism "denies that Jesus must be the object of saving faith."[29]

Pinnock would be right if he meant that faith was not merely some magic phrase recited without personal commitment. Just to mouth the words, "Lord Jesus, save me!" would not result in salvation. A parrot could do that. Rather, a person's faith in Jesus Christ as sin-bearer and God-man are mandatory, whether or not they are expressed audibly. But Pinnock does not mean this. He suggests that a Buddhist might truly be seeking God, even though he knows nothing of Christian truth. Pinnock asserts, "What God really cares about is faith and not theology, trust and not orthodoxy."[30]

The New Testament teaches, however, that God is interested not merely in sincere faith, but in the object of faith. He is interested not merely in people trusting in some vague divine being, but rather that they trust in the person of Jesus Christ. John 3:14–16 makes it clear that faith must be in him (the Son of Man who was lifted up). In the end the one "who does not believe the Son shall not see life, but the wrath of God abides on him" (John 3:36 NKJV). As Paul replied to the Philippian jailer's question, "Believe"—place your faith—"on the Lord Jesus Christ" —the only God-given Savior—"and you will be saved" (Acts 16:31 NKJV). In the same vein Paul reminded the Roman Christians that it was necessary to hear and understand the gospel in order for a person to place his faith in the only Savior, Jesus Christ (Rom. 10:13–15). Biblical faith is a believing response to God's Word. The gospel revealed in the New Testament is the content of our faith. The person and work of the Lord Jesus Christ, as revealed in the gospel, is the object of our faith.

True salvation (eternal life) is granted only to those who place genuine faith in the unique and divinely sent Savior, the Lord Jesus Christ. Is God interested in our orthodoxy? Obviously so![31]

Conclusion

Jesus Christ is unique. This is both the assertion and the theology of the New Testament. He is unique as God who has joined His creation. His divinity is set forth in the New Testament. God became man. The Incarnation was achieved by means of the Virgin Birth. This ontological fact (His uniqueness of being) qualified Him to accomplish the divine plan of redemption. No other person qualifies. He alone is Savior. Acceptance of Him as Savior is the only divinely offered means of eternal life. Jesus said, "Enter by the narrow gate; for wide is the gate and broad is the way that leads to destruction, and there are many who go in by it. Because narrow is the gate and difficult is the way which leads to life, and there are few who find it" (Matt. 7:13–14 NKJV).

The proclamation of the biblical gospel is not politically correct in our pluralistic and ecumenical world. Exclusivists have been accused of being cold and hard-hearted. They have even been accused of being immoral for excluding good people of other religions from heaven (but "There is none righteous, no, not one," (Rom. 3:10 NKJV). We must remind ourselves that "objections to the doctrine of salvation through Christ alone are based upon sentimentality and human reason, not upon the statements of Scripture."[32] Christians must continually ask themselves, "To whom am I accountable?" If I am accountable to the social influences around me (pluralistic philosophies, the ecumenical movement), then I need to change my views to what would be acceptable, even fashionable. But if my accountability is to the Almighty, who has revealed Himself in the Bible and through the incarnation of His Son, I cannot but echo the voice of the Master when He said, "Unless you repent you will all likewise perish" (Luke 13:3, 5 NKJV).[33]

Study Questions

1. What will our source of authority be for determining answers to questions about salvation?
2. Investigate the New Testament evidence for the deity of Jesus Christ.

3. What makes Jesus Christ like us (a fellow human being)?
4. What makes Jesus Christ unique (not merely special, but categorically unique)?
5. What does it mean to be saved?
6. From what are we saved?
7. To what are we saved?
8. For Christians, what are our obligations in respect to the gospel of Jesus Christ?

Chapter Notes

1. William James, *The Varieties of Religious Experience: A Study in Human Nature* (New York: New American Library, 1958), 157.
2. Ronald H. Nash, *Is Jesus the Only Savior?* (Grand Rapids: Zondervan, 1994), 9.
3. Ibid.
4. Jacob A. Loewen, "My Pilgrimage in Mission," *International Bulletin of Missionary Research* 22, no. 2 (April 1998): 72.
5. Clark H. Pinnock and John Sanders are notable inclusivists within evangelicalism. See their cited works for an exposition of their ideas.
6. Nash, *Is Jesus the Only Savior?* 107.
7. James Davison Hunter, *Evangelicalism: The Coming Generation* (Chicago: Univ. of Chicago, 1987), 36.
8. Clark H. Pinnock, "The Finality of Jesus Christ in a World of Religions," in *Christian Faith and Practice in the Modern World* (Grand Rapids: Eerdmans, 1988), 153.
9. Clark H. Pinnock, *A Wideness in God's Mercy* (Grand Rapids: Zondervan, 1992), 157.
10. Ibid., 97.
11. John Sanders, "Is Belief in Christ Necessary for Salvation?" *Evangelical Quarterly* 60, no. 3 (July 1988): 259.
12. The author begins with two presuppositions: (1) that God is; and (2) that God has revealed Himself. Upon investigation the Bible self-authenticates itself as divine revelation, which discloses the truth of who God is and what He expects of man as His image-bearer.
13. When a scholar wanders from the investigation of biblical revelation to mere human speculation, he has moved from theology to philosophy.
14. Examples would be the translation of the word in John 1:18 made by J. B. Phillips, trans., *The New Testament in Modern English* (New York: Macmillan, 1961); Charles B. Williams, trans., *The New Testament: A*

Private Translation in the Language of the People (Chicago: Moody Press, 1957); and William F. Beck. trans., *The Holy Bible in the Language of Today: An American Translation* (Nashville: Holman Bible Publishers, 1976).

15. William F. Arndt and F. Wilbur Gingrich, *A Greek-English Lexicon of the New Testament,* 2d ed. (Chicago: Univ. of Chicago, 1979), 527. See also F. Buchsel, "μονογενης," in *Theological Dictionary of the New Testament,* vol. 4 (Grand Rapids: Eerdmans, 1967), 738.

16. J. A. Fitzmyer, "μονογενης," in *Exegetical Dictionary of the New Testament,* vol. 2 (Grand Rapids: Eerdmans, 1991), 440.

17. D. R. Bauer, "Son of God," in *Dictionary of Jesus and the Gospels* (Downers Grove, Ill.: InterVarsity, 1992), 775. In a similar vein MacLean stated, "Our Lord is Son in a unique sense." A. J. MacLean, "Only-Begotten," in *Dictionary of the Apostolic Church,* vol. 2 (Edinburgh: T & T Clark, 1918), 113.

18. One might also note John 1:18. An alternative textual reading would speak of Jesus as "the unique God" (μονογενης θεος) who is in intimate fellowship with the Father.

19. See Richard A. Young, *Intermediate New Testament Greek: A Linguistic and Exegetical Approach* (Nashville, Tenn.: Broadman & Holman, 1994), 63; and Bruce A. Baker, "Granville Sharp's Rule," *The Journal of Ministry and Theology* 1, no. 2 (fall 1997): 46.

20. Augustus Hopkins Strong, *Systematic Theology* (Valley Forge, Penn.: Judson, 1907), 305–15.

21. Pinnock, *A Wideness in God's Mercy,* 31–32.

22. As an inclusivist, Clark H. Pinnock has suggested that exclusivists have distorted the meaning of this verse. "Acts 4:12—No Other Name Under Heaven," *Through No Fault of Their Own? The Fate of Those Who Have Never Heard,* ed. William V. Crockett and James G. Sigountos (Grand Rapids: Baker, 1991), 109. Pinnock argued that salvation is grounded in the provision and authority of Jesus Christ ("in His name"), but that does not require that the sinner hear the name and gospel of Jesus in order to be saved.

23. John Sanders, *No Other Name: An Investigation into the Destiny of the Unevangelized* (Grand Rapids: Eerdmans, 1992), 64.

24. Tertullian, "On the Flesh of Christ," *The Ante-Nicene Fathers,* vol. 3 (New York: Charles Scribner's Sons, 1905) ch. 5.

25. John Piper, *Let the Nations Be Glad! The Supremacy of God in Missions* (Grand Rapids: Baker, 1993), 115.

26. "Papyri receipts for taxes have been recovered with the word *tetelestai*

written across them, meaning 'paid in full.'" Edwin A. Blum, "John," *The Bible Knowledge Commentary,* ed. John F. Walvoord and Roy B. Zuck (Wheaton, Ill.: Victor, 1983), 340.

27. T. Leonard Lewis, "Redemption by Christ," *The Word for This Century,* ed. Merrill C. Tenney (New York: Oxford Univ., 1960), 80.

28. Pinnock, *A Wideness in God's Mercy,* 158.

29. Sanders, *No Other Name,* 265.

30. Pinnock, *A Wideness in God's Mercy,* 112.

31. How is it that so many within the broad evangelical community have drifted so far from orthodoxy? The process of drift began two generations ago when the emerging New Evangelicals, in response to theological liberalism's denial of divine self-disclosure in the Bible, felt the need to question the doctrine of inspiration (see, for example, "Is Evangelical Theology Changing?" *Christian Life,* April 1956, 20–22). This was viewed as necessary in order to enter into scholarly dialogue. One result of this questioning of biblical inspiration was a succeeding generation theologically weak on bibliology, many of whom were willing to deny the biblical doctrine of inspiration and inerrancy. (This phenomenon among second generation New Evangelicals was lamented by Harold Lindsell, a first generation New Evangelical. See *The Battle for the Bible* [Grand Rapids: Zondervan, 1976]; and *The Bible in the Balance* [Grand Rapids: Zondervan, 1979]). Now another generation of evangelicals has arisen who is willing to deny the specifics of the gospel revealed in the Bible, which they inherently deny is inerrant revelation. Clark Pinnock, inspired by the ecumenical spirit of the Second Vatican Council, grounds his inclusivistic gospel on the need for "evangelical civility" and "a spirit of openness and hope in regard to all people of the earth" ("The Finality of Jesus Christ in a World of Religions," 154, 168).

32. Ernest Pickering, *Will People Go to Hell Who Never Heard of Christ?* (Decatur, Ala.: Baptist World Mission, n.d.). See also Millard J. Erickson, *The Evangelical Left* (Grand Rapids: Baker, 1997), 111–12, where Erickson observes that among the reasons for a rise in pluralistic theology are cultural and emotional motivations.

33. The reader desiring an in-depth treatment of this subject is referred to the 600-page treatise by Donald A. Carson, *The Gagging of God: Christianity Confronts Pluralism* (Grand Rapids: Zondervan, 1996).

7

DAVID W. RONAN

LORDSHIP AND MISSIONS

Conversion in Japan

In Japan's evangelical churches, when a person claims to have saving faith in Jesus Christ church leaders look for signs of conversion that include an aversion to ancestral practices.[1] For Japanese people who struggle with ancestral customs, conversion involves both a turning *from* former "lords" or "masters" and a turning *to* God (1 Thess. 1:9). Many who convert to Christianity struggle to remove themselves from ancestral practices fostered through family traditions. To leaders of Japanese churches, this separation or turning from ancestral rites to Christ seems to be the strongest indicator of genuine conversion. Because the church leaders view actions and attitudes as indicative of one's primary spiritual relationship, they require evidence of a clear turning away from former ancestral practices to one's new Lord, Jesus Christ. A person should no longer desire to serve the family's ancestors, but naturally desire to separate from them (2 Tim. 2:19). It can be concluded, then, that church leaders in Japan understand conversion to Christianity in primarily relational or "lordship" terms.

Introduction

Japan has never experienced a prolonged national turning from indigenous beliefs to Christianity. Yet, many individuals do believe and experience new life (John 3:3). When these people receive new life from God, signs of change emerge. New believers learn more of Scripture, pray to God, attend church faithfully, share Christ with others, and contribute to the church's growth.

Many Japanese converts struggle with the ancestral practices. Oldest sons assume the responsibility for maintaining the family altar, before which household members pray and make offerings to deceased relatives. Seasonal family gatherings invariably include a visit *en masse* to the ancestral tomb. Spirits of deceased family members are said to live in the tomb and they return to the family home to visit at other times.[2] On these, as well as other occasions, living family members offer incense, food, and drink to the deceased ancestor to acknowledge the spirit's presence and to comfort or console that spirit. During this time, family members normally burn incense and verbally address the deceased person's spirit, speaking out loud in a direct conversational tone as if the deceased person were right there. The living report family activities and express gratitude to the spirit. Funerals include similar behaviors embellished with grief and feelings of loss. Refusal to participate in these rituals is tantamount to turning your back on your family, because the departed spirit needs these rituals to help it on its journey.

Consequently, Japanese Christians who refuse to perform these rituals risk harming or even losing family relationships. Japanese church leaders realize that when believers risk family relationships because of their new relationship to Christ, those individuals demonstrate genuine conversion. Rarely would Japanese people refuse to serve their families' ancestors unless they served a new "master." In other words, they would have to value the new spiritual relationship with their new master more highly than their old spiritual relationships with their families. Conversely, church leaders are reluctant to confirm saving faith in one who claims Christ yet performs actions or demonstrates an attitude void of repentance concerning the ancestral rites and beliefs.

Japanese Ancestral Practices as Religion

Saving faith for Japanese people involves a change in religion. While the term "religion" is often used to describe various phenomena, from cultic behavior to Buddhist beliefs, religion as an academic notion provides some structure to measure the shifts people experience when they receive new life in Christ. Missionaries have sought to understand the impact of religious thought and belief in order to communicate the gospel in culturally relevant terms.

Emile Durkheim defines religion as "a unified system of beliefs and practices relative to sacred things, that is to say, things set apart and forbidden—beliefs and practices which unite into one single moral community called a Church, all those who adhere to them."[3]

"Beliefs" identify intellectual and intuitive aspects that explain what people think and how they feel. "Practices" identify rituals or what people do. "Sacred things" refer to the objects or the recipients of the rituals or practices. "Moral community" signifies those who believe and perform rituals or practices relative to or directed toward sacred things.

Japanese ancestral practices meet Durkheim's definition of religion. First, Kunio Yanagita says that Japanese people "feel a strong conviction" that their ancestors return. He suggests that every Japanese person understands the ancestors' return, arguing that "our countrymen have believed it from the unknown past . . . none of them showing attitudes denying that hope." He summarizes by saying, "People have never thought about there being no proof for it, or rather, the faith itself is the basis for evidence of many facts."[4]

Yanagita describes "conviction" in a more affective or perceptive sense as compared with the Western notion of cognitive intellectual resolution. He argues that Japanese people have always had this intuitive sense of ancestral presence. Because all Japanese people have held this conviction or belief, further evidence is unnecessary since the faith itself is proof enough. Therefore, Japanese ancestral practices parallel Durkheim's religious criterion of "an organized system of beliefs."

Second, Durkheim says that religion includes practices, that is, specific rituals. At funerals, Japanese people make offerings of food, flowers, or incense, burn candles, say prayers, and bow to the body of the deceased.[5] At festivals, Yanagita describes *Bon* (the ancestral spirits' midsummer return to the family home) and *Shogatsu* (the New Year's return of family spirits) as a time to visit graves,[6] offer rice and food at the altar,[7] burn incense, and bow before the tablet as if the ancestor were there.[8] Hori says Japanese people feel that their daily lives require religious rites, festivals, and ceremonies.[9] In short, funerals and festivals involve specific rituals that are performed at certain times and are consistent with deeply held beliefs.

Third, Durkheim classifies the sacred as that which is "set apart." Yanagita refers to deceased ancestors as deities throughout his writings.[10] Hori speaks of the Japanese belief that the dead become gods.[11] Ushijima denotes that each rite in the funeral process moves the spirit of the dead upward as it becomes more purified, clearly suggesting that the deceased becomes sacred through the funeral rituals by which they are set apart.[12]

Finally, Durkheim's fourth element of religion involves the community, the church, or "those who adhere." Living family members comprise those who conduct the "practices" on behalf of the "sacred," their ancestors. Those who perform rituals consistent with the role of "community" do, by those actions, acknowledge their own relationship to the sacred. That is, people perform rituals for their ancestors because they are related or bound spiritually. Yanagita explains the subtle nuances of one's obligation to venerate. He says that many learned the meaning of the word *senzo* by watching the example of their elders. These people, he says, "regard an ancestor as one who should be venerated, the soul of a person who would not be worshiped elsewhere than in his own family itself."[13] Furthermore, Yanagita narrowly defines worship responsibility to specific lines in the family. He says, "It may be correct to say that all the Taira families are descendants of Kammu, but he was an Imperial ancestor, and other than the noble family in the direct line of emperors, none should count him in his genealogy and none should venerate him."[14]

A number of points resonate from Yanagita's conclusions. First, he equates "venerate" with "worship" in the context of ancestral practices. Second, his usage of worship would be less likely to include notions of "respect." After all, who would argue that one refuse to respect a former Japanese emperor? Or who would suggest that only the direct descendants of a deceased emperor could show respect?[15] Ultimately, people—the "profane"—perform rituals for deceased relatives—"the sacred"—because the living and the dead are connected through genealogical and spiritual relationships. Responsibility to perform these rituals has less to do with respect in the social understanding of courtesy or honor.

In summary, Japanese ancestral practices contain all four elements that Durkheim defines as religion. Japanese people comprise "one moral community." They hold a set of beliefs and conduct ritual practices involving the setting apart of ancestral spirits into the realm of the sacred. Therefore, Japanese ancestral practices are religion, not just a cultural form or custom.

Using Durkheim's four basic components of religion, we can see that a person who experiences a religious conversion would evidence a change in each of the four areas of religion: (1) direction (who or what gets worshiped); (2) action (rituals or practices performed); (3) attitude (what one thinks or feels regarding the object); and (4) relationship (how one is connected to the object of religious action, feeling, and thought). Before we explore the quality of these four components, we must first understand basic elements of worldview (the basic map of a religion),

Japanese ancestral rites and their meaning, the theology of worship, and the significance of conversion.

Japanese Religion and Worldview

Yanagita refers to ancestor worship as the core of the Japanese religious experience.[16] Hori defines ancestral practices as the *raison d'être* for a Japanese person.[17] In other words, Japanese ancestral beliefs and practices express the core of what it means to be Japanese. Worldview, according to Nash, is a conceptual scheme into which people place events and beliefs, and by which they interpret or judge reality.[18] Hiebert says that religion provides people with the content of reality, indicating the relationships between things.[19] Altogether, this suggests that Japanese ancestral practices express the reality of the Japanese worldview. McGuire says that conversion is a transformation of one's basic meaning system.[20] The degree to which the content changes remains unclear. Yet since ancestral practices constitute the core of Japanese religion, and since this religion comprises the content of their worldview, then religious conversion for Japanese people would strongly suggest a change in their understanding of and relationship to the ancestral system.

Rituals in Japanese Ancestral Practices

Religious rituals combine myth with drama in a symbolic expression of belief.[21] They bestow sacredness, separating the sacred from the profane,[22] and they express "a relationship with a divine being or beings."[23] Because rituals embody beliefs and express relationships, a religious change or conversion would also involve a corresponding change in the rituals that proclaim the old spiritual relationships and beliefs.

Ritual Possesses Independent Meaning

Hiebert indicates that ritual behaviors carry meaning independent of participant intention.[24] Reader argues that actions are religious when performed in a religious context and resemble other commonly accepted religious forms.[25] Many cultures dichotomize between form and meaning, while others do not.[26] Japanese people often refer to behavior such as bowing before the family altar, clapping the hands together at a shrine, or inscribing prayers on an *ema* at a temple as worship.

Ritual Bestows Sacredness

Ayabe said that Japanese people answer the question "Are you a Christian?" according to whether or not they have been baptized.[27] In other words, one is a Christian based upon whether one has gone through the initiation rite or ritual. This suggests that Japan might be a culture that does not separate form from meaning in religious practices. It appears that form gives clear meaning to the participant—the one who performs or receives the rite receives a different status or undergoes some type of transformation for having experienced the rite.

Ritual Expresses Relationship

On January 3, 1997, the *Japan Times,* a popular English newspaper in Japan, featured a photo of people at the Meiji Shrine over New Year's with heads bowed and hands clasped. The headline read, "People Welcome the New Year with Prayer." By all accounts, the Japanese media, viewing people performing ritual actions in a religious shrine and without any understanding of the performers' cognitive or emotional disposition, conclude that these people are praying. In other words, in the case of the *Japan Times* headline, it mattered little to the reporter what people thought or intended in their hearts. The reporter saw people behaving in specific ways (folding their hands and bowing their heads) in a defined context (a temple) and concluded that they were praying. Since prayer is part of worship, whether to God (Acts 2:42) or to Baal (1 Kings 18:26), ritual performance seems to express ritual relationship with a deity. Action and meaning seem linked.

Second Kings 5:15–19 illustrates the link between form and meaning. Naaman, the commander of Assyria's army and a presumed follower of animistic practices, converts and believes in Israel's God. The passage indicates a problem when newly converted Naaman suggests that he must still bow down to a pagan god in the course of his professional duties. Elisha, by his response, appears to sanction Naaman's conduct.

> Then Naaman and all his attendants went back to the man of God. He stood before him and said, "Now I know that there is no God in all the world except in Israel. Please accept now a gift from your servant." The prophet answered, "As surely as the LORD lives, whom I serve, I will not accept a thing." And even though Naaman urged him, he refused. "If you will not," said Naaman, "please let me, your servant, be given as much earth as a pair of mules can carry, for your servant will never again make burnt offerings and sacrifices to any other god but the LORD. But may the LORD forgive your servant for this

one thing: When my master enters the temple of Rimmon to bow down and he is leaning on my arm and I bow there also—when I bow down in the temple of Rimmon, may the LORD forgive your servant for this." "Go in peace," Elisha said. (NIV)

Four significant insights emerge from Naaman's brief response at this point of conversion. First, he acknowledges that there is only one God, "Now I know that there is no God in all the world except in Israel." Naaman essentially disavows his own nation's deities, calling them what amounts to "not-gods" and embracing Israel's God. Second, Naaman concludes that only Israel's God, now his God too, deserves offerings and sacrifices: "Your servant will never again make burnt offerings and sacrifices to any other god but the LORD." Deity deserve offerings and he intends now to give those to Israel's God. In other words, whereas before he gave gifts to his pagan deities, now "never again" will he do so. This suggests that Naaman understands the significance of offerings and implies a relationship between him, as an individual, and the Deity at the moment of his conversion. Third, Naaman realizes even at this moment that his behavior, "when I bow down in the temple of Rimmon," would be inconsistent with the testimony he has just given, "there is no other God in all the world," and that he "will never again make burnt offerings and sacrifices to any other god but the LORD." Bowing to a "not-god" is incongruous behavior for one who serves the God of heaven. In other words, people do not bow to a god that is not their deity (Daniel 3). Conversely, people do bow to that which is their deity. They demonstrate their relationship with the deity by bowing (Daniel 3). Fourth, Naaman seeks forgiveness for his anticipated bow: "But may the LORD forgive your servant for this one thing." People do not seek pardons for that which is lawful or pleasing to God. No one in Scripture asks God to forgive them for obedience. People seek forgiveness for disobedience, especially after they understand their disobedience. Naaman knows that bowing, even in the course of his professional duties, requires forgiveness. He knows it is wrong. Finally, Elisha replies, "Go in peace." While it seems that the prophet permits this inconsistency, it is more reasonable to suggest that Elisha simply dismisses Naaman without addressing the problem.

Therefore, Naaman the animist made a profession of faith—"there is no other God"—and demonstrated repentance—"will never again make burnt offerings and sacrifices"—at the moment of his conversion. For an animist, repentance means separating from former gods.[28] Naaman separated from his former gods by refuting their validity, refusing to give them offerings and sacrifices, and desiring not to bow before them.

Biblical Significance of Worship

Clark Offner argues that a person's inner motivation determines if an act is worshipful.[29] Yet Scripture indicates that actions themselves constitute worship. Abraham said, "We will worship and then we will come back" (Gen. 22:5 NIV), as he prepared to sacrifice Isaac. Sacrifice meant worship. God forbade Israel to bow before graven images. "You shall not bow down to them or worship them" (Ex. 20:5; 23:24 NIV). Bowing before an image also indicated worship. Shadrach, Meshach, and Abednego refused to bow before Nebuchadnezzar's image (Dan. 3). From all indications, the king cared little about their inner attitudes; he cared only for their external compliance—bowing! The act of bowing communicated worship and service in the context. They refused to bow because the action of bowing meant they would be worshiping the image, even if their inner thoughts were very much fixed on their own God.

Though the quality of worship seems to differ throughout Scripture, the John 4:23 "spirit and truth" quality of worship hardly seems a possible standard for the worship of Baal, Molech, or Chemosh. In Isaiah 44, God ridicules mindless idolatrous acts, calling them worship: "From the rest he makes a god, his idol; he bows down to it and worships. He prays to it and says, 'Save me; you are my god'" (v. 17 NIV). God says that this type of behavior and these specific actions constitute worship even though the participant is ignorant of the significance of his acts: "They know nothing, they understand nothing; their eyes are plastered over so they cannot see, and their minds closed so they cannot understand" (v. 18 NIV). Such behavior, though uninformed and without knowledge, would not meet a John 4:23 "spirit and truth" test. Yet even as God condemns such idolatrous behavior, He calls it worship.

Scripture further suggests that pagan ritual acts constituted worship, again apart from the performer's intention. To us as believers, drunken feasts before pagan deities, orgies as part of fertility cults, and child sacrifices to fiery gods do not meet our standards of true worship and to refer to them as such seems ludicrous. But if pagan rituals needed to meet the John 4:23 criterion in order to be called worship,[30] then God's ridicule and judgment for following such practices make little sense.[31]

While Japanese ancestral practices do not include orgies and child sacrifices, their rites do involve very prescribed behaviors directed toward spirits that are not God. The following section explains the nature of some ancestral rituals in relation to worship, including bowing, offering gifts, and serving idols.

Bowing Equals Worship

Offner argues that while Abraham bowed in worship to God (Gen. 22:5), he also bowed to his guests (Gen. 18:2). Joseph's brothers did the same when they met in Egypt (Gen. 24:26). Since people performed the same action before God and others, the action itself cannot mean worship.[32]

Direction helps define an action's meaning in such cases. Halbertal and Margalit insist that when the object of the bow is ritually worshiped, as in the case of Japanese mortuary tablets,[33] "the context and the fact that this idol is one that is religiously worshiped define the act as an act of worship rather than a gesture of respect, independently of the intention of the person performing the action."[34]

All three criteria apply to Japanese memorial tablets or *ihai*. First, bowing before the *ihai* is consistent with prescribed ritual behavior. Second, Japanese people consider the *ihai* a religious object. Third, regardless of a person's internal mind-set, Japanese people still refer to bowing before the family altar, *butsudan,* as an act of worship, *suhai.*

Ian Reader advances the directional or locational argument by saying that religious actions (bowing, burning incense, and prayer) performed in a religious setting (before a family altar while viewing the mortuary tablet or at a grave site location of understood religious activity) are religious.[35] Therefore, cultural customs may be religious as well as cultural. For example, Japanese people may refer to ancestral rituals as customs.[36] Yet the custom can still be religious. Reader argues that, in many Western countries, Sunday morning church attendance is a cultural custom, though most would see this as a religious practice as well.

Theologically, Aune insists that the New Testament difference between prostrate bowing and worship is a false distinction when a religious object is involved. He argues that prostrate bowing and worship are the same in that case:

> One of the simplest and most basic actions connected with worship is that of "bowing down." Various forms of bowing, whether bending forward at the waist with eyes downcast, kneeling, or prostration, are all symbolic actions which indicate subjection or subservience, i.e., the inferior status of the one who bows in comparison with the one to whom one bows. The ritual expressions

of superior/inferior status, such as bowing, are often
identical with social expression of such status. Further,
bowing gives behavioral expression to the experience
of religious awe. . . . Conclusion: in every instance but
Rev. 3:9, cultic worship is in view, and the supposed
contrast between the attitude of worship and adoration
and that of external physical bowing or prostration is
untenable.[37]

In summary, an action has meaning apart from participant intention.
One man can shake hands with another and insist that he intended nothing more than to show friendship. Yet when that man happens to be the
president of the United States, and the one receiving the handshake is
Fidel Castro, the president of Cuba, and when the handshake takes place
before television cameras in the White House Rose Garden, the action
takes on a meaning all its own, wholly apart from what either participant
intends. Therefore, when someone follows a cultural custom and bows
before the *ihai,* Scripture, not culture, determines the action's meaning.
In the case of bowing before a generally understood religious object, the
action should be considered worship regardless of the person's intention.

Offering Gifts Equals Worship

Israelites burned incense, baked cakes, and made drink offerings to
the queen of heaven (Jeremiah 44). For that, God said, "They provoked
me to anger by burning incense and by worshiping other gods" (v. 3 NIV).
In worshiping the queen of heaven, the remnant actually expressed their
dependence on this deity rather than on God. The worship of Molech
consisted of human sacrifices (Lev. 18:21; 1 Kings 11:7–8), signifying
the people's allegiance and identification with their god. Even the biblical
worship of Yahweh included various types of animal sacrifices and food
offerings (Lev. 3:3, 9; 7:16) designed to express identification, allegiance,
and dependence upon their God. Regardless of the object of the form,
ritual offerings expressed a relationship between the worshiper and the
deity to whom the worshiper sacrificed.[38]

Japanese ancestral practices involve burning incense, making offerings
of food and beverages, and saying prayers to the deceased relative. Therefore, when Japanese people conduct these types of rituals for their
deceased relatives, they express the spiritual relationship between themselves and the object of the form, the ancestor. Scripture describes this

type of relational identification, involving offerings of food, drink, incense, and prayer, as worship.

Serving Idols Equals Worship

Graven images, *pecel* in Hebrew, always referred to carved or shaped images that represented a deity and were used in religious worship.[39] This word was most frequently translated as "idols" in Scripture, and the second commandment prohibited the use of such images in any kind of worship, including the worship of Yahweh.[40]

Mortuary tablets, *ihai,* consist of shaped pieces of wood, four to six inches high, and are believed to represent the spirit of the dead.[41] The *kaimyo* (the new heavenly name of the deceased person)[42] is "carved into" the surface of a tablet.[43] This tablet becomes "the object of veneration by family members and of prayers offered."[44]

Therefore, the *ihai* is a carved image, representing the spirit of a deity or the "sacred." It is placed in a religious altar *(butsudan)* and used in religious worship.[45] The *ihai* is therefore an idol.

Meaning of Conversion in Scripture

Pendulum-like conversion occurs when people reject their past and accept a new religion.[46] The conversion of the animistic, idol-worshiping Lycaonians from paganism to Christ (Acts 14:20) illustrates this kind of conversion. The Lycaonians rejected their former idolatrous beliefs and practices for a radically different future. Japanese conversions closely resemble the Lycaonian, pendulum-like experience, because Japanese worship seems to be animistic,[47] and any conversion involves a clear rejection or break with the past.[48]

Conversion is "the fundamental decision of an individual in response to God's call to repentance and faith,"[49] a turn from the many gods, or from no god, or from "belief in" a distant, unknown, or inactive god to belief in "the living God,"[50] "a change in allegiance in which Christ is accepted as Lord and center of one's life,"[51] "involving both repentance from sin, and faith toward Christ."[52]

Therefore, when a Japanese person who previously served ancestors converts in repentance and saving faith, that individual turns from old beliefs ("we must serve the ancestors"), from former practices (ancestral rituals), and from past deities (the ancestors), to believe, obey, and serve the God of the Bible (1 Thess. 1:9; 2 Tim. 2:19). In other words the ancestors, as they are embodied in the living family and symbolized in the family altar *(butsudan),* in the mortuary tablets *(ihai),* and in the respective rites of the spiritual household *(ie)* cease to function as the center of a converted person's life. Jesus Christ replaces the spiritual center or core of the individual, and that changed Japanese person lives his or her life in allegiance to Christ as Lord, serving only Him.

Repentance and saving faith are the constituent components of conversion. Therefore, to understand the essential characteristics of spiritual change, we must study both.

Repentance

If repentance is part of conversion, what is repentance? Second, for what sins did the nations repent? Jesus said, "But unless you repent, you too will all perish" (Luke 13:3 NIV). Luke 24:47 says that "repentance and forgiveness of sins" (NIV) will be proclaimed in His name to all nations. Jews had to repent of their part in Christ's crucifixion. When they repented of this, they would be incorporated into the body of believers (Acts 2:36–40) and saved "from this corrupt generation" (NIV). Gentiles had to repent of their idols (Acts 14:15; 17:29–30). Later, Zaccheus repented and announced before everyone his intention to return stolen money. To that Christ said, "Today salvation has come to this house . . ." (Luke 19:9 NIV). The rich young ruler had great wealth. Scripture indicates that because he would not separate from this wealth, the source of power with which he identified himself, he did not manifest the repentance necessary to enter the kingdom of God (Matt. 19:23). Gentiles who practiced magical arts "brought their scrolls together and burned them publicly" (Acts 19:19 NIV).

Without having defined the term, the text indicates that there is no life without repentance. Christ also said—and thus Scripture supports—that repentance would be part of God's worldwide message of eternal life and an essential component of salvation.

Also, it appears that public separation from one's source of power or identity is the commonly shared element in the examples above. Jews separated themselves from those who crucified their Messiah and identified themselves as Christ's follower by their baptism: "Repent and be baptized, everyone of you, in the name of Jesus Christ" (Acts 2:38 NIV). Gentiles separated themselves from their idols (1 Thess. 1:9). Zaccheus separated himself from his money and in the process announced a separation from his corrupt business practices. Ephesians involved in the occult separated from their power sources by openly burning their very expensive magical tools.

The Old Testament notion of repentance (Heb. *shuv*) is rendered "turn," or "return" in English and translated *epistrepho* in the Septuagint. France notes that the term is used "in connection with men's relationship with God."[53] He says that in the New Testament, *epistrepho* signifies "both 'from' and 'to,' replacing an old way of life and an old loyalty with a new and opposite allegiance."[54] "Turning" symbolized spiritual allegiance to God, expressing relationship with Him.

We define repentance as "separating or turning from one's source of power or identification to God." When idols or spiritual forces comprise the power source, then one must separate from those idols or forces and turn to Christ. Likewise, those who depend on money or corrupt influences demonstrate repentance by separating or turning away from those things and depending on Christ's teachings. This could explain why Simon the sorcerer, coming as he did from an animistic background (Acts 8:9–25), probably had not yet been converted, because he had not properly rejected his first source of power, magic.[55] Peter scolded him, saying, "Repent of this wickedness. . . ." Peter described Simon's dependence on power and perhaps his desire to influence others as "wickedness." Peter's tone suggests that Simon had not yet fully left his past power source, had not completely turned to God, and, therefore, had not experienced true repentance.

In Japan, repentance in the context of ancestral practices might look like a clear separation or turning from dependence on one's ancestors as one's source of power and a turning to Christ as Lord. Whereas a Japanese person's identity formerly might have rested in the relationship maintained with the family ancestors, now it would come from his or her new relationship with Christ as Lord.

Saving Faith

Saving faith describes the positive or the "turning to" side of conversion. It answers the question, "To what does a person turn in conversion?" After all, people can stop following Japanese ancestral practices only to follow some other humanistic belief. In that case, they are forsaking ancestral rites without true biblical conversion because they have not embraced Jesus Christ (John 14:6).

Saving faith distinguishes itself from other forms of *pistis* faith both in content and character. Scripture says that demons have "faith" (James 2:19), but it is incomplete. James says that complete faith is accompanied by deeds. Demonic deeds do not correspond to saving faith.

Simon the sorcerer may have expressed "faith" (Acts 8:13), but the content and character of his faith seemed to be driven by "the great signs and miracles he saw." Even the Jews at the wedding ceremony "believed [pisteuo] in his name" (John 2:23–24 NIV), but "Jesus would not entrust himself to them, for he knew all men." Jesus seemed to realize that those who believed at the wedding feast did not possess saving faith.

Our Lord said, "Now this is eternal life: that they may know you, the only true God, and Jesus Christ, whom you have sent" (John 17:3 NIV). God sent Jesus so that the world through Christ would be saved. Faith in Him, then, corresponds to obeying Him. As MacArthur said, "The ultimate test was whether this man would obey the Lord."[56] Saving faith knows God through Jesus whom God sent. Saving faith is a gift from God (Eph. 2:8–9). People do not generate it themselves. In John 3:36, "believe" [pisteuo] is synonymous with "obedience" [apeitho]: "He who believes in the Son has eternal life; but he who does not obey the Son will not see life, but the wrath of God abides on him" (NASB). Specifically, that obedience must be to Christ: "Why do you call me 'Lord, Lord,' and do not do what I say?" (Luke 6:46 NIV). Therefore, saving faith is a gift from God that brings people into a personal knowing relationship with God. This knowing relationship involves willingly obeying what Christ says.

In summary, conversion involves two theological components: repentance and saving faith. Repentance can be understood as a separation from or a turning from old deities, and saving faith is a turning toward Christ and an obedient relationship with Him. Both repentance and saving faith constitute the same act viewed from different perspectives. In an animistic context, "Conversion means participating in a genuine decision for Christ, a sincere turning from the old gods and evil spirits, and a determined purpose to live as Christ would have men live."[57]

Conversion and Religious Change

Scripture identifies conversion as repentance and faith. Hans Kasdorf expands these two states into four elements of change relative to religious conversion: direction, action, attitude, and relationship.[58]

Direction

Direction identifies the from/to formula—referred to theologically as repentance/faith—of Japanese persons who performed religious acts of worship directed toward their ancestors. With repentence these former practices cease. New believers no longer direct their worship to or serve these "not-gods" (Gal. 4:8). Those who repent have changed "from" following in the direction or way of former deities.[59]

Nevertheless, biblical conversion includes a change "to" the God of the Bible: "You turned to God from idols" (1 Thess. 1:9b NIV). Simply stopping former ancestral practices does not constitute conversion. A Japanese person must embrace Christ, "to serve the living and true God" (1 Thess. 1:9b NIV). Therefore, biblical conversion for a Japanese person involves a change in direction from the "not-god" to the "living and true God."

Action

True faith produces actions consistent with belief. Abraham offered up his son (Gen. 22); Zaccheus gave half of his estate to the poor and offered to repay those he had cheated (Luke 19:8); Jews who repented at Pentecost were baptized (Acts 2:41).

Those who are converted from animistic backgrounds also demonstrate their repentance and faith through specific actions, including both a rite of separation—formally putting away the idols (Eph. 2:12–13; Josh. 24:14–15; Acts 19:18–19; Eph. 4:22–24),[60] and a rite of passage[61] or transformation,[62] most commonly understood as baptism (Acts 2:41; 16:33; 22:16).[63]

Attitude

Attitude encompasses both intellect and emotion. Those who repent see that the ancestors are not gods (Gal. 4:8), and that the God of the Bible is the Creator God (Acts 17). Normally confession (Rom. 10:9–10) and a commitment to obey, "as a child," Christ (Matt. 18:3) accompany belief.

Emotion accounts for an individual's feelings. Yanagita writes, "Recalling what they had seen and heard when they were little and the talk of former people, they would feel a strong conviction and begin to practice it. . . ."[64] Hori states, "Either consciously or unconsciously, the people feel that their daily lives require several kinds of rites, festivals, and ceremonies. . . ."[65] Smith claims that the "folk" nature of ancestor worship's makes Japanese ancestral practices difficult to systematize. The Japanese people have just "always felt" the rites were necessary.[66] Conversion requires that people's emotions or feelings about ancestral practices change. They may even express a strong aversion toward ancestral customs.

Beliefs evidence objective thought. Feelings, however, are more illusive. The roots of ancestor worship seem to lie at the deeper affective or "feeling" level. For that reason, objective analysis becomes all the more problematic.

The feelings of Japanese people toward their ancestors would change after conversion, therefore, because they are new creatures (2 Cor. 5:17) with new desires (Rom. 7:18) and a will to obey God (Acts 5:29). In other words, Japanese people who used to worship their ancestors would not want to continue to worship them after experiencing biblical conversion.

Relationship

Lordship identifies roles and relationships.[67] A master's disciples willingly follow him, giving active testimony to their own status as disciples (2 Kings 2:6) and to their master's status as teacher. In other words, an individual can only be a disciple in relation to a master. Without a husband, a woman could not be a wife. Service manifests itself in a spirit of total surrender. When people become Christ's disciples, they must be willing to forsake family (Matt. 8:22; Luke 9:60; 14:26–27, 33), material goods (Matt 19:21), and even their lives (John 11:16). Thus, for a Japanese person, accepting Christ as Lord means forsaking all, including ancestral rites, and willingly becoming His disciple.[68]

Paul Hiebert illustrates the lordship-relationship most clearly in his presentation of category types,[69] specifically pointing to the "extrinsic centered-set" analogy.[70]

Intrinsic well-formed (bounded) sets establish membership based upon intrinsic qualities. In other words, people are converted when they experience changes internally.[71]

Intrinsic fuzzy sets, like bounded sets, are based upon intrinsic quality, yet by contrast they have no exact boundaries.[72] Fuzzy sets defy two-valued bounded set systems and encompass qualitative descriptions such as bright, tall, clear, intelligent, and so forth.

Extrinsic well-formed (centered) sets differ from intrinsic set characteristics in how they define membership. Extrinsic sets are formed on the basis of how they relate to other things rather than what they are in and of themselves.[73] Extrinsic centered sets have sharp boundaries and a well-defined center. Membership within the set is determined by the element's relationship to the central point of reference.[74] As kinship groups share common ancestors, so biblical converts share a common spiritual ancestor in Christ. In this case, Jesus is their Lord; they are His disciples.

Therefore, centered-set thinking suggests that Japanese people who experience conversion depart "from" their earthly family and lineage "to" a spiritual family with membership based upon their relationship to the center or reference point, Jesus Christ. Hiebert adds,

> Clearly, following Jesus requires some basic knowledge about him. The Jesus we follow is not the creation of our minds, but the Jesus of history as recorded in Scripture. But mental assent to the facts of biblical history does not make us Christians. We need to know Jesus personally, in the biblical sense of knowing another person (Deut. 34:10; Judg. 2:10; John 17:3). . . . It is a covenant commitment to the other as a person, not a contract to join forces to accomplish a task.[75]

The preceding body of literature clearly indicates that people from animistic backgrounds who convert to Christianity understand the conversion process in personal or relational terms. The following section turns from secondary research to primary field research, and consists of interviews with leaders of Japanese churches. These leaders say what behavior they believe most clearly indicates a conversion to true Christian faith.

Field Research

Since some Japanologists argue that Western missionaries may have influenced the Japanese church's aversion to ancestral practices,[76] the following sample consists of two groups, composed equally of foreign-born missionaries and Japanese-born pastors. Most of the first group are Euro-American. The second group are ethnically and culturally Japanese. Not only were these men born in Japan but they speak Japanese as their first language and consider themselves Japanese. While many of them could speak English very well, some chose to speak only Japanese. Since I have lived in Japan for eight years I could speak Japanese fluently enough to conduct a structured interview and engage the respondent in meaningful discussion. There was no need for an interpreter, and nothing in the interviews seemed to be misunderstood or considered incomplete by either side.

The responses below are representative of the data. Qualitative research invites descriptive rather than statistical responses. Therefore, supporting information appears in narrative rather than quantitative format. The sample consisted of twenty respondents—ten veteran foreign missionaries to Japan and ten Japanese national pastors—to whom I put the following questions:

1. From what to what does a Japanese person convert?

The responses indicated that the most important qualitative measure of conversion was that of "relationship." The Japanese people seemed to see the to/from formula in conversion as a change in relationship *to* God and *from* the ancestors rather than a simple intellectual shift. Missionaries and pastors, in describing this change, used animated hand gestures, personal life stories, and emotional expressions of delight, including smiles, direct eye contact, and uplifted voices accompanying virtually every reply. One respondent said, "Socially, it's converting from your old friends to your new friends." The new friends referred to were new Christian friends that the believer had at church. Another said, "Really, he converts from no connection with religion to a personal relationship with God."

A Japanese pastor beamed as he related the story of a man whose conversion became clear in his aversion to false worship. As a new Christian the man had been worried because, as he said, "Now I have Jesus my Savior and Lord. But every year, I have to lead two hundred people of my government to worship at the shrine in Tokyo. I have to do this in two days." God answered this man's prayer, and he did not have to go. But his struggle actually validated his conversion testimony to the Japanese pastor. This pastor realized the man was a true believer because he "knew God as his Father."

Another Japanese pastor related that conversion brought a woman to a new perception of herself. As she said, "I had no value before, but now I have value in God's eyes. I am His."

In each case, the clearest descriptions of conversion fell into the relationship category. When a Japanese person becomes a Christian, his or her personal and spiritual relationships change. Pastors used chopping, slicing, cutting, and waving motions to signify that any relationship with the ancestors was finished.

2. What is "saving faith" as you have seen it in people's lives when they confront ancestral practices?

The findings seem best exemplified in a story involving a twenty-year old Japanese woman who had recently professed Christ. As she celebrated her twentieth birthday with her parents, her father insisted that she show respect to her grandparents, because she was "here because of them." She replied, "No. I'm here because of Jesus Christ, not them. I'm not going in there!" He said, "Listen, you're my daughter and you're going to show the respect!" She said, "I am not [going to do this]!"

The struggle seemed to be rooted in the different perceptions of primary relationships. Her father felt her primary relationship was with her grandparents. She understood her primary relationship was with Christ. She would not perform the traditional ritual of burning incense and reporting to her grandmother, because she realized that her relationship to Christ had wrought a change. Behavior that expressed a relationship with her ancestors would be completely inconsistent with the reality of her relationship with Christ.

One Japanese pastor succinctly said, "Saving faith means that you cut off your relationship with ancestors. You don't need ancestors."

3. What does "repentance" in the Japanese church mean in relation to ancestral practices?

Representative responses included, "Repentance means that people stop doing [pause] the bowing, the prayers, the incense, *matsuri* [religious festivals], *iroiro* [various things like that]." Another said, "It means a 180- degree change from the old ways of worshiping to the new ways. Instead of worshiping the ancestors, the old ways, they worship God, the new ways. Partial turning or mostly turning is not repentance. It must be a complete 180-degree turn." One included an affective quality: "They think differently. They seem sad about worshiping the ancestors. They don't want to do that any more. But, for many people, this takes time."

Action seemed to validate repentance in conversion. Japanese pastors strongly associated action with attitude, suggesting that repentance constitutes a change of mind that naturally relates to changed behavior. In all cases, action or behavior changes correlated to another category, which suggests that changed behavior is related to changed attitudes and allegiances and also suggests that attitude changes would be indiscernible apart from behavioral changes.

4. In the context of ancestor worship, what must a Japanese person understand about Christ's lordship to confirm a genuine conversion as you see and understand it?

Virtually all the references to Christ's lordship indicated a relationship, primarily and initially vertical in nature (God to human) but often horizontal (human to human). That is, Christ's lordship over a person's life impacts horizontal relationships. One said, "It's leaving community."

Another said, "Jesus Christ is Lord, rather than the ancestors." A missionary added, "It's Jesus Christ and no others." Another emphasized that "trusting Christ as your Lord and Savior" means that "He [Christ] must be the one you worship. It's not the Savior now, and later the Lord." A Japanese pastor linked Christ's lordship with service, obedience, and a public profession of faith. He said, "You cannot claim the lordship of Christ and serve ancestors." Having spent over forty years in Japan, one missionary said, "Lordship is Christ as Lord at the moment you believe [Japanese word *Shu*]. He must be your Master or else you are not a true believer." Another added, "Before someone is baptized he must understand Christ's lordship."

5. What do you think baptism means in the minds of Japanese people?

A national pastor told the story of a woman who asked her father to come watch her baptism. The pastor said, "I remember lowering his daughter into the water. He closed his eyes. He could not watch, because he knew at that moment he was losing his daughter." Others said, "you join the group"; "you enter the church family"; or "you desert your family." One Japanese pastor said, "I think it helps them to feel Christian." He meant that they felt part of the group; they belonged.

The responses strongly emphasized relationship. Japanese people view water baptism as indicative of a new relationship. The ceremony seems to function as a rite of passage[77] or a transformational rite,[78] bringing them into the local body of Christ.

Research Summary

Conversion in the context of Japanese ancestral practices appears as repentance, a turning from ancestral practices, and is closely associated with a change in attitude and direction. Repentant people stopped taking part in ancestral practices. Saving faith suggests a spiritual shift in a person's primary relationships away from the earthly family and deceased ancestors to Jesus Christ as Lord. Lordship speaks of an exclusive relationship. Japanese believers serve Christ, seeking human relationships and performing acts only if they conform to that understood relationship. Finally, baptism testifies to an existing relationship with Christ and His people. Therefore, Japanese church leaders do not administer baptism to those whose relationship with Christ and believers is unclear.

Conclusion

Christ identifies actions as evidence of a relationship with Him: "Why do you call me 'Lord, Lord,' and do not do what I say?" (Luke 6:46). Relationship seems to precede actions. When Paul met Christ in Acts 9:6, Paul said, "Lord, what do You want me to do?" (NKJV) Lordship and obedience go together. When Paul referred to Christ as "Lord," he clearly saw himself as Christ's servant, having a responsibility to obey. Christ's reply certainly indicated that as well: "Arise and go into the city, and you will be told what you must do" (Acts 9:6b NKJV). Jesus told the rich young ruler in Matthew 19:21, "If you want to be perfect, go, sell your possessions and give to the poor, and you will have treasure in heaven. Then come, follow me" (NIV). If the young man had correctly understood his relationship to Christ, that of disciple/Lord, he would have obeyed and followed Jesus. He did not. Christ seemed to use this example to say that failure to obey Him denotes the absence of a primary relationship with Him. The words "lord" and "master" are synonymous English renderings of the Greek word *kurios*. Thus, when Jesus said, "No one can serve two masters" (Matt. 6:24 NIV), He was saying that no one can serve Christ as Lord and another master as well, whether it be money or family or a former deity. In Japan, that would suggest that people cannot serve Jesus and their family's ancestors.

Because Japanese ancestral practices indicate the possibility of a spiritual allegiance to someone other than Christ, it seems reasonable to question the internal quality of a Japanese person's spiritual conversion or faith if that person claims to be Christ's disciple yet continues to perform rites to his or her ancestral "lord." In the New Testament, those who followed Jesus as Lord forsook all: "We have left all we had to follow you!" (Luke 18:28 NIV). Genuinely converted idol worshipers manifested spiritual fruit in the form of deliberately separating themselves from deities or powers that were "not-god" (Acts 19). Scripture teaches that fruit indicates what is inside: "Each tree is recognized by its own fruit" (Luke 6:44 NIV). A fig tree bears figs, not apples. Trees that bear oranges on the outside are orange trees on the inside. This fruit-bearing criterion seems scripturally valid, suggesting that those who experience new life as Christ's disciples will manifest fruit consistent with that spiritual change.

Christ expects total, complete surrender to His lordship. Serving Christ does not mean 95 percent commitment to Him and 5 percent reserved for former ancestral practices, regardless of how indifferent the participant is to the rites. Christ's call to leave one's family strikes a clear note with those who view ancestor worship as the family bond. In essence, Christ requires His followers to forsake even family to become His disciples (Matt 8:21).

If ancestor practices constitute the worship of "not-gods" or spiritual fornication, then those who willingly desire to observe such practices may not have experienced new life (Luke 6:46). In other words, it seems that the "fruit of idolatry" manifests a heart not yet converted. Japanese people might formerly have burned incense to ancestral spirits, offered food, drink, and prayers before ancestral tombs, and bowed in acts of worship before the ancestors, but regardless of their level of sincerity in doing these thing, Scripture indicates that this behavior should cease at conversion (1 Thess. 1:9). When a person receives new life from God, that seems to include an aversion toward serving ancestral spirits or any other "not-god," which would include a desire to not follow ancestral worship forms (Ex. 20:2–5; Gal. 4:8).

The research indicates that Japan's church leaders understand conversion and saving faith as primarily relational. That is, when Japanese persons experience new life in Christ, they understand themselves to be primarily related to Christ as their new Lord. They recognize that their spiritual relationship with their former ancestral line completely ends the moment they enter this new relationship with Christ. Furthermore, these converts seem to understand that they are no longer obligated to serve and obey their ancestors, because they now belong to Christ. Finally, this primary spiritual relationship quite naturally and without explanation requires obedience to Christ's commands. Japan's church leaders realize that people cannot claim to have saving faith and yet perform acts of service or worship to deceased ancestral spirits.

In the context of the discussions of "lordship salvation," this study suggests that the lordship position seems more supportable in view of the Japanese conversion experience.[79] Furthermore, these findings suggest that the "no-lordship" position may come from a very narrow Western cultural perspective. It stands to reason that if the "no-lordship" position were theologically valid, those conclusions would be universally supportable from a number of different cultural perspectives and worldviews. Yet even a small sample from two other Asian nations indicates that the "no-lordship" position lacks any broadly based advocates, as the "lordship" position is culturally understood.

Christian Alternatives

Having established what church leaders believe is indicative of an individual not truly converted, we now will suggest in this section some ways of demonstrating ancestral respect that accommodate the natural Japanese (and human) desire to honor relatives.

A Korean Christian lady married a Japanese man. He became a Christian as a result of her influence. She came to Japan with her husband following their marriage. His mother became angry when she realized that her son would not worship at the *butsudan* and blamed her son's Korean wife. Though they lived in separate homes, their co-location suggested to the matriarch that her son should soon take over the *butsudan* and keep it in his house. The son's wife refused.

Instead, the wife erected a large wall plaque of the family's genealogy, illustrating ancestors far back into history. The wife placed the plaque right over the *genkan* (entryway) so that every time family members entered or exited the house they would see and be reminded of their heritage.

Some Christian families build a running history of their family tree. In Japan, this demonstration of commitment to family history seems very acceptable. When children and adults in Christian families can discuss grandparents and great-grandparents in vivid detail, they gain the respect of their relatives and community and demonstrate that they have not forgotten their ancestors because of their Christian conversion.

Modern technology affords families the opportunity of putting together photo albums and libraries of family videos. Family portraits and personal handwritten notes pasted into a family scrapbook do much to reassure relatives and build a sense of "family" among siblings.

Japanese pastors strongly encourage their members to visit their parents and to foster good relationships with them. Along with the visits, people must demonstrate love, kindness, and concern for their parents and for the welfare of their family. In this way, Christian love can become a universally acceptable way to establish relationships, build trust, and enjoy the richness of family life in Japan.

Study Questions

1. What four elements seem to constitute a religion?
2. Define and explain "religious conversion."
3. How would you respond to someone who felt that Elisha told Naaman in 2 Kings 5 that it was acceptable for Naaman to bow down in the temple of Rimmon as part of his service to the king?
4. Explain the significance of form and meaning as they relate to bowing and Shadrach, Meshach, and Abednego in Daniel 3.
5. How would you respond to individuals who claimed that, because

they did not truly believe in a religious practice, they were not performing a meaningful act by bowing before an idol?

6. Explain the significance of Christ's lordship in the context of an animist's conversion to Christianity.

Chapter Notes

1. Japanese church leaders also look for positive signs of conversion —a passion for Bible reading and renewed comprehension of Scripture, willing church attendance, a desire to pray and witness, a teachable spirit— as well as the negative aspects of conversion that include acts of separation from the ancestral practices.

2. Tetsuo Yamaori, "The Metamorphosis of Ancestors," *The Japan Quarterly* 33, no. 1 (January–April 1986): 50.

3. Emile Durkheim, *The Elementary Forms of Religious Life,* trans. Karen E. Fields (New York: Free Press, 1995), 44.

4. Kunio Yanagita, *About Our Ancestors: The Japanese Family System,* trans. Fanny Hagin Mayer and Ishiwara Yasuyo (Tokyo: Japanese Society for the Promotion of Science, 1970), 140.

5. Noboru Yamaguchi, "What Does the New Testament Say About Ancestral Practices?" in *Christian Alternatives to Ancestor Practices*, ed. Bong Rin Ro (Taichung, Taiwan: Asian Theological Association, 1985), 44.

6. Yanagita, *About Our Ancestors,* 44.

7. Ibid., 50.

8. Robert J. Smith, *Ancestor Worship in Contemporary Japan* (Stanford: Stanford Univ. Press, 1974), 79–80.

9. Ichiro Hori, *Folk Religion in Japan: Continuity and Change,* ed. Joseph Kitagawa and Alan L. Miller (Chicago: Univ. of Chicago, 1968), 2.

10. Yanagita defines "ancestors" as "all those souls that the household has the exclusive right and duty to venerate" (*About Our Ancestors,* 10).

11. Hori, *Folk Religion in Japan,* 13.

12. Iwao Ushijima, *Ihai siashi to nihon no kazoku. Shinzoku: Izu hanto. Toshima o chushin to shite* ("Ihai" Cult in Relation to Japanese Kingship and Family—Ancestor Worship in Toshima Island, Izu Archipelago). *Minzokugaku kenkyu* 31:3:169–78. Cited in Robert J. Smith, *Ancestor Worship in Contemporary Japan.*

13. Yanagita, *About Our Ancestors,* 23.

14. Ibid., 24.

15. Ibid., 23–24.

16. Ibid., 6. Yanagita suggests that perhaps deities worshiped in local festivals are actually family ancestors venerated as territorial protectors as well as

individuals who existed as part of a family. Yet ancestral practices essentially constitute all Japanese religion.

17. Hori, *Folk Religion in Japan,* 2.

18. Ronald H. Nash, *World-Views in Conflict: Choosing Christianity in a World of Ideas* (Grand Rapids: Zondervan, 1992), 16.

19. Paul G. Hiebert, *Cultural Anthropology* (Grand Rapids: Baker, 1983), 371.

20. Meredith B. McGuire, *Religion: The Social Context,* 3d ed. (Belmont, Calif.: Wadsworth, 1992), 71.

21. Hiebert, *Cultural Anthropology,* 374.

22. Durkheim, *The Elementary Forms of Religious Life,* xlvi.

23. David Reid, *New Wine: The Cultural Shaping of Japanese Christianity* (Berkeley, California: Asian Humanities Press, 1991), 3.

24. Hiebert, *Cultural Anthropology,* 374.

25. Ian Reader, "What Constitutes Religious Activity? (II)" *Japanese Journal of Religious Studies* 18, no. 4 (1991), 373–76.

26. Hiebert, *Cultural Anthropology,* 374.

27. Henry Ayabe, *Step Inside Japan: Language, Culture, Mission* (Tokyo: Japan Evangelical Missionary Assoc., 1992),189.

28. Alan R. Tippett, *Introduction to Missiology* (Pasadena: William Carey Library, 1987), 323–36.

29. Clark B. Offner, "Continuing Concern for the Departed," *Japanese Religions* 11, (December 1979): 5–6. Offner said, "Until the missionary understands the inner motivation and moral character of the act of *sosen suhai* [ancestor worship], his judgment should be reserved. According to the teachings of both Jesus and Paul, it is the inward quality which stimulates the external acts that should be the object of moral judgment." Offner went on to describe "motivation and moral character" as a "sense of a continuing relationship with family members and respected leaders who have departed this life (but who remain nearby rather than journeying to some distant spirit world)."

30. Clark B. Offner, "'Worship' in the Bible and in Japan," *The Japan Missionary Bulletin* 35 (March 1981): 93–99. Offner argues from the position that worship consists of the internal heart condition and that those who worship God must do so in "spirit and truth" (John 4:23). He points to 1 Samuel 15:22—"to obey is better than sacrifice"; Micah 6:7–8—that God does not want "thousands of rams" as sacrifices as much as for people "to act justly and to love mercy and to walk humbly with your God"; and Isaiah 66:2–3—God esteems "he who is humble and contrite in spirit" rather than the one who sacrifices animals and burnt offerings. Offner's point is that God wants internal consistency more than outward compliance.

While Scripture does indicate that one's internal disposition toward God determines the quality of worshipful acts, Offner seems to misapply God's rebuke to Israel for worshiping Him without a right heart. The worship of God never was the same in Scripture as the worship of an idol or a "not-god." God was not rebuking them for bringing sacrifices per se, but for bringing them without the right heart and thinking that they satisfied God only by conforming to prescribed forms. Forms still mattered to God, which is why He condemned Jeroboam's golden calves in Bethel and Dan as syncretistic (1 Kings 12:28–30). Many may have come with a heart to worship Jehovah, but they used the wrong form, i.e., a calf. God said, "this thing became a sin." Even the worship of God was sinful when done in the wrong form (cf. Ex. 32). Therefore, we cannot separate form from worship though the worship of God required more than outward forms but also inward conformity to God's rule. Pagan worship, however, nowhere prescribes internal spiritual congruity, which makes it quite different from the worship of God. Yet God's Word refers to ritual outward acts performed before idols as worship, albeit false worship.

31. God judged Israel and Gentile nations for false worship and for failing to obey and serve Him. First Chronicles 5:25: "But they were unfaithful to the God of their fathers and prostituted themselves to the gods of the peoples of the land, whom God had destroyed before them." Then in 9:1, "The people of Judah were taken captive to Babylon because of their unfaithfulness." Ephraim's name evoked fear in other nations. Yet Hosea 13:1 adds, "But he [Ephraim] became guilty of Baal worship and died." Psalm 106:28–29 clearly indicates that Israel "yoked themselves to the Baal of Peor" when they "ate sacrifices offered to lifeless gods." Their identification with Baal roused God's indignation—"they provoked the Lord to anger by their wicked deeds"—and judgment—"and a plague broke out among them." The passage seems to refer to Numbers 25:2–3 where "the people ate and bowed down before these gods. So Israel joined in worshiping the Baal of Peor. And the Lord's anger burned against them." This Scripture passage suggests that the acts of eating and bowing identified and connected the actor with the deity. God judged even Gentile nations for such wicked practices when He destroyed Babylon, because Belshazzar praised the false gods of silver and gold and not the true God (Dan. 5:23).

32. Offner, "'Worship' in the Bible and in Japan," 94.

33. Herman Ooms, "A Structural Analysis of Japanese Ancestral Rites and Beliefs," *Ancestors,* ed. William H. Newell (The Hague: Mouton Publishers, 1976), 61–90. See also J. M. Berentsen, *Grave and Gospel* (The

Netherlands, Leiden: E. J. Brill, 1985). Yanagita, *About Our Ancestors;* and Hori, *Folk Religion in Japan.*

34. Moshe Halbertal and Avishai Margalit, *Idolatry,* trans. Naomi Goldblum (Cambridge: Harvard Univ. Press, 1992), 204–5.

35. Ian Reader, "What Constitutes Religious Activity? (II)," 373–76.

36. Yanagita describes unconscious ancestral traditions as follows: "A well known *custom* at Chinkoji in Matsubara, Kyoto is of going to meet the spirits with a small branch of fir, and they let it rest one night in the well at the house. . . . A more unusual *custom* was in the country of the southern part of Kyushu where they went to meet spirits at the *Bon* market," *[italics added].* He refers to ancestral rituals simply as cultural "customs." Ibid., 134–35.

37. D. E. Aune, "Worship: Lesser Ritual Actions: Bowing or Prostration," *The Anchor Bible Dictionary,* vol. 6, ed. David Freedman (New York: Doubleday, 1992), 987. Aune agues that there exists no difference between "worship" and "physical prostration" with the use of *proskynein* followed by either the dative or the accusative.

38. Lawrence O. Richards, "Offering and Sacrifice," *Expository Dictionary of Bible Words* (Grand Rapids: Zondervan, 1985), 464–69.

39. W. Barnes Tatum, "The LXX Version of the Second Commandment (Ex. 20:3–6 = Deut. 5:7–10): A Polemic Against Idols, Not Images," *Journal of the Study of Judaism* 17 (1987): 181.

40. Abel L. Ndjerareau, "The Theological Bases for the Prohibitions of Idolatry: An Exegetical and Theological Study of the Second Commandment" (unpublished Ph.D. dissertation, Dallas Theological Seminary, 1994).

41. Smith, *Ancestor Worship in Contemporary Japan,* 79.

42. According to a Buddhist priest who mentioned this in a personal conversation with the author, the *kaimyo* is deliberately changed from the person's name in this life to a different name so as to fool the individual who sits at heaven's gate with the book of wrongdoings. When the recently deceased appears, the person with the book allows the individual entrance into heaven because the new name or *kaimyo* inscribed on the *ihai* does not correspond with any names in the book of wrongdoings.

43. Smith, *Ancestor Worship in Contemporary Japan,* 79.

44. Ibid., 81.

45. "It is a fact that the Japanese hold a deeply rooted, though somewhat vague belief or feeling that the spirits of their ancestors and family dead actually live in the mortuary tablets; consequently to the Japanese, the mortuary tablets are the ancestors themselves and their beloved deceased.

There is the reason why most Japanese cannot bear to part with the mortuary tablets, or allow them to be burned, and feel a terrible reproach, and an unbearable sense of loneliness when such things happen." Tatsumi Hashimoto, *Ancestor Worship and Japanese Daily Life (Sosen suhai to nichijo seikatsu)*, trans. Percy T. Luke (Tokyo: Word of Life Press, 1962), 10.

46. Beverly Roberts Gaventa, *From Darkness to Light: Aspects of Conversion in the New Testament* (Philadelphia: Fortress, 1986), 9–10.

47. Gailyn Van Rheenen, *Communicating Christ in Animistic Contexts* (Grand Rapids: Baker, 1991), 26.

48. Gaventa, *From Darkness to Light,* 9–10.

49. Hans Kasdorf, *Christian Conversion in Context* (Scottdale, Penn.: Herald, 1980), 11.

50. David A. Shank, "Towards an Understanding of Christian Conversion," *Mission-Focus Magazine* 5:2 (November 1976), 6.

51. David J. Bosch, *Transforming Mission: Paradigm Shifts in Theology of Mission,* American Society of Missiology Series, no. 16 (New York: Orbis Books, 1991), 488.

52. Rene C. Padilla, *The New Face of Evangelicalism,* An International Symposium on the Lausanne Covenant (Downers Grove, Ill.: InterVarsity, 1976), 75.

53. R. T. France, "Conversion in the Bible," *The Evangelical Quarterly* 65, no. 4 (1993): 293.

54. Ibid., 295.

55. Tippett, *Introduction to Missiology,* 329–30. He mentions that many animists often confuse the gospel with another source of power.

56. John MacArthur, *The Gospel According to Jesus: What Does Jesus Mean When He Says, "Follow Me"?* (Grand Rapids: Zondervan, 1994), 93–94.

57. Donald A. McGavran, *Understanding Church Growth,* rev. ed. (Grand Rapids: Eerdmans, 1980), 340.

58. Kasdorf, *Christian Conversion in Context,* 55, 57.

59. Tippett, *Introduction to Missiology,* 327.

60. Ibid., 328–29.

61. Arnold van Gennep, *The Rites of Passage* (Chicago: Univ. of Chicago Press, 1960). First published in 1909.

62. Paul G. Hiebert, *Anthropological Reflections on Missiological Issues,* (Grand Rapids: Baker, 1994), 169–72.

63. Ayabe, *Step Inside Japan,* 189.

64. Yanagita, *About Our Ancestors,* 140.

65. Hori, *Folk Religion in Japan,* 2.

66. Smith, *Ancestor Worship in Contemporary Japan,* 2–5.
67. Charles R. Taber, "God vs. Idols: A Model of Conversion," *Journal of the Academy for Evangelism in Theological Education* 3 (1987–1988): 21.
68. Ibid., 30; Tabor notes, "For persons who worship idols, whether exclusively or in combination with the worship of God, conversion entails, in the words of Paul, both a radical turning *from* and a radical turning *to*. This requires that the idols be *named* and *forsaken*. Let no one imagine that this can be untraumatic, the mere substitution of one label for another. Forsaking an idol is forsaking that which was the core of one's existence, the ultimate point of reference for belief and behavior."
69. Hiebert, *Reflections*, 107–36.
70. Ibid., 122–30.
71. Ibid., 111–18.
72. Lofti Asker Zadehh, "Fuzzy Sets," *Information and Control* 8 (1965): 338–53.
73. Hiebert, *Reflections,* 122.
74. Ibid., 123.
75. Ibid., 125.
76. Clark B. Offner, "Continuing Concern for the Departed," Japanese Religions 11 (December 1979), 14.
77. Van Gennep, *Rites of Passage.*
78. Hiebert, *Reflections,* 169–72.
79. John Piper, *The Pleasures of God* (Portland: Multnomah, 1991), 279–305, succinctly and clearly expresses a view that this author considers consistent with the Japanese attitude specifically and the general Asian sentiment on the lordship issue. Piper rightly identifies this "two-stage, Savior-Lord sequence" as perhaps the problematic (may I suggest *American*) source of this debate. Asian church leaders with whom this author has spoken suggest that this recent question is simply a non-issue to them and their people. One Chinese church leader said, "I do not see what the problem is. We Chinese understand right away that Jesus is Lord." On October 12, 1998, in Bangkok, five Thai church leaders commented about this very debate and said, "A person cannot be a true Christian unless they surrender to Christ as Lord. . . . Of course Jesus is the Lord. . . . Every person who converts to Christianity believes that Jesus is the Lord. . . . They must put away the old gods and ways and follow their new master." In other words, Japanese, Chinese, and Thai church leaders seem to understand Christian conversion, in their cultural experience, to be primarily a shift of allegiance from former deities to the Lord Jesus. Furthermore, Piper points

out, and most every Japanese pastor I have met would likely concur, that people cannot truly be saved if they say, "No, I don't want to bow to him as Lord, and I do not accept his claim on my life as authoritative Guide and Teacher" (ibid., 285.) In Japan, such an attitude would likely result in people simply adding Christ to their array of spiritual deities, since Jesus has no claim to their exclusive worship. Finally, Piper forcefully asserts that "Christ *is* Lord whether we acknowledge that or not . . . he is the Lord *of every true believer* whether we grasp this fully or obey him fully or not" (italics included; ibid., 286).

8

WILLIAM H. SMALLMAN

THAT WE MAY BE ONE . . . THAT THEY MAY BE WON

Fundamentalists are united in their opposition to the ecumenical movement, but they are certainly not on the same page in understanding what it is. We will examine this movement, historically and theologically—especially as it impacts world missions—from its own source materials so that our comprehension and opposition will be biblical in direction and attitude.

Some writers use the term *ecumenical* accurately in reference to the unification movements among churches of the major Christian traditions, whether Protestant, Roman Catholic, or Eastern Orthodox.[1] That confluence of professing Christians is primarily embodied in the World Council of Churches (WCC). Although WCC's attendant organizations and movements overlap with those of some Catholics and evangelicals, the Roman Catholic Church as a body continues to remain outside the WCC by its own choice.

Others use the term *ecumenical* in referring to broadly evangelical activities, when the more accurate descriptor would be *interdenominational*. Still, many of these broadly evangelical activities do rather carelessly cross over into cooperation with churches that are in the National Council of Churches and the WCC, in which case they do represent truly ecumenical cooperation.

This chapter will address the history and some key attributes of the WCC. It will then measure the implications of some of its claims and tendencies as they affect fundamentalist and evangelical missionary efforts around the world. There is a crying need for convictions based on an accurate knowledge of Scripture and history. Looking back a century or more may keep the next generation of missionaries from repeating mistakes and help them advance the spread of the biblical gospel around the world. Too much progress has been made in evangelization to give in to a pluralistic context that rejects the biblical authority behind the gospel.

What has caused the turnaround from a biblically based gospel to the ecumenical movement within two generations? How did it all begin during the heyday of evangelical world missions? How can we keep from repeating the same tragic errors? How can we carry on biblical missionary service without entanglement or compromise?

We begin with a quick historical survey.

Missionary Roots of the WCC: IMC, F&O, L&W
1. World Conferences

Pioneer Baptist missionary William Carey proposed that all of the evangelistic mission boards of his day should meet for a global strategy conference. He suggested in 1804 that the first such meeting be convened in Capetown, South Africa, in 1810. A conference of this nature at last took place in 1854, twenty years after Carey's death, with twin conferences in London and New York.

Thereafter conferences were open to evangelistic missionaries of all Protestant denominations about every ten years through the remainder of the nineteenth century, though they were largely Anglo-American with some continental participation. The final such fully evangelical conference was held in New York in 1900. The turning point for ecumenism took place in Edinburgh in 1910, when the evangelical mission leaders sought guidance from known modernists for help in missionary methods.[2]

John R. Mott, the architect of the ecumenical movement, invited known modernist speakers to the 1910 Edinburgh conference to help plan social ministries, not for their theology. Notable among the modernists in attendance was Dr. Walter Rauschenbusch, best known for his definitive work on the social gospel, *Christianity and the Social Crisis* (Macmillen, 1907). The ship of world-level missions organizations then began to list and to sink. From that point on, a fully evangelical world missions conference was not held again until our lifetime. Even then, "Berlin 1966," sponsored by the Billy Graham Evangelistic Association, was rather broad in its definition of who might participate as evangelicals.[3]

2. Major Organizations and Organizers

Out of that watershed congress in Edinburgh in 1910, and following the devastation of World War I, there arose three new organizations that would go on to reshape the Protestant mission world. Despite their best intentions, all three would shortly abandon biblical missionary principles.

a. IMC: International Missionary Council, 1921

While Europe was still reeling from the impact of the war, the continuing committee from "Edinburgh 1910" assembled in Lake Mohonk, New York, in 1921 and formed the International Missionary Council (IMC). The modernist-fundamentalist controversy was raging, so most of the gospel-preaching missionaries had already separated from the mainline denominations that were sinking into modernism. It was then that these newly modernized denominational missions determined to keep the old missions ship afloat, even without a gospel cargo to give it purpose. Without a message of redemption, missions quickly degenerated into socio-political activism and relief work, with a major focus on unity. Meanwhile, the fundamentalist mission agencies, denominational and nondenominational, carried on the bulk of church planting missionary work apart from the new IMC.

b. F&O: Faith and Order, 1927

The purpose of Faith and Order (F&O) was to examine the doctrines and traditions that separated the member churches from each other. F&O actively sought ways to foster unity and cooperation among the member churches, even promoting mergers. Global conferences of F&O began in 1927 in Lausanne, then continued with "Edinburgh 1937," where its members cautiously helped to design a world council of churches.

c. L&W: Life and Work, 1925

The Universal Christian Conference on Life and Work (L&W) fo cused its resources on the practical issues addressed by the churche especially in the practice of the social gospel. The L&W agenda, direct from the premier conference in Stockholm in 1925, included labor lav racism, women's rights, disarmament, church-state relations, globali and similar moral and social issues. In the shadow of Hitler's ascent t convened again in Oxford in 1937, as "the motor of advance, seein the dangerous and tumultuous social situation of the world the compe reason for moving decisively towards a dynamic and informed ecume council of churches."[4]

The motto of L&W was "Doctrine divides while service unites," leaning on a half-truth. It is false doctrine that causes division, while true biblical doctrine gives a foundation for mutual respect and even joint activity. Over the previous century, missions of differing ecclesiastical traditions, those that agreed on foundational doctrines of biblical Christianity, got along well, working parallel to each other. L&W looked away from the theological boundaries between churches to the moral issues that could unite them in action. That old motto is being resurrected today, with a focus on warmth over truth.

3. The World Council of Churches, 1948

After F&O and L&W had carried out their separate agendas for about twenty years, they recognized the value of uniting their organizations. They realized that they were already working together extensively on matters of common interest. At the initiative of the more liberal and aggressive L&W, the two organizations held parallel conferences in England in 1937. In 1938 they cooperated in drawing up the constitution of the proposed world council of churches.

The International Missionary Council had determined to remain outside the strictures of ecumenical structures. It continued to have its own global conferences with a focus on missionary interests from its less traditionally orthodox viewpoint. In international conferences the IMC gathered momentum as neo-orthodoxy flourished in the aftermath of the collapse of old modernism and the growing sense of spirituality in all religions. [5]

World War II interrupted the flow of its progress for another decade and killed off several of the key leaders of the burgeoning ecumenical movement.

The WCC General Assemblies

The World Council of Churches has only convened in general assembly eight times in its fifty years of history, about every seven years.

1. WCC1 Amsterdam, 1948

The WCC was constituted as the religious equivalent of the newly formed United Nations (1945) and as a forum for churches to discuss matters of common interest. The first general secretary, Dr. Willem Adolf Visser 'tHooft of the Netherlands Reformed Church, insisted that the purpose of the WCC was *not* to form a "superchurch" that would supersede the variety of traditions in the churches.[6] The WCC would have no

authority over the constituent churches. The theme of this first assembly was "Man's Disorder—God's Design," playing off the disorder left around the globe by World War II.[7] The general theological environment was a mixture of idealistic liberalism and idealistic liturgical churches bringing a tolerant nominal orthodoxy to the table.

2. WCC2 Evanston, 1954

In the only assembly to convene in the USA, the second general assembly essentially affirmed the continuing existence of the WCC. The assembly theme, "Christ—the Hope of the World," focused on eschatological hope in the aftermath of the Korean Conflict and in the heart of the Cold War then underway. The theological stance of the Council was the neo-orthodoxy then rampant in its liberal member churches, and it was presented by key speakers including Karl Barth, the Neibuhrs, and other lesser lights. Evangelism was crowded out by the move to political activism to end racial and economic discrimination.

3. WCC3 New Delhi, 1961

The third general assembly, with the theme "Jesus Christ—the Light of the World," was one of the most significant and was marked by three major events.

a. IMC Integrated into the WCC

The International Missionary Council had operated parallel to the WCC but with many common interests. After long consideration, the IMC integrated into the WCC as the Commission on World Mission and Evangelism (CWME). The intent was to bring missions into the heart of the ecclesiastical machinery. The unforeseen result, however, was the smothering of the missionary spirit of the denominations within two decades. The presiding elder of a small reformed evangelical denomination within the WCC expressed his strong lament: "No one in New Delhi could possibly have predicted the virtual demise of the missionary movement—much less within the next fifteen years."[8]

b. EOC Joined the WCC

Virtually all of the national Eastern Orthodox churches (EOC) joined the WCC at New Delhi 1961. They had always considered themselves to be the Una Sancta, the one apostolic holy catholic church. They joined in order to witness to the truth of ancient orthodoxy to liberal Protestants. The Orthodox had hoped that the evangelical bloc would join with them as a counterweight to the liberal Protestants, who denied the essence of historical Christianity. The evangelicals would not join, however, but the EOC joined anyway. The one concession the EOC demanded was the modification of the Basis Statement to include the Trinity and the authority of the Scriptures.

c. Basis Statement Modified

The Basis Statement is the only doctrinal standard of the WCC and may be interpreted in any way the member churches wish. This 1961 Basis Statement is still in effect:

> The World Council of Churches is a fellowship of churches which confess the Lord Jesus Christ as God and Savior according to the scriptures and therefore seek to fulfill their common calling to the glory of one God, Father, Son and Holy Spirit.[9]

Jesus had long ago issued the disclaimer that not all who called Him "Lord, Lord" would be recognized as those whom He knows personally and allowed into heaven (Matt. 7:21–23).

4. WCC4 Uppsala, 1968

The fourth assembly, hosted in Sweden in the social upheaval of the 60s, brought an even more radical theological distancing from the biblical understanding of the gospel and of evangelism. The focus was that "evangelization is humanization," as a better society reflects the kingdom of God more clearly. The newly arising theology of liberation was getting its first showing in interecclesial conferences before the publication of its key first books within the next three years. Under the theme, "Behold, I Make All Things New," Uppsala was the most broadly representative gathering of various Christian groups in nearly a millennium, especially with the new and significant participation of EOC.

5. WCC5 Nairobi, 1975

The fifth general assembly, the first in Africa, marked a conservative backlash. The recently completed International Conference on World Evangelization in Lausanne in 1974 had fostered a global awareness of evangelical missions. Many new denominations from the newly liberated nations came into the WCC, not knowing how little gospel was there, and demanded that the Council identify its truly Christian nature.

Dr. John Stott, a "conciliar evangelical" as a conservative Anglican, preached in a plenary session. His message was "Five Things the WCC Needs to Restore" to its ministries: the lostness of man, confidence in the gospel, the uniqueness of Christ, the urgency of evangelism, and personal experience of Christ.[10] Did this revivalist preaching rattle the WCC? No. Shortly before Dr. Stott was to present his message his speaking time was cut from thirty minutes to eight minutes. Then WCC totally ignored the message—no rebuttal, no argument, no forums, no serious attention given to a lone biblical message.

In 1974 the United Nations had promulgated the "New International Economic Order," which the WCC theologians quickly identified with the kingdom of God, or global socialism. This was emerging as a major theme of the liberation theology, which was by now well entrenched in conciliar theology of mission. A related term in "ecumenese" is JPSS, or a "just, participatory, and sustainable society," designed as a model for opposing the [capitalist] imperialism that left many peoples oppressed and voiceless.[11]

6. WCC6 Vancouver, 1983

By 1983 the Council was committed to pluralism and welcomed dialogue with fifteen representatives of "other living faiths" to learn from their spirituality. Rhetoric about "God's preferential option for the poor" was commonplace, along with demands that Western economic imperialism be curtailed. The Council was openly advocating mergers among churches of similar traditions and seeking to remove barriers of communion and doctrine between all Christians along the lines of the BEM document from Faith and Order in 1982. Roman Catholic participation was highly visible but self-limited.

A new action unit was set in motion with "the Vancouver call" for JPIC: justice, peace, and the integrity of creation.[12] This new, major thrust would formalize the treatment of economic, disarmament, and environmental issues as theological issues for church attention, following an essentially leftist orientation. Through this structural unit, the New Age advocates have a field day promoting their views, with a pantheistic and evolutionary emphasis.

Key ecumenical documents were formally presented to the constituency at Vancouver, discussed below as BEM and MEEA. These remain at the heart of WCC discussions, with serious implications for world missions.

7. WCC7 Canberra, 1991

The seventh general assembly included a parade of practitioners of "other living faiths," the politically correct term rather than "non-Christian religions." The Eastern Orthodox church leaders expressed offense that non-Christians should be instructing the Christians on spirituality, but the assembled WCC was committed to a fuller exercise of pluralism.[13]

The assembly theme was "Come Holy Spirit—Renew the Whole Creation," so charismatics of all stripes had their day in the sun. A key plenary speaker was a Korean female seminary professor who led a liturgy invoking the spirits of oppressed women and minorities from biblical and secular history, who referred to the Holy Spirit as "she," and who demonstrated the burning of written prayers to ancestors.[14] Her message was that experience matters far more than doctrine, since there is no final authority for moral or spiritual questions. This doctrine fits postmodernism, which is sweeping the philosophical circuits of the contemporary world.

8. WCC8 Harare, 1998

The most recent general assembly returned to Africa, in Harare, capital city of Zimbabwe, in December 1998. Some specific expectations are in view as a result of this second assembly in Africa, though the most significant changes normally take place after personnel are newly appointed in the general assemblies and the central committee.

1. A proposal was presented for a major reorganization of the WCC, so that the structure in place since 1991 became unrecognizable.[15] Part of the restructuring was motivated by severe budget shortages in the WCC, though an upturn in its financial picture was announced late in 1998. The activities of the Geneva headquarters have run far ahead of the contributions of the member churches, and newer members have less resources to share. There is also strong interest in lowering any barriers that keep the RCC from becoming a full partner in the WCC. Such a partnership would create a truly global ecumenical church with a strong political voice, the playground of the coming Antichrist. Financial proposals included the idea that the rich capitalist nations should forgive the indebtedness of the poorer nations, since the burden of interest payments perpetuates the poverty of those nations.

2. The restructuring may allow the Commission on World Mission and Evangelism to quietly disappear. There will be properly equivalent subunits, but nothing branded with the offensive term "evangelism." True

biblical evangelism is coming to be scorned in WCC literature as proselytizing, individualistic, otherworldly, imperialistic, and arrogantly disrespectful of other religions' spirituality. In the Harare assembly, evangelism was labeled *proselytism* and was mentioned since it "still causes pain and is a problem."[16] Missionary work becomes mere fraternal cooperation, sharing of resources, and dialogue with other living faiths, particularly since all countries are now mission senders rather than mission fields.

3. The WCC formally considered a proposal to encourage the establishment of a Universal Christian Forum open to all types of Christian churches that can accept the *Basis:* Roman Catholic, Orthodox, Protestant, Evangelical, Pentecostal, and new churches. Many of the subunits of the WCC already have Roman Catholic members, even though that church is not a member of the WCC through its own self-limitations. The proposed forum would leave the RCC a greater measure of autonomy, allowing it to participate freely without compromising its own doctrine of the primacy of the pope.[17]

4. This fiftieth anniversary celebration encouraged additional forms of less subtle repudiation of the uniqueness of Christ and Christianity as God's self-revelation and way of salvation. This is already common currency in the WCC, but in the wake of Harare there will be a more blatantly anti-biblical posture toward moral authority and the definition of true spirituality.

5. The new CUV document was presented as a foundational statement of ecumenical interest, fully titled, "Towards a Common Understanding and Vision of the WCC." This responds to complaints of the Orthodox and evangelicals about doctrinal slippage, among other issues, after seven years of deliberations in the central committee.

Recent Key Developments in the WCC
1. 1982 BEM

At its own conference in Lima in 1982, Faith and Order first presented a draft of a document (commissioned at Nairobi 1975) seeking to lower the barriers among all churches. *Baptism, Eucharist, and Ministry* makes three radical proposals that member churches have been debating ever since. There are several published volumes of the responses from and to the various churches around the world. All nominally favor the notions, but none are eager to give up their distinctives. The *BEM* principles are:

a. Baptism

Any person baptized as a Christian in any church should be recognized as a baptized Christian by all other churches of any tradition. No one should be required to submit to rebaptism upon changing to a church (denomination) of different tradition. This is clearly an anticonversion measure, taking offense at the notion that a person who wants to move, say, from a Lutheran church to a Baptist church, has been "converted" and needs to be baptized as if a heathen.

b. Eucharist

Any baptized Christian from any church should be welcomed at the communion table of any other church without having to submit to any other screening, practices, baptism, or traditions. All such Christians should be free to cocommune as they wish.

c. Ministry

Any person ordained to the ministry by any Christian church should be recognized as qualified to be invited to minister the Word and the sacraments in any other churches of all traditions. This does not demand that any church accept any minister, but that all be considered acceptable for such an invitation as a visiting minister. It makes no difference if a minister is a woman, or is a practicing homosexual, or has completely different theological convictions and ecclesiastical practices. Those are trivial matters before the compelling principle of Christian unity.

A recent news item illustrates the very spirit of compromise and cooperation that is fostered by *BEM* as four American denominations completed an accord for mutual recognition.[18] Around the world there are reports of growing numbers of serious negotiations between pairs of churches of similar traditions, exploring possible mergers. In too many cases, their common heritage in Christian orthodoxy is ignored in order to follow a liberal agenda together in theological unbelief.[19]

When Jesus prayed in John 17 that Christians might be one that the world might be won, the primary objective was missiological.[20] Unity was to be an instrument in world evangelism. The WCC has turned this around to make mission an instrument of unity, their real goal.

2. 1983 MEEA

In 1982, the central committee of the WCC issued a statement prepared by CWME to stand as a statement of the WCC's theology of evangelism. *Mission and Evangelism, an Ecumenical Affirmation* is difficult to critique because it is laden with evangelical terminology and with references to Scripture. One needs to know how to read ecumenese, since the interpretation of their own statements is so fluid. Some naive evangelical leaders have casually expressed deep satisfaction at the biblical nature of *MEEA* as a mandate for evangelism. This is a dangerous effort to placate a notably anti-evangelistic body.

Even the famed *Dictionary of the Ecumenical Movement* understands *MEEA* to represent a brand of evangelism that no evangelical would identify as such. Emílio Castro, then general secretary of the WCC, writes there that *MEEA*

> makes clear that the spiritual gospel and the material gospel are one and the same gospel of Jesus Christ. Liberation, development, humanization and evangelism are all integral parts of mission.[21]

In the original *MEEA* booklet there are two types of printing. There is the document itself on a colored background to highlight it, and there is running commentary on plain white paper, with case studies to illustrate the realities of the policy statements. Often you feel like you are reading messages from two different worlds.

For example, *MEEA* offers a rather broadly acceptable definition of evangelism, including "The church is called to announce Good News in Jesus Christ, forgiveness, hope, a new heaven and a new earth," and then illustrates it. The case study is about the wives of Bolivian tin miners who staged a hunger strike, demanding more humane working conditions for their husbands in the mines. The demonstration is called evangelism, because they did this on Christmas Day. "The Name was named" as they invoked the name of Christ in their demands for justice.[22] The case shows nothing of the kerygmatic content of a gospel message. The repentance sought was for the bad working conditions, not for being sinners before God. The only ones who were deemed in need of repentance were the rich, exploitative mine owners, while the poor workers were presumed to be the people of God by virtue of their poverty. That is the CWME's real intention in defining evangelism, and that is not evangelism in any biblical sense. Their organizations' interpretations of their statements show how fluid their assertions are.

If *MEEA* represents the theology of mission and evangelism of all of the member churches (and debate will go on for years to come), then conciliar missionary activity will degenerate into social work with a religious front. Fundamentalist and evangelical missions need to study *MEEA* and formulate responses that repudiate its unbiblical foundations, along with continuing their own proactive missionary efforts in biblical evangelism.

4. RCC and WCC

Back in 1965, during Vatican II, the JWG, or Joint Working Group, was formed of members of both the RCC and WCC—six Catholic members and eight WCC members—with powers for serious negotiations.[23] Both sides have been interested in having the WCC represent *all* major Christian blocs, including the Eastern Orthodox churches, who joined the WCC in 1961. The Orthodox have always hoped that the evangelical bloc would also join but gave up on that expectation after the formation of the World Evangelical Fellowship in 1951.

The Catholics themselves have resisted overtures to enter the WCC due to their own doctrines that (1) define the RCC as the one true church (as the Eastern Orthodox do as well) and (2) define the pope as the unique Vicar of Christ, so he cannot be *inter pares* with the Ecumenical Patriarch and the Archbishop of Canterbury. (If there is a quintessential Protestant, it is either that top Anglican archbishop or Billy Graham.) The Ecumenical Patriarch of all Orthodox confessions recommended that the Roman Catholic Church join the WCC on the Council's fiftieth anniversary in 1998.[24]

5. Increased Interaction of WEF with WCC, and NAE with NCC

In 1987, in Cleveland, Ohio, this writer personally observed a very friendly dialogue between Dr. Emílio Castro, then general secretary of the WCC, with Dr. John White, then president-elect of the National Association of Evangelicals and a vice-president of Geneva College in Pennsylvania. While White gave a good accounting of evangelical doctrines from the NEA statement of faith, the two men expressed regret that they did not talk so frankly on many other occasions, and they wanted similar forums. They hugged and called each other "brother" to a round of pathetic applause.

The continuing committee of the Lausanne Conference on World Evangelization [1974] convened a second International Congress on World Evangelization in Manila in 1989, known commonly as Lausanne II. This was a global gathering of evangelical missions and church leaders concerned about completing the task of world evangelization during this millennium.[25] Enthusiasm was high; strategies proliferated. There was a strong charismatic element in the meetings and a sense of urgency that made notions of noncooperation with any missionary effort a serious problem. The "Manila Manifesto" noted that separatism was not an allowable option.

> Some of us are members of churches which belong to the World Council of Churches and believe that a positive yet critical participation in its work is our Christian duty. Others among us have no link with the World Council. All of us urge the World Council of Churches to adopt a consistent biblical understanding of evangelism.[26]

The manifesto deserves serious reconsideration as it repeats the tragedy of Edinburgh 1910 in graciously but carelessly erasing the lines between those who preach the gospel and those who need the gospel, as if they could evangelize others together. It is not a plan that is derived from Scripture, and historically it has not worked.

At the conclusion of the seventh general assembly of the WCC in 1991 a letter was presented containing "Evangelical Perspectives from Canberra" from twenty-nine self-identified evangelical participants from around the world. They did have some quite proper criticisms of the proceedings, seeking a high Christology and reprimanding the Council for pursuing syncretism. They reminded the WCC leadership that at the previous assembly in 1983 there had been much greater participation by evangelicals in WCC activity. "The WCC expressed this commitment by seeking greater involvement from evangelicals within the member churches of the WCC, promoting interchange with evangelical consultations such as Lausanne II at Manila [1989], and increased input in WCC consultations and working groups from those in charismatic, evangelical and Pentecostal movements both within and beyond the WCC."[27]

Continuing their complaints that "evangelicals remain underrepresented at Canberra, at the level of plenary presentation and in leadership of sections," they asked for evangelical representation (just as there was for women and Eastern Orthodox) within every commission and a bilateral monitoring commission.

"Evangelicals need to take a more active part in ecumenical events, both evangelicals who are part of member churches and those who are outside." They went on to explain that, as the situation worsened, "the experience provided by the assembly of work in sub-sections enabled evangelicals and those from other perspectives to discover each other not as antagonists but as believers together." They continued this incredible complaint, "We strongly urge that conversations and encounters between evangelicals and Orthodox be fostered as soon as possible to explore common ground and address differences."[28]

The growing eagerness of some evangelicals to interact deeply with ecumenicals presumably arises from evangelistic impulses, but their interaction is hindered by a naïve expectation that the uniqueness of the gospel message will be clearly maintained through such witness. The ecumenical impulse is to embrace the evangelical message as it eagerly embraces all types of spirituality, but in doing so it would smother it. Ecumenical optimism for inclusive action is to be regarded as dangerous for evangelical witness.[29]

In a growing number of countries, there are national Christian councils with a distinctly ecumenical flavor, with or without Roman Catholic participation. They are offering the governments of non-Christian nations the "favor" of screening the visa applications of those who want to enter the country as religious workers. Since they claim to represent all Christian bodies before the government, they claim they can promote harmony by screening out the troublesome workers (i.e., all of the evangelistic ones, among them the fundamentalists and evangelicals, along with the cults). Fundamentalists then have to repudiate the way ecumenical bodies represent them and request their own visa quotas and favors before governmental agencies.

6. Fellowship Versus Cooperation

There is increased carelessness by some evangelicals in defining who they will formally cooperate with, informally associate with, or personally fellowship with, in missionary ministry. The high priority given to evangelism can easily lead to a setting aside of biblical guidelines for cooperation or noncooperation and opposition of error. In Jesus' prayer for unity in John 17:21, the pattern for unity was truth: "As thou, Father, art in me, and I in thee." The ontological oneness of the Trinity, with the Spirit unmentioned here, is the model and basis of the oneness of believers. There are not three gods bundled together like sticks but a spiritual unity comprised of three Persons of the Godhead. Similarly, the unity for which Jesus prayed was answered in the coming of the Holy Spirit to fill up His body, the church, and unite by spiritual baptism all who are true believers. Whatever organizational unity we enjoy, it is only a weak portrayal of the permanent, involuntary, organic, ontological unity that we already enjoy with all true believers. Granted, there is vast room for improvement in how that unity is projected to a watching world, but we know that a cluster of over three hundred denominations, struggling in harness with their varying degrees of belief and unbelief, is definitely not the answer to Jesus' prayer. Union is not unity.

Since holding to the truth together was the pattern of the unity for which Jesus prayed, it is clear that any religious movement that denies the essence of biblical orthodoxy is not a candidate for biblical cooperation with biblical believers.[30]

The present-day ministry environment does not favor a particularity of conviction that limits cooperation among believers in Christ. Even at a new evangelical college where I studied back in the 1970s, a faculty member complained of "sloppy agape," which encouraged people to forget their important convictions and just enjoy one another on common ground. We cannot forget the difference between *fellowship* (which allows us to recognize any true brother or sister in Christ regardless of their church connections) and *cooperation* (in which we combine our resources and reputations with others of like faith and order).

Large parachurch movements like Promise Keepers casually talk and sing of "tearing down walls" with little regard for the important reasons why fellow Christians have built the walls. Granted, racial reconciliation is long overdue, but the notion that it is sinful to have convictions that keep Christians from cooperating together across denominational lines is hopelessly naïve. The issue of seeking or refusing to cooperate with people who are rooted in the WCC is crucial, as is the identification of ministry as favoring or disfavoring charismatic phenomena. When some Christians cannot conscientiously cooperate with other Christians who insist on unbiblical strategies in their ministries, that is not to be construed as the party spirit that Paul attacks as sub-Christian.[31]

I conclude with a quotation from a prayer letter mailed out by a young missionary couple who served under the mission board of a respected evangelical denomination, baptistic in nature. They had gone to another country to work with a tribal group for evangelism and church planting. Observe their generous defection, though I leave them unnamed.

> When we searched to see if there might be an existing group which had like faith and vision to reach the [tribe], guess what we found? Our exciting discovery was to find the Anglican Church (AC) to be the evangelical influence [here]. We knew the AC represented a strong presence, but it wasn't until we had the opportunity to

> fellowship with the director of the region and under-
> stand the church's ministry purpose that we recognized
> the possibility of working together to reach the [tribe]. . . .
> After much prayer, we came to a unified decision that
> we . . . should move [there] to work alongside the AC to
> focus on youth ministry, along with relationship build-
> ing and [language] study. Notice that our focus has
> changed from church planting to *church strengthening
> & transforming.* (Why build a Burger King next to a
> McDonald's, right?)

Is there anything deeply disturbing here?

1. Their work will strengthen churches who are at the heart of the
WCC. Even if (granting for the sake of argument) those Anglican workers
were Bible-believing evangelicals, there is every assurance from history
that the future will lead to increasingly ecumenical and liberal connections. There is no guarantee that the successors to the present missionaries
will agree with the gospel. Their work is virtually guaranteed to fail in a
generation.

2. They abandoned the very ministry purpose for which their Baptist
and baptistic churches had sent them to the field. They are strengthening
the very churches from which their senders are seeking to win lost souls.

3. They offer no word on whether those evangelical Anglicans are
charismatic in their practice and ministry.

4. They overlook the fact that Burger King and McDonald's *do* rather
commonly build near to each other. There is a nearby market for each,
and each has an appeal the other does not offer. In that large, tribal society
there still is room for an evangelical church alongside the Anglican
Church. If the workers in the Anglican Church are really presenting the
gospel, they will rejoice that others are reaching their target people.
Comity arrangements, such as dividing up territories for exclusive
franchise, was a part of the old colonial missions mentality. Mission
churches today hold true to their own convictions and are respectful of
their neighbors.

Where Do We Go from Here?

The burden of the Pastoral Epistles is the necessity of handing down
the true tradition to another generation of faithful pastors/teachers. If
that message is confused, diluted, or distorted, our ministry efforts can

be undone in a single generation. Concern for the purity of our ministry associations is costly but vitally necessary.[32] Organizational unity is only one of many concerns found in Scripture, and it must take its place in the prioritizing of ministry responsibilities. We are separated unto God, unto His holiness, unto His yearning to embrace a lost world in reconciling grace.

We serve the God who cried out for Adam in the garden, who was seen in the father of the prodigal running out to the shadow on the horizon, who descended into this vile world as the Lamb of God to die on a sinner's cross, who descended to empower the new body of Christ, who moved holy men to write the perfect message of the Word of God destined for all peoples. As we serve such a God of grace, are we not compelled to measure our mission by His mission, our holiness by His holiness, our standards for ministry by His standards for ministry, our relationships with true and false teachers by His relationships with true and false teachers? The work of world evangelization is so vitally important that it must be driven by biblical convictions, not just by convenience.

The current evangelical disregard for the dangers of ecumenism stems from a sublime ignorance of the antipathy of much of that movement for the basic positions of the Bible. The evangelistic movements can continue their forward impulse without selling their souls to the very people who need the message they preach. We don't convince people of their need for salvation by recognizing them as fellow Christian leaders. All of the many traditions of biblical Christians can freely work in the liberty of their own convictions, with strong mutual respect, and without compromising the foundational biblical convictions that drive them.

The ecumenical movement is no friend of world evangelism, despite its roots in the global missionary movement. Awareness of the anti-evangelistic nature of ecumenical mission theology and practice will arm church planting missionaries and missions-minded churches, as they prepare for fully biblical missionary service.

Sources Used

Douglas, J. D., ed. *Proclaim Christ Until He Comes: Lausanne II in Manila.* Minneapolis: World Wide Pub., 1990. These official proceedings of the International Congress on World Evangelization, Manila 1989, summarize addresses, workshops, Bible studies, video scripts, statistics, and the Manila Manifesto.

Fey, Harold E., ed. *A History of the Ecumenical Movement, 1948–1968.*

Vol. 2. Geneva: WCC, 1970. (Vol. 1 see Rouse.). Continuation of the standard history, a vitally important resource, now more topical. Volume 3, slated for 1999, has not appeared.

Henry, Carl F. H.; and Mooneyham, W. Stanley, eds. *One Race, One Gospel, One Task.* Two volumes. Minneapolis: World Wide Pub., 1967. These are the Official Reference Volumes of the papers and reports of the World Congress on Evangelism, Berlin, 1966.

Hoekstra, Harvey T. *The World Council of Churches and the Demise of Evangelism.* Wheaton, Ill.: Tyndale, 1979. A conciliar evangelical insider critiques the leftward moves of the WCC.

Kinnamon, Michael, ed. *Signs of the Spirit: Official Report of the Seventh Assembly.* Geneva: WCC, and Grand Rapids: Eerdmans, 1991. Official proceedings of the 1991 General Assembly in Canberra, Australia.

Lossky, Nicholas, et al., eds. *Dictionary of the Ecumenical Movement.* Geneva: WCC Publications, and Grand Rapids: Eerdmans, 1991. Here are 1,100 pages of authoritative resource material on the ecumenical movement from primary sources: history, conferences, personalities, movements, theological and ethical topics, ecclesiastical bodies and movements, principles. Valuable.

Meyer, Harding; and Vischer, Lukas, eds. *Growth in Agreement: Reports and Agreed Statements of Ecumenical Conversations on a World Level.* Faith & Order paper no. 108. Geneva: WCC, and New York: Paulist, 1984. This massive collection of bilateral dialogs records the workings of major church groups as they converse about their common and different doctrines and traditions, and as they seek mutually acceptable grounds for cooperation and even possible merger. Primary documents from WCC and RCC sources.

Noll, Mark A. *Turning Points: Decisive Moments in the History of Christianity.* Grand Rapids: Baker, 1998. This fine scanning of Christian history focuses on twelve hinges of secular and ecclesiastical history that shaped the church of today, along with reflections on major events of the twentieth century.

Paton, David M., ed. *Breaking Barriers: Nairobi 1975.* Grand Rapids: Eerdmans, and London: SPCK, 1976. This volume is the official proceedings of the fifth general assembly in Kenya.

Rouse, Ruth; and Neill, Stephen Charles, eds. *A History of the Ecumenical Movement, 1517–1948.* Vol. 1. 2d ed. Philadelphia: Westminster, and Geneva: WCC, 1970. (Vol. 2, see Fey.) The standard history of the EM and the WCC. Competent, critical, and sympathetic to ecumenism as the official history.

Visser 'tHooft, W. A. *The Genesis and Formation of the World Council of Churches.* Geneva: WCC, 1982. The patriarch of the ecumenical movement tells its history from his personal perspective. Formative and informative.

WCC, eds. *Man's Disorder and God's Design.* New York: Harper & Brothers, 1949. Here is "an omnibus volume" of four books in one of the official proceedings of the first assembly of the World Council of Churches, presented to and resulting from the assembly meetings.

————. *Baptism, Eucharist and Ministry.* Faith and Order paper no. 111. Geneva: WCC, 1982. One of the key current issue documents as F&O explores three vital issues that keep churches from formally uniting.

————. *Mission and Evangelism: An Ecumenical Affirmation.* Geneva: WCC, 1983. An official statement on mission from CWME, loaded with evangelical terminology and humanization goals; text plus interpretations, a key current issue document. It was probably drafted by Emílio Castro.

————. *And So Set Up Signs: The WCC's First 40 Years.* Geneva: WCC, 1988. A wonderfully concise history of the WCC from its formative meetings up to preparations for Canberra 1991, with pictures and bios of key persons, timelines, and summary sidebars, all based on official WCC historical publications.

Study Questions

1. What meaning should we properly attach to the term *ecumenical* today? Why?
2. How could the ecumenical movement arise out of the very heart of the world missionary movement? Could such a thing happen again in our generation?
3. In what ways were the third and fourth general assemblies of the WCC the most significant?
4. How has pluralism been increasingly manifest in the most recent general assemblies of the WCC?
5. How does the *BEM* document minimize the apparent need for true spiritual conversion?
6. Describe the impact of the Roman Catholic Church in the future strategies and structures of the ecumenical movement.

Chapter Notes

1. There is little effort to define formally the amorphous term *ecumenical movement*. Visser 'tHooft prepared a notable study on "ecumenical"

through Scripture and history, listing seven distinct usages of the term. The last of these was "that quality or attitude which expresses the consciousness of and desire for Christian unity" (Ruth Rouse and Stephen Charles Neill, eds., *A History of the Ecumenical Movement, 1517–1948*, vol. 1, 2d ed. [Philadelphia: Westminster, and Geneva: WCC, 1970], 735).

2. Mark Noll agrees with the impact of the three new movements in an excellent new survey of church history, noting, "The missionary conference in Edinburgh was, therefore, the beginning of the twentieth-century ecumenical movement" (*Turning Points: Decisive Moments in the History of Christianity* [Grand Rapids: Baker, 1998], 271). He goes on to comment, "Edinburgh marked a turning point because it represented just about the last moment when 'worldwide Christianity' could in any meaningful sense be equated with the Christianity of Europe and North America. The wave of the future was toward a world Christianity; the wave of the future was the indigenization of Christianity in countless regional cultures; the wave of the future pointed toward the Lausanne Conference on World Evangelization in 1974" (272–74). What the Wheaton historian fails to mention is the takeover of the world missionary movement by the liberal elements of the denominations early in this century, and that Lausanne was needed because the CWME of the WCC has failed to carry out the biblical mandate for evangelism because of its defection to humanization and liberation as mission.

3. The official reference volumes show that among the "conciliar evangelicals" (that is, from churches in the Council, the WCC) on the program of Berlin 1966 were Anglicans, United Methodists, United Presbyterians, and Germans from organizations called ecumenical in their self-designations. There was a willingness to ignore structural connections and loyalties to bring in evangelical preachers from the heart of the ecumenical movement. In his opening greetings, chairman Dr. Billy Graham commented, "The elements of spiritual fire are here and could make this Congress as significant in the history of the Church as the World Missionary Conference which was held in Edinburgh in June, 1910" (Carl F. H. Henry and W. Stanley Mooneyham, eds., *One Race, One Gospel, One Task*, vol. 1 [Minneapolis: World Wide Pub., 1967], 10). It did repeat the major error of Edinburgh by bringing in representatives from the very bodies it sought to evangelize to instruct them in missionary work! Edinburgh 1910 truly was very significant, but as a turning point away from distinctly evangelical missionary cooperative efforts.

4. Paul Albrecht, "Life and Work," in *Dictionary of the Ecumenical Movement*, ed. Nicholas Lossky et al. (Geneva: WCC, and Grand Rapids: Eerdmans, 1991), 614.

5. Conferences of the IMC were held in Jerusalem, 1928; Madras, 1938; Whitby, Ontario, 1947; and Willingen, Germany, 1952, before these denominational missionary boards as a body united with their parent denominations in the WCC in 1961 as a subunit.

6. The WCC Central Committee reflected in 1950 on what the WCC is not. "1. *The World Council of Churches is not and must never become a superchurch.* It is not a superchurch. It is not the world church. It is not the Una Sancta of which the Creeds speak. . . . If the Council should in any way violate its own constitutional principle, that it cannot legislate or act for its member churches, it would cease to maintain the support of its membership." Noted in the memoirs of the first general secretary. W. A. Visser 'tHooft, *The Genesis and Formation of the World Council of Churches* (Geneva: WCC, 1982), 113–14.

7. "Two world wars have shaken the structure of the world. Social and political convulsions rage everywhere. . . . The word 'faith' has acquired a new context. . . . A formidable obstacle to Christian faith is the conviction that it belongs definitely to a historical phase now past. . . . And yet there is an earnest desire for clearly formulated truth. . . . So the Church sees the World. What does the World see when it looks at the Church? . . . It is a church awakening to its great opportunity to enter as the minister of the redemption wrought by Christ into that world with which God has confronted us. It is a Church that today desires to treat evangelism as the common task of all the churches, and transcends the traditional distinction between the so-called Christian and the so-called non-Christian lands. . . ." This excerpt is from the report to Amsterdam for Section II, in *Man's Disorder and God's Design,* ed. WCC (New York: Harper & Brothers, 1949), 2:212–14.

8. The fuller comment was, "The new CWME was given a stated aim which, surprisingly the IMC never had: 'To further proclamation to the whole world of the Gospel of Jesus Christ, to the end that all men may believe and be saved (IMC and CWME minutes 1961a).' The statement was in the finest tradition of understandings and assumptions that ever undergirded the missionary movement. In the light of it, no one in New Delhi could possibly have predicted the virtual demise of the missionary movement (so far as WCC member churches from the West are concerned), much less within the next fifteen years. No one at that time could have foreseen the totally redefined goals of mission" (Harvey T. Hoekstra, *The World Council of Churches and the Demise of Evangelism* [Wheaton, Ill.: Tyndale, 1979], 50).

9. From the WCC Constitution cited in Michael Kinnamon, ed., *Signs of the Spirit: Official Report of the Seventh Assembly* (Geneva: WCC, and Grand Rapids: Eerdmans, 1991), 358. Nothing indicates whether writing *scriptures* without capitalization is intended to include revelation other than the Bible.

10. The official proceedings of the fifth assembly include a one-page summary of Stott's message, as of other plenary sermons, noting "It was unfortunate that time allowed neither for Dr. John Stott to give the whole of his response nor for the discussion which his firm but courteous statement would have provoked" (David M. Paton, ed., *Breaking Barriers: Nairobi 1975* [Grand Rapids: Eerdmans, and London: SPCK, 1976], 18). The record shows Stott's conclusion: "We are all conscious . . . of the wide gap of confidence and credibility which exists today between the ecumenical leaders and evangelicals, between Geneva and Lausanne. . . . Ecumenical leaders genuinely question whether evangelicals have a heartfelt commitment to social action. . . . Evangelicals question whether the WCC has a heartfelt commitment to worldwide evangelism. They say they have, but I beg this Assembly to supply more evidence of it."

11. Article on JPSS in Lossky, *Dictionary of the Ecumenical Movement,* 550.

12. The concluding report of the Vancouver Assembly notes, "Jesus Christ is the life of the world. This life is to be expressed through justice and peace for the whole world and respect for the integrity of all creation. . . . The urgency of this situation calls for cooperation with all others who share the hope for a just and peaceful social order and the well-being of all creation and especially with those who confess and act in direct opposition to the powers of death." The actual formation of a study unit for JPIC was accomplished through the Central Committee following the sixth assembly. See David Gill, ed., *Gathered for Life: Vancouver 1983,* (Grand Rapids: Eerdmans and Geneva: WCC, 1983), 251. The noted "powers of death" are generally the Western capitalist movements.

13. In the Canberra proceedings volume, a response document of "Reflections of Orthodox Participants" includes their complaint that, "The Orthodox note that there has been an *increasing departure from the Basis* of the WCC . . . in some specific doctrinal areas." They continue, "The Orthodox follow with interest, but also with a certain disquiet, the developments of the WCC towards the broadening of its aims in the direction of *relations with other religions.* The Orthodox support dialogue initiatives . . . [but] . . . when dialogue takes place, Christians are called to bear witness to the integrity of their faith. . . . It is with alarm that the Orthodox have heard some presentations on the [Pneumatological] theme of this assembly. . . . Some people tend to affirm with very great ease the presence of the Holy

Spirit in many movements and developments without discernment. The Orthodox wish to stress the factor of sin and error which exists in every human action, and separate the Holy Spirit from these. We must guard against a tendency *to substitute a 'private' spirit, the spirit of the world or other spirits for the Holy Spirit* who proceeds from the Father and rests in the Son. . . . Pneumatology is inseparable from Christology" (Kinnamon, *Signs of the Spirit,* 279–82, emphasis original).

14. Dr. Chung Hyun Kyung said, "As for me the image of the Holy Spirit comes from the image of *Kwan In.* She is venerated as the goddess of compassion and wisdom by East Asian women's popular religiosity. She is a *bodhisattva,* enlightened being. . . . Perhaps this might also be a feminine image of the Christ who is the first-born among us, one who goes before and brings others with her" (Kinnamon, *Signs of the Spirit,* 46). Only the Eastern Orthodox expressed their outrage at such bold heresy, often remaining outside the tent where worship sessions were held (21–22).

15. WCC, eds., *And So Set Up Signs: The WCC's First 40 Years* (Geneva: WCC, 1988), 71. After the sixth assembly in 1983, the WCC was structured in three program units, and their respective subunits. Much of this has been modified before and during the eighth assembly in 1998.

A. FAITH AND WITNESS
1. Faith and Order
2. World Mission and Evangelism
3. Church and Society
4. Dialogue with People of Living Faiths

B. JUSTICE AND SERVICE
1. Churches' Participation in Development
2. International Affairs
3. Programme to Combat Racism
4. Inter-Church Aid, Refugee and World Service
5. Christian Medical Commission

C. EDUCATION AND RENEWAL
1. Education
2. Women in Church and Society
3. Renewal and Congregational Life
4. Youth
5. Theological Education

16. http://www.wcc-coe.org/wcc/assembly/fpgc-4.html, p. 4.

17. "4/30/98 Ecumenist renews call for universal Christian council Kampen,

the Netherlands, 28 April (ENI). Dr. Konrad Raiser, general secretary of the World Council of Churches, has renewed his call for the main Christian churches to start, in the year 2000, a process to lead to a universal Christian council uniting all churches and Christians." (*Ecumenical News International*, e-mail edition, 30 April 1998).

Dr. Raiser said that in the year 2000, leaders of the Roman Catholic, Orthodox, Protestant, Anglican, and Pentecostal churches should make a solemn promise not to rest until such a council had been achieved.

It would not be necessary to resolve all outstanding issues between the main Christian traditions to achieve a universal Christian council, Dr. Raiser said, but among those that needed to be tackled were the issues of tradition in the Orthodox church, the question of ministry and authority in the churches of the Reformation, and the primacy of the pope in the Roman Catholic Church.

Despite evangelical participation in the official programme, many evangelicals stayed away from the Kerkendag. According to Teun van der Leer, chairman of the evangelical alliance, "Evangelicals are not very enthusiastic about ecumenism. My people have a preference for ecumenism of the heart and less about ecumenism between churches." Van der Leer said that the year 2000 should mark the start of re-evangelizing Europe rather than bringing church organizations together. *Ecumenical News International,* no. 8 (30 April 1998): Bulletin #98-0184, pp. 15–16.

18. The Evangelical Press News Service of June 26, 1998, Charlotte, N.C.: "'Full communion'" between the Presbyterian Church (USA), Reformed Church in America, United Church of Christ, and the Evangelical Lutheran Church in America (LCA) became official June 17 when the PCUSA approved the accord.

"PCUSA Stated Clerk Clifton Kirkpatrick called the full communion agreement 'a major breakthrough' and said the historic agreement 'culminates a 30-year search to together find a way to the glory of God to express the unity of Christ's church.'

"At a news conference . . . ELCA bishop . . . said 'out of our shared commitment to the gospel, we've come together after 450 years to say, "There is nothing that should divide us. We can be in full communion. This is a united witness we make to the world.'"

"The agreement opens the communion celebrations of each denomination to members of the others, commits the churches to closer cooperation in worship and mission, and provides for the exchange of ministers between the churches in accordance with its own polity and requirements.

"The clergy exchange provision is the key to the agreement. 'The agreement will be most felt at the local level when there's interchange of clergy,' he explained.

"[Presbyterians have been in full communion with the United Church of Christ and the Reformed Church of America for many years, working together in a number of ways]: joint orientation and training of overseas mission personnel, conversations between Christian educators of both churches about sharing curriculum materials, and talks between various mission agencies of both churches about joint projects."

19. The major collection of such "ecumenical conversations" is Harding Meyer and Lukas Vischer, eds., *Growth in Agreement: Reports and Agreed Statements of Ecumenical Conversations on a World Level,* Faith & Order paper no. 108 (Geneva: WCC, and New York: Paulist, 1984). Bilateral groups considering mergers or other bridge building include Anglican-Lutheran, Anglican-Roman Catholic, Baptist-Reformed, Lutheran-Roman Catholic, and even Pentecostal-Roman Catholic, among many others. Few are eager to surrender their distinctives, but all are eager to dialogue about deepening relationships and shared ministry.

20. Both John 17:21 and 23 have *hina* clauses that specify final purpose: *"that* the world may believe, and *that* the world may know that you have sent me." The ultimate purpose of unity was missiological, the recognition of Jesus Christ as the unique Savior from God in open display before a watching (or indifferent) world.

21. Castro in the article "Evangelism" in Lossky et al., *Dictionary of the Ecumenical Movement,* 397. Castro is the probable main drafter of the MEEA document itself, during his tenure as director of the CWME subunit.

22. See WCC, eds., *Mission and Evangelism: An Ecumenical Affirmation* (Geneva: WCC, 1983), 28–34. A parallel case has a quite acceptable definition of conversion ("The proclamation of the Gospel includes an invitation to recognize and accept in a personal decision the saving lordship of Christ. It is the announcement of a personal encounter, mediated by the Holy Spirit, with the living Christ, receiving his forgiveness, and making a personal acceptance of the call to discipleship and a life of service"), but the defining illustration is of a factory worker in Hong Kong who got help from Christian friends in getting a fair settlement in a labor dispute so came to believe in "the God of justice who disapproves of injustice," and became an activist in the Christian Industrial Committee as an outlet for his new faith (18–26).

23. Harold E. Fey, ed., *History of the Ecumenical Movement,* vol. 2, 340. At the fourth assembly in Uppsala 1968, the JWG was specifically instructed

to pursue the membership of the RCC in the WCC (p. 442), and such mutual quests have escalated since then. By 1990 the JWG had twelve members each from the RCC and the WCC.

24. 11 April 1997 Ecumenical Patriarch raises issue of Catholic membership of WCC (e-mail edition).

> Geneva (ENI). A suggestion by the Ecumenical Patriarch, the spiritual leader of the world's Orthodox Christians, that the Roman Catholic Church join the World Council of Churches in time for the WCC's fiftieth anniversary next year, takes on a particular significance because of the wide-ranging review the WCC is conducting of its activities and structure, according to observers in Geneva. One proposal being considered by WCC member churches is that *the WCC could help create a new ecumenical forum which could include the Roman Catholic Church and other churches which are not WCC members."* The Ecumenical Patriarch made his remarks to journalists visiting Istanbul earlier this year. (ENI-97-0143, 670, emphasis added)

25. Charismatic missiologist C. Peter Wagner of Fuller's School of World Mission marked Lausanne II as a watershed conference that marked the acceptance of the Signs and Wonders Movement as a legitimate option by the larger evangelical movement.

26. J. D. Douglas, ed., *Proclaim Christ Until He Comes: Lausanne II in Manila* (Minneapolis: World Wide Pub., 1990), 35. One of the workshops recorded in the proceedings grappled with some key issues of relationships with other global bodies: World Evangelical Fellowship, LCWE, WCC, RCC. The questions were more courageous than the responses. Question 5 was "The Lausanne Covenant affects cooperation with 'non-Protestant evangelicals.' Are we saying this supersedes the Creeds as definitive in clarifying who are in Christ? This affects both Roman Catholics and Orthodox." Question 7 was "How can we avoid evangelicals within the Lausanne movement creating closed networks which resist cooperation? This is a real problem in some countries." It continues, "Dialogue between evangelicals and Roman Catholics was reviewed. Many areas of common concern, including world evangelization, are apparent. Often charismatic renewal spurs cooperation. Lausanne must endorse this obvious movement of the Holy Spirit." Other such statements reveal a basic posture: evangelicals seek to cooperate with anyone who claims to be a Christian, and any who resist free cooperation are a problem. Those who denominate themselves as separatists or fundamentalists seem to be a greater problem to the evangelicals than are the Catholics and charismatics.

27. The published proceedings of the seventh general assembly include a special section of "Evangelical Perspectives from Canberra" from which the comments are excerpted. Kinnamon, *Signs of the Spirit,* 282ff.

28. Ibid., 284–85.

29. The ecumenical news wire ENI noted recently,

Official sees signs of hope for relations between two big Christian groups New York (ENI). A Canadian church leader who represented the World Council of Churches (WCC) at the recent assembly of the World Evangelical Fellowship (WEF) is optimistic about the possibilities of future relations between the two groupings. The WCC has as members mainstream Protestant, Anglican and Orthodox churches around the world, while the WEF represents most of the world's major evangelical churches. Although there has long been dialogue between churches in both groupings, there have sometimes been sharp differences of opinion in the past on subjects such as evangelization and ethical issues. (ENI-97-0208, 770, *Ecumenical News International*, e-mail edition, 22 May 1997)

30. There are clear commands not to associate in ministry with those who are identified as teachers (not just victims) of false doctrines: 2 Corinthians 6:14–18; Ephesians 5:11; 1 John 4:1–4; and 2 John 9–11 among others noted from the Pastoral Epistles. Christian leaders are to oppose the false doctrines of such teachers and not share in their ministry efforts, nor they in ours.

31. First Corinthians 3:3 clearly identifies "divisions among you" as "carnal," along with envy and strife. To be thus *sarkikos,* or governed by the flesh or fallen nature, is just the opposite of being *pneumatikos,* or spiritual, governed by the spirit and by the Spirit. But Paul clarifies in verse 4 that those illicit divisions are not licit differences of doctrine and practice within the larger principle of obedience to the Word of God. Those divisions related to pride in the identity of the preacher under whom they were converted, a totally unacceptable basis for breaking fellowship.

32. Titus 1:9–16 commands that church planting pastor to rebuke false teachers in the community by dialogue and confrontation, to expose the truth and error, and not to share in common ministry. The language gets more direct by Titus 3:10, calling for the godly missionary to reject a heretic as one who is committed to error and not to invite him onto his platform.

There are milder admonitions for those who cause disputes over trivia (1 Tim. 1:4–7), presuming that the new ministers can discern and maintain sound doctrine (1 Tim. 1:18; 3:9, 16; 4:1, 6, 11, 16; 6:3–5, 12, 20) for the health of the growing churches.

9

KEVIN T. BAUDER

A PRELUDE TO A CHRISTIAN THEOLOGY OF CULTURE

As a child, I anticipated our church's missionary conference as the most interesting event of the year. Missionaries would tell tales of adventure and escape. They would stock their display tables with headdresses, spears, and gigantic snakeskins. They would show photographs of exotic places and peoples. Consequently, I was very young when I realized that missionaries regularly dealt with folk who lived quite differently from those in my comfortable Michigan town. Such people dwelt in structures that appeared remarkably odd and uncomfortable to me. They ate things that I certainly hoped would never show up on my dinner table. They sometimes wore strange clothing or, what was even stranger, no clothing at all. That posed a mighty puzzle: I could not understand how a missionary could, without any evident sense of inconsistency or embarrassment, display pictures of Christian converts in stages of undress for which people in my town would have been jailed.

Once I even asked my pastor how Christians could act so differently in other places. My pastor, a missionary himself, told me that that was "just the way they do things over there." Clearly, my pastor believed that certain allowances had to be made for "the way they do things." But this, too, puzzled me, for my pastor also taught that I was supposed to behave differently from non-Christians in our community. It seemed to me that we were willing to grant certain concessions to "the way they do things over there," but we were pretty restrictive in "the way we do things around here."

Years later, I learned that there was a name for "the way they do things," and that it also applied to "the way we do things." That name is *culture,* and it is at the center of one of the problems that missionaries face. Simply posed, the problem is this: must people abandon their culture in order to live as Christians, or can the Christian faith be adapted to fit different cultures? This is not just a question for missionaries. It is a question that we all have to answer, because we all must balance the habits and perspectives of our culture against the demands of our Christian faith.

Niebuhr's Typology: Solution or Complication?

In trying to work out the relationship between Christianity and culture, only a limited number of combinations are possible. H. Richard Niebuhr charted the major combinations in his book, *Christ and Culture.*[1] Niebuhr summarized five ways in which Christians have tried to solve the problem of balancing the demands of their faith against those of their culture. First, Christians might withdraw from their culture in order to live the Christian life (separatism). Second, they might redefine Christianity in terms derived from their culture (accommodation). Third, they might try to appropriate the best in their culture in order to combine it with their Christianity (synthesis). Fourth, they might be forced to live paradoxically, participating in both the Christian world and their own sinful, cultural world, even though they recognize that the two cannot ultimately be reconciled (dualism). Finally, they might try to live out the ideals of Christianity within their sinful culture in such a way that the culture would be transformed (conversionism).

Which of these five possibilities is the biblical answer? Should Christians live as separatists, as accommodationists, as synthesists, as dualists, or as conversionists? The Bible appears to give different answers to this question. For example, 1 John 2:15 commands, "Love not the world, neither the things that are in the world"; which looks a lot like separatism. But then 1 Corinthians 9:22 speaks of becoming "all things to all men," which strongly resembles accommodation or at least synthesis. Passages could be advanced that appear to substantiate each of the five options. In fact, orthodox Christians have implemented and defended all five.

What is the problem here? Why does the Bible seem to give such conflicting answers to such a seemingly simple question? Perhaps it is because the question is more complicated than it looks. Perhaps it cannot be answered plainly because it has not been asked clearly. Perhaps the confusing answers arise from confused assumptions.

Suppose one begins by assuming that culture is created by God. The opening chapter of Genesis teaches that God's creation is good. Even making allowances for the effects of the Fall, if culture is God's creation, then it is basically good and ought to be embraced. But suppose one assumes that culture is what the New Testament means when it talks about *the world*. The Bible clearly condemns the world as a center of opposition to God. If culture is, or is part of, the world, then it is basically evil and it must be shunned.[2]

Either or both of these assumptions may be flawed, but for the moment one need only note that these two approaches get opposite answers, because they begin with different definitions of culture. Therefore, to find out what the Bible has to say about the problem of Christianity and culture, one must begin with a clear idea of what culture is. This definition will not arise from the text of Scripture, because the Bible offers no definition or even discussion of culture in the abstract.

This observation underscores a difficulty with Niebuhr's five approaches: none of them can be applied to culture in general. Each solution has to be applied by particular Christians to particular cultures. This difficulty leads to another question: Might the way in which we solve the problem of Christianity and culture depend upon the particular culture, or perhaps even the particular cultural phenomenon that we have in view?

In order to answer this question, we must first take steps toward a useful definition of culture. A useful definition is one that will permit us to discuss culture without landing us in contradictions or inanities. During the past century or so, at least three significant attempts have been made to offer such a definition. Since one or the other of these definitions is often assumed by those who write about culture, we should examine them briefly before proceeding.

Three Ways of Defining Culture
The Scientific Theory of Culture

The first way of defining culture is employed by the social sciences. The point of a science is to describe the way things are, not to prescribe the way things ought to be. A social scientist, then, *as a scientist* is not supposed to make judgments about cultural values but is supposed to observe and quantify human cultural activity. This requirement, however, catches every would-be social scientist on the horns of a dilemma. On the one hand, if he does not have a way of saying which human activities and institutions belong to the category called *culture,* then he has no way of limiting his study. He has defined nothing. He literally does not know what he is talking about. On the other hand, if he begins with a definition that distinguishes what he thinks ought to qualify as culture, then his treatment is not free of his own values. He has already inserted an *ought,* a value judgment that skews the scientific process toward a particular set of outcomes—the very thing that a scientist is not supposed to do.

This is the inner contradiction that plagues all attempts to study human cultures scientifically. Unless there is some definition of culture already in place before the study begins, the study cannot proceed at all. But if that definition is already in place, then the study is not really scientific. It becomes the outworking of the scientist's own opinions about what culture ought to be.

Anthropologist Elmer S. Miller has candidly acknowledged this problem. He admits that, "A basic problem of formulating theories is knowing where to look to find things that fit together. There are so many things we might observe about people . . . that to generate theories we have to focus on only those phenomena that will tell us most about human behavior in society." In other words, some leap of the imagination lies at the heart of every social science. How important is this leap? Miller admits that amongst anthropologists, "anyone who has proposed a different way of looking at human behavior has begun by redefining the subject matter."[3] This is a frank admission by a social scientist that all attempts to treat culture scientifically are really exercises in circular reasoning.

Increasingly, social scientists have been driven to admit that neither cultures nor their definitions are value-free. Ervin Laszlo, one of the pioneers of general system theory, writes bluntly, "Cultures are, in the final analysis, value-guided systems."[4] But as soon as this is recognized, the discussion of culture drops largely out of the domain of science and into a different realm altogether.

All of this underlines one of the problems with Niebuhr's discussion of Christianity and culture. Niebuhr assumes a scientific definition of culture, which helps to explain why his categories are so difficult for real Christians to apply to real cultures.[5] Jack Schwandt speaks for a growing number of Christians, in stating that the scientific approach renders the whole concept of culture questionable. He points out that under the social-scientific definition, one may speak of academic culture or of the culture of a mental hospital, but by definition one is not allowed to make value judgments between them. He states flatly, "We need a different basis for assessing the 'problem' of culture than the one we see Niebuhr borrowing here from today's social sciences."[6]

One cannot conduct a value-free discussion of a value-laden phenomenon. This is particularly true for Christians, who do not pretend that they are just observing and describing cultures. Christians intend to make ethical decisions about their involvement with culture. They aim to judge the value of one thing (Christianity) against another (culture). For a task like this, a scientific definition of culture would be useless, even if it were possible. It would be like asking bacteriologists to express an opinion about the value of microorganisms in general, without permitting them to make any distinction between those that are beneficial for people and those that make people sick. Defining culture in terms that are acceptable to the social sciences will not help Christians decide how they should relate to own culture. A scientific definition of culture leads into contradiction.

The Critical Theory of Culture

The second definition of culture has been attempted by cultivated critics who spell culture with a capital C. For them, *culture* means *high* culture: art museums, great poets, symphonic music, philosophy, jurisprudence, and so forth.

The English poet Matthew Arnold developed such a critical view of culture during the nineteenth century. He began with the understanding that fewer and fewer people lived according to a belief in God or in anything transcendent. He feared that this loss of faith was leaving the world without "joy, nor love, nor light, nor certitude, nor peace, nor help for pain." The world had become a "darkling plain," filled with chaos and disorder, "where ignorant armies clash by night."[7] Arnold thought that culture might take the place of faith as a way to hold the darkness and disorder in check.

For Arnold, culture was a pursuit or study of human perfection, a way of getting past the savagery that threatened civilization in the absence of faith. To be cultured was to be aware of and to reflect upon the best that had been thought and said by artists, poets, philosophers, composers, jurists, and so forth. As cultured people were exposed to refined thought, they would reject the prejudices that they had absorbed through their upbringing. When enough people from every class had done this, civilization would be led by a humane spirit rather than by prejudice or class interest.[8]

Arnold saw two possible approaches to culture, and he viewed them as fundamentally incompatible. Both of these approaches aimed for human perfection and salvation, but they employed different ways of achieving them. *Hebraists* focused upon conduct and obedience; they were governed by strictness of conscience. *Hellenists,* on the other hand, were driven by the desire to see things as they really are; they were governed by spontaneousness of consciousness. If this seems unclear, it may help to note that the Hebraism of Arnold's system corresponds to the separatism of the "Christ against culture" position in Niebuhr's work, while the religious form of Hellenism is very similar to Niebuhr's "Christ of culture" accommodationism. To Arnold, the only useful religion is one that merges with culture, while a religion that submits itself in unquestioning obedience to God and to His Law is a threat to culture and to civilization. Such Hebraism was so authoritarian that it would necessarily stifle the free play of ideas that was necessary to culture. Incidentally, Arnold named his contemporary, Charles Haddon Spurgeon, the quintessential Hebraist.

The critical theory of culture, as articulated by Arnold, continues to have an influence today. Jacques Barzun, for example, defines culture as "the traditional things of the mind and spirit, interests and abilities acquired by taking thought; in short, the effort that used to be called cultivation—the cultivation of the self."[9] For Barzun, civilization exists to guide thought and conduct at large.[10] This is almost pure Arnold, and Barzun is one of the leading contemporary defenders of the critical view of culture.

Such a view of culture also seems to be assumed by some evangelical writers. For example, Leland Ryken, in *Culture in Christian Perspective,* limits his discussion to Christian participation in the fine arts[11]. Along the same line, Mark Noll's book, *The Scandal of the Evangelical Mind,* laments the fact that evangelicals have lost their voice in the centers of cultural power (whether political, scientific, or educational).[12] The critical theory of culture is alive and well in these evangelical books.

Does the critical theory of culture provide a helpful definition for discussing the problem of Christianity and culture? Two reasons indicate that it does not. First, this theory is elitist in the negative sense. According to the critical definition, most of the world's population has never had any culture at all. Contrary to this theory, culture is not just art museums, symphony halls, and political institutions. It also includes such matters as the traditions, customs, cuisine, clothing, homes, and recreations of different peoples. The problems that most Christians confront in their relationship to culture are not at the level of high culture (which is the *only* culture, according to the critical definition), but at the level of lived, everyday culture. The critical definition of culture gives those Christians little help in discussing *ordinary* culture.[13]

Second, if we restrict our discussion to the relationship between Christianity and high culture, the critical definition of culture is not very useful. Arnold's Hebraism and Hellenism are only the extreme views. We know from Niebuhr that mediating positions are possible. If we reject Arnold's view that culture must take the place of faith, then the critical definition of culture gives us no hint as to the best criteria for choosing between the possible options. Thus, while the critical definition is an advance over the social-scientific definition, we need something more complete if our discussion is to go forward.

The Organic Theory of Culture

The third attempt to define culture is represented by the thought of laureate T. S. Eliot. Eliot was acquainted with the writings of the early social scientists, and he also knew Arnold's work. His theory of culture was intended to challenge and correct both of these inadequate conceptions.[14]

Eliot emphasized that cultures are organic, growing structures that emerge when different interests (for example, class and region) intersect and interact within a society. Thus, culture is not the creation of an elite but an outgrowth of a society taken as a whole. In Eliot's view, the unifying point of a culture is always a religion. Religion is not simply one aspect of culture. On the contrary, a culture must be regarded as an incarnation of a particular religion. Religion and culture are different modes of viewing the same thing. Thus, Eliot flatly contradicted Arnold's view that culture could be perpetuated in the absence of religion. On the other hand, he ruled out the notion (summed up by Niebuhr as "Christ against culture") that the products of culture were "frivolous obstructions to the spiritual life."[15]

Still, Eliot did not want a complete identification of religion with culture in actual practice. In his view, if either is completely accommodated to the other, the result will only be an inferior religion and an inferior culture. While culture embodies a religious worldview, most of culture is not specifically religious. Culture should be defined so broadly as to embrace all of the characteristic activities and interests of a people. All of those interests and activities when added together, however, do not by themselves equal a culture. They are like the parts of the human body: in order to live, they have to be animated by something immaterial and nonquantifiable. This soul of a living culture is its religion.

The implication of Eliot's theory is that cultures are significant. Each culture embodies the worldview of a particular people. Each cultural phenomenon will somehow express that worldview. Thus, culture is not just for the elite (as in the critical definition); it is a part of everyday life for every person. But culture is not open-ended (as in the social-scientific definition): culture and its manifestations are to be defined by their relationship to a way of perceiving reality. And while culture may take in a very broad spectrum of interests and activities, it becomes culture (as in *high* culture) when people deliberately attempt to articulate their worldview through art, literature, music, law, and other recognizably cultural activities.

One might object to Eliot's insistence that each culture incarnates a religion, inasmuch as contemporary secular cultures seem to incarnate a *rejection* of religion and transcendence. Arguably, however, even this rejection of religion is itself a religious view. At any rate, secular cultures do incarnate a worldview or a way of perceiving reality. Thus, the organic theory of culture is applicable even to contemporary, secular developments.

Implications of the Organic Theory

The organic theory of culture offers several advantages to the Christian who wishes to think about cultural issues. One advantage is that it helps to guard against the two confusions discussed earlier in this chapter. First, in Eliot's view, cultures are not the creation of God; they are the creations of humans. Therefore, the Christian can expect to find evidence of both grace and depravity in every culture. No culture can be embraced as an unqualified good, and most cultures cannot be rejected as unqualified evils.[16] Second, if Eliot is right, then Christians must not naïvely equate *culture* with the *world*. When the New Testament writers use the term in its ethical sense, the *world* is a system of opposition to God, and to be a friend of the world is to be an enemy of God (James 4:4; 1 John 2:15–17). Cultures need not embody such opposition, but one would be naïve to deny that they might. Thus, while Christians should not regard their cultures as synonymous with the world, they must be alert for the world as it comes to expression within their cultures.

The organic theory of culture provides a means of evaluating cultures. One can judge cultures as being better or worse. One need not conclude that every culture is as good as every other culture. To use Schwandt's terms, academic culture and the culture of a mental hospital are not at the same level. Such a view of culture permits Christians to offer a mean-ingful rebuke to Nazi culture or Mafia culture.

Similarly, the organic definition of culture permits Christians to evalu-ate various cultural phenomena. Whatever carries meaning is capable of being evaluated. At the very least, one finds reason here to approach poetry, the arts, architecture, and music as significant phenomena. Thus, Christians have a privilege and duty to understand every aspect of the cultures in which they live. Media, forms, traditions, customs, institu-tions, and manners of expression are all matters in which the Christian must become interested.

Most importantly, Eliot's definition provides a way of dealing with cultures in biblical terms. If cultures are significant—if they embody meaning—then that meaning is subject to the canons of truth or false-hood. Such expressions can be evaluated for their propriety. If the organic definition of culture is correct, then all cultures (and all the phenomena of each culture) stand under the judgment of God's Word. People are accountable for the meaning of what they do.[17]

Of course, Christians should not expect the Bible to specify the meaning of every symphony, poem, or custom. Whole ranges of critical disciplines exist to help us explore those meanings, and Christians should recognize those who are skillful in those disciplines. Once Christians know the meaning of a thing, they are able to bring it under the authority of God's Word and to evaluate its usefulness.

This explains how the Bible can give such seemingly contradictory answers to the cultural question. Paul can command Titus to rebuke the Cretans because of several cultural tendencies (Titus 1:12–13), while he remains willing to defer to many of the cultural preferences of his dif-ferent audiences (1 Cor. 9:19–22). It is not culture *per se* that is to be rejected or embraced but the meaning of a particular culture or cultural phenomenon.

Does this mean that the only aspects of culture that Christians can enjoy are those that explicitly communicate a biblical content, such as sermons, hymns, and tracts? Not at all. A Christian view of reality will permeate one's way of speaking about politics, science, law, love, work, and so on. A love poem, for instance, does not need to mention the gospel in order to be thoroughly Christian in its outlook. But Christians do need to beware of affirming false views of love in the poetry that they write or recite.

Does this mean that the Christian must reject all cultural phenomena that do not embody a specifically Christian worldview? Again, the answer is no. Because of God's common grace, because all people share the image of God, and because all peoples have access to a natural revelation, all cultures embody some part of the truth. Christians may find surprising flashes of insight in cultures that have developed without specifically Christian influences. Christians should not assume that everything in such cultures is necessarily incompatible with Christianity.

The implication for missionaries is twofold. On the one hand, they must not simply adopt "the way they do things over there." On the other hand, they need not enforce contemporary North American culture upon a people in order to teach that people a vital Christianity. To the greatest extent possible, missionaries should allow the meaning of Christianity to permeate the cultural phenomena of the people among whom they minister.[18] Each aspect of "the way they do things" must be parsed for its meaning. In each culture, whatever expresses a meaning that contradicts the Christian worldview must be rejected; everything that affirms the Christian worldview should be embraced, and anything that is compatible with (though not necessarily expressive of) the Christian worldview may be retained.[19]

These same principles apply to those of us who are not missionaries and to "the way we do things around here." We are not to assume that our own culture embodies and expresses a Christian way of looking at the world. We are not to pick up habits of expression just because they have become dominant within our culture as a whole. We are called upon to make the same evaluation that the missionary makes.

We must become serious about significance. We must take up our own traditions, institutions, and artifacts in order to examine them for meaning. We must discipline ourselves to bring every aspect of our culture under the judgment of the Word. And we must teach those to whom we minister to do the same.[20]

Study Notes

1. Which (one or two) of the five patterns for the interaction of gospel and culture, as delineated by Niebuhr, do *you* prefer? Why?
2. How do our own values influence our understanding of culture, both cultures in general and our own particular culture?
3. Of the three models of culture offered in this chapter (scientific, critical, organic), which do *you* think provides the best platform

for a thorough comparison of the pressures from both culture and Scripture in shaping our lifestyle?

4. Just what is "the world," in both the positive and negative senses, as a systemic object of emulation or avoidance for Christians?

5. Describe how religion, as a key element of worldview, drives the other layers of any culture.

Chapter Notes

1. H. Richard Niebuhr, *Christ and Culture* (New York: Harper Colophon Books; Harper and Row, 1951). It should be noted that Niebuhr wrote about *Christ* and culture, not *Christianity* and culture. Niebuhr distinguished Christ from the historical Jesus, speaking of Christ as the One who lives in the remembered history that shapes Christian faith and action. "Christ," for Niebuhr, involves a binary movement, first from the world to God in radical faith and love, and then back from God to the world, loving the world for God's sake. It is the second half of this movement that requires Niebuhr to work out the implications of Christ for culture (11–29). In the present essay, I am not concerned to expound the technical aspects of Niebuhr's thought, which would require an examination of several of his other works as well as the religious sociology of Max Weber and Ernst Troeltsch. I am interested in his typology as a summary of possible solutions to a particular problem that Christians face.

2. Such confusions are extremely common amongst evangelical writers. Perhaps in previous generations the latter confusion was the more prevalent, but the former is currently dominant. It is one (but only one) of the failures of clear thought that bespeckle Leland Ryken's argument in *Culture in Christian Perspective* (Portland, Ore.: Multnomah, 1986), 14. An evangelical writer who manages to deploy both of these confusions simultaneously is Michael Scott Horton, who ends up equating the biblical categories of *creation* and *world*, thereby eviscerating the term κοσμος of the ethical sense in which it is sometimes used in the New Testament; see Michael Scott Horton, *Where in the World Is the Church? A Christian View of Culture and Your Role in It* (Chicago: Moody, 1995), 9–13.

3. Elmer S. Miller, *Introduction to Cultural Anthropology* (Englewood Cliffs, N.J.: Prentice-Hall, 1979), 38.

4. Ervin Laszlo, *The Systems View of the World* (New York: George Braziller, 1972), 101.

5. Charles Scriven wrote an entire book to offer this criticism: *The Transformation of Culture: Christian Social Ethics After H. Richard Niebuhr*

(Scottdale, Pa.: Herald, 1988). Scriven argued that Niebuhr employed a value-neutral definition of culture when dealing with the first four types, but that he subtly shifted the definition in order to expound "Christ Transforming Culture." According to Scriven, Niebuhr's definition of culture for the transformationist type was geared more toward the *prevailing* culture. In Scriven's view, any of the four preceding types might become legitimate strategies for implementing the conversionist type, depending upon what prevailing culture one had in view. Scriven was not the first to express dissatisfaction with Niebuhr's typology. For example, see Robert E. Webber, *The Church in the World: Opposition, Tension or Transformation* (Grand Rapids: Academie Books, Zondervan, 1986), 262–64.

6. Jack Schwandt, "Niebuhr's *Christ and Culture:* A Reexamination," *Word and World* 10 (1990): 371.

7. Matthew Arnold, "Dover Beach," in *Literature: Structure, Sound and Sense,* ed. Laurence Perrine, 2d ed. (New York: Harcourt, Brace, Jovanovich, 1974), 833–34.

8. Arnold set forth his theory of culture in *Culture and Anarchy* (New Haven: Yale Univ. Press, 1994). My brief synopsis of Arnold's thought is, of course, woefully truncated (though not, I hope, inaccurate as far as it goes). Many important aspects of Arnold's thought (such as his notion of "sweetness and light" or his contrast between Barbarians, Philistines, and the Populace) simply cannot be discussed here. Readers who are interested in the problem of Christianity and culture should take the time to familiarize themselves with Arnold's thought.

9. Jacques Barzun, *The Culture We Deserve* (Middletown, Conn.: Wesleyan Univ. Press, 1989), 3.

10. Ibid., 111.

11. Leland Ryken, *Culture in Christian Perspective: A Door to Understanding and Enjoying the Arts* (Portland, Ore.: Multnomah, 1986).

12. Mark A. Noll, *The Scandal of the Evangelical Mind* (Grand Rapids: Eerdmans, 1994).

13. This is one of the matters that troubles me about Noll's argument in *The Scandal of the Evangelical Mind.* Noll builds upon the notion of loving the Lord our God with our whole mind, which is a biblical imperative. But he seems to equate this love with what is called "the life of the mind," which he then identifies with high culture (especially academe). I reject both of these equations. Are we unable to love the Lord with our whole mind until we have been to a university?

14. The key work in which Eliot developed his theory of culture is "Notes Towards the Definition of Culture," in *Christianity and Culture* (New York:

Harcourt, Brace and World, 1949). The study of this essay is imperative for all Christians who wish to make sense of cultural issues.

15. Ibid., 102.

16. One of the strengths of the statement on Evangelism and Culture in the Lausanne Covenant is that it embodies this ambivalence toward cultures: "Because man is God's creature, some of his culture is rich in beauty and goodness. Because he has fallen, all of it is tainted with sin and some of it is demonic" (clause 10), from J. D. Douglas, ed., *Let the Earth Hear His Voice* (Minneapolis: WorldWide Publications, 1975).

17. It is unclear what the Lausanne Covenant means when it says, "The gospel does not presuppose the superiority of any culture according to its own criteria of truth and righteousness, and insists on moral absolutes in every culture" (clause 10). If moral absolutes are applicable to culture, then cultures can be evaluated (recognized as superior or inferior) according to those absolutes. Perhaps this sentence would have spoken more clearly had the syntactical ambiguity been eliminated from the clause "according to its own criteria of truth and righteousness." What is the antecedent of *its*? If the framers of the covenant simply intended to say that the Bible does not state *a priori* which cultures are to be recognized as superior, then I am in agreement.

18. This statement must be tempered by the recognition that it is naïve to speak (as the Lausanne Covenant does) of Christ's evangelists humbly seeking to "empty themselves of all but their personal authenticity in order to become the servants of others" (clause 10). I, at least, am unsure how an acultural evangelist would speak, or what the gospel would look like if it could be reduced to formless aculturality. I agree with the Covenant that "missions have all too frequently exported with the gospel an alien culture, and churches have sometimes been in bondage to culture rather than to the Scripture" (clause 10). The solution, however, seems to lie not so much in divesting oneself of one's culture as in becoming aware of the implications of one's own inculturation.

19. While it forms the matter of a separate essay, this raises the question of how cultural phenomena come to be invested with meaning and whether it might be possible for some phenomena to be reinvested with a different meaning than they once carried. For the moment, I will simply state that I regard this as a possibility in some, but not all, cases.

20. [Editor's note: From the viewpoint of cultural anthropology it is helpful to describe culture as multilayered complex of concentric spheres with *worldview* at its burning core, consisting of the commonly held philosophical elements of reality (ontology, epistemology), nature vs. supernature

(giving the basic divisions of worldviews as secular, spiritual, or composite —and those subdivided as dualistic or balanced), and identity (corporate self-concept, individualistic vs. communal concepts). Proceeding outward from worldview is the layer of *values* (ethics, aesthetics), which drives the next layer, *organization or institutions* of the culture (family, religion, war, health, learning, economy, sex roles, governance, etc.). The outermost layer of this cultural "onion" is made up of the specific *behaviors,* practices, customs, status symbols, protocols, and artifacts which are the most visible and transitory elements of culture. A formal description of culture (ethnology) often proceeds from the outside inward, focusing on the institutional level and neglecting the spiritual dimensions which integrate a culture from its worldview outward. WHS]

10

LEIGH E. ADAMS

MARIOLATRY

A Study of Satan's Program
to Elevate Mary to Preeminence

The cover of *Newsweek's* August 25, 1997, issue featured an artist's portrayal of Jesus' mother, subtitled "The Meaning of Mary—A Struggle Over Her Role Grows Within the Church." Lead contributor Kenneth L. Woodward's article "Hail, Mary" introduced the subject with the following statement and rhetorical question, "A growing movement in the Roman Catholic Church wants the pope to proclaim a new controversial dogma: that Mary is a Co-Redeemer. Will he do it, maybe in time for the millennium? Should he?"[1]

The editor's choice of the word *struggle* in the subtitle seems appropriate when we consider Woodward's observation that "rumors of the potential new dogma have triggered blistering criticism from other Christian denominations and ignited a battle within the church itself."[2] Obviously, not all theologians are agreed as to the timing and perhaps the authenticity of this proposed dogma.

Pope John Paul II has strong support to proceed with yet another elevation of Mary. Consider the Vatican Information Service press release (July 30, 1998) report: "At today's general audience . . . the Pope recalled that the Second Vatican Council presents Mary 'as a member of the Church, specifying that she is so in a pre-eminent and altogether singular way. Mary is the figure, model and Mother of the Church.'"[3]

Dr. Ludwig Ott, in his volume *Fundamentals of Catholic Dogma*, which bears the imprimatur of the Roman Catholic Church, provides the

following definition of theology that acknowledges tradition as one of
the sources of doctrine:

> Theology is a science of faith. It is concerned with faith
> in the *objective sense (fides quae creditur)* that which is
> believed, and in the *subjective sense (fides qua creditur)*
> that by which we believe. Theology, like faith accepts,
> as the sources of its knowledge, Holy Writ and Tradition
> (remote rule of faith) and also the doctrinal assertions
> of the Church (proximate rule of faith).[4]

This chapter, however, will address the changes in the worship and
devotion of Roman Catholics resulting from the succession of announced
dogmas and other doctrinal assertions that contribute to a theology of
Mary. As noted in the following table, each doctrinal emphasis in
Mariology corresponds to one in Christology—the theology of Jesus
Christ. The *Mariology* of Roman Catholic dogma has become the
Mariolatry of Roman Catholic devotion.

Christology	Mariology
Christ: God	Mary: Mother of God *(Theotokos)*
Christ: Worship	Mary: Veneration
Christ: Birth/Incarnation	Mary: Birth/Immaculate Conception
Christ: Earthly Family	Mary: Perpetual Virgin
Christ: Redemption/Death	Mary: Co-Redeemer
Christ: Resurrection/Ascension	Mary: Bodily Assumption
Christ: Priestly Intercession	Mary: Mediatrix of All Graces
Christ: Return as King of Kings	Mary: Queen of Heaven

Infiltration of the Church

Believers should remember that Satan has a well-designed strategy to oppose the Great Commission. Corinthian Christians were reminded by Paul as he wrote: "But if our gospel be hid, it is hid to them that are lost: in whom the god of this world hath blinded the minds of them which believe not, lest the light of the glorious gospel of Christ, who is the image of God, should shine unto them" (2 Cor. 4:3–4).

Satan's Challenge

In Genesis chapter 3, the serpent discovered that Eve misquoted God as she responded to his question. Aware that she was not quite certain of God's command, he contested the truth of God's command saying, "Ye shall not surely die: for God doth know that in the day ye eat thereof, then your eyes shall be opened, and ye shall be as gods, knowing good and evil" (Gen. 3:4–5). From that moment Satan realized that opposition to God could be effectively undertaken by appealing to man's desire for knowledge. What about the future? Is there life after death? Is the paint still wet? Finances, health, family, and a myriad of subjects daily pass though man's thought patterns. Satan would use man's curiosity to direct his thoughts within the world system, which was and is under his control. He would provide man with answers through the many religious systems including Christianity.

Increase in Spiritism

Spiritism, one of Satan's counterfeits, is one of the world's major religions. Even Saul, Israel's first king, turned to an agent of the god of this world when he approached a medium in Endor to contact Samuel (1 Samuel 28). Today, nominally Roman Catholic countries like Brazil and France have experienced tremendous expansion in spiritism. Brazil alone numbers "14,000 spiritist centers and 420,000 mediums. There are seven million Brazilians practicing Kardecism ('High' spiritism) and millions more practicing Umbanda and Macumba ('Low' spiritism with African roots). A majority of Brazilians are involved—most still claiming to be Christian."[5]

Opposition to Missions

Government leaders such as Pilate, Herod Agrippa, Festus, and Caesar strongly opposed the organization of the early church. The high priest and members of both the Sadducees and Pharisees used every tactic to silence those who were spreading the good news. The apostles and deacons were imprisoned. Stephen and James gave their lives. Following Saul's conversion, Satan opposed his missionary efforts and sought to kill him. In Philippi, he and Silas were imprisoned after being accused by spiritists. Philosophers in Colosse and Athens, while curious, directed their efforts to discredit early missionaries. The early church was engaged in warfare.

Missionary Efforts to Prepare for Spiritual Warfare

However, the Lord had not left His disciples without instructions. Had not Paul repeatedly cautioned pastors and missionaries to hold fast, to resist Satan's efforts to infiltrate the church? His words to the Ephesian leaders were very clear.

> Take heed therefore unto yourselves, and to all the flock, over the which the Holy Ghost hath made you overseers, to feed the church of God, which he hath purchased with his own blood. For I know this, that after my departing shall grievous wolves enter in among you, not sparing the flock. Also of your own selves shall men arise, speaking perverse things, to draw away disciples after them. (Acts 20:28–30)

Timothy, who later served as missionary pastor in Ephesus, was encouraged to "Put on the whole armor of God, that ye may be able to stand against the wiles of the devil" (Eph. 6:11). Satan was not standing by idle. In Galatia, Paul admonished believers for having turned from the truth (Gal. 3:1).

Jude, the Lord's brother, cautioned all believers to exercise extreme care in administration of the local church as he wrote: "For there are certain men crept in unawares, who were before of old ordained to this condemnation, ungodly men, turning the grace of our God into lasciviousness, and denying the only Lord God, and our Lord Jesus Christ" (v. 4).

Constantine Opens the Door

Following his game plan, Satan's agents had effectively infiltrated a number of the first-century churches. During the ensuing years, numerous heresies plagued Christianity. However, it was not until the fourth century that Satan gained the opening he had sought. Following the victory at Milvian Bridge, Constantine the Great issued the "Edict of Milan confirming the religious toleration proclaimed by Galerius, extending it to all religions, and ordering the restoration of Christian properties seized during the recent persecutions."[6] Soon he issued another decree uniting the Christian church to the Roman State.[7] F. F. Bruce comments, "Christianity thus became fashionable, which was not really a good thing. It meant a considerable ingress of Christianized pagans into the church—pagans who had learned the rudiments of Christian doctrine and had been baptized, but who remained largely pagan in their thoughts and ways."[8]

The Sacred Deposit

Many of the pagan religions included the worship of female deities, thus providing the ideal opportunity to direct attention and worship to Mary. This did not prove too difficult since

> The Catholic Church teaches that the normative revelation of God, for all times and situations, comes to us from the Holy Spirit through two channels: sacred Scripture and sacred tradition. The Second Vatican Council's Dogmatic Constitution on Divine Revelation states that "Sacred tradition and sacred Scripture form one *sacred deposit* of the word of God, which is committed to the church" (no. 10). The phrase "the word of God" is used by many Christians to refer only to the Bible, but Catholics understand that both the Bible and sacred tradition are God's revealed word.[9]

The official decision to accept both the Bible and tradition as divine revelation to the sacred deposit provided the opportunity to adopt many "pious opinions" as church dogma. The recognition of such opinions as part of the sacred deposit, however, required that the teaching be elevated to successively higher degrees of authenticity. Ott describes the stages of the progress of tradition into the sacred deposit.

> As to the Formal side of dogma, that is, in the knowledge and in the ecclesiastical proposal of Revealed Truth, and consequently also in the public faith of the Church, there is a progress (accidental development of dogmas) which occurs in the following fashion: (1) Truths which formerly were only implicitly believed are expressly proposed for belief. (2) Material Dogmas are raised to the status of Formal Dogmas. (3) To facilitate general

understanding, and to avoid misunderstandings and dis-
tortions, the ancient truths which were always believed
. . . are formulated in new, sharply defined concepts. (4)
Questions formerly disputed are explained and decided,
and heretical propositions are condemned (5) There may
be also a progress in the confession of faith of the individual believer through the extension and deepening of
his theological knowledge.[10]

But what is a dogma? The American Heritage Dictionary defines it
as "a doctrine or a corpus of doctrines relating to matters such as morality
and faith, set forth in an authoritative manner by a church." Its definition
remains sufficiently confusing, however, when a person discovers that
Roman Catholic Canon Law mentions eight types of dogma, each with
varying degrees of authority: General, Special, Pure, Mixed, Formal,
Material, Necessary, and Unnecessary.[11]

Ott, in *The Fundamentals of Catholic Dogma,* provides (in descending
order) a list of "The Theological Grades of Certainty."

1. *Revealed Truth of Scripture or dogmas* as pronounced by the
   Pope or General Council of the Church.
2. *Catholic Truths or Church doctrines* on which the infallible
   Teaching Authority of the Church has finally decided.
3. *Teaching proximate to Faith,* is a doctrine, which is regarded
   by theologians generally as a truth of Revelation, but which
   has not yet been finally promulgated as such by the Church.
4. *Teaching pertaining to the Faith,* that is, a doctrine on which
   the Teaching Authority has not yet finally pronounced, but
   whose truth is guaranteed by its intrinsic connection with the
   doctrine of revelation (theological conclusions).
5. *Common Teaching* is doctrine, which in itself belongs to the
   field of free opinions, but which is accepted by theologians
   generally.
6. *Theological opinions* of lesser grades of certainty are called
   probable, more probable, well-founded. Those which are regarded as being in agreement with the consciousness of Faith
   of the Church are called *pious opinions.* The least degree of
   certainty is possessed by the *tolerated opinion,* which is only
   weakly founded, but which is tolerated by the church.[12]

It appears that the authenticity of its sacred deposit is directly proportional to the acceptance by clerics of a particular doctrine. "A point of doctrine ceases to be an object of free judgment when the Teaching Authority of the Church takes an attitude which is clearly in favor of one opinion. Pope Pius XII explains in the Encyclical 'Humani generis' (1950): 'When the Popes in their Acts intentionally pronounce a judgment on a long disputed point then it is clear to all that this, according to the intention and will of these Popes, can no longer be open to the free discussion of theologians.'"[13]

Introduction of False Teaching

Capitalizing on man's curiosity, Satan conceived a devious scheme to satisfy man's desire to know the future. It involved infiltrating the church. Paul cautioned the Corinthians regarding his crafty tactics:

> But I fear, lest by any means, as the serpent beguiled Eve through his subtlety, so your minds should be corrupted from the simplicity that is in Christ. . . . For such are false apostles, deceitful workers, transforming themselves into the apostles of Christ. And no marvel; for Satan himself is transformed into an angel of light. Therefore it is no great thing if his ministers also be transformed as the ministers of righteousness; whose end shall be according to their works. (2 Corinthians 11:3, 13–15)

Let's review some of the facts Satan used in his efforts to deceive the church. Seven hundred years before Mary's visit to Elizabeth, the Lord told King Ahaz, "Behold, a virgin shall conceive, and bear a son, and shall call his name Immanuel" (Isa. 7:14). God would come to earth and dwell with man!

"All Generations Shall Call Me Blessed"

As prophesied, Mary hurriedly made her way across the Judean hills heading for the home of her cousin Elizabeth. Before she could tell her the good news, the Holy Spirit moved Elizabeth to greet her with the words, "Blessed art thou among women, and blessed is the fruit of thy womb. And whence is this to me, that the mother of my lord should come to me?" (Luke 1:42–43). The two women had much to discuss concerning their pregnancies. Mary told her, "From henceforth all generations shall call me blessed. For he that is mighty hath done to me great things; and holy is his name" (Luke 1:48–49).

Tradition Has Added Other Titles

Mary's prophetic statement, "All generations shall call me blessed" (Luke 1:48), has certainly been true. However, many have done more than simply call Mary "blessed." She has become the one to whom they pray and worship as evidenced by her many titles: Mary, Refuge of Sinners; Mary, Mediatrix of all Graces; Our Lady of Perpetual Help; Queen of All Saints; Mother of Sorrows; The Madonna; Mary, Queen of Heaven; and so forth.[14]

Having established matriarchal systems of worship such as the Canaanite Ashtoreth and Corinth's Aphrodite, Satan seized his opportunity to inaugurate his plan. The infiltration of the church would unfold its nefarious dividends through the development of this doctrine in the Roman Catholic Church.

Mary: Mother of God

In A.D. 431, the leaders of the early church convened a Council in Ephesus to resolve a problem relating to Nestorius's teaching that there were two separate persons, one human and the other divine, in the incarnate Christ. In an effort to correct this heresy, the Council accorded Mary the title *theotokos* or "Mother of God." However, there was no Scripture support for this action. Mary is referred to only as the "mother of Jesus" (John 2:1, 3; Acts 1:14) and by Elizabeth as "the mother of my Lord" (Luke 1:43). W. C. G. Proctor comments, "Unfortunately, the term soon came to be regarded as expressing an exaltation of Mary, and by the sixth century false notions about Mary, originally framed by Gnostics and a sect known as Colyridians, were taken up by the church itself, and the way was open for the worship of Mary, which has since grown so greatly, especially in the Roman Catholic Church."[15]

Pope John Paul II Honors Mary as "Mother of God"

Pope John Paul II, during a general audience at St. Peter's Square on April 29, 1998, said,

> From the moment in which "the Son of God came into the world and began to live as man, although being fully God, . . . Mary became the Mother of God. This was the highest honor that could be attributed to a human creature.

Mary's total surrender to the work of her Son manifested itself particularly in the participation in His sacrifice" for the salvation for all. "This association in Christ's sacrifice gave new motherhood to Mary." The Holy Father concluded by extending an invitation to "love Mary as Christ loved her, to welcome her as Mother in our lives and to let us be guided by her on the paths of the Holy Spirit."[16]

Mary: Immaculate Conception

Was it possible that a sinner could give birth to the Messiah? Clerics and laity alike pondered how this could happen. Oblivious to the clear teaching of Scripture, theologians and cloistered monks had debated this for many years, seeking a rational explanation. Their pious opinions were gradually accepted as revealed truth. On December 8, 1854, Pope Pius IX decreed that "the Most Holy Virgin Mary was, in the first moment of conception . . . preserved free from all stain of original sin."[17] The pious opinions of those fifth and sixth century ecclesiastics had thus ascended the ladder of authenticity resulting in the dogma of the Immaculate Conception.

Eadmer's Axiom

Interestingly, Dr. Ludwig Ott comments, "The doctrine of the Immaculate Conception of Mary is not explicitly revealed in Scripture."[18] Yet, this dramatic pronouncement by Pius IX was and is universally adhered to by Catholics. In view of the lack of scriptural support, the following scholastic axiom, found in the writings of Eadmer, is suggested, "God could do it, He ought to do it, therefore He did it." Ott adds, "This, it is true, gives no certainty, but still, it rationally establishes for the dogma a high decree of probability."[19]

Mary's Testimony

It is important to remember that the dogma of the Immaculate Conception has reference to the birth of Mary, not Jesus. One only has to consider Mary's own testimony to recognize the error. She had told her cousin Elizabeth, "My soul doth magnify the Lord, and my spirit hath rejoiced in God my Savior" (Luke 1:46–47). Had Mary been sinless she would not have referred to her need of a Savior. She was a sinner! The Bible clearly declares that, "All have sinned, and come short of the glory of God" (Rom. 3:23). There are no exceptions. In addition, the apostle

Paul wrote, "for what the law could not do, in that it was weak through the flesh, God sending his own Son in the likeness of sinful flesh, and for sin, condemned sin in the flesh" (8:3). Christ was born of Mary, in the "likeness of sinful flesh." His mother was keenly aware of her need for a Savior.

Mary: Perpetual Virgin

In A.D. 649, the Lateran Council declared that Mary "conceived without seed, of the Holy Ghost, generated without injury (to her virginity), and her virginity continued unimpaired after the birth."[20] The Roman Catholic Confraternity translation of Scripture does not support this teaching since it uses both the words *brothers* and *sisters*. It reads, "Is this not the carpenter, the son of Mary, the brother of James, Joseph, Jude, and Simon? And are not also his sisters here with us?" (Mark 6:3, paraphrase).

"Brother" or "Cousin"?

Catholic theologians contend that the word "brother" should be understood as "cousin"—an extremely weak argument since there was a Greek word for cousin in use at that time. In fact, it was used to describe Elizabeth's relationship to Mary in Luke 1:36. It seems quite clear that Mary and Joseph, after the birth of Jesus, had at least six children.

Consider also the fact that Joseph ". . . knew her not till she had brought forth her firstborn son" (Matt. 1:25). Had there been only one child, the word *monogenes* (translated "only begotten" in John 3:16, with its essential meaning, "unique one") would have been the word chosen by the Holy Spirit in this passage. However, since there were other children born to Mary, the Holy Spirit directed John to use *prototokos* or firstborn. Christ was Mary's firstborn son, not her unique, only begotten son. Jesus, the firstborn, had four brothers and at least two sisters.

Mary: Co-Redeemer

As the sinless "Mother of God," Mary is considered by Roman Catholics to have participated actively in redemption. St. Bonaventure prayed, "And why, O Lady, didst thou also go to sacrifice thyself on Calvary? Was not a crucified God sufficient to redeem us, that thou, His Mother, wouldst also go to be crucified with Him?"[21] A large wooden cross can be seen in front of an Italian church testifying to Bonaventure's unscriptural prayer. The sculptured torso of Christ is nailed to one side; a likeness of Mary's body on the other side. According to Scripture,

Mary was not crucified with her son but placed under the care and keeping of the apostle John (John 19:27).

Ott, after quoting Ambrose as saying, "Christ's passion did not require any support" comments, "In the power of the grace of Redemption merited by Christ, Mary, by her spiritual entering into the sacrifice of her Divine Son for men, made atonement for the sins of men, and (de congruo) merited the application of the redemptive grace of Christ. In this manner she co-operates in the subjective redemption of mankind."[22]

Who Crushed the Serpent's Head?

Addressing the serpent, God said, "And I will put enmity between thee and the woman, and between thy seed and her seed; it shall bruise thy head, and thou shalt bruise his heel" (Gen. 3:15). Most Roman Catholic churches display a statue of Mary with her foot crushing the head of the serpent. The church maintains that Mary fulfilled that prophecy. St. Alphonse de Liguori also refers to this as he recites the words of the *Little Rosary of Mary Immaculate:* "The Holy Virgin Mary, conceived without sin. The Virgin's foot has bruised the serpent's head."[23] However, according to Scripture, victory over Satan is made possible because of Christ's death on the cross (1 Cor. 15:55–57).

Mary: Bodily Assumption

Four years following a query addressed to his bishops (May 1, 1946) as to whether the bodily assumption of Mary into heaven could be defined as a proposition of faith, Pope Pius XII (November 1, 1950) decreed that "Mary, the immaculate perpetually Virgin Mother of God, after the completion of her earthly life, was assumed body and soul into the glory of heaven."[24] Dr. Ott, commenting on this dogma, admits that, "Direct and express scriptural proofs are not to be had."[25] That was the last instance of *ex cathedra* promulgation of new dogma in contemporary Catholic history, but the way remains open.

Mary Waited in Jerusalem

The final reference to Mary in the Bible is found in Acts, where we read that she and other disciples had gathered together in Jerusalem to await the promise of the Holy Spirit (Acts 1:14). Doubtless, they recalled the comforting words of the Lord who earlier had said, "Let not your heart be troubled. . . . In my Father's house are many mansions. . . . I go to prepare a place for you. And if I go and prepare a place for you, I will come again, and receive you unto myself; that where I am, there ye may be also" (John 14:1–3). There is no special reference to a "bodily assumption." Mary, as a believer, will be "taken up" at the Rapture along with other Christians (1 Thess. 4:13–18).

Mary: Mediatrix of All Graces

In the seventh century, a noted difference is seen in the attitude of the church toward Mary. While not having been elevated to equality with the Trinity, she was considered of higher rank than ordinary saints or angels. This was evidenced by the Latin terminology used to define the type of prayer used in worship. Worship of the Trinity was defined as *latria*. The worship of saints and angels was referred to as *dulia*. Mary, regarded as above the saints and angels, was accorded worship defined as *hyper-dulia*. This was associated with the teaching that Mary is the Mediatrix of all grace. Ott comments, "The title Mediatrix is attached to Mary in official Church documents also, for example, in the Bull 'Ineffabilis' of Pope Pius IX (1854); in the Rosary Encyclicals 'Adiutricem' and 'Fidentem' (D 1940 a) of Pope Leo XIII (1895 and 1896)."[26]

Millions of faithful Roman Catholics believe that Mary, as "Mother of God," has special privileges no one else could ever possess. A Roman Catholic nun, Mary Amatora, O.S.F., wrote,

> Never believe, dear child of God, that it is better to go directly and straight to God. Without Mary, your action and your intention will be of very little value; it will not be worth much in the sight of God. But when you go to God through Mary, your work will be Mary's work; your intentions will be Mary's intentions. In this way it will be great and noble and worthy of God. He will never refuse what Mary offers to Him.[27]

Bernadine, a Catholic saint, blasphemously declared, "At the command of Mary, all obey, even God!"[28] Considering such a statement, it is not difficult to understand why so many Roman Catholics maintain unwavering devotion to the recitation of the Rosary. However, it must be emphasized that, although Mary is blessed, she is not the one who blesses. Access to the Father is clearly defined in Scripture as being through the Son, not the mother. "For there is one God, and one mediator between God and men, the man Christ Jesus" (1 Tim. 2:5). Jesus said, "I am the way, the truth, and the life: no man cometh unto the Father, but by me" (John 14:6).

Roman Catholic theologians do not readily admit the elevation of Mary to a place of preeminence equal to the Trinity. Its practical reality, however, is demonstrated by the millions of devoted individuals kneeling before her image to recite "vain repetitions" (Matt. 6:7).

Mary: Queen of Heaven

The dogma of the Bodily Assumption of Mary (A.D. 1850) opened the door to further presumptions. Pius XII declared, "Mary's sublime dignity as the Queen of Heaven and Earth make her supremely powerful in her maternal intercession for her children on earth."[29]

It is not surprising, after centuries of increasingly higher levels of worship, that she would be elevated to status as Queen. Ott remarks,

> After being assumed into Heaven and being raised above all angels and saints, Mary reigns with Christ, her Divine Son. The Fathers from ancient time honoured her as the Patroness, Lady, Queen, Queen of the creation, Queen of Men. The Liturgy honors her as the Queen of Heaven and Earth, and so do the Popes in their Encyclicals (Pius IX, Leo XIII, Pius XII). Mary's right to reign as Queen of Heaven is a consequence of her Divine Motherhood. Since Christ, because of the hypostatic union, is as man the Lord and King above all creation, so Mary as "the Mother of the Lord" shares in the royal dignity of her Son, even if only in an analogical way. Furthermore, Mary's royal merit is based on her intrinsic connection with Christ in His work of Redemption.[30]

After the expression of such high regard from leaders of the Church, it is not surprising that Sister Mary Amatora would write,

> We ought also to believe that toward the end of time, God will raise up great and holy persons full of the Holy Spirit and formed by the work of Mary. It is through this powerful Sovereign, the Holy Spirit will work great wonders in the world. By this means sin will be destroyed, and the kingdom of Jesus Christ will come. On the ruins of the corrupt world will Mary set up the kingdom of her Son.[31]

Mary: Expected Jubilee Declarations

Four years prior to his 1854 *ex cathedra* declaration of the Immaculate Conception as dogma, Pope Pius IX queried his bishops to ascertain whether the church was ready to receive another revelation concerning Mary from the sacred deposit. While not having issued a similar query, Woodward reported that the present pope has received strong support to encourage a papal decree that the Virgin Mary is Co-Redemptrix, Mediatrix of All Graces, and Advocate for the People of God.

> This week, a large box shipped from California and addressed to "His Holiness, John Paul II" will arrive at the Vatican. The shipping label lists a dozen countries—from every continent but Antarctica—plus a number, 40,383, indicating the quantity of signatures inside. Each signature is attached to a petition asking the pope to exercise the power of papal infallibility to proclaim a new dogma of the Roman Catholic faith: that the Virgin Mary is "Co-Redemptrix, Mediatrix of All Graces and Advocate for the People of God."
>
> If this drive succeeds, Catholics would be obliged as a matter of faith to accept three extraordinary doctrines: that Mary participates in the redemption achieved by her son, that all graces that flow from the suffering and death of Jesus Christ are granted only through Mary's intercession with her son, and that all prayers and petitions from the faithful on earth must likewise flow through Mary, who then brings them to the attention of Jesus. This is what theologians call high Mariology, and it seems to contradict the basic New Testament belief that "there is one God and one mediator between God and man, Christ Jesus" (1 Timothy 2:5).[32]

This movement to elevate these teachings to the status of dogma should come as no surprise since the majority of Catholics have believed these doctrines for hundreds of years. To proclaim them as dogma simply would establish them at the same level of authenticity as Scripture.

According to a number of Roman Catholics, the proclamation of a Marian dogma during the Jubilee celebration is very possible. Woodward further indicates that, "John Paul has declared a jubilee celebration for the millennium—a perfect occasion for defining a new dogma."[33]

Archbishop Sergio Sebastiani, secretary general of the Vatican's Jubilee Committee, presented the plan for welcoming pilgrims to Rome and the Vatican. His committee released information that an estimated 21.2 million visitors are expected to attend the special Jubilee events.[34]

Professor Mark Miravalle, leader of the petition drive and a lay theologian at Franciscan University in Steubenville, Ohio, says "Personally, I'm confident that there will be this recognition of Marian truth before the year 2000."[35] Woodward's report comments that "Miravalle has met with the pope several times and published three books since launching his bold initiative at a Marian conference in 1993. An infallible papal definition, he says, 'would put these doctrines "at the highest level of revealed truth."'"[36]

Interdiction of the Truth

Fundamentalism has long been a special target of the Roman Catholic Church. The persecution of Protestants was practiced in most countries where the Church was considered as the religion of the state. Ignatius Loyola founded the Society of Jesus, better known as the Jesuits. Pope Paul III, in granting his approval in 1540, provided them with a twofold objective, "to support the Papacy and Catholic truth against prevalent heresy and to undertake missionary work among the heathen."[37] Many governments feared the intrusion of the Jesuits into the political arena. The *Oxford Dictionary of the Christian Church* comments,

> In England, where the Jesuits first arrived in 1578, they were feared as the most redoubtable advocates of the Papacy and held in abhorrence as teaching that the end justified the means, that the Pope had the right to excommunicate and depose sovereigns, and that excommunicated sovereigns might be assassinated.[38]

Ignatius Loyola and Martin Luther

Displayed prominently in Quebec City, capitol of Canada's French-speaking province, is a statue of Ignatius Loyola standing with one foot on the body of Martin Luther. Loyola, in proclaiming victory, is seen holding a book dedicated to the Virgin Mary. A defeated and fearful Martin Luther cringes under foot as he holds a copy of the Bible. Obviously, this does not reflect Mary's view of Scripture. In the portion of Luke's gospel (1:46–56) known as the Magnificat, we see that Mary quoted from fifteen Scripture verses. She had committed the Word of God to memory. Surely Mary did not reject Scripture.

The Roman Catholic Church and Fundamentalism

Opposition to those who believe that the Bible is God's complete revelation should not be surprising. This position denies any continuing postcanonical revelation whether through the "sacred deposit" as taught by the Roman Catholic Church or through cults such as the Jehovah's Witnesses, the Church of the Latter-Day Saints, Scientology, Christian Science, and so forth. Father George MacRae was appointed to the Charles Chauncy Stillman Chair of Roman Catholic Studies at Harvard Divinity School. In his address to the Massachusetts Leaders' Conference held at Boston University (June 1978), he stated:

> The exaggerated reverence for the Word of God in the Bible that is characteristically attributed to what we call fundamentalism is a misapprehension of the central reality of Christian faith, and that, after all, is fairly important. . . . The fundamentalist doesn't recognize it as God's word in human words but treats it as a non-human product, a kind of a magic attitude, by refusing to study and analyze it as a human document. The Bible is full of contradictions and if they refuse to study it as a human document then God is all mixed up and that is not our image of God. . . .
> Fundamentalism denies that the Bible should be interpreted; it is of the essence of the fundamentalistic attitude to say you don't have to interpret God when He's talking to you, just listen. The fundamentalists' refusal to get involved in interpretation eventually results in private interpretation, that each person is his or her own interpreter. That comes down to say that the Bible will mean what I choose it to mean at any given time and that's terribly arrogant and dangerous. . . .
> Fundamentalists say only the Bible gives access to God. Prayers, sacraments, the community of Christian believers united together, as Jesus said, give us access to God. It is by no means only the Bible that does that. The Bible is an alien book from a different time and culture, different period of history, written in languages we no longer use and that must be interpreted to find out what it is saying to us today.[39]

MacRae, in his attack on Protestant biblical hermeneutics, resorted to declaring the Bible to be an alien book that must be interpreted to be properly understood. As believers, we do not deny the need for interpretation but reject the allegorical approach of Catholicism.

Ramm maintains that "what is not a matter of doctrinal revelation cannot be made a matter of faith."[40] Ramm discusses errors resulting from establishing doctrine on tradition:

> The greatest violators of this principle are Catholic theologians because according to their view all they need is an allusion in the Bible to their doctrines to make them Scriptural. The full teaching of the doctrine is formed from unwritten traditions. For example, there need only be a vague reference to purgatory for the entire Catholic doctrine of purgatory to be Scripturally justified. The same is true of Peter's popedom, prayers for the dead, and their additional ordinances.
>
> This is seen in actions so clearly in one passage of Newmans' *Apologia pro vita sua* in which, on the flimsiest of Scriptural evidence, he "proves" the Catholic doctrine of nuns and monks (Everyman's Library edition, pp. 253–4). Coming to the Bible with a full-fledged dogma about nuns and monks, he finds verses that bear a resemblance to the dogma; but if the dogma were based on what the Scriptures clearly taught in terms of substantial exegesis, the dogma would collapse.[41]

The same liberties have been taken by Catholic clerics and theologians to establish dogmas elevating Mary to preeminence as set forth in Mariolatry.

Missionary Efforts in Roman Catholic Countries

During the early decades of this century, increased missionary efforts in Roman Catholic countries such as Spain, Portugal, Brazil, and Colombia resulted in the conversion of many souls. Roman Catholics were invited to read the Bible for themselves. Many realized for the first time that the doctrines they had been taught were not from the Bible but based on tradition. Radical changes in the liturgy, the removal of numerous patrons from the list of saints, and other clarifications served to pave the way for the ecumenical overtures initiated by Pope John XXIII. In French Canada the introduction and association of the *Nouveau Testament* to the catechism in the parochial schools was but one of the many evidences of the attempt to assuage the curiosity of its adherents. This effort, however, proved to further reveal the tremendous gulf between the Bible and tradition. The editor, Father Achille Brunet, included in the preface a papal directive from Pope Pius XII quoting Jerome as saying, "Ignorance of Scripture is ignorance of Christ."[42] Not often is a missionary able to suggest that the inquirer follow advice from Rome! In addition only 347, or 35 percent, of the 992 catechism questions found at the end of the *Nouveau Testament* indicated scriptural support—a fact frequently used in evangelism.

Conversions Cause Catholic Concerns

The Roman Catholic Church is concerned over the increasing number of its members who have accepted Christ. Every effort is being made to retain them in its membership. The Liturgical Press, Collegeville, Minnesota, has published a brochure by Fr. Eugene LaVerdiere titled *Fundamentalism: A Pastoral Concern,* which candidly admits the problem.

> In recent years fundamentalism has been making significant inroads in the Roman Catholic Church, not that we have ever been altogether free of it. Never before, however, have we experienced it in its present form, where Catholics personally opt for a fundamentalist stance toward Scripture and its bearing on Christian life. A committed fundamentalism, as opposed to unconscious fundamentalist influence, is new for us. Having little experience with it, many do not know how best to approach it."[43]

Notre Dame: "Our Lady's" University

To illustrate, following many years as a church planter in Roman Catholic Quebec, this writer was involved in campus evangelism with Baptist Mid-Missions' Campus Bible Fellowship (CBF) ministry. After being appointed in 1974 as the North America administrator, I felt the Lord would have us establish a ministry at the University of Notre Dame. Subsequently, we shared this burden with pastors from several independent Baptist churches in the South Bend area and were ready to proceed.

Having requested a meeting with the administration, I was graciously received by a vice president. Inviting me into his office he asked, "What can I do for you?" Briefly we reviewed our national CBF program and asked about the possibility of conducting Bible studies on the Notre Dame campus. Peering over the top of his glasses, he said, "You mean you want to come on this campus and make proselytes?" My reply was simply, "Yes, that is one of the words we would use to describe our goal." (We had already noted campus bulletin boards displaying notices and messages from Catholic charismatic groups and a number of Eastern mystic groups.) After a moment or two of reflection he responded, "I don't see why not. Maybe you can help our students."

However, several years later this door closed when students began to tell others about Christ and how to know for certain that they could go to heaven. Their assurance directly contradicted the Catholic position on the need for sanctifying grace obtained through the sacraments. When families and parish priests became aware of the ministry of "fundamentalists" on campus, it was not long before complaints began to pour into the alumni office. Responding to such pressures, the administration removed its recognition of Campus Bible Fellowship as an approved on-campus student organization.

But God opened another door across the street from the main campus. Local independent Baptist churches, which had formed the CBF Area Liaison Committee, provided funds for purchase of a nearby property, thus insuring a continuing ministry to reach lost students at Notre Dame.

Roman Catholics Cautioned Not to Debate "Fundamentalists"

LaVerdiere's solution to the dilemma (mentioned earlier) resulting from missionary efforts to reach Roman Catholics is simply that parish priests should recognize that "fundamentalism is primarily a pastoral problem, not one of biblical interpretation." He cautions,

> By engaging fundamentalists on their own ground, we too easily slip into fundamentalism ourselves. We might outwit a fundamentalist in public debate, but our position on the Scriptures would then have little value beyond the *ad hominem* argument which supports it. It would do little to nourish the Christian community. . . .
>
> The Scriptures belong to all of us. Like the fundamentalist, we too appropriate the Scriptures and find life through them. Outwardly, both the fundamentalist and the nonfundamentalist stand on the same ground:

the Scriptures. However, denied the right to interpret the Scriptures, we find ourselves deprived of one of our most basic resources for articulating and orienting Christian life. Since in their insecurity, fundamentalists find it necessary to impose their interpretation on everyone else, they also threaten our entire pastoral effort.[44]

Papal Appeal to Young People

One of the major concerns of the Roman Catholic Church is the lack of young people needed to fill the ranks of priests and nuns. Pope John Paul II, during his visit to Cuba in January of 1998, challenged the youth saying:

> Today the church turns to Mary and constantly invokes her as a helper and a model of generous charity. The young people of Cuba look to her. . . . Entrust your hearts to Mary, dear young men and women, you who are the future of these Christian communities which have been so tried through the years. Never be parted from Mary; walk always with her at your side. Thus you too will be holy, imitating her and being strengthened by her help, you will accept God's word and promise, you will treasure it deep within you and you will become heralds of a new evangelization for a society which is also new: the Cuba of reconciliation and love.[45]

Imperfection of the Sacred Deposit

Timothy, as a young missionary, was assigned to oversee the mission church in Ephesus, capital of the Roman province of Asia. In addition to government offices, it was also the location of the temple of Diana, who was also known among the Greeks as Artemis. The temple was actually "a shrine devoted to her service."[47] The proclamation of the gospel in this pagan community resulted in a riot. Worshipers of Diana rejected the truth as they chanted, "Great is Diana of the Ephesians!" (Acts 19:28, 34).

As the one responsible for this newly established mission church, Timothy, no doubt, came under attack from every quarter. Satan sought to discourage this young missionary and discredit his message. In his letter to the church at Corinth, Paul reminded believers of the possibility of infiltration by Satan's workers.

For such are false apostles, deceitful workers, transforming themselves into the apostles of Christ. And
no marvel; for Satan himself is transformed into an
angel of light. Therefore it is no great thing if his ministers also be transformed as the ministers of righteousness; whose end shall be according to their works.
(2 Corinthians 11:13–15)

Timothy and members of the Ephesian church had been cautioned
to be ready for the battle (Eph. 6:11–18). A personal appeal is directed
to the young missionary as Paul wrote, "O Timothy, keep that which is
committed to thy trust, avoiding profane and vain babblings, and opposi-
tions of science falsely so called: which some professing have erred
concerning the faith. Grace be with thee. Amen" (1 Tim. 6:20–21, emphasis added). The acceptance and addition of extra-biblical doctrines,
that is, "profane and vain babblings," serves Satan's purposes in the pol-
lution of the truth.

The expression "committed to thy trust" refers to the deposit of a
sacred trust (*parakatatheke,* "something put down alongside") that the
Lord had entrusted to him—His Word, the Bible. The profane and vain
babblings of "religion" that some considered as additional revelation
deceived many professing Christians. Similarly the sacred deposit of the
Roman Catholic Church, which equates the progressive revelation of
tradition as equal to or as a clarification of Scripture, is part of Satan's
plan to blind the "minds of them which believe not, lest the light of the
glorious gospel of Christ, who is the image of God, should shine unto
them" (2 Cor. 4:4).

The Veneration of Mary

The introduction of the doctrines of Mariolatry by the Roman Catholic Church have resulted in the preeminence and worship of Mary. In his
book *Our Lady Among Us,* Rev. Valentino Del Mazza comments,

On April 24, 1970, the Pope paid a visit to the shrine at
Bonaria in Cagliari, Sardinia. On this prophetic occasion
Paul VI affirmed that "dangerous hesitancy" in devotion
to Mary is contrary to the teaching of the Council. Christ,
he went on, came to earth through the vital mystery of
the incarnation in the womb of the Virgin, and it is she

who gave Him to men. We must acknowledge, therefore, the essential relationship that links Jesus with Mary
and opens up the way that takes us to Him. "If we want
to be Christians," the Pope concluded, "Mary must be
our example in the following of Christ."[48]

Some time later (October 17, 1971), Pope Paul VI further defined
Mary's role in God's plan of redemption in his address to those present
at the beatification service of Friar Maximilian Kolbe. The pope, in re-
viewing the friar's spiritual qualifications, said,

And Kolbe sees Mary, like the whole of Catholic doctrine, liturgy and spirituality, inserted in the divine plan,
as the fixed term of eternal counsel, the fullness of grace,
the seat of wisdom, the predestined Mother of Christ,
the queen of the messianic kingdom, and at the same
time the Lord's handmaid, the one chosen to offer the
Incarnation of the Lord her irreplaceable cooperation
as the Mother of the Man-God, our Savior.[49]

Having anticipated the possibility of negative reaction from some
Roman Catholics as well as the Protestants, Del Mazza comments,

. . . . We here summarize the Pope's thought—we cannot reprove the Franciscan [Friar Maximilian Kolbe] of
his dedication to the veneration of the Virgin: our cult
will never equal her dignity, rooted in her close communion with Christ, as the New Testament witnesses it.
There is no danger of a so-called mariolatry, just as the
moon can never overshadow the sun.[50]

Del Mazza and the pope were mistaken. Mary is worshiped by
millions who kneel before her statue in blind devotion. Millions do not
know the differences among the Latin words used by Roman Catholic
theologians to distinguish levels or types of worship. They do know,
however, what their priests have taught them in catechism about the
Immaculate Conception and Mary's part in redemption. They remember
the stories they have heard and read in their literature, such as the following
chronicle from the Franciscan Fathers.

> A certain brother Leo saw in a vision two ladders, the one red, and the other white. On the upper end of the red ladder stood Jesus and on the other stood His holy Mother. The brother said that some tried to climb the red ladder; but scarcely had they mounted some rungs when they fell back. They tried again, but with no better success. Then they were advised to try the white ladder and to their surprise they succeeded for the Blessed Virgin stretched out her hand and with her aid they reached heaven.[51]

St. Bernard also referred to Mary as the sinner's "ladder" and wrote, "the most compassionate Queen, extending her hand to them, draws them from an abyss of sin, and enables them to ascend to God."[52] Certainly Mary would never have approved such teaching.

Mary knew her Son taught His disciples to pray to the Father (Luke 11:2). She would not want millions to be praying to her because she had been elevated to the status of divine Mother. Mary knew her Son would die for the sins of His people (Luke 9:22) but could not know that one day she would be mistakenly considered by millions as the "co-redemptrix." Mary knew Jesus would come again (John 14:3) but did not know that one day people would be taught that she would return to establish His kingdom here on earth.

Mary's advice to those in Cana was simply, "Whatsoever he saith unto you, do it" (John 2:5). May the Lord enable us to remain true to the fundamentals of the Word of God as we obey our Lord in carrying the good news to a lost world.

Study Questions

1. Summarize the essential commonalities shared by the worship of Christ and the veneration of Mary in the mind and practice of Catholics.
2. How might the veneration of Mary continue ancient pagan worship of female deities?
3. At what level of Catholic teachings are key dogmas and traditions about Mary?
4. Pope John Paul II sees himself as a Marian missionary. How has his influence furthered the cause of Mariology?
5. Describe how a Catholic person's occupation with Mary might interfere with his or her being biblically evangelized.

Chapter Notes

1. Kenneth L. Woodward, "Hail, Mary," *Newsweek* report on "The Meaning of Mary," 25 August 1997, 49–56.
2. Ibid., 49.
3. VIS-Press release, Internet: http://vatican.va/vis/dimamiche/b0_en.htm.
4. Ludwig Ott, *Fundamentals of Catholic Dogma* (St. Louis: Herder Book, 1956), 2.
5. Patrick Johnstone, *Operation World* (Grand Rapids: Zondervan, 1993), 129–30.
6. Will Durant, *Caesar and Christ* (New York: Simon and Schuster, 1944), 634.
7. F. L. Cross, ed., *Oxford Dictionary of the Christian Church* (London: Oxford Univ. Press, 1958), 334.
8. F. F. Bruce, *The Spreading Flame* (Grand Rapids: Eerdmans, 1958), 295.
9. Alan Schreck, *Basics of the Faith: A Catholic Catechism* (Ann Arbor: Servant, 1987), 120 (emphasis added).
10. Ott, *Fundamentals of Catholic Dogma,* 7–8.
11. Ibid., 7–8.
12. Ibid., 9–10 (italics mine).
13. Ibid., 9.
14. Fr. Valentino Del Mazza, S.B.D., *Our Lady Among Us* (Boston: Daughters of St. Paul, 1978).
15. Everett F. Harrison, ed., *Baker's Dictionary of Theology* (Grand Rapids: Baker, 1972), 365–66.
16. Internet: Press Release Vatican News Service, http://www.vatican.va/index.htm.
17. Ott, *Fundamentals of Catholic Dogma,* 199.
18. Ibid., 200.
19. Ibid., 202.
20. Ibid., 203–4.
21. St. Alphonse de Liguori, *The Glories of Mary* (Brooklyn: Redemptorist Fathers, 1931), 477.
22. Ibid., 213.
23. Ibid., 667.
24. Ott, *Fundamentals of Catholic Dogma,* 208.
25. Ibid., 208.
26. Ibid., 211–12.
27. Sister Mary Amatora, *The Queen's Secret* (Chicago: J. S. Paluch, 1954), 35.
28. Liguori, *Glories of Mary,* 181.
29. Encyclical Ad Caeli Reginam, 1954.

30. Ott, *Fundamentals of Catholic Dogma*, 211.

31. Amatora, *Queen's Secret*, 44.

32. Woodward, "Hail, Mary," 49. See also www.maxkol.org/mdogma04.htm about the proclamation of the dogma of Mary's maternal mediation as Co-Redemptrix.

33. Ibid., 55.

34. VIS-Press release, Internet: http:/www.vatican.va/vis/dimamiche/a0_en.htm.

35. Woodward, "Hail, Mary," 49.

36. Ibid.

37. Cross, *Oxford Dictionary of the Christian Church*, 722.

38. Ibid.

39. Father George MacRae, "Missing The Word," *Catholic Charismatic,* vol. 3, no. 5 (December–January 1979): 15.

40. Bernard Ramm, *Protestant Biblical Interpretation* (Boston: W. A. Wilde, 1950), 109.

41. Ibid., 91–92.

42. Achille Brunet, ed., *Le Nouveau Testament* (Montreal: Société Catholique de la Bible, 1959), 7.

43. Fr. Eugene LaVerdiere, S.S.S., *Fundamentalism: A Pastoral Concern,* reprinted from *The Bible Today* 21, no. 1 (January 1983) 5–11, (Collegeville, Minn.: Liturgical Press, n.d.), 1.

44. Ibid., 3–6. See also Karl Keating, *Catholicism and Fundamentalism* (San Francisco: Ignatius Press, 1988) for instruction from an outspoken Catholic apologist opposed to fundamentalism.

45. *L'Osservatore Romano,* January 1998, Internet: http://www.vatican.va/index.htm.

46. *Cleveland Plain Dealer,* September 2, 1995 (site address is http://www.udayton.edu).

47. James Orr, ed., *International Standard Bible Encyclopaedia* (Grand Rapids: Eerdmans, 1960), 2:843.

48. Fr. Valentino Del Mazza, S.B.D., *Our Lady Among Us* (Boston: Daughters of St. Paul, 1978), 71–72.

49. Fr. Del Mazza, *Our Lady Among Us,* 72.

50. Ibid.

51. Liguori, *Glories of Mary,* 246.

52. Ibid., 83.

SECTION THREE
STRATEGIC STUDIES

11

DOUGLAS R. McLACHLAN

ANTIOCH

A Missional Model

The church at Antioch was a missional giant. Its history as a Great Commission launch pad and a cross-cultural communication center is recorded by Luke, primarily in Acts 11–15.

It was from Antioch that the first real-world, formal missionary outreach "to the end of the earth" (NKJV) was launched (Acts 1:8). And it was from Antioch that the gospel first reached into Europe on Paul's second missionary journey (Acts 16:8–10). So it is not inaccurate to say that it is because of Antioch that the gospel finally came to us on this side of the Atlantic. Antioch saw to it that the Christian Good News arrived in Europe, and in the providence of God and the flow of history Europe brought it to the shores of North America.

What do missional giants look like? What shape does a missionary church take? Is it possible to duplicate such a church in our kind of world? We hope to answer these questions in this chapter, as we develop an overview of the city and church of Antioch.

Antioch the City: Strategically Significant

Antioch of Syria, situated on the Orontes River at the foot of Mt. Silpius, was founded in 300 B.C. by Selucus Nicator, "first ruler of the Selucid dynasty, and was named by him after his father, Antiochus. He had already given his name to Selucia Pieria at the mouth of the Orontes, the port of Antioch (cf. 13:4)."[1]

R. N. Longenecker defines the magnitude of this city in Luke's day:

> Because of its strategic location, political importance,
> and great beauty, it was referred to in antiquity as "Fair
> Crown of the Orient" or "The Queen of the East." During
> the first Christian century it was, after Rome and
> Alexandria, the third largest city of the Roman Empire,
> with a population of over 500,000.[2]

Antioch was located some three hundred miles to the north of Jerusalem and eighteen to twenty miles east of the Mediterranean up the Orontes. In this setting, it was the point of contact between "the urbanized Mediterranean world and the eastern desert."[3] As such, it flourished as a commercial center. Commerce flowed down the ancient rivers and traversed the main thoroughfares from east to west, and Antioch was perfectly situated to accommodate both.

Antioch's political prestige was no less significant than her commercial prosperity. In the beginning, she had served as the capital of the Selucid monarchy, and later in the Roman reorganization of western Asia she served as the seat of administration for the Roman province of Syria.[4]

Antioch's sophistication was enhanced by its architectural splendor. Longenecker paints a graphic picture of this sophistication:

> Probably the most noteworthy architectural feature of
> the time was the great colonnaded street that ran north-
> east to southwest along the line of an earlier Selucid
> street and formed the main street of the Roman city. It
> was two miles long, about thirty-one feet wide, and had
> flanking porticoes that were each about thirty-two feet
> wide. Its more than thirty-two hundred columns sup-
> ported the porticoes on each side and the vaulted stone
> roofs at each intersection, with these structures being
> highly ornamented. The surface of the road was paved
> with marble. Some of the porticoes led to the entrances
> of public buildings; some to the homes of the wealthy.
> Others protected shoppers and a variety of merchants,
> whose booths were set up between the columns. There
> was in fact, no other city in the world where one could
> walk for two miles in such splendor under porticoes.[5]

Although Antioch was Greek in its roots, it became a very cosmopolitan city. John Stott describes her cosmopolitan character as follows:

> It had a large colony of Jews, attracted by Selucus' offer of equal citizenship, and Orientals too from Persia, India and even China, earning it another of its names, "the Queen of the East." Since it was absorbed into the Roman Empire by Pompey in 64 B.C., and became the capital of the imperial province of Syria . . . its inhabitants included Latins as well. Thus Greeks, Jews, Orientals and Romans formed the mixed multitude of . . . the . . . city.[6]

It would be difficult to imagine a more cosmopolitan setting anywhere in the world of antiquity. Antioch provided fertile soil for the planting of a New Testament church that would be, from its very inception, international in its composition and global in its vision.

But despite the fertility of its cosmopolitan setting and the prosperity of its political, commercial, and architectural status, Antioch was known throughout the Greco-Roman world for its terrible moral debauchery. "The city's reputation for moral laxity was enhanced by the cult of Artemis and Apollo at Daphne, five miles distant, where the ancient Syrian worship of Astarte and her consort, with its ritual prostitution, was carried out under Greek nomenclature."[7] Barclay affirms that Antioch was a lovely and cosmopolitan city, but she was also a byword for luxurious immorality. She was famous for chariot racing and a kind of deliberate pursuit of pleasure that went on literally day and night. But most of all she was famous for the worship of Daphne, whose temple stood five miles out of town. The priestesses of the temple were "sacred prostitutes," and "the morals of Daphne" was a phrase that all the world knew for loose living.[8]

Like our own culture, Antioch manifested the absence of all moral restraints and practiced the unfettered pursuit of pleasure. In all such indulgence, it is not freedom and fullness that emerge but moral bondage and poverty of spirit. There is something revelatory in the fact that it was to such a people that the liberating power and justifying righteousness of the gospel was introduced (Romans 1:16, 17). Something new and wonderful was about to happen in Antioch that would showcase the dynamism of the gospel and provide a phenomenal launch pad for the expansion of the Christian faith across all geographical, cultural, and racial lines, all the way out to "the end of the earth" (NKJV), precisely as Jesus Himself had mandated in Acts 1:8.

Antioch the Church: Spontaneously Generated

Michael Green is right when he comments on what was happening in Acts 11:19–30:

> What can we learn from the planting of the faith in Antioch? How was it won for Christ? One might imagine that it was the target of careful planning, of a major crusade or a five-year plan. No. Or was it converted through the brilliance and self-sacrifice of the leading apostles? No. It was won through a handful of wandering Christians moving up the coast from Jerusalem. They had no money, no plans. They simply loved Jesus very much and wanted to share Him with others. So they did. It was all very spontaneous.[9]

In one sense the words "spontaneous eruption" provide a very good definition for personal evangelism and church planting. While some structure is necessary for the efficient carrying out of mission, it must never come at the expense of spontaneity. There is no substitute for the natural overflow of the gospel into the lives of people who are a regular part of our daily world. Christians who are overjoyed with the reality of the divine presence in their lives are simultaneously overwhelmed with a sense of divine mission to their world. Clearly, that was a significant part of what was happening in Antioch.

This model of spontaneous church planting seems to unfold in several simple but challenging steps.[10] First, the church was *birthed* by unknowns (Acts 11:19–21). This is perfectly consistent with the emphasis in Acts that God accomplishes His goals on earth through a variety of people. The complex and beautiful mosaic of people whom God used in the rapid expansion of the Christian faith is thrilling. It means that there was no singular mold for ministry in the New Testament church, and that God is prepared to use ordinary people to accomplish extraordinary objectives, if they will make themselves available. The result was the conversion of a great number of individuals who then solidified into a community of faith, a local assembly of believers in Jesus Christ, a biblical church!

But if the church was birthed by unknowns, it was *nurtured* by Barnabas (vv. 22–24).

> The leaders of the Jerusalem church recognized the novelty of the situation in Antioch when news of it reached them. They considered themselves responsible for the direction of the movement in all its extensions. Therefore, as Peter and John had earlier gone to Samaria to investigate Philip's missionary service there, so now Jerusalem sent a delegate to Antioch to look into the strange events that were being enacted in that city. [11]

One can hardly imagine a more perfectly suited delegate. Barnabas was "a good man, full of the Holy Spirit and of faith" (v. 24 NKJV). As a Cypriot Jew by birth, he was less Judaistic than his compatriots in Jerusalem and more open to Gentile inclusion in the body of Christ.

The impact of God's grace through the gospel was so radical that it could be seen (v. 23). So Barnabas's strategy was to celebrate their conversion ("he was glad" NKJV) and encourage them in their growth, urging them to be resolute in their adherence to the Lord ("that with purpose of heart they should continue with the Lord" NKJV). The result of Barnabas's efforts was spiritual growth for the believers and numerical growth for the body: "And a great many people were added to the Lord" (v. 24 NKJV).

Third, the Antioch church was *matured* by the apostle Paul (vv. 25–26). The magnitude of the task soon overwhelmed Barnabas, so he "departed for Tarsus to seek Saul" (v. 25 NKJV). Bruce defines this as "a task of some difficulty, perhaps since Saul appears to have been disinherited for joining the followers of Jesus and could no longer be found at his ancestral home."[12] It is likely that Paul had been living and ministering in Syria and Cilicia for some seven to ten years, having been sent to Tarsus for his own safety by the Jerusalem church (9:28–30). Barnabas's actions on this occasion reveal a combination of rich personal humility and wise missional strategy. The apostolic band and those who assisted them were always into the systematic communication of truth as the ground of Christian maturity and growth. The results in Antioch were phenomenal: "For a whole year they assembled with the church and taught a great many people. And the disciples were first called Christians in Antioch" (v. 26 NKJV).

And finally, the church at Antioch was *authenticated* by cross-cultural *agape* (vv. 27–30). The Jerusalem-based New Testament prophet, Agabus, communicated by revelation an approaching famine, which was to spread over the Roman world in the days of Claudius Caesar (v. 28).

Claudius reigned from A.D. 41–54, and there are historical notations of frequent famines during this period.[13] The church at Antioch responded to this revelation, sending a contribution for the relief of the Jewish brethren in Jerusalem (vv. 29–30).[14] Already the familial bond between Jew and Gentile, which exists uniquely within the framework of the body of Christ, was becoming apparent (cf. Eph. 3:6). The ability of the church at Antioch to manifest such qualities so early in her spiritual journey authenticated her claim to be genuinely Christian. The combination of a spontaneous birth, sensitive nurturing, and systematic training equipped this community of faith to fulfill its purpose and mission. The launchpad was now in place for a high-octane kind of ministry that could and would support a Great-Commission strategy. The target would be the entire Greco-Roman world. Antioch was to become not only "the metropolis of Gentile Christianity" but the mission base for world evangelization.[15]

Antioch the Church: Missionally Driven

Everybody agrees that the believers in Antioch represent a missional milestone. Their ministry, both at home and abroad, established a benchmark by which all the rest of us should be measured. Their ministry is prototypical for missions today.

In this final section, I want to focus on the missional qualities of this dynamic body of believers. The list of qualities that I will identify is selective, not exhaustive. Much more could and should be said about this robust model of authentic ministry. For our purposes, I will focus on only four qualities. They are unmistakably evident in Antioch and define the shape of a truly missional body.

Missional Churches Celebrate Diversity

It appears that the cosmopolitan nature of the city of Antioch was reflected in the composition of the church that was planted there (Acts 11:19–30). Doubtless, the first strategy of the refugee witnesses to Jesus Christ who reached Antioch with the gospel was to connect with the Jewish populace of the city, probably via the synagogue (v. 19). This was a perfectly natural alliance since they all were Greek-speaking Jews and part of the Christian diaspora—Christians from Jerusalem who had been "scattered" on account of the persecutions that accompanied the martyrdom of Stephen (cf. 8:1). The unique thing about the strategy in Antioch, however, was that it did not end in the synagogue. The Antioch missionaries and their converts appear to be the first Christian congregation that took seriously the Lord's mandate to engage in Christian witness and church planting cross-culturally (11:20; cf. Luke 24:47). They were capable of digesting diversity and assimilating multiple ethnicity. This was critically important in the rudder-setting stage of New Testament church history. They took a bold step across ethnic lines and began to flesh out this ideal, which would be debated and clarified in Acts 15 by the Jerusalem conference and canonized later by the apostle Paul in Ephesians 3:6. They developed an intentional and fruitful strategy to reach the *Gentile* populace in their immediate locale (Acts 11:20–21).

There has been some debate as to whether or not this act was really as cross-cultural as it first appears. Some have argued that the Greek word for "the Grecians" (v. 20) may refer to Hellenistic Jews and not necessarily to Gentiles in the classical sense.[16] It seems to us, however, that the evidence for radical, cross-cultural outreach, the kind which crosses the line into wholesale Gentile evangelism and discipleship, is overwhelming:

1. The whole context of Acts 10 and 11 supports the concept of Gentile inclusion in the body of Christ. Cornelius's conversion under the ministry of the apostle Peter led the Jerusalem church to concede that "God has also granted to the *Gentiles* repentance to life" (Acts 11:18 NKJV, emphasis added). This paved the way and opened the door for a fuller manifestation of Gentile inclusion in Antioch (vv. 19–30).
2. Stott acknowledges that the language is inconclusive: "Linguistically, we can be sure only that *Hellenistas* denotes people whose language and culture are Greek; the word does not indicate their ethnic origin."[17] However, F. F. Bruce concludes that "since Jews in Antioch had already been evangelized, the sense of the passage requires . . . pagan Greeks (cf. 16:1; Rom. 1:16)" rather than Greek-speaking Jews.[18]
3. Stott argues further that "it is clear from both Acts 15:1 and Galatians 2:11ff. that in the church of Antioch Jews and Gentiles, the circumcised and the uncircumcised, were at that time enjoying table fellowship with one another."[19] This can only mean that Gentile evangelism and discipleship were going on in Antioch.

4. The Jerusalem church's interest in this whole episode would not have been piqued if the converts at Antioch had only been Hellenistic Jews (cf. Acts 15:4–5). The inclusion of Hellenistic Jews had already been experienced by the early church (6:1ff.). What was happening in Antioch was entirely new.
5. The Acts 15 disputation dealing with law and grace, circumcision and uncircumcision, Jew and Gentile, and the church at Jerusalem and the church at Antioch presupposes a Gentile constituency in Antioch.

There can be no doubt at all. The believers at Antioch were not provincial in perspective. They celebrated the diversity of ethnicity that God intended for Christ's body (Gal. 3:28; Rom. 1:14–16; 3:22; 10:12; Eph. 2:14; Col. 3:11), and their missional strategy demonstrated it. Pride of race, language, or culture must never be allowed to shut down the urgent biblical evangelism that is mandated by Jesus on behalf of all the people groups of the world.

Missional Churches Manifest Unity

The church at Antioch demonstrated an amazing familial unity in the midst of rich interpersonal diversity (Acts 13:1–3). The unity seems to surface in two ways.

First, the ability of the leadership of this church to connect and serve together harmoniously is a reflection of Spirit-induced missional oneness. I have always appreciated Michael Green's analysis of this ministry team:

> They had Barnabas, a Cypriot landowner and Levite; Simeon, nicknamed "the swarthy," who was clearly black; Lucius from Cyrene in North Africa, who was probably black too; Manaen, one of the intimates of the Herod family, and therefore very much an aristocrat; and a fiery intellectual from Tarsus by the name of Saul. I do not imagine it was very easy for this lot to live together in peace.[20]

This can only mean that they had been richly endowed with the superabundant quality of interpersonal *agapé* (Rom. 5:5; Gal. 5:22).

Barnabas and Saul are well known to us, but we know very little for certain of Simeon Niger, Lucius of Cyrene, and Manaen. Simeon's Latin surname, Niger, clearly identifies him as a black man.

It is tempting to identify him with Simon of Cyrene, who was made to carry Jesus' cross on the way to the place of execution, but Luke does not suggest the identification, although he mentions Simon in his passion narrative (Luke 23:26); moreover, it is Lucius, not Simeon, who is here called the Cyrenaen.[21]

Not much more is known of Lucius of Cyrene. Some have sought to define this as a veiled reference to Luke himself, who may very well have been indigenous to Antioch and perhaps one of its original converts. Evidence to justify such a connection, however, is completely inadequate. I believe Stott is correct when he writes, "The conjecture of some early church fathers that Luke was referring to himself is extremely improbable, since he carefully preserves his anonymity throughout the book."[22] Doubtless, Lucius was one of the Cyrenaens who formed the original band of refugee witnesses who had planted the church in Antioch (cf. 11:20). As for Manaen, we know only that he was "brought up with Herod the tetrarch." The term translated "brought up" is *syntrophos*. It describes someone who is "a companion in education, playmate, intimate friend.[23] The various lexical aids suggest that this term can mean "foster brother," and that it "was given to boys of the same age as royal princes, who were taken to court to be brought up with them."[24] Others suggest that *syntrophos* "literally referred to someone suckled by the same nurse as a baby. Later it came to mean someone 'reared together' with someone."[25] The Herod to whom Luke refers is "Herod Antipas, youngest son of Herod the Great, who ruled Galilee and Peraea as tetrarch from 4 B.C. to A.D. 39."[26] More than all the other authors of the Gospels, Luke seems to have the most intimate knowledge of the Herod family. Very likely it was Manaen who supplied him with his inside information.

F. F. Bruce's comment regarding Manaen and Herod Antipas is stimulating:

> What a commentary on the mystery and sovereignty of divine grace that, of these two boys who were brought up together, one should attain honor as a Christian leader, while the other should be best remembered for his inglorious behavior in the killing of John the Baptist and in the trial of Jesus![27]

How could five men so radically different from one another possibly get along with each other? How could they minister and live together under the common umbrella of one church in peace and harmony? While little may be known of the particular roots and backgrounds of some of these leaders, what is perfectly clear is that none of them behaved as a prima donna. There was none of that smallness of soul that spends its time belittling others while boasting of itself. Among the dynamic leaders of the Antioch church, self-promotion was wholly absent and self-abnegation was fully present. These are always the hallmarks of authentic, biblical love, and they define the shape of missional leaders and their churches.

But what was true of the leadership at Antioch was true, secondly, of the general populace of the church. The unity of the body was not only modeled in the familial oneness of its leadership but also in the body's apparently unanimous and obedient response to the Spirit's sovereign selection of Paul and Barnabas for missionary work (13:2–3). No strident voices are raised in opposition to this directive from God, given no doubt through one of the "prophet-teachers" who formed the leadership team. Even though obedience to such a directive would ensure for the church a certain level of deprivation due to the absence of its most prominent teachers, there is every evidence that its individual believers were in unity with God and in harmony with one another when it came to this most significant contribution to Christ's cause. Without exception, this is the shape a missional people take. Irreconcilable differences within the body always shut down any attempt to fulfill our ministry of reconciliation to our fractured and alienated world (cf. 2 Cor. 5:18–21). No such differences plagued the church at Antioch.

Missional Churches Anchor to Theology

The commitment of Antioch to absolute truth and biblical theology becomes apparent first in the systematic discipleship that was evident in the ministries of Paul and Barnabas. The net result of Barnabas's journey to Tarsus was the rediscovery and eventual employment of Saul in the ministry at Antioch. Together they formed a part of the ministry team in the church, whose members were defined as "prophet-teachers." Polhill is correct in affirming that, "The gift of prophecy can be that of foretelling future events, as with Agabus (Acts 11:27). More often it is that of speaking an inspired word from God for the edification and direction of the community."[28] The words of the prophets were the voice of God and were written down in the pages of Scripture. It is obvious from the entire context in Acts that, as the prophet-teachers exercised their giftedness as mediators of God's truths, the believers in Antioch took what was being said very seriously. They listened carefully and respectfully and responded obediently to God's Word. Clearly, there was no thinning of theology going on in Antioch. This was a church that was absolutely loyal to absolute truth. Before Barnabas and Saul left on their first missionary journey, Luke describes their ministry in this way: "So it was that for a whole year they assembled with the church and taught a great many people . . ." (11:26 NKJV). And following the successful completion of their first journey, and their special conference in Jerusalem, Luke says again, "Paul and Barnabas also remained in Antioch, teaching and preaching the word of the Lord, with many others also" (15:35 NKJV).

Jesus Himself had taught that truth was the only agent that could effect liberation and transformation (John 8:32; 17:17). Perhaps the most profound evidence that the theology of the New Testament, the absoluteness of its truth-claims, had worked its liberation and transformation in Antioch is Luke's claim that "the disciples were first called Christians in Antioch" (Acts 11:26 NKJV). Contextually, this phenomenon is the direct result of the year-long communication of truth by Barnabas and Saul. Stott is probably right to say that

> Now it seems to have been the unbelieving public of Antioch, famed for their wit in nicknaming skill, who . . . coined the epithet *Christianoi*. . . . Although it does not seem to have caught on initially, since elsewhere it appears only twice in the New Testament (Acts 26:28; 1 Peter 4:16), it at least emphasized the Christ-centered nature of discipleship. . . . It marked out the disciples as being above all . . . the followers, the servants of Christ.[29]

But Antioch's commitment to absolute truth and biblical theology can be seen in a second way. It was the church at Antioch that took the initiative in finding a solution to the weighty theological disputation between law and grace in Acts 15. This was a watershed issue, a blockbuster theological debate, which could have shattered for all time the Christian household of faith had it been processed wrongly. When Luke records that "*they* determined that Paul and Barnabas and certain others *of them* should go up to Jerusalem, to the apostles and elders, about this question," there can be no doubt that he is referring to the Antioch congregation as a whole, for he goes on to say, "So, being sent on their way *by the church* . . ." (Acts 15:2–3 NKJV, emphasis added). These were people who cared about precision in theology and accuracy in their understanding of the gospel. And they were prepared to take whatever steps were necessary in order to define accurately, defend courageously, and declare lovingly the rich content of God's Word.

Their model bears special relevance for modern mission work. The world of today does not simply passively ignore truth, it actively assaults it. At the heart of postmodernity is the rejection of the existence of the absolute—an outright denial of truth. Evidence mounts that this perspective controls not only the secular academy but, almost unbelievably, huge segments of concessive evangelicalism as well.[30] In the modern world, and in particular in the theological milieu, there is a desperate need for passionate truth-bases, that is, New Testament local churches that remain absolutely loyal to absolute truth. This is the shape that effective missional ministries always take.

Missional Churches Evidence Spirituality

The spiritual disciplines and devotion that surface in Acts 13:1–3 all point to a spiritually-minded body of believers. Very clearly, "the Antioch Christians are at worship (13:2). They are concentrating on the Lord, adoring Him. The Greek suggests that they were 'holding liturgy' to the Lord. They were serious about it, so serious that they gave themselves to fasting."[31] Luke's word for serving or worshiping in verse 2 is *leitourgeo*. In antiquity it described a worship and service that came at great personal cost to the participant. There is in it a nuance of sacrifice, as there is in the other key components of worship that are evident here: fasting and prayer (vv. 2–3). The believers at Antioch were prepared to say "no" to themselves in very disciplined and sacrificial ways so that they could say "yes" to God when He spoke and "yes" to others who had needs.

It should come as no surprise that a call to mission grew out of a context of worship. Worship is a high-octane activity, a high-energy event, a high-voltage experience. In authentic and passionate Christian worship, our connection with God is firsthand and immediate, having both an inspirational and a transformational impact on our lives. We always go away from that connection changed and challenged. Worship is unique in that it is an engine and not a caboose, a drive-mechanism and not a trailing vehicle. Worship is the cause; everything else is an effect—including urgent biblical evangelism and global mission. When you love God you begin loving what God loves. God loves lost souls. In fact, He loves a lost world—and He gave Himself for it when He gave "His only begotten Son" (John 3:16 NKJV). When God is worshiped rightly, Christians are driven to taking risks and doing unthinkable things. Like Jesus Christ, who accomplished the Atonement through His loving sacrifice of Himself, Christians now announce the Atonement through the loving sacrifice of themselves. He died sacrificially to achieve it; we live sacrificially to proclaim it. There is a sense in which our whole faith-manifesting, love-exhibiting, risk-taking life is nothing other than a liturgy, an act of high-octane, high-energy, high-voltage worship issuing in high-impact service and outreach. In our day, we need to recover the reality of such worship if we ever hope to fulfill our mission in our generation.

It is important to affirm that authentic worship is anchored to truth, and truth was undeniably present in the Antioch church. Passion in worship must always be supported and directed by reverence for God and, along with His truth, reverence was also undeniably present in the Antioch church. It was the Holy Spirit who connected with this spiritually minded, worshiping body of believers, and it was the Holy Word—probably mediated through one of the prophet-teachers—that gave direction to the body: "As they ministered to the Lord and fasted, the Holy Spirit said, 'Now separate to Me Barnabas and Saul for the work to which I have called them'" (Acts 13:2 NKJV). The reason we must emphasize a worship and a spirituality that are truth-based is because so much of the evangelical world is severing this natural and biblical connection. Stanley Grenz is among of evangelical theologians who are drifting toward a New Age-like spirituality. In his book *Revisioning Evangelical Theology,* Grenz argues that we should shift from a "creed-based" evangelicalism to a "spirituality-based" postmodern evangelicalism. He says, "In recent years we have begun to shift the focus of our attention away from doctrine, with its focus on propositional truth in favor of a renewed interest in what constitutes the uniquely evangelical vision of spirituality."[32] I agree with Albert Mohler's critique of such a view. He says,

> Grenz would liberate evangelicalism from propositional truth so that 'a uniquely evangelical vision of spirituality may flourish.' But without doctrine, without propositional truth, without the truth of God's Word, the vision of spirituality may indeed be unique but it cannot be evangelical.[33]

In Antioch, the disciples' vision of spirituality and their act of worship were grounded, not in feel-good experiences that were severed from truth, but in the exaltation of God, which was anchored to, supported, and directed by the exegesis and the exposition of truth. For them, God Himself was the central figure, the critical component, the ground and support, the beginning and end, the sum and substance, the center and core, the turbo-charged energy source that was driving the life and ministry of that missional body. Their biblically based spirituality spawned effective service, and their God-honoring worship birthed global witness. Productive missional bases always look like that!

Conclusion

If we were all honest, we would acknowledge that there are not many churches in our twenty-first century Western civilization like the community of faith at Antioch. All the more reason to aspire to such an ideal. Here was a church planted in one of the most cosmopolitan cities of the first-century world. It was a church that had experienced a spontaneous birth at the hands of refugee witnesses expelled from Jerusalem. Moreover, that church had developed under the influence of sensitive nurturing from Barnabas and systematic training from Paul and others of the prophet-teachers, whom God in His sovereignty had placed there.

The net result was a robust and dynamic body of believers who were upward looking and outward reaching. In their celebration of diversity, their manifestation of unity, their exaltation of theology, and their demonstration of spirituality, they modeled for us the kind of Christians we should be and the kind of churches we should plant and grow. I challenge us all to probe more deeply the nuances of Antioch's missional qualities—including the ones we could not mention here—and to practice them more authentically ourselves and in our churches. Then, perhaps once again, a vision for and commitment to world evangelization will break out among the people of God.

Study Questions

1. How did the commercial and political significance of ancient Antioch enhance its influence as a missional sending center?
2. Summarize the phases of apostolic impact that shaped the infant church in Antioch.
3. Explain how the ethnic diversity within the Antioch congregation amplified its suitability as a launching site for international ministry.
4. What does the Antioch experience teach us about the interactivity of sound doctrine and sound missiology?

5. Describe how outreach is to be driven by worship, as modeled by the church in Antioch.

Chapter Notes

1. F. F. Bruce, *The Book of Acts,* rev. ed. (Grand Rapids: Eerdmans, 1998), 224.

2. R. N. Longenecker, "Antioch of Syria," in *Major Cities of the Biblical World,* ed. R. K. Harrison (Nashville: Nelson, 1985), 9.

3. Bruce, *Book of Acts,* 224.

4. Ibid.

5. Longenecker, "Antioch of Syria," 13–14.

6. John R. W. Stott, *The Spirit, the Church and the World* (Downers Grove, Ill.: InterVarsity, 1990), 203.

7. Bruce, *Book of Acts,* 224.

8. William Barclay, *Ambassador for Christ* (Valley Forge: Judson, 1973), 64.

9. Michael Green, *Evangelism Through the Local Church* (Nashville: Nelson, 1992), 87.

10. Cf. Stott, *The Spirit, the Church and the World,* 201–6, who provides the stimulus for this development.

11. Bruce, *Book of Acts,* 225.

12. Ibid., 227. Cf. his footnote, no. 30.

13. Homer A. Kent Jr., *Jerusalem to Rome* (Grand Rapids: Baker, 1972), 99–100.

14. Bruce, *Book of Acts,* 230. Here Bruce says: "We know that Judea did in fact suffer severely from a famine at some point between A.D. 45 and 48. At that time Helena, queen-mother of Adiabene, a Jewish proselyte, bought grain in Egypt and figs in Cyprus and had them taken to Jerusalem for distribution, while her son King Isates sent a large sum of money to the authorities in Jerusalem for famine relief. The church of Antioch similarly organized a relief fund for the mother-church."

15. Bruce, *Book of Acts,* 225.

16. See Stott's discussion of this, *The Spirit, the Church and the World,* 201–3.

17. Stott, *The Spirit, the Church and the World,* 202.

18. Bruce, *Book of Acts,* 223.

19. Stott, *The Spirit, the Church and the World,* 203.

20. Michael Green, *Evangelism Now and Then* (Downers Grove, Ill.: InterVarsity, 1979), 39.

21. Bruce, *Book of Acts,* 244–45.

22. Stott, *The Spirit, the Church and the World,* 216.

23. Fritz Reinecker and Cleon Rogers, *A Linguistic Key to the Greek New Testament* (Grand Rapids: Zondervan, 1980), 291.

24. Bruce, *Book of Acts,* 245.
25. John B. Polhill, *Acts,* in The New American Commentary (Nashville: Broadman, 1992), 289.
26. Bruce, *Book of Acts,* 245.
27. Ibid.
28. Polhill, *Acts,* 289.
29. Stott, *The Spirit, the Church and the World,* 205.
30. cf. John H. Armstrong, ed., *The Coming Evangelical Crisis* (Chicago: Moody, 1993); and James Montgomery Boice and Benjamin E. Sasse, eds., *Here We Stand* (Grand Rapids: Baker, 1996).
31. Green, *Evangelism Now and Then,* 43.
32. Stanley Grenz, *Revisioning Evangelical Theology* (Downers Grove, Ill.: InterVarsity, 1993), 56–57.
33. Albert Mohler, "Contending for Truth in an Age of Anti-Truth," in *Here We Stand,* 55. [Editor's note: This shift is a rerun of one a few generations back in which Friedrich Schleiermacher, son and grandson of leading Pietist pastors of deep spirituality, came to be known as "the father of modernism." Passionate godliness based on biblical doctrine morphed into passionate spirituality loosed from the moorings of Bible truth. This soon spiraled downward into man-centered churchianity, and modernism turned great evangelical denominations into spiritual deserts by the beginning of the twentieth century. WHS]

12

JOHN E. STAUFFACHER

EVANGELISTIC METHODS USED BY BAPTISTS AND ANABAPTISTS

What is the difference between seeing an event on film and witnessing an event in person? One difference is that witnessing involves the whole person. In New Testament usage, *martus* denotes one who can confirm facts or give information about something. But the same word applies to those who suffer death as a consequence of their testimony for Christ, who is Himself called "the faithful witness" (Rev. 1:5).

The notion of witness in our day has fallen upon bad times. Dozens of bystanders see an accident or a crime take place. Unwilling to bear testimony, they all disappear. Even in Christian circles, in which we speak so highly and constantly of deep commitment to Christ, we are often content simply with words, or a role, or an appearance of involvement. True witnesses are concerned about truth and facts. But they are burdened with something more—an intimate value judgment about those facts. They are willing to die to affirm the message. True witnesses must know and love the Person of whom they witness, for without love, Christian testimony shrivels into fanaticism or a mechanical exercise. And just as human affection manifests itself in many different ways, so love for Christ expresses itself in new trends and creative directions. But in the end, the methods count for little; it is the love and passion for Him that make the impact. The short glimpses this chapter gives of Anabaptist and Baptist witnessing illustrate this truth.

Anabaptist Evangelism

From January 21, 1525, the moment that the Zurich "radicals" de-cided to break with Zwingli and establish a believers' church by practicing believers' baptism in Thomas Manz's house, the program of the "Anabaptist" Christians was evangelism. No Bible text was more frequently cited in confessions of faith and in court testimonies than Matthew 28.[1] The story of the brutal repression of their revival movement is often ig-nored, played down, or unappreciated. They remain an embarrassment to tranquil Christendom. For four centuries, people have relied on the polemics of Luther, Calvin, and Bullinger for their opinion of the Anabaptists. Neither Roman Catholic nor Protestant authorities have yet pronounced any formal apologies to the descendants of the lowly Anabaptists whom they drowned, burned, and tortured by the thousands.

Successful Evangelism. The rapid extension and heroic resistance of Anabaptists prove that their evangelism was uncommonly successful. Curiously, their methods were not spectacular and, for the most part, consisted of nothing more than *functioning as assemblies of believers* organized along the lines of the New Testament—worshiping wherever they could; baptizing genuine believers; observing the Lord's Supper in sincerity and simplicity, often in a home setting. The martyr churches themselves, functioning according to the New Testament pattern, be-came "the method," the powerful spiritual magnet that drew people from all ranks of society to experience salvation in Christ and to bear the cross for Him. In spite of excesses, occasional moral failures, and some doctrinal errors that appeared in the decades after 1525, the biblical Anabaptists were a manifestation of genuine spiritual revival.[2]

Conventicles. In contrast to the Reformers, Anabaptists stressed free-dom of the will and the decision for or against Christ. What were the means they used in propagating the gospel message? Because they were persecuted and because their message required discretion, thought, and conviction, the "conventicle" or small house-meeting for Bible study, discussion, questions, and prayer was always the preferred evangelistic method. As in New Testament times, men and women in Zurich met for reading, questioning, and Bible study several times weekly. This was going on all around Zurich, particularly in Zollikon, where the first Anabaptist church was established, but also in Hongg, Kusnacht, Schaffhausen, St. Gall, Chur, Zofingen, and Gruningen.[3] Believers' bap-tism and the Lord's Supper were also observed.[4] These are the normal functions of a free church—but were condemned as crimes by Zurich's

Reformed church and city council, because they knew of the Anabaptists' power to attract adherents.

The spiritual revolution that created the revival expressed itself in a multitude of other ways—almost all of them natural, biblical, and uninvented. Were brothers Roubli, Haetzer, Castelberger, and Brotli to be banished from Zurich? This was an occasion to invite them to a farewell supper on January 25, 1525 (only four days after the first believers' baptism), to which others also came—nine men in all.[5] At this meeting Hans Bruggbach fell under deep conviction of sins and requested believer's baptism. It is impossible to recount the thousands of conventicles or house meetings organized during this period for the intense study of Scripture, for prayer, for baptism, for the Lord's Supper, and for the practice of church discipline.

Small meetings sometimes grew to larger assemblies and had to change their addresses. An example was John Kessler's Sunday evening home Bible study. He was a Zwinglian with Anabaptist sympathies and the author of *Sabatta.* His group, in only a few months, needed a meeting hall to accommodate one thousand people. When the worried authorities forced him to stop his teaching, the Anabaptist Ulimann took charge of the group.[6]

Open-Air Evangelism. At times in the earlier stages of the movement, when discretion was no longer possible, the message had to be proclaimed in the open air. Bolt Eberli, the peasant preacher from Schwyz, was particularly eloquent and boldly proclaimed the gospel for a few weeks in the spring of 1525 in the fields around St. Gall. Catholic authorities seized him and burned him at the stake on May 29, 1525, the first martyr of the Swiss brethren.[7] Yet others took his place, using this method that shook the region and centuries later brought salvation to hundreds of thousands under the ministry of Wesley and Whitfield. G. H. Williams states,

> By now the exhortations of the Anabaptist revivalists every evening and on holidays, in the mountains, woods, fields, and at the gates of the city, had become so frequent and exciting that the town churches were drained of their attendants, divided in their counsel, and deprived of alms for the sustenance of the poor. The town council thereupon reversed itself and demanded that all preaching and disputing take place *in the churches,* and that there be no more gatherings in or around the town.[8]

Even as George Blaurock was being led away to prison on a horse, following his intervention in the services of the village church of Hinwil, he exhorted the throng and sang hymns. The sympathetic crowd tried to arrange a service then and there in the open air. It was easier to take a bone from a dog, said Kessler, than to take field preaching away from the Anabaptists.

Baptism and the Lord's Supper. Naturally, baptisms (by pouring, at first) were also conducted in the open air, or in rivers and streams. One notable case was the Easter 1525 baptism of three hundred people by Balthasar Hubmaier in the public square of Waldshut. He used a milk bucket with water from the town fountain. These meetings were often followed by the Lord's Supper, observed by the baptized. The Supper, "as an expression of genuine brotherly togetherness," was regularly and frequently practiced as an important part of the inner dynamics of the communal life of the church.[9] The Table also provided the ideal occasion for church discipline, as the leaders supervised the purity of the assembly through the ban or exclusion, an integral part of the common life of these believers. In an important study of Anabaptists, Jean Seguy concludes that "the Supper collectively seals the non-worldliness of the group . . . and proclaims the purpose of practical conformity to Christ (*Nachfolge Christi*) in the daily, individual and collective life of the members of the assembly."[10] Since the Spirit-given communion of the brethren extended also to their lives *before* the Supper, many practiced community of goods and offerings for the poor among them. Baptism and the Lord's Supper could be powerfully attractive, practiced in unadorned simplicity as a regular internal function of the revived church. As intended by God, they gave profound identity and communion to a spiritually deprived people, tired of liturgy and form and thirsting for a return to realities.

Public Meetings. For these Anabaptists, being a witness was no longer the job of professionals. The simplest believer could be an evangelist. Artisans and farmers might, in fact, be better at it than intellectuals. Thus, the gospel spread through both the haphazard wanderings of lay preachers and the organized missions of recognized evangelists.[11] Early-stage Anabaptists persevered in other forms of open-air evangelism such as door-to-door witnessing. This was done in the Zurich area but also in Holland, where the authorities complained that "several hundred people would go out to preach and to convert people to their sect. . . . They already are sending people to that end."[12] Roelandt was a resistant Dutchman who had often been invited by the Mennonites to their meetings.

They would use the curious phrase, "You will hear something there which will please you very much!"[13] A certain Guysperre from Ghent announced his meetings by distributing notices throughout the city.[14] On several occasions Anabaptists organized demonstrations[15] but not always to good effect, as in Amsterdam.[16]

Public Debates. Anabaptists quickly learned the evangelistic value of the public debate. The Reformers considered them easy prey at first, but frequently the keen wit and extensive Bible knowledge of the accused preachers turned public opinion in their favor.[17]

Commercial Missionaries. Witnessing through commercial contacts was another type of Anabaptist evangelism. The Dutch, in 1532, were particularly good at this. Verheyden notes that "merchants from Zeeland stopped to visit Flanders, ostensibly for business reasons, but really, under the pretext of their trade, to help the new ideas take root in the broad and receptive Flemish field."[18] The Waldensians had also spread the gospel in this manner. Three hundred years later in France, Baptist pioneer Esther Carpentier, seller of sewing notions, was used of God to evangelize the populations of scores of towns and villages in Picardy. Peddlers were often effective evangelists, as were wandering journeymen and artisans.[19]

Martyrdom. Certainly the most spectacular—and perhaps the most effective—Anabaptist method of witness was martyrdom and cross-bearing. Reading of the various court trials and testimonies of the despised Anabaptists (from Michael Sattler's calm, measured, biblical answers to the frenzied authorities, to the accounts of hundreds of victims recorded in Van Braght's *Martyrs' Mirror*) one begins to understand that these brave men and women had carefully prepared for these moments.[20] Suffering—and the occasion for testimony—was understood as the normal lot of a disciple of Christ, the once-in-a-lifetime chance that could not be missed, for the Christian was one with Christ in spiritual union and also in cross-bearing. A veritable theology of suffering is taught in nearly all Anabaptist writing.[21]

The persecution process could begin when an Anabaptist refused to "baptize" an infant or swear by oath in court. Both refusals shocked society. Subsequent testimony under trial often meant declaring that Catholic baptism had no value, that the Mass was idolatry, that the worship of Mary was useless, that purgatory did not exist, that the pope was the Antichrist, and that Christian belief was to be based solely on the Word of God. Once the sentence was pronounced, Anabaptists usually refused the counsels of a monk and, on the way to burning or drowning, declared loudly the real reason for their martyrdom. They often cried at the very end, "We're neither heretics nor Lutherans!"[22] Many trials included questions about fellow believers. Only rarely did any valuable information escape the victims' lips.

The burnings, drownings, and tortures had no marked effect upon the growth of the Anabaptists; at worst, the persecutions caused great sufferings or initiated a move to another region. Often the population was moved to sympathy for the Anabaptist cause, and sometimes their torturers were converted. *The Chronicle of the Hutterite Brethren* recounts hundreds of cases of grievous suffering. Hans Purchner endured torture for two days at the hands of monks and priests, yet he did not flinch. At his execution he called the crowd to repentance. The heart of Leonhard Dax, one of the priests who had tortured him, was softened; he was converted and became a Hutterite.[23]

Anabaptists seemed convinced that martyrdom was the supreme evangelistic method and that, in any case, it was their destiny. Benefits were gained from cross-bearing. It liberated the believer and destroyed sin (Leonhard Schiemer; see 1 Peter 1:4, 4:1); it was the sign of being a member of the true church (Jacob Hutter); it was the surest way of gaining eternal life (Balthasar Hubmaier).[24] One oft-recounted incident reveals this spirit at its finest. An accused Dutch Anabaptist was fleeing from his captors across a frozen pond. The ice broke under his pursuers, and they plunged to certain death. The believer turned back to pull them out of the icy water to safety. The authorities he had saved arrested the Christian on the spot and had him put to death.

Silent Witness. Did Anabaptists believe in silent evangelism? After the considerable sufferings of the first century of their existence, Mennonites tended more and more to this form of witness. Their simple lifestyle, high morals, hard work, honest dealings, good relations with their neighbors, brotherly help—all combined to make them singularly different from the rest of the population. In this sense, they were an effective witness. But their historians are severe: In time, they became a spiritual ghetto of closed circles and, in general, did not seek to make converts.[25] Jean Seguy is even more harsh. Because they became tolerant and lacked the will to make converts, they were "totally incapable of evangelizing outside their ethnic context."[26] Mennonites did not disappear, however, because new recruits came from family tradition, immigration of brethren from other dangerous regions, and occasional individuals unhappy with the official churches. It took the revival movement of pietism to bring an evangelistic spirit back to some Mennonite churches.

In spite of its diversity, the biblical branch of sixteenth-century Anabaptism stands out as a genuine and deep movement of spiritual revival. With the exception of the Waldensians, Anabaptists were the first Christians since the early church to devote themselves fully and creatively to evangelizing the lost and teaching that the Great Commission was binding upon all church members. Claiming a total return to the Bible for their doctrinal foundation, Anabaptists lived and died by the Word of God. Once this spiritual dynamic was in place, these men and women needed only to fill it out with the "forms" of the believers' church, the two scriptural ordinances, Bible study in conventicles, open-air witness of several varieties, testimony through public debates, disputations, commercial contacts, cross-bearing, and martyrdom. Biblical Anabaptism's thousands of martyrs testify to the soundness and authenticity of their own evangelism and spiritual life, expressed in healthy evangelistic methods.

Baptist Evangelism

The birth of this church in 1608 launched a movement that put world evangelism into high gear. This evangelistic dynamic is still extremely active today, not only in the forty million or so Baptists, but in the multitudes of other churches built along Baptist lines that are active in winning non-Christians to faith in Christ.

The First Baptist Church

The word *baptist* was first applied to the Church of English separatists. Under the leadership of John Smyth and Thomas Helwys, they fled as a group to Amsterdam in 1608 because of persecution by the Church of England. The group found lodging in the "Great Bakehouse" of Jan Munter, a Mennonite; this gave Smyth his first contact with continental Anabaptists and provided an occasion for him to thoroughly reflect on his own beliefs. It is beyond the purpose of this article to note the numerous, varied, and important doctrinal questions raised and decided by Smyth, Helwys, and this little congregation between 1608 and Smyth's death in 1612. It is enough to say that, in his quest for the primitive church, Smyth was creative, open-minded, and determined at all costs to find, or found, a church that was as close as possible to the New Testament model. In the process, his examination of the Scriptures convinced him that infant baptism, which had tied church and community together for a thousand years and which he and his brethren had received in the Church of England, was worthless. Baptism upon profession of faith and repentance was the only right method of admitting adults to church fellowship. "There was nothing to do but to begin again and to reconstitute the Church, not on a basis of mutual covenant between its members *[the Separatist method]*, but by the baptism of all professed believers."[27]

Thus, the officers of the church—Smyth, Helwys, and the deacons—"laid down" their offices, the members annulled their former church organization, and during the same evening they reconstituted their assembly by baptizing each member upon profession of faith in God and repentance of sins. To begin the process, Smyth baptized himself, then he baptized Helwys and the other members of the new church. Immersion was as yet unknown to these believers, so the mode of baptism was affusion, or pouring from a basin, according to the Mennonite practice. Perhaps unconsciously, these pioneers had recovered one of the basic evangelistic methods built into the Great Commission by the Lord Himself. Millions, after hearing and believing the gospel, have been confronted by Christ's command and have obeyed by receiving baptism in the name of the Father, Son, and Holy Spirit. The missionaries, evangelists, and philanthropists who have ignored or side-stepped this ordinance have always diminished the glory of Christ by treating His words lightly and have hampered true evangelism by removing the health-giving test of voluntary obedience to Christ's command.

Thus, the first Baptist church was composed of Englishmen and was founded in exile on foreign soil. It does not appear to have been otherwise active in evangelism. Language and cultural differences were obstacles. And once they had reconstituted themselves into a professing church, their main preoccupation was to unite with the Waterlander Mennonite assembly where Jan Munter was a member. Smyth began negotiations with these brethren, but they were long and difficult, and he died before the English were finally accepted. The fires of evangelistic zeal, however, were dampened by more than the language barrier and other interests. There was now dissension inside Smyth's own church. Doctrinal arguments centering around Hoffmannite Christology, and the succession of elders was weakening the unity of the brethren. Helwys caused the final split. He separated from Smyth and his friends and returned to England with a small group to plant, in Spitalfields, just outside the walls of London, the first English Baptist church of modern times.

Baptist Growth in England from Helwys to Carey

After being thrust into notoriety in 1612 by the publication of *A Short Declaration of the Mistery of Iniquity,* Helwys was thrown into prison because of this very bold plea for universal religious liberty, which was understood by King James I as a provocation. By 1616 Helwys had died. John Murton now assumed leadership and by 1626 four other Baptist churches had taken root in England—in Lincoln, Coventry, Salisbury, and Tiverton.

Underground Methods. Obviously, effective evangelism was taking place, but the methods appear to have been those of the clandestine church. People were attracted to it by their own spiritual thirst, by one-on-one evangelism, by persecution from the authorities, by the love and fellowship of the members, and by intense study of Scripture. The Anabaptists had benefited from these "methods" largely during the long years of their deep sufferings.

By 1640 changes in the political and religious situation in England permitted a degree of liberty for Baptists and Independents. Signs of active evangelism began to show in England during a period of strong church growth (1640–1660). Independents and Baptists had constituted the main body of the New Model Army under Cromwell, and they were now in a position to demand liberty of conscience for all, something very distasteful to the Presbyterians and the authorities of the established church.

Printed Witness. This period of liberty, but also of civil and religious chaos (several sects were born, the king was assassinated, the Civil War broke out), found the Baptists evangelizing by means of pamphlets and tracts in favor of tolerance and against infant baptism and the forced tithe. Even some who never became Baptists were influenced by their ideas (John Milton, Colonel and Mrs. John Hutchinson, John Tombes, Francis Cornwell, Christopher Blackwood, and others). One is struck by the courage of the authors of these Baptist publications, which not only contained devotional sermons and doctrinal themes but also spoke on issues facing the nation and on matters about which Baptists were falsely accused, such as their attitude toward the magistrate. To distance themselves from the rebellion of Venner, the hotheaded cooper, Baptists of all opinions disclaimed any association with him in *The Humble Apology of Some Commonly Called Anabaptists* (1661). In 1647, in response to Thomas Edward's hostile and slanderous book, *Gangraena* (1646), both Baptists and Congregationalists collaborated in a reply affirming full support of the civil magistrate, as established by God. *A Declaration* reaffirmed the class structure of that period and the right to private property, and it rejected polygamy—all issues on which the Baptists had been falsely represented. The primary concern in this defense was to prevent possible harm to the whole movement and any hampering of evangelism.

Public Debates. Some of the Baptist growth must also be credited to public debates. These discussions were organized with all who would accept the challenge. One of the most famous debates, which drew great crowds, was held in Southwark in 1642 between William Kiffin (a Baptist) and the Rev. Daniel Featley, D.D., who wrote up his version of the arguments in *The Dippers Dipt, or, the Anabaptists Duck'd and Plunged over Head and Eares*. He testified, in spite of himself, to the methods and effectiveness of Baptist evangelism in the introductory epistle to the lords and citizens of Parliament:

> [They] . . . preach, and print, and practise their heretical impieties openly; they hold their conventicles weekly in our chief cities, and suburbs thereof . . . they flock in great multitudes to their Jordans, and both sexes enter into the river and are dipt. . . . And as they defile our rivers with their impure washings, and our pulpits with their false prophecies and fanatical enthusiasms, so the presses sweat and groan under the load of their blasphemies.[28]

Openly is the key word. Baptists were saying "Come and see for yourselves. We're not hiding anything. We're in agreement with the Bible." Taking only this testimony, one notes the effective use of preaching, literature, and public outdoor baptismal services as ways of attracting men and women to Baptist assemblies and to the gospel.[29]

Military Missionaries. An unusual feature of the growth of the English Baptist churches at this period was the missionary work of believing soldiers in the New Model Army under Cromwell. Preferring prayer meetings to taverns, ordinary soldiers as well as officers "fought the good fight of faith" and left behind a testimony that changed lives. W. T. Whitley provides details:

> Colonels Rede and Dean traversed South Wales to stamp out a rising in Pembroke, and Baptist churches sprang up along their route. A Lancashire rising in May was quelled by Robert Lilburne, and within a month John Wigan had planted a Baptist church in Manchester. When the Scotch Army evaded Harrison and came to grief at Preston, Brigadier-General Deane did fine service, while Rede helped capture the last infantry at

> Warrington; here again a Baptist church appears within
> three years. In November the cavalry besieged Pontefract,
> and soon after its fall a Baptist church was found there.[30]

The same things occurred in Ireland, where Baptist soldiers were stationed. The beginnings of Baptist work in France in the early 1800s can be traced to British soldiers billeted in the village of Nomain who left Bibles in the homes of their hosts as they prepared for the battle of Waterloo. Far from loved ones, these men found their fulfillment in prayer, testimony, and Bible study. Yet this was no planned strategy hammered out in the offices of an English Baptist missionary association. The key was in the dynamics—the basic sincerity and zeal of humble soldiers to make the best use possible of their situation and the present moment for Christ.

Conventicles. Accompanying the more visible methods for propagating the Baptist message, the "conventicle" was widely used during both the clandestine period and in later times. These religious assemblies consisted usually of a few people (they could also be numerous) meeting for Scripture reading, study, and explanation. Their effectiveness is shown by governmental opposition expressed in several decrees, especially the Conventicles Acts of 1664 and 1670, which "punished all persons of sixteen and upwards attending a Nonconformist service, at which more than four persons joined the family."[31] Those who broke the law could expect heavy fines and long imprisonments. An interesting sidelight was the imprisonment of a Seventh-Day Baptist, Francis Bampfield, at Dorchester Jail for nine years (1662–1671). While in jail, he and other ministers preached to townspeople who crowded into the prison courtyard once every day and twice on Sundays to hear the Word. Finally, the exasperated authorities ordered the jailer to bar people from coming into the prison to hear preaching.

Pastoral Ministry as Evangelism. While not specifically a "method," pastoral ministry among the early Baptists was clearly oriented toward evangelism. A notable example is the well-known Henry Jessey, who was "ejected" in 1662 from the pastorate of the Baptist church in Southwark, which he had occupied since 1637. In addition to his morning and afternoon sermons he preached every week to wounded and maimed veterans. He worked on a more correct translation of the Bible and raised large amounts of money to relieve the sufferings of the Jews, being greatly interested in their conversion. When he died in 1663, nearly five thousand people attended the funeral. Benjamin Keach, pastor of a

Baptist church in Winslow, an enthusiastic advocate of congregational hymn-singing and author of several books, was also deeply concerned about winning the young to the Lord. He was condemned in 1664 for having published *Child's Instructor; or a New and Easy Primer,* in which the judge found that he had taken "damnable positions contrary to the Book of Common Prayer." All copies of this book were burned, but Keach rewrote it from memory. *Child's Instructor* later enjoyed several editions.

Evangelistic preaching in the churches and itinerant evangelism in the small towns and countryside gained hundreds of new converts during the first century of English Baptist history. Effective preachers almost always drew sizable congregations. Not a few of these were the despised "mechanic preachers," untaught but full of zeal and marvelously able to communicate with the common people. A well-known example was Thomas Lambe, a soap-boiler who served two prison sentences because of his Baptist convictions but nevertheless evangelized the region around Gloucester, immersing converts in the Severn. By 1645 he was pastor of a London church at Bell Alley, to which flocked large groups of noisy and lively young people as well as older folk who enjoyed the preaching and the debates.[32]

Doctrine Is Important. It would be a mistake to omit reference to the doctrinal and spiritual undergirding of historic Baptist evangelism. As the second century of Baptist history began, doctrinal errors and sinful practices bore bitter fruit in the form of dying evangelism and fractured churches. Religious indifference in the nation filtered into the Baptist churches through attacks against the doctrine of Christ—chiefly Arianism and Socinianism. Many General Baptist churches became extinct, or adopted Unitarianism, reducing their message to mild moral precepts. As Dan Taylor observed, "They degraded Jesus Christ, and He degraded them." Particular Baptist churches at first suffered less because of their more Calvinistic background, yet they declined later because of a growing antinomianism. In the eighteenth century, many Particular Baptists became hyper-Calvinists and supralapsarians. The preaching of the gospel was devitalized, and evangelism was paralyzed. Invitations were no longer extended to sinners to repent, and applications were not given to sinful situations. Prominent pastors like John Skepp (pastor of the Curriers' Hall Baptist Church); John Brine, his successor; John Gill (pastor of an important London church for over fifty years and a doctor of divinity in Aberdeen); and John Johnson of Liverpool refused to address sinners about the necessity of repentance and faith. Faith, they felt, was "not a duty which God requires of a man, but a grace which it is impossible to convert into a duty. Faith cannot . . . be required of any man and want of faith is no sin. It is not the soul of man which believes but the principle of grace within him."[33] Under this teaching, many churches declined or closed.

Reaction to weakened doctrine and the decline of spiritual life was bound to occur. It came in the form of persistent prayer meetings, spiritual revival, and evangelistic missions. The ministry of John Wesley and George Whitfield brought new stirrings of life among the Baptists. Robert Hall, Andrew Fuller (the best theologian of the English Baptists and the one who dealt the mortal blow to hyper-Calvinism in England), John Sutcliff (pastor of Olney Church, which sent William Carey into the ministry), John Ryland, and John Fawcett were gifted preachers who evangelized sinners. Andrew Fuller and John Sutcliff gave solid backing to William Carey's mission to Serampore, India. As the 1700s drew to a close, Baptist evangelism revived and developed. Doctrine had regained its soundness and spiritual life its authenticity.

William Carey's Evangelistic Methods

Carey's church-planting strategy in India in the 1790s at first seems to have drawn its inspiration from methods he had known in England. Seeking individual conversions, Carey, Marshman, and Ward distributed literature, translated and published the Bible, and engaged in open-air preaching sessions, doctrinal debates, and disputes with local Brahmins. They felt that the general Indian population could be converted only if the Brahmin caste were first won to the Lord. Torrents of abuse and obscenity often greeted the missionaries during these meetings.[34] Carey was perhaps borrowing a method pioneered by Raymond Lull with the Muslims in the thirteenth century and also used by the Jesuit missionary Robert de Nobili, who became a Christian Brahmin, studying the major schools of Hindu philosophy in order to present Christian doctrine as much as possible in Hindu terms. Carey's method differed from that of Christian Frederick Schwartz, who had been sent by the Danish-Halle Mission to South India in the early 1700s. A man of remarkable piety, Schwartz's strategy was to become a Christian guru or spiritual teacher. The strategy worked to the extent that people from all sorts of religions and castes gathered around him—he had adapted his ministry well to the Indian culture—but he planted no churches.[35] "Uncompromising and confrontational" are words that describe the approach Carey used at the beginning. In time, the missionaries learned to moderate their attacks on Hinduism and concentrate on preaching the gospel more thoroughly. Carey and his friends also worked for social reform and publicly opposed the *sati* (burning of widows on the funeral pyre of their husbands), the temple prostitutes, the cruel exposure of infants, and the dying on the banks of the Ganges. This social reform, too, can be seen as an evangelistic method, as it drew attention to the message of the Bible and the grace of God available to sinful men. The Serampore missionaries also saw clearly the urgent need for native preachers and leaders and for long-term investment in their training. This was no substitute for evangelism but the necessary complement. They felt the missionary's role was to be neither pastor nor evangelist of a local church but a blend of apostle and elder, planting new churches and overseeing the doctrine and discipline of established churches.

In 1843, however, after fifty years of heroic effort, the Baptist Missionary Society could only count about fifteen hundred members in their Indian churches, and half of these were Europeans. Crowds were relatively easy to assemble—the Indians were polite—but few were willing to pay the price of following Christ. The heavy social pressures inherent in the caste system prevented people from breaking with Hinduism. One who did, (a former Hindu holy man and reformer), converted to Christ and ministered for twenty years as an itinerant evangelist living an extremely simple life, and devoting himself to prayer. The result was a mass movement of the Nomo Sudra caste to Christ.[36] Large central mission stations were developed where converts could settle to avoid the drastic effects of severance from their caste. These converts became economically dependent on the missionaries, working as servants, teachers, and evangelists. The churches became professionalized, and missionaries ruled the communities. In 1854 to 1855, an American Congregationalist, Rufus Anderson, organized the breakup of large stations in order that priority could be given to village churches with native pastors.

Carey's methods were certainly excellent—drawn from the Scriptures and adapted to the culture and the times—but they were not perfect. His spiritual zeal was exemplary. He and his friends invested all they had in a desperate struggle with Hinduism, yet the spiritual results in their eyes were quite meager. One lesson is that authentic zeal and good methods will not necessarily gain an abundant harvest. The receiving culture can be extremely difficult for Christians to penetrate. Time, perseverance, waiting for the moving of the Holy Spirit, and learning the way a culture functions—all are necessary for evangelists. Carey and his friends had, nevertheless, laid the indispensable groundwork.

Gerhard Oncken's Evangelistic Methods

Johann Gerhard Oncken can be safely called the greatest church-planter in Europe. McBeth says of him, "Seldom has one person contributed so much to the development of a denomination, nor left his stamp more indelibly upon it. Not only in Germany, but also throughout Europe much of Baptist work stems either directly from Oncken or from others whom he trained and sent out."[37] Born in Oldenburg, Germany, in 1800 Oncken spent several years in Edinburgh, Scotland, where he came into contact with evangelicals influenced by the Haldane brothers. Converted in London, young Oncken immediately began distributing tracts and witnessing. In 1823 he returned to Germany as an agent of the Continental Society and later the Edinburgh Bible Society, whose objective was to distribute Bibles and gospel tracts far and wide. This method of evangelism was Oncken's favorite, and by 1879 he reported that he had given out 2 million Bibles in Europe.[38] Oncken had apparently had no contact with British Baptists but by 1826 had come to Baptist convictions, primarily through his own study of the New Testament. In the absence of a baptized person to perform Oncken's baptism, an American professor on sabbatical, called Barnas Sears, baptized him and six others in the Elbe River on April 12, 1834. The next day, they organized a Baptist church. By 1836 the membership of this extremely active Hamburg church had climbed to sixty-eight. Oncken's motto, "Every Baptist a missionary," was practiced from the beginning as he and his church witnessed not only to the Hamburg residents but also to the foreign workers who migrated there to rebuild the city after the devastating fire of 1842. In 1843, Oncken baptized 273 people, and more than three hundred for each of the next two years.

Oncken's vision, strategy, and energy were as wide as the European continent. He conducted preaching tours in most of the countries of eastern and western Europe and visited groups of believers more or less marginally linked to Protestant denominations. Convincing them to constitute a Baptist church, he enlisted their leaders and trained their workers in a seminary he founded in 1849. Immigrant laborers, converted during their time in Hamburg, returned to evangelize and found Baptist churches in their homelands. These churches became part of a vast network of churches and mission efforts, all more or less linked to Oncken and the Baptist church of Hamburg.

What made Oncken so effective? He had natural zeal and enthusiasm; he held firm convictions about believer's baptism and the church; he used the Bible and the printed page persistently in spreading the gospel message; he was a gifted evangelist and preacher in his own language and culture; he was sensitive to the sufferings of those made homeless by the fire of 1842 and used this tragedy for the cause of the gospel; he saw the great opportunities immigrants afforded for the gospel (foreigners in Germany and vice versa); he was bold in persuading other Christians to join his movement; he believed training workers and leaders was important; he had a gift for organization; and, most important of all, he had a grand vision of what God could and would do. Oncken was Europe's greatest church-planter, not because of any spectacular or creative methods he used, but because he had abounding zeal, deep conviction, and a profound faith. God crowned his efforts with exceptional success.

Conclusion

The related but distinct evangelistic methods used by Anabaptists and the Baptists illustrate two critically important elements in any evangelistic endeavor: (1) the dynamic, or power behind it, and (2) the method or means used to express the dynamic. Our generation tends to give undue importance to method, deemphasizing the love, inner power, and zeal that make all true evangelism possible. Zealous people always find a method. "Method" people do not always find zeal. Methods can be extremely diverse, according to the personalities of those who employ them and the cultures and contexts in which they are employed. There are many options, and some give better results than others. Rigorous care and Bible study must determine the proper choice.

Past methods can sometimes be reused and adapted. Take public debate, for instance. Why couldn't pastors, missionaries, and converts in certain countries try the public forum (or the media) again as a place to engage in the battle for minds and hearts? Have missionaries in hostile western cultures understood the great advantages in using the tried and true conventicle method? What about the power of open-air meetings, as used in recent years in communist countries? Are we exploiting the press to the best of our ability? Should we not at least occasionally print and distribute our Baptist convictions on public issues? Have we not devalued the local church? Does it function biblically as a powerful evangelistic tool? Has our craving for musical embellishment and our lip-service to God's holiness robbed Baptist worship of the stark beauty and power of believers' baptism and the solemn joy of the Lord's Supper? Are we practicing biblical discipline, and are we preparing our people for martyrdom and other forms of cross-bearing? Or are they merely learning pulpitry and make-believe?

Past zeal must be renewed and coldness to Christ must be abandoned, for the "salt has lost its savor," and the light is under a bushel. "Remember therefore from whence thou art fallen, and repent, and do the first works; or else I will . . . remove thy candlestick" (Rev. 2:5).

Study Questions

1. What does it take to be a true witness for Christ?
2. What features of Anabaptist evangelism made it so effective? Compare their methods with those in common use today.
3. As you compare Anabaptists with Baptists, do you feel that Baptists innovated in evangelism?
4. What basic differences do you find between the evangelistic situation of the early Baptists and that of the missionaries in European countries today?
5. Which of these "old methods" would you like to try in your own ministry?

Chapter Notes

1. Franklin H. Littel, *The Origins of Sectarian Protestantism* (New York: Macmillan, 1964), 109.
2. Four or five types of Anabaptists can be distinguished: the biblical, church-oriented movement such as the South-German and Swiss Brethren, the North-Germans and the Mennonites; the community-life groups such as the Hutterites; the spiritualist-individualist fellowships such as those who followed Caspar Schwenckfeld; rationalists like Sebastian Franck; and the apocalyptic movement following teachers like Melchior Hofmann.
3. At least five homes in Zollikon are mentioned in the court records. Fritz Blanke, *Brothers in Christ* (Scottdale, Pa.: Herald, 1961), 53. See also Littel, *The Origins of Sectarian Protestantism,* 12–13, for the use of the conventicle.
4. Ibid., 53–54.
5. Ibid., 25.
6. G. H. Williams, *The Radical Reformation* (Philadelphia: Westminster, 1962), 128–29.
7. Ibid., 129.
8. Ibid., 130.
9. Robert Friedmann, *The Theology of Anabaptism* (Scottdale, Pa.: Herald, 1973), 125. See also Littel, *Origins of Sectarian Protestantism,* 98–100.

10. Jean Seguy, *Saisons d'Alsace,* no. 76 (1981): 14.

11. Littel, *Origins of Sectarian Protestantism,* 120–22.

12. A. L. E. Verheyden, *Anabaptism in Flanders, 1530–1650* (Scottdale, Pa.: Herald, 1961), 105.

13. Ibid., 114.

14. Ibid., 89. He once used the same method, however, to protest the ban placed on him by other Mennonites!

15. Blanke, *Brothers in Christ,* 60.

16. G. H. Williams and A. M. Mergal, eds., *Spiritual and Anabaptist Writers* (Philadelphia: Westminster, 1957), 218–22.

17. Littel, *Origins of Sectarian Protestantism,* 159, lists nine famous disputations between 1525 and 1578 in which Anabaptists took part.

18. Verheyden, *Anabaptism in Flanders,* 16.

19. Littel, *Origins of Sectarian Protestantism,* 123–25.

20. Williams and Mergal, *Spiritual and Anabaptist Writers,* 140–43.

21. Littel, *Origins of Sectarian Protestantism,* 132–34.

22. Verheyden, *Anabaptism in Flanders,* 114.

23. *The Chronicle of the Hutterite Brethren,* 2 vols. (Rifton, N.Y.: Plough, 1987), 1:322.

24. W. Klaasen, ed., *Anabaptism in Outline* (Kitchener, Ontario: Herald, 1981), 85–86.

25. C. Mathiot and R. Boigeol, *Recherches historiques sur les Anabaptistes* (Flavion, Belgium: Le Phare, 1969), 252.

26. Jean Seguy, *Les Assemblées Anabaptistes-Mennonites de France* (Paris: Mouton, 1977), 428.

27. A. C. Underwood, *A History of the English Baptists* (London: Baptist Union Publication Dept., 1947), 37.

28. Ibid., 67.

29. For another well-known public debate held in 1653 on infant baptism between an Independent (Richard Carpenter) and a Baptist (John Gibbs), ibid., 98. Carpenter's title: *The Anabaptist washt and washt, and shrunk in the washing.*

30. W. T. Whitley, *A History of the British Baptists* (London: Baptist Union Publication Dept., 1932), 78.

31. Underwood, *A History of the English Baptists,* 95.

32. Ibid., 76.

33. Ibid., 135.

34. Brian Stanley, *The History of the Baptist Missionary Society, 1792–1992* (Edinburgh: T & T Clark, 1992), 44.

35. R. Pierce Beaver, "The History of Mission Strategy," in Ralph D. Winter and Steven C. Hawthorne, *Perspectives on the World Christian Movement* (Pasadena, Ca.: William Carey Library, 1992), B–64.

36. Stanley, *The History of the Baptist Missionary Society,* 141.

37. H. Leon McBeth, *The Baptist Heritage: Four Centuries of Baptist Witness* (Nashville, Tenn.: Broadman, 1987), 470.

38. Ibid., 471.

13

DANIEL K. DAVEY

THE LOCAL CHURCH IN WORLD EVANGELIZATION

Getting a Right Perspective

A candid appraisal of the involvement of Western Christianity in world missions is anything but complimentary. Whether through arrogance or ignorance, Western local churches are giving less to mission work than they did ten years ago, and they are committing fewer of their members to cross-cultural ministries. In short, Christians in the West are losing interest in reaching other nations with the gospel message of Jesus Christ.

One reason for the decline in missions is Western Christianity's own decline in evangelicalism. Johnstone determined that in 1900, 25 percent of Canada claimed to be evangelical. By 1990 the figure dropped to less than 8 percent.[1] South of the border, evangelicals comprise a mere 11 percent of the 500 million people in that part of the North American continent.[2] Meanwhile, Sjogren and Stearns chronicle a deterioration of local churches in the United States.[3] They communicate disturbing statistics: 85 percent of all America's churches are either stagnant or dying, nearly sixty thousand American churches annually report no conversions to Jesus Christ, sixty churches a week are closing their doors for lack of attendance, and for the first time in fifty years the number of American career missionaries has significantly dropped (50,500 in 1988 to 41,142 in 1992).[4]

To illustrate this current breakdown of American churches, John and Sylvia Ronsvalle of Empty Tomb, Inc., a research organization in

Champaign, Illinois, note that "while total giving rose in 1995, giving as a percentage of churchgoers' income has steadily declined over the past three decades."[5] This decline is most telling in the shrinking of mission work in many local churches. The Ronsvalles explain that earlier in this century, when incomes were not nearly what they are today, giving percentages were higher. In the past, Americans built large churches, established extensive mission outreaches, created mission boards, and constructed schools and even hospitals. Today, however, many churches are struggling to maintain the facilities and ministries built by earlier generations.[6]

As a pastor, I am deeply concerned about the meaning and significance of these statistics, especially as they relate to American church life. Over the last fifteen years, I have talked to many people who have observed the difficulty that American missionary candidates face getting to their desired fields of ministry. A few have wondered if it is even worth the hassle and expense for an American to become a foreign ambassador for Christ. If local churches in America continue to falter in investing in and sending career missionaries, will the United States play any significant role in world missions in the next millennium? Sjogren and Stearns state that already a "fundamental shift" has taken place in world missions.[7] While the United States continues its decline in its world evangelization efforts, many other countries in the Eastern Hemisphere are rising to take its place both in raising monies and sending missionaries.[8] It has been conservatively estimated that by A.D. 2000 there will be about two thousand non-Western mission agencies in existence.[9] The question is, then, What is the future role of the American church in world evangelization? Does it still have a significant place in world ministry? If so, how can the current trend in declining mission-related activities be reversed? Will the United States ever again become the dominant force in world evangelization?

These alarming statistics are only the manifistations of the root cause for the lack of energy for missions. The real problem is theological. American churches seem at a loss to clearly define their nature and purpose. Many churches have shifted their focus from God's Word to battling social agendas, increasing attendance numbers, meeting significant needs within the secular community, and developing novel worship services. In so doing, they have often ignored truth and, thereby, broadsided the very character of God. Many local churches in America stand in need of a revival of mission and a change of direction.

The Source and Boundary of Definition

At this crossroads in history, many voices are calling for the church to redefine itself and clarify its strategy and function. Repeatedly some voices demand that the church look to modern American culture to find significance. If the church is to thrive, they speculate, then it must adapt to its culture. This contemporary formula, however, is anything but original. In 1934, explains David Wells, a major study was done to identify the ministerial role.[10] This study concluded that pastors were, and needed to be, teachers, preachers, worship leaders, administrators, and shepherds. Several years later another "clerical study" of forty-seven American denominations added four things that a pastor needed to be able to do: "[with] an open affirming style, know how to foster friendship in the church, be aware of denominational activities, be able to lead the church's participation in political discussion of matters of moment, and provide a witness against the world's injustice."[11]

In 1986, the list was expanded to fourteen items. Wells writes, at that point, "Evangelical churches gave their top priority to planning ability, facility in leading worship, and sensitivity to the congregation."[12] According to Wells, "the new clerical order" had redefined the pastoral role in terms of technical and managerial skills. Wells concludes, "The older role of the pastor as broker of truth has been eclipsed by the newer managerial functions."[13] The conclusion of Wells's study demonstrates that the American church has a changing face. Its change is closely tied to the capricious character of modern culture. Those who espouse cultural identification as the means to enhance church life erroneously surmise that if the church is to remain a force in the American culture it must change with the culture. Therefore, books are being generated by the score to help the modern church keep up with the changes.[14] Is culture, however, the guiding light for discovering the nature, purpose, and emphasis of the church? How one answers this question will significantly affect how one defines the church and its strategy to multiply itself around the world.

Of necessity, the church operates on the foundation of revealed truth recorded in the Word of God. This Word distinguishes it from all other religious societies, sects, or cults. If the church conducts itself apart from scriptural principles, it is reduced to the same level as every other humanly sourced "ism" that meets a passing cultural fancy but is short lived.[15]

If the Bible, however, is the church's ultimate standard for existence and significance, then the church's role and function will be manifested

within God-fixed borders. These divine boundaries will inevitably intersect with a morally fluid culture and generate abundant cultural controversy. But if Scripture is unerringly observed, the church will fulfill its
divine purpose, escaping both theological error and eventual disaster.

What are the God-fixed borders for the church? Rather than human
explanations or justifications for the existence and nature of the church,
what are God's expectations—for the American church or any other
church? To answer these questions we must first discover from Scripture what constitutes the nature of the church. Only then may we proceed to follow God's strategy or plan. Second, this chapter will search
Scripture to unlock God's established intention for the church. This will
clear the way for the church aggressively to spread the gospel of Christ
to all nations and, in doing so, fulfill its divine mission.

The Nature of the Church

A study of the church should begin with defining its nature or essence.
Some begin ecclesiological study with an examination of the church's
function rather than its constitution.[16] For them, the essential element is
not theology—what the Scripture says—but methodology—how the
church relates to its culture.[17] Such a pragmatic approach breeds general
confusion and creates multiple opinions on the purpose of the church.
As Walvoord points out, however, if the nature of the church is clearly
defined by Scripture, then seeking students will not only have God's
clear teaching on the subject, but the present task of the church will be
properly identified.[18]

Since it is impossible to study all the biblical information on the
nature of the church, we will concentrate on the New Testament book of
Ephesians, aptly called by one contemporary author "a mini-course in
theology, centered on the church."[19] The apostle Paul divides this book
into two parts. Hendriksen notes the clear-cut division and explains that
church doctrine dominates the first chapters while exhortation to church
members encompasses the final three chapters.[20] Numerous church-
related themes occupy Paul's opening chapters: election (1:4), adoption
(1:5), redemption (1:6–7), eternal security of the believer (1:13–14),
God's power working in the believer (1:19–21), grace (2:1–10), the theological relationship between Christian Gentiles and Christian Jews
(2:11–22), the significance of the dispensation of grace (3:1–12), and
the love of Christ toward His people (3:13–21). The distinctive element
of these chapters, however, is the way Paul weaves together key ecclesiological truths to emphasize the nature of the church. These truths state

that (1) the church is a divine creation, (2) the church is Christ's body, (3) the church operates on divine energy, and (4) the church exists to bring glory to God.

The Church Is a Divine Creation

Three times in the first three chapters of Ephesians Paul uses the Greek verb κτίζω meaning "to create or produce" (2:10, 15; 3:9).[21] This verb, Wood correctly asserts, "is used only of God and denotes the creative energy he alone can exert."[22] Accordingly, the church, like God's creation of the heavens and the earth (Gen. 1–2), is the sole production of God. Ephesians reveals that His construction of the church began before the world itself was created (1:4); His Son was sent into the world at God's appointed time to create in Himself this new entity (1:7–11; 2:15); He created a divine path of good works upon which He places every member of the new community (2:10); and He protects every member of the new creation by sealing them with His Holy Spirit (1:13–14). Since God has taken such care to plan, create, maintain, and secure His church in this world, then we may conclude that God has left nothing to mere chance or human speculation. In fact, Paul announces that God's church is so thorough in every detail that it clearly manifests the "wisdom of God . . . according to the eternal purpose which He accomplished in Christ Jesus" (3:10–11 NKJV). In other words, Paul views the divine design of the church, in both its inauguration and maintenance, as complete and eternally sufficient. Therefore, as a creation of God reflecting the wisdom of the infinite God, the essential nature of the church stands in need of nothing.

The Church Is Christ's Body

There are several metaphors by which Paul describes the church in the book of Ephesians.[23] None so distinctly portrays the nature of the church as does Paul's usage of the phrase *body of Christ*. Witmer writes, "The distinctiveness of the church rests in its identity as 'the body of Christ.'"[24] Walvoord goes one step further when he states, "Much of the modern confusion on the doctrine of the church comes from a failure to understand the Scriptural revelation of the church as the body of Christ."[25] While other Pauline metaphors give added light on the nature of the church none so clearly portrays the essence so intimately as does the term *the body of Christ*.

By definition, the physical σῶμα is made up of many parts and is the seat of mortal life.[26] It is the exterior that houses the life principle, and is fully animated by the same. In like manner, the spiritual σῶμα (meaning, the church) has many parts and is the visible expression of Christ's life. By using the term *body of Christ,* Paul is expressing the role of the church as the observable expression of Christ to a world that was not privy to the historical incarnation of Christ. Paul's meaning is deeper, however, than mere outward form. This body is filled with the "fullness of Him who fills all in all" (1:23 ɴᴋᴊᴠ).[27] In other words, Jesus Christ is not just physically represented on this earth by His church like a foreign ambassador would represent his Sovereign to another; rather, He is the very life principle within the church. The church is complete because Christ's complete presence resides within it. As one translation put it, "The Church is his body, and in that body lives fully the one who fills the whole wide universe."[28] For this reason Paul considered the church to be "a dwelling place of God" (2:22 ʀsᴠ). Surely, the place where God dwells is sufficient to meet every need its residents have and protect those residents from any kind of evil assault. This is, in fact, exactly what Christ promised while He was with His disciples when He said, "I will build My church, and the gates of Hades shall not prevail against it" (Matt. 16:18 ɴᴋᴊᴠ). Therefore, Christ's abiding presence within the church ought to greatly encourage the visible body, especially when its surrounding culture views the church as outdated or even unnecessary.[29] The truth is, because Christ is living within the body, it is virtually unstoppable—all it can do is increase and develop (cf. 4:12–15).

The Church Operates on Divine Energy

Ephesians 1 can be divided into two parts. The first part relates to Paul's praise of God for all the spiritual blessings each Christian receives the moment he trusts Christ as his personal Savior (1:3–14). These incomparable blessings drive Paul to his knees in prayer for the saints who make up this body of Christ in Ephesus and possess such wonderful gifts from God (1:15–23). One of the key requests in this prayer is that each Ephesian believer would mentally grasp God's resource of supernatural power for body living (1:18–21). The same power, which raised up Christ from the dead, (1:20) is "the exceeding greatness of His power toward us who believe" (1:19 ɴᴋᴊᴠ). Again, in Paul's second prayer for these same believers (3:15–21), he exalts the exceeding abundance of such power, which is possessed by every saint (3:20).[30] The *Expositor's Greek Testament* correctly concludes that Paul is describing the absoluteness of God's power ("able to do beyond all things"), and therefore, this powerful God is able to go "superabundantly beyond the utmost requests we can make in prayer."[31]

The importance of the absolute power of God in the body of Christ cannot be overstated. It is God's absolute power that chose us before the creation of this world (1:4). It grants us life, who were formerly dead in trespasses and sin (2:5). It prepares us for good works (2:10); places us into the body of Christ (2:15–16); provides us access to the heavenly Father (2:18); builds us into a proper home for the dwelling of God on earth (2:22); and uses us to manifest the wisdom of God to all principalities and powers (3:9–10). Paul's intent is clear: The church exists solely by divine power. This divine power is absolute. This divine power is incomparable. This divine power is far more than the church will ever need to meet its own needs, to conquer all its enemies, and to overcome all the fiery darts of the Evil One. Therefore, the body of Christ is fully empowered to accomplish all that God intends. It is not necessary for the church to look to pagan culture to provide "energizing extras" in order for Christ to be more of a force in this world. The church is a cultural dynamism by virtue of its inherent power, not because of any pragmatic methodology. Christ's body does not need to be reinvigorated by some synthetic assistance. Interestingly, Paul concludes his letter to the Ephesian church with the words, "Be strong in the Lord and in the power of His might" (6:10 NKJV). Clearly, Paul considers this power of Christ to be sufficient for every possible circumstance the body may face.

The Church Exists to Bring Glory to God

The ultimate priority of the church is to bring glory to its Creator. Since Paul declares the church to be of divine origin, it seems only fitting that the church should respond in praise to His work. Paul leaves no room for the church to glorify itself, for humanity had nothing to do with the planning, creating, maintaining, and developing of the church. Likewise, the church is not to glorify various methodologies, since clever human techniques are without Pauline endorsement. Paul is careful to claim that all praise belongs to Christ.

When Paul begins his letter, he expresses joy that every saint in the body is blessed with "every spiritual blessing in the heavenly places in Christ" (1:3 NKJV). He then recites at least eight theological blessings, which are punctuated by one phrase found three times: "to the praise of His glory" (1:6, 12, 14 NKJV).[32] Paul expects all of the spiritual investments in the body of Christ to result in God's receiving all the praise and glory.

Near the end of the Ephesian letter, Paul states the divine goal of all God's effort in creating the spiritual σῶμα: "That (ἵνα) He might present it to Himself a glorious church, not having spot or wrinkle or any such thing, but that it should be holy and without blemish" (5:27 NKJV). God has accomplished in Christ all that is necessary to make the body ready for the glorious future presentation. Hendriksen explains:

> The *presentation* here referred to must be viewed as definitely eschatological, that is, referring to the great consummation when Jesus returns upon clouds of glory. . . . Christ himself readies [the church] in order to present her to himself. The point stressed is, of course, that she, the church, can do nothing in her own power. She owes all her beauty to him, the bridegroom.[33]

The unveiled truth about the body of Christ is that from start (Pentecost) to finish (the Rapture of the church), the church is a magnificent handiwork of God. For this reason, Paul concludes his doctrinal portion of the letter with these words of doxology: "To Him be glory in the church by Christ Jesus to all generations, forever and ever. Amen" (3:21, paraphrase).

Summary

The book of Ephesians masterfully weaves together various ecclesiological themes into a beautiful tapestry, showing the nature of the church to be a complete and sufficient design of God. God Himself has properly prepared the church for all that it needs or could ever want (1:3). This truth is the theological anchor for our understanding of any other truth about the church of God. In fact, writes Walvoord, to misunderstand the above facts on the nature of the church will blur not only one's theological perspective on church issues but "make impossible a practical approach to the present task of the church."[34] Once Paul's basic church concepts are accepted, however, then the strategy or mission that God has laid out for His church can be properly developed. This strategy, moored to Paul's Ephesian explanations of church truth, will provide the body of Christ with its divine method for aggressively reaching the world with the gospel of Christ. Keep in mind, Paul views the church as unstoppable. This strategy, then, guarantees that the church will successfully accomplish God's eternal purpose (cf. Eph. 3:9–11).

The Strategy of the Church

Since God has clearly established the nonnegotiable theological parameters of His church, does He also have a plan for its function within society? Or, to phrase it differently, if we accept God's blueprint in the book of Ephesians for the nature of the church, can we also discover God's clear intention for its daily operation? Will this plan of God supply all the much-needed energy for missions many American churches seek? Again, just as God revealed His thoughts on the nature of the church in Scripture, so also has He unfolded His divine strategy for the daily operation of the church. He has not left the church without His plan and power to accomplish His mission strategy. The question is, Do we, in modern American Christianity, really understand God's strategy for His church?

The English term *strategy* is military, associated with the theater of war.[35] It is the "science and art of military command" whereby one military leader seeks to outthink and then outmaneuver the other to gain a victory.[36] Strategy is a carefully laid plan that is usually kept secret from the majority of troops until the time of immediate implementation. By such tactics the enemy's spies will be caught unawares, and the enemy itself will be caught off guard.

In the final days of Christ before He ascended into the third heaven, He laid out His strategy to the disciples. Unlike standard military procedure, Christ openly announced His scheme, and it is recorded in Matthew 28:18–20:

> And Jesus came and spoke to them, saying, "All authority has been given to Me in heaven and on earth. Go therefore and make disciples of all the nations, baptizing them in the name of the Father and of the Son and of the Holy Spirit, teaching them to observe all things that I have commanded you; and lo, I am with you always, even to the end of the age." Amen. (NKJV)

Matthew's explanation of Christ's strategy "connects itself with the missionary assignment of the apostles and the universal church,"[37] clearly marking a "turning point in the operation of God's redemptive program in the world."[38] The majority of Matthean chapters finds Christ offering Himself as the fulfillment of the promised Old Testament Messiah to the Jewish people (1:21; 2:1–6; 4:12–17; 10:1–7; 11:3–19; 12:6, 38–42; 20:20–28; 21:1–11). Until this particular commission, which Christ issued, He had limited His disciples' activity to the Jews (10:7–15). Now He advances a clear call to "make disciples of all the nations." Christ's objective is clear—to reach every nation with His teachings.

There are many ways to dissect this strategy of Christ. As one carefully studies the passage, however, a dominate word appears and ties the entire passage together.[39] The key word in this passage is πᾶς and is usually translated "all." Christ's strategy can be understood by studying the four usages of πᾶς: πᾶσα ἐξουσία (all authority), πάντα τὰ ἔθνη (all the nations), πάντα ἐνετειλάμην ὑμῖν (all things I commanded you), and πάσας τὰς ἡμέρας (all the days).

All Authority

The full statement Christ gave His disciples is, "All authority has been given to Me in heaven and on earth." In the Greek New Testament this statement begins with the aorist passive verb ἐδόθη, translated "has been given." The aorist tense, writes Hiebert, "records this bestowal of authority as a definite fact, but no indication of time is given."[40] Several questions come to mind when this verb is examined in its context. Since the time element seems fluid, when did Christ receive this authority? Also, what is meant by the specific term *authority*? And finally, why does Jesus now make public that He has all authority?

Christ did not have to wait until after His resurrection to exercise authority. Throughout the gospel account, Matthew shows that Christ displayed divine power: He taught with distinguished authority (7:29); He had power to immediately heal leprosy (8:1–4); He commanded the demonic world (8:28–34); He forgave sin (9:1–8); He was able to confer His power on the disciples to work miracles (10:1); and He defied the laws of nature (14:25–33). These particular acts of authority, however, were for a specific purpose. The apostle John identifies that purpose as twofold: (1) that all may believe that Jesus is the Messiah; and (2) that all may know He is God (20:30–31). Hiebert writes that Christ's manifestations of power were "limited demonstrations"[41] and "served as confirmatory signs establishing His identity as the incarnate Son of God sent to be the Savior of sinful humanity."[42] In Matthew 28, when Jesus announces He has all authority in heaven and on earth, He is really declaring that He is no longer restrained to sporadic outbursts of power. Now, without restriction, He has "universal sovereignty," which He will exercise from this moment forward.[43]

The phrase *all authority* has two strong emphases. First, the word ἐξουσία is a legal term that denotes a high court granting "the right to do something or the right over something."[44] Once the high court grants the privilege it cannot be revoked. When Christ rose from the dead, God the Father "put all things under His feet" (Eph. 1:22 NKJV) and "highly exalted Him" by giving Him "the name which is above every name, that at the name of Jesus every knee should bow, of those in heaven, and those on earth, and those under the earth" (Phil. 2:9–10 NKJV). No person, space, or being is exempt from the authority of Christ, and no one has more power than He. This, then, is the second emphasis of the phrase *all authority*. The term πᾶς "declares the complete and unlimited scope of the bestowal of [Christ's] power, while 'in heaven and on earth' delineates the two spheres of power bestowed on the risen Jesus."[45]

Christ's official announcement of His unrestricted authority is of utmost consequence to the disciples. Christ's absolute authority over the earth grants His disciples access to their nation as well as to any population group in the world. In other words, Christ's authority makes the phrase *restricted access people groups* insignificant. This means the disciples and the future church have every right to speak the gospel message any place on the globe. In Acts 4 and 5, Christ's established authority was severely tested by the religious leaders. True to form, however, the apostles declared the message of life and properly charged the religious leaders (4:19–20):

> Whether it is right in the sight of God to listen to you more than to God, you judge. For we cannot but speak the things which we have seen and heard. (NKJV)

The disciples were convinced of their authority to speak the wonderful words of life. Neither man nor law could stop their mission, for it had been commissioned by the highest authority in the universe. It is on the basis of this authority that men throughout church history have accomplished the most difficult of tasks in the face of seemingly insurmountable human and demonic roadblocks. David Livingstone exercised Christ's authority and opened Africa to the gospel; William Cary opened India; Hudson Taylor opened China; John Paton opened the New Hebrides Islands; and Jim Elliot, with his companions, opened the hearts of savage Indians in Ecuador. In each case, these men expended their toil, sweat, and even blood. They eventually reached a people-group, and even nations, that had been considered by many of their contemporaries as hopelessly unreachable, with the gospel. Their success lay not in human determination or resolve but in Christ's absolute authority.

All the Nations

Once Christ expresses His complete authority, His attention turns to the disciples' responsibilities. Christ commands His disciples to, "Go . . . make disciples of all the nations." Hiebert asserts, "This is the heart of Jesus' purpose in arranging this mountainside meeting with His disciples."[46] The revelation of His comprehensive authority was not the reason for this meeting; rather, Christ wanted His disciples to begin implementing His new strategy.[47] The newness of Christ's command is seen in the words "make disciples of all nations." First, the verb μαθητεύσατε is an aorist imperative, which shapes this verb as a "brisk command, or order."[48] Second, this command does not specifically say "make sinners saved," though this is surely implied in the disciple-making process. What Christ does command is: "Make pupils or learners" of Me out of all nations. Broadus says,

> To disciple a person to Christ is to bring him into the relation of pupil to teacher, "taking his yoke" of authoritative instruction (11:29), accepting what he says as true because he says it, and submitting to his requirements as right because he makes them.[49]

This verb, then, means far more than just seeing people come to Christ in salvation. It means the disciples of Christ are to help ("make") other people "hear, understand, and obey Jesus' teaching."[50] Third, disciples are to be made from every nation of the world. Since all four usages of πάντα τὰ ἔθνη in Matthew (24:9, 14; 25:32; 28:19) refer to all peoples without regard to ethnicity, we may assume the Jews are included with the Gentiles in the command to reach all nations.[51] This was not a Gentile commission but a worldwide commission. Because of its overwhelmingly broad scope, these final words of Christ in Matthew are often called the Great Commission.

The disciples were not without a method to accomplish their task. Christ's universal formula is stated in two attendant present participles: βαπτίζοντες (baptizing) and διδάσκοντες (teaching).[52] The first participle presupposes that people have accepted and submitted to Christ's purpose for coming into the world as stated in Matthew's opening chapter: "He [Jesus] will save His people from their sins" (1:21 NKJV). Once people have privately come to believe in Christ as their Savior, they are publicly baptized, which brings them "into open fellowship with the acknowledged body of believers."[53] Also, by baptism new believers openly declare their willing submission to the lordship of the Father, Son, and Holy Spirit.[54]

The second participle is not prefaced by the conjunction *and* (καὶ) or any other connecting particle, which, as Hiebert asserts, "indicates that this program of 'teaching' is not strictly coordinated with 'baptizing.'"[55] It is possible, then, that "teaching" may take place before the baptism occurs.[56] It is clear, however, that teaching is to be an on-going process after one's baptism. The teaching-learning motif is of paramount importance in the Christian life.

This method of disciple making that Christ announced remains unchanged. A disciple is made by two definite means: personal baptism and being taught to observe Christ's commands. These means cannot be improved upon or added to. They worked powerfully in the first century and will work just as powerfully today. In effect, together they are God's ordained formula to bring about supernatural and lasting change in the hearts of men.

All Things I Have Commanded You

All teaching has content. What Christ demanded to be taught was everything (πᾶς) He had commanded His disciples. This means several things to those who desire to follow Christ's words. First, the focus of the teaching-learning model is not on Old Testament Law, but on the words of Jesus.[57] The book of Hebrews supports this truth, explaining that all revelation culminated in God's Son (1:1–2). The coming of Christ is "the fulfillment of everything to which the Old Testament Scriptures pointed."[58] Therefore, who Christ is and what Christ says is crucial for all of Christ's followers.

Second, the phrase *all things* (πᾶς) is all-encompassing. Each command Christ intended His disciples to communicate is important for the lives of new disciples. Christ was not placing in the hands of His original disciples the power to indiscriminately pick and choose from the commands that He placed in their safekeeping. On the contrary, everthing He imparted to His chosen few was to be passed on in its entirety to the nations.

Third, Christ assumed His words were sufficient to accomplish the task of making disciples of all nations. His commands did not need additional human genius or creative new terms. Interestingly, years later the apostle Paul writes that if anyone goes beyond the words of Christ in his personal teaching methods, "he is proud, knowing nothing, but is obsessed with disputes and arguments over words." (1 Tim. 6:4 NKJV).

Clearly, Paul considered Christ's words sufficient to make sinners spiritually whole until "the end of the age."

Fourth, the teaching process is more than pouring facts into the minds of those who desire to be Christ's disciples. Christ used the Greek verb τηρέω, meaning "to watch over, guard, keep, hold, preserve, or protect."[59] Christ did not expect His disciples to be informational machines. He meant them to be personal disciples. This means true believers will manifest a new character that matches their new belief. They practice in life what Christ commanded in truth. In baptism new disciples announce their willingness to obey Christ, and as they learn the truth of Christ's words, they immediately desire to exercise that truth in their lives. This means, then, that Christ's teachings are all-sufficient and need only be explained within the teaching-learning model for spiritual results to take place. Accordingly, since His teachings are eternally sufficient, they need not be repackaged or even replaced to make Christianity more palatable to the modern intellect (cf. Rom. 10:14–15).

All the Days

The strategy of Christ is for the long haul—until the end of all the days. Christ promises His disciples that He will literally be with them, as Hendriksen translates, "day in [and] day out."[60] God will never take a vacation from His disciples. Hiebert writes,

> It assures His disciples that there is no need for doubts or misgivings on their part in accepting the commission given them. He declared that He is no absentee lord who leaves [H]is people to carry out their assignment unaided and alone.[61]

The Great Commission is great not just because of its universal scope but also because of what Christ actually promises: "I will be with you all the days." Christ is saying that no one is alone when taking His words to the nations and making new disciples. The very presence of Christ attends each disciple-maker. His personal presence makes possible the overwhelming task of His church—to reach every nation with His gospel. Nothing could be more encouraging to the church than this divine promise. Christ's presence is the church's guarantee that His strategy is more than mere methodology. It gives assurance that the disciple-making process is a divine undertaking and is God's way of reaching all nations with the truth.

Summary

The sum total of Jesus' words in Matthew 28 is that the church is fully equipped to function without hindrance in any generation. Christ's unrestricted authority paves the way for every nation of the world to be touched with the gospel. Christ expects that all who follow Him in discipleship will publicly demonstrate their commitment through the waters of baptism and openly embrace every word that Christ passed on through His original core of disciples. His disciples need not fear, because Christ promises His full presence will be with each one. This strategy of Christ is guaranteed by His personal presence, and He expects the outcome to affect all nations.

One final nuance of this strategy is that Christ's plan for His disciples, and ultimately for His church, is the only one He announced to His people. In other words, there is no other strategy to reach the world with the gospel apart from the one given by Christ. The early church, in the book of Acts, took these words of Christ very seriously. They soon "filled Jerusalem with [their] doctrine" (5:28 NKJV); they made disciples among the Gentiles (10:44–48); they cultivated new nations in Syria and Asia Minor (11:22–26; 13–14); and eventually impacted "all who dwelt in Asia" (19:10 NKJV). Everywhere the first generation of believers went they made disciples and established local bodies of Christ (14:21–23). They were convinced of two important facts: (1) They had Christ's plan, which was sufficient to make disciples of all the nations, and (2) there was no other plan of operation. In other words, Christ's plan was the only method by which they were to reach the world with His truth.

The Challenge to the American Church

In May 1976, a tenth printing of Francis Schaeffer's book, *The God Who Is There,* was issued.[62] In the opening pages Schaeffer lamented "the tragedy of our situation today."[63] The problem facing Christianity, as Schaeffer saw it, was "the drift" of "many pastors, Christian educators, evangelists and missionaries" from absolute truth to the modernization of truth.[64] In other words, Schaeffer was decrying the shift of focus in Christian churches from what Scripture taught (propositional truth) to a more modern methodology, void of clear absolutes.[65] Schaeffer believed that if this horror were not checked a whole generation of young people—and churches—would be swept away by the tide of modern culture. Now, more than twenty years later, Schaeffer's prophetic scare is our modern reality. MacArthur writes,

The visible church in our generation has become aston-
ishingly tolerant of aberrant teaching and outlandish
ideas—and frighteningly *in*tolerant of sound teaching.
The popular evangelical conception of 'truth' has become
almost completely subjective. Truth is viewed as fluid,
always relative, never absolute.[66]

Having exposed the state of the American church, we can well understand why its energy for missions is at an all-time low. We are sending
out fewer foreign missionaries, allotting less funds to global evangelization,
and, in general, are less concerned about the spiritual condition of other
nations. American Christians have adopted a careless attitude about others
while spending an exorbitant amount of time on personal cares, felt needs,
and financial security. Biblical truth has been replaced in the church
with cultural relativism and a feel-good psychology. But, as sinister as
all this may sound, there is hope.

This chapter is offered as a solution to the theological and missional
crisis of the American church. It is a call back to the absolutes of Scripture.
It is a reflection upon the scriptural boundaries that clearly define the
nature (form) and strategy (function) of the church. If the American
church, or any church outside this country, refuses to live within the
God-fixed borders of Ephesians 1–3 and Matthew 28, it will flounder
spiritually and miss its God-intended purpose. Modern methods are incapable of rejuvenating a drifting church. There must be a return to God's
Word.

In this past century, American churches were privileged to play a
major role in reaching the world with the gospel of Christ. God entrusted
them with financial resources, multiple Bible colleges and seminaries,
mission boards, millions of professed church members, numerous career
missionaries, and media outlets without number. Now, however, many
of these once prosperous churches seem to be at a historical crossroads.
Many are in danger of fitting God's description of the church at Sardis:
"You have a [reputation] that you are alive, but you are dead" (Rev. 3:1
NKJV). Either these American churches are going to experience a revival
of truth and enter a new dawn of theological integrity and missional
energy, or they will die with the culture they have been called to save.
The choice lies in the lap of every reader. May God help you to choose
wisely.

Study Questions

1. In what ways have you seen a spiritual decline in American churches?
2. What are some of the problems facing missionaries as they relate to the American culture?
3. Do you see the young people in your church wanting to be Christian workers or career missionaries? Why or why not?
4. What is the importance of theology to the life of the church?
5. What do the other gospels add to the explanation of the Great Commission in Matthew 28?
6. What important practical church issues does Paul deal with in Ephesians 4–6 that heighten your understanding of the function of the local church?
7. Does your church have the right understanding of God's boundaries for its form and function?

Chapter Notes

1. Patrick Johnstone, *Operation World* (Grand Rapids: Zondervan, 1993), 151.
2. Ibid., 65.
3. Bob Sjogren, and Bill and Amy Stearns, *Run with Vision* (Minneapolis: Bethany House, 1995), 68–69.
4. Ibid.
5. David Briggs, "American Protestants Are Getting Stingy with Church Donations," *Virginia Pilot Daily Newspaper,* 20 January 1998, E1–2.
6. Ibid.
7. Sjogren and Stearns, *Run with Vision,* 70.
8. Ibid.
9. Ibid., 67–68. Sjogren and Stearns reveal that in 1990 there were over twelve hundred non-Western mission agencies in existence. This number, they conclude, will be near two thousand by A.D. 2000.
10. David Wells, *No Place for Truth* (Grand Rapids: Eerdmans, 1993), 231–35.
11. Ibid., 232.
12. Ibid., 233.
13. Ibid.
14. Four pastors who illustrate this propensity to adapt the church to modern culture are Leith Anderson, *Dying for Change* (Minneapolis: Bethany House, 1990); David Fisher, *The 21st Century Pastor* (Grand Rapids: Zondervan, 1996); Ed Dobson, *Starting a Seeker Sensitive Service* (Grand Rapids: Zondervan, 1993); and Rick Warren, *The Purpose Driven Church* (Grand Rapids: Zondervan, 1995).

15. Gary L. W. Johnson makes this point clear in his chapter, "Does Theology Still Matter?" *The Coming Evangelical Crisis,* ed. John Armstrong (Chicago: Moody, 1996), 57–73.

16. Millard Erickson, *Christian Theology,* 1028–30, stresses the fact that much of modern theology is less interested in the essence of the church (form) and greatly concerned with the dynamics of church life (function). Erickson correctly assesses that "the church is now studied through disciplines and methodologies other than dogmatics or systematic theology."

17. Ibid., 1029.

18. John Walvoord, "The Nature of the Church," *Bibliotheca Sacra* 116 (1959): 291.

19. James Boice, *Ephesians: An Expositional Commentary* (Grand Rapids: Zondervan, 1988), 9. Also, John MacArthur, *Ephesians* (Chicago: Moody, 1986), *viii:* "Ephesians focuses on the basic doctrine of the church—what it is and how believers function within it." William Hendriksen, *Ephesians* (Grand Rapids: Baker, 1967), 62–63, "Careful study of Ephesians has led an ever-increasing number of exegetes to arrive at the conclusion that the concept of *the church* receives such emphasis in this epistle that the entire contents can be grouped around it without superimposing one's own subjective opinions upon the apostle's thinking."

20. Hendriksen, *Ephesians,* 62–63.

21. W. Bauer, W. F. Arndt, and F. W. Gingrich, *Greek-English Lexicon of the New Testament,* 4th rev. ed., s.v. "κτίζω," 456; and *Dictionary of New Testament Theology,* s.v. "Creation," by H. H. Esser, 1:383.

22. A. Skevington Wood, "Ephesians," *Expositor's Bible Commentary* (Grand Rapids: Zondervan, 1978), 11:36. Also, for other biblical examples of this fact see Mark 13:19; Colossians 1:16; 1 Timothy 4:3; Revelation 4:11 and 10:6.

23. Ibid., 63. Wood offers three metaphors: a body (1:22–23; 4:4, 16; 5:23, 30), a building (2:19–22), and a bride (5:25–27, 32).

24. John Witmer, "A Review of *Wrongly Dividing the Word of Truth,*" Part 2, *Bibliotheca Sacra* 149 (1992): 263.

25. Walvoord, "The Nature of the Church," 292.

26. Bauer, Arndt, and Gingrich, *Greek-English Lexicon of the New Testament,* s.v. "σῶμα," 806.

27. Hendriksen, *Ephesians,* 103, "The argument with respect to the exact meaning of fullness in this particular case covers many pages in scores of commentaries." In opposition to Hendriksen and the other Reformed writers who have followed Calvin's interpretation ("This is the highest honor of the church, that, until he is united to us, the Son of God reckons himself in some measure imperfect."), I believe Wood, "Ephesians," 32, offers a more reasonable explanation: "But is Christ in any sense incomplete? To make

the church essential to the full being of Christ is to reverse the true relationship. The New Testament regards Christ as essential to the full being of the church, not vice versa."

28. J. B. Phillips, *The New Testament in Modern English* (New York: Macmillan, 1958).

29. Wood, "Ephesians," 32, "This carefully balanced statement [1:23] of Christ's role was designed to encourage the church militant here on earth."

30. S. D. F. Salmond, "The Epistle to the Ephesians," *The Expositor's Greek Testament,* ed. W. Robertson Nicoll (reprint, Grand Rapids: Eerdmans, 1983), 3:317, takes the phrase "exceeding abundantly above all that we ask or think" and translates it as "able to do beyond all things, superabundantly beyond what we ask or think."

31. Ibid.

32. These blessings may be counted as (1) chosen before creation (v. 4), (2) adoption (v. 5), (3) made us accepted (v. 6), (4) redemption through His blood (v. 7), (5) forgiveness of sins (v. 7), (6) knowing His will (vv. 8–9), (7) an inheritance (v. 11), and (8) the sealing of the Holy Spirit (vv. 13–14).

33. Hendriksen, *Ephesians,* 253.

34. Walvoord, "The Nature of the Church," 291.

35. *Webster's New International Dictionary Unabridged,* 2d ed., 2490.

36. Ibid.

37. D. Edmond Hiebert, "An Expository Study of Matthew 28:16–20," *Bibliotheca Sacra* 149 (1992): 338.

38. Ibid., 339. Also, D. A. Carson, "Matthew," *Expositor's Bible Commentary* (Grand Rapids: Zondervan, 1984), 8:595. Carson writes that 28:18 marks "a turning point in redemptive history." For another treatment of Matthew 28:18–20, see ch. 4.

39. Carson, "Matthew," 594: "'All' dominates vv. 18–20 and ties these verses together. . . ."

40. Hiebert, "An Expository Study of Matthew 28:16–20," 346.

41. Ibid.

42. Ibid. Also, it is important to note that these displays of authority caused the scribes continual concern. In fact, they questioned Christ on "his authority" in Matthew 21:23–27. The answer Christ gave them left them frustrated and without the answer they sought.

43. Hendriksen, *Ephesians,* 998.

44. *Theological Dictionary of the New Testament,* s.v. "ἐξουσία," by W. Foerster, 2 (1964): 562.

45. Hiebert, "An Expository Study of Matthew 28:16–20," 346.

46. Ibid., 347.

47. This chapter will not deal with the grammatical significance of πορευθέντες,

which is correctly translated "go" in the NKJV (see the same construction in 28:7 with the aorist participle followed by the aorist imperative, translated "go tell"). See the excellent discussion of this adverbial participle by Daniel Wallace, *Greek Grammar Beyond the Basics* (Grand Rapids: Zondervan, 1996), 645.

48. Hendriksen, *Ephesians,* 999.
49. John Broadus, *The Gospel of Matthew* (Philadelphia: American Baptist Pub. Society, 1886), 593.
50. Carson, "Matthew," 596.
51. Ibid.
52. There are differing views on how these two participles relate to the main verb μαθητεύσατε. Though Carson takes a slightly different approach than I, he clearly recognizes that whatever view is taken "their precise relationship to the main verb is not easy to delineate" (ibid., 597). It seems best, as Hendriksen concludes (ibid., 1000) that the "concepts 'baptizing' and 'teaching' are simply two activities, in co-ordination with each other, but both subordinate to 'make disciples.' In other words, by means of being baptized and being taught a person becomes a disciple, with the understanding, of course, that this individual is ready for baptism and is willing to appropriate the teaching."
53. Hiebert, "An Expository Study of Matthew 28:16–20," 350.
54. Ibid., 351: "The baptism characterized as 'in the name of the Father and the Son and the Holy Spirit' is distinctive by the name invoked. It distinguishes Christian baptism from proselyte baptism or the baptism of John the Baptist. The expression would also distinguish it from all forms of baptism performed in the pagan world."
55. Hiebert, "An Expository Study of Matthew 28:16–20," 352.
56. Ibid., also see Salmond, "The Epistle to the Ephesians," 340.
57. Carson, "Matthew," 598–599, makes this point.
58. Ibid., 599.
59. Bauer, Arndt, and Gingrich, *Greek-English Lexicon of the New Testament,* s.v. "τηρέω," 822.
60. Hendriksen, *Ephesians,* 1003.
61. Hiebert, "An Expository Study of Matthew 28:16–20," 353.
62. Francis Schaeffer, *The God Who Is There* (Downers Grove, Ill.: InterVarsity, 1976).
63. Ibid., 13.
64. Ibid., 13–14.
65. Ibid.
66. John MacArthur, *Reckless Faith* (Wheaton: Crossway, 1994), 19.

14

GERALD K. WEBBER

THE WELL-EQUIPPED SENDING CHURCH

There is a discernible gap between the missionary methods of first-century Antioch and those of many North American churches at the close of the twentieth century. Given roughly two millennia of intervening church history, this is understandable. But is it good?

Bible students with a sound hermeneutic know that much of what is described in Acts is not meant to be applied to the entirety of the church age. The sign gifts, after all, passed away with the apostles who administered them. Still, that same student will see in primitive church practice some valid and suggestive principles. Those principles should guide contemporary churches in the execution of their missionary programs.

One critical concern should be the relationship between sender and the person sent—the local commissioning church and the front-line missionary. Unfortunately, the nature of this vital alliance is often obscured in popular practice. Mission agencies, a comparatively recent development, have no doubt usurped, on occasion, the role of the sending church. It is equally clear that some churches have unwittingly, or sometimes consciously, surrendered their rightful niche. The question is, Who does what? Allowing that the mission agency, though not biblically prescribed, is not *un*biblical, how can we ensure that it does not invade the ground of local-church prerogative?

Perhaps the most enlightening biblical passage addressing these conflicts is Acts 13. This text chronicles what is referred to today as the "commissioning" of the first New Testament missionaries. The narrative establishes the primacy of the local church, and the attentive reader can draw some very enlightening principles from the first four verses:

> Now there were in the church that was at Antioch certain prophets and teachers; as Barnabas, and Simeon that was called Niger, and Lucius of Cyrene, and Manaen which had been brought up with Herod the tetrarch, and Saul. As they ministered to the Lord, and fasted, the Holy Ghost said, Separate me Barnabas and Saul for the work whereunto I have called them. And when they had fasted and prayed, and laid their hands on them, they sent them away. So they, being sent forth by the Holy Ghost, departed unto Seleucia; and from thence they sailed to Cyprus. (Acts 13:1–4)

Missions is the local church reaching beyond its own geographical and cultural boundaries in response to Christ's command to go into all the world and preach the gospel to every creature. At Antioch, the Holy Spirit unveiled God's strategy for separating and sending specially called representatives to do just that. As the account unfolds, the principles emerge.

Principle #1: The Church Is Where God's Servants Are Developed

Today, the validity and value of Bible institutes, colleges, and seminaries is unquestioned. They have proved their usefulness in preparing those who will handle the precious truths of the Word of God and deal with the complex issues of Christians living in a post-Christian society. But these places of learning were never meant to supplant the local church. God established the latter to be the birthplace and incubator for missionaries.

Nor is the modern missionary agency to be the fountainhead of missions. Some very well-intentioned people do not grasp this fact. They believe these agencies are responsible for populating the mission fields of the world. One can almost hear the thoughts of callers who ask, "Would you send us a missionary?"—as if the mission had a high-tech machine in the back room ready to receive detailed specifications at one end and turn out a finished missionary product at the other.

While the ministry schools may assist in preparing missionaries, and the mission agencies may give valuable counsel and assistance to missionaries in the performance of their duties, it is the local church that actually *produces* these servants of the Lord.

Pastors and church leaders might well ask themselves two critical questions: (1) How many missionaries (and other vocational Christian workers) has our church produced in its history? (2) What are we doing *today* to develop the next generation of missionary workers?

It does not require a large church, a multiple staff, and a full-orbed program to create an atmosphere where missionaries are born. This writer knows of a fledgling church in New York state that, in its six-year journey from birth to independence, prepared *three* committed families for missionary service. In the mid-1940s, a home missionary went door-to-door in a remote wooded area in Michigan's Upper Peninsula, seeking children for his newly established Sunday school. Living in a shabby, one-room log cabin, its only conveniences a flowing well, a single incandescent bulb, and an external "two-holer," was a little boy who would accept that invitation. Soon he trusted Christ as his Savior and came under the loving discipleship of a small community of believers with great faith and long vision. God ultimately called that young man into missionary service. The result of his thirty-five years of evangelism and church planting among the hill tribes of Bangladesh was more than one-hundred national churches and the salvation of thousands of precious Bengali souls.

When it comes to producing servants of the Lord, the size of a church is immaterial. What makes the difference is its vision for what God is able to do in terms of developing workers for the mission fields of the world.

Principle #2: The Church Is Where Spiritual Gifts Are Discovered and Implemented

The text from Acts declares that there were in the church "certain prophets and teachers." Nor should one be surprised. Gifted people *should* be found in the church. While some of the gifts present in the early church have ceased, many yet remain and are meant to be used for the building up of the body (Eph. 4:11–16).

We cannot fully discuss the *charismata* here. Others have done so with great meticulousness, if not consistency.[1] While there is scant agreement on which gifts belong in what list and how each is to be used, there *is* considerable accord that spiritual giftedness is a fact of life for the church today.

Knowing that God oversees the construction of the body and placement of its members (1 Cor. 12:18, 28) and that the Holy Spirit gives to each member a gift (Eph. 4:7; 1 Peter 4:10–11) that is necessary for that particular body's development, we should expect to find individuals in the church whose spiritual gifts need to be implemented, both for their own benefit and that of others. Should it not also seem likely that God is developing some of these gifted souls for work beyond local borders?

The congregation aspiring to be an effective sending church ought to have acceptable procedures for helping its people to identify their spiritual gifts. A variety of "spiritual gift surveys" and instructional materials are obtainable for this purpose.[2] Creative teachers can even produce their own teaching aids. However it is accomplished, there must be some specific and intentional way to help believers recognize their spiritual gifts.

It is apparent in Scripture that these "certain prophets and teachers" not only possessed spiritual gifts but were *using* them. A discovered grace-gift is inert until it is implemented. Prophets are to prophesy, and teachers are to teach. Those who serve most effectively on the mission field are those whose gifts have first been effectively employed in the ministry of a sending church. As gifts are exercised, they are strengthened, and so are their users. These growing servants of God often become the stuff of which fine missionaries are made.

Principle #3: The Church Is Where Ministry Is Shared

Verse 2 relates that the missionaries-to-be "ministered to the Lord and fasted." The root of the word *leitourgeo,* here translated "ministered," describes the activity of the Old Testament priest before the altar. It indicates participation in public worship.[3]

The effective sending church is a place where others besides the pastor share in the functions of the worshiping body. Young men will be given opportunity to publicly read Scripture, pray, and perhaps even preach on occasion. Shunning the lure of professionalism, the concerned pastor will allow children to participate in special music and dramatic presentations. Youth nights will not be uncommon, and teenagers may be employed from time to time in ushering and greeting visitors. In short, this will not be the "church of the one-man ministry" because a "one-man ministry" kills incentive in potential ministers and missionaries.

The greatest impediment to a shared ministry is fear on the part of the one who must do the sharing—in this case, the pastor. His unwillingness to take risks in training and building disciples may keep him from reproducing a fine ministry. Gary McIntosh, in his thought-provoking book, *The Exodus Principle,* says,

> The most challenging risk that leaders often have to take is investing their ministry in the people. Even though we know that the clergy-laity gap is unbiblical, putting into practice the truth that we are all servants of Christ has proven difficult. Too many pastors and other church

> leaders hold their people down, fearing the mistakes they
> might make if given freedom to serve. . . . Leaders are
> risk-takers encouraging every member to bring their ac-
> tions and behavior into agreement with what God has
> made them—a minister of Christ.[4]

Blessed is the church where ministry is shared and where people
have the opportunity to publicly grow in the grace of service. The selfless
provision of room to fail—and thus room to succeed—creates a climate
where missionaries can be developed.

Principle #4: The Church Must Sense the Spirit's Direction

Acts 13:2 reveals that, in an environment of sharing in spiritual ministries, the Holy Spirit communicates (perhaps to the assembled church; at
least to the leadership) the divine will for His chosen workers. The church,
then, must see and recognize the hand of God. While always active in the
process of identifying, preparing, and sending missionaries into Great
Commission service, the church is nonetheless secondary. God Himself is
always cast in the lead role in this divine/human cooperative.

If the calling of servants in Acts is consistent with the calling of servants throughout biblical history (and there is no reason to assume otherwise), God's part in the preparation of these individuals can be backdated
to eternity past. King David declared in Psalm 139 that God had known
him, possessed him, covered him, and shaped him in his mother's womb.
At the time of Jeremiah's conscription into prophetic service, God said,
"Before I formed thee in the belly I knew thee . . . I sanctified thee, and I
ordained thee . . ." (Jer. 1:5). Paul implies in Ephesians 1 that predestina-
tion, God's foreknowledge of his salvation, also covered his call to service.

This theological understanding of the ways of God with His chosen
servants prompts an inescapable conclusion: The church is to be so in
tune with what God is doing that it quickly recognizes His calling in the
lives of its membership and authenticates on earth what has already been
decreed in heaven.

Principle #5: The Church Must Release Its Members to Serve Beyond Its Boundaries

As the narrative continues, the Holy Spirit speaks, giving the direct
order to which the church must respond. He says, "Separate [to] me
Barnabas and Saul . . . "(v. 2). There is no mystery in this vocabulary.

The original word rendered "separate" means to mark off with a boundary.[5] These two who have so faithfully served in local ministry are now, in a manner of speaking, to be cut out from the herd, branded, and moved to another corral. The congregation must willingly "release" them for new responsibilities in other places.

Missions, once again, is the local church reaching beyond its own geographical and cultural boundaries in response to Christ's command to go into all the world and preach the gospel to every creature. Once God had marked out Paul and Barnabas for extension ministries, the church had to release them with an official and heartfelt blessing.

The sending church must respond to God's direction for its ambassadors. They must gird themselves to suffer the loss with grace. It is not painless to dispatch much-loved servants of God. A writer vividly recalls the bittersweet feelings when he and his family were called from a happy and fruitful pastorate to a church planting ministry on the other side of the world. The songwriter's words, "When we asunder part, it gives us inward pain," were more than mere poetry. Who could doubt that Paul and Barnabas and the Antioch congregation paid an emotional price when they were separated?

This process of separation can also be a struggle for a congregation planting a new church in its own vicinity. In such cases, more than just one or two may be called upon to loosen or sever the ties that bind. Several families, or even several dozen members, may be needed as the nucleus for the new work. Anticipation of such loss prevents many churches from doing the right thing in their own "Jerusalem." But God is honored, and His work can be multiplied when a church body is willing to pay the price. Witness God's blessing upon such churches as Bethesda Baptist in Brownsburg, Indiana. This congregation has planted nine new churches in and around the Indianapolis area over a recent ten-year span. Far from suffering loss, the mother church has continued to grow and prosper throughout the process. Each separation resulted in pain but also produced fruit for the glory of God.

Effective sending churches willingly, if not eagerly, acknowledge God's orders to separate out those whom He calls to other places and responsibilities.

Principle #6: The Church Must Recognize God's Callings

There is but a slight shift in nuance between sensing the Spirit's direction (principle #4) and recognizing God's callings. But the difference, while slight, is significant and worth noting. The former emphasizes the activity of the Holy Spirit in planning and executing the missionary call of Paul and Barnabas. The latter underscores the need, on the part of the church, to see the hand of God in the *continuing* ministries of the missionaries, even after they depart.

Some years ago, a book about knowing and doing the will of God appeared in bookstores. It attracted immediate attention, especially in Bible colleges and seminaries. Popularized by Garry Friesen in his *Decision Making and the Will of God,* the central premise was that everything that could be known about the will of God was already revealed in the pages of the Bible.[6] Friesen postulated that the believer today should not be looking for God to provide individualized direction and leadership for his critical choices (marriage, ministry, and so on). As long as the Christian walked in concert with biblical guidelines, any number of valid choices could express the good and acceptable and perfect will of God.

Credit should be given to Friesen for magnifying the importance of the Word of God in any search for the will of God. Still, there is ample evidence in Scripture and human experience that God *is* interested in directly influencing the specific decisions of His servants as to where they will work, what they will do, and with whom they will do their work. He may use His Word, and He may use providential circumstances. He may employ external counsel, and He may apply unexplainable internal promptings. However it is accomplished, the servant of God may expect "callings." There may even be "callings within callings," such as Luke cites in Acts 16:10. Already *en route* on their second missionary journey, Paul's missionary team embarked for Macedonia, "assuredly gathering that the Lord had *called us* for to preach the gospel [specifically] unto them."

The effective sending church will recognize the call of God upon its missionary and acknowledge the leadership of the Lord, even in the smaller matters of specific placement in time and space.

Principle #7: The Church Treats the Sending of Missionaries Seriously

Luke indicates in Acts 13:3 that it was only "when they had fasted and prayed" that the commissioning was effected. Whatever else may be deduced from this statement, it is certain that the body understood that they were dealing with holy matters when sending out their missionaries. Holy matters require intense spiritual preparation.

Thus, they fasted and prayed. Others are better schooled and prepared to comment on the place of spiritual fasts in the contemporary church. But certainly fasting need not be eliminated when a contemporary church seeks God's face.

There is no indication in the text as to the number, format, or time frames for the church's seasons of prayer over this matter. Nor is there any hint as to the span of time over which their praying took place. It was surely more than a brief, solitary, isolated event, or else the matter of fasting becomes irrelevant.

An unavoidable conclusion is that Antioch took seriously its privileges and responsibilities as a sending church. Prayer, undergirded and intensified by fasting, set the stage for carrying out the commissioning. Their approach seems preferable to the cursory prayer preceding a potluck supper in the church fellowship hall.

Principle #8: The Church Identifies with and Authorizes Its Missionaries

A missionary, by definition, is one who is sent by another. Woe be unto the missionary who presumes to go forth without the biblical authority of a sending church, symbolized here in verse 3 by the "laying on of hands." George Peters says of this act,

> By the laying on of hands, the church and the individual missionary become bound in a bond of common purpose and mutual responsibility. It is thus not only a privilege and service; it is also the exercise of an authority and the acceptance of a tremendous responsibility. The identification of the church with the sent-forth representative is inclusive doctrinally, spiritually, physically and materially. It is the constituting of a rightful representative who will be able and who is responsible to function as a representative of the church. The church, therefore, by the laying on of hands, declares herself ready to stand and make such representation possible. This should include the prayers and finances required for such a representative ministry.[7]

Peter's recurring use of the word *represent,* or variations thereof, is not merely a case of accidental redundancy. The word is probably the best choice to express what really happens in the commissioning. The sending church identifies itself with the missionary to such a degree that, when the latter goes forth, it is as if the former goes *with* him, *in* him, to his work.

For this reason, it is perhaps significant and advisable for the sending church to actually perform the rite of the laying on (imposition) of hands with its missionaries. Although the significance of this ceremony has varied throughout biblical history, it was a common practice all the way back to the days of the patriarchs. With Jacob, it was a sign of transference of blessing. Later, the tribe of Levi was set aside by the imposition of hands. In the sacrificial system, the hands of the offerer were laid on the head of the vicarious animal. Moses appointed Joshua as his successor, symbolically transferring his authority with the laying on of his hands. The practice continued into New Testament times, when Jesus laid hands on the little children in blessing and upon the sick for healing. The apostles laid hands upon those who would receive the Holy Spirit in the transitional experiences of Acts 8 and 19. The appointment of the seven in Jerusalem was done with imposition of hands. Later, Timothy is told to "stir up the gift of God, which is in thee by the putting on of my hands" (2 Tim. 1:6), and "neglect not the gift . . . which was given thee by prophecy, with the laying on of the hands of the presbytery" (1 Tim. 4:14). He is also cautioned to "lay hands suddenly on no man" (1 Tim. 5:22).[8]

It would be hard to conceive of a more fitting way to portray the relationship between the missionary and his sending church than this setting aside of a special service wherein duly appointed representatives of the assembled church lay hands on the sent one, symbolizing the identification and transference of authority taking place in the commissioning. Memories of this solemn observance will keep the relationship fresh and meaningful through the years while the parties are separated. When significant issues arise and decisions must be made concerning the missionary's ministries or personal concerns, one and all will be prompted to remember that it is the sending church, not the mission agency or other supporting churches, whose authority flows in and through the life of the missionary.

Principle #9: The Church Enables and Underwrites Ministry

Just before declaring that "the Lord ordained that they which preach the gospel should live of the gospel" (1 Cor. 9:14), Paul asks the rhetorical question, "Who goeth a warfare any time at his own charges?" (1 Cor. 9:7) Or, as rendered in the *New American Standard Bible*, "Who at any time serves as a soldier at his own expense?"

The intention and commitment to underwrite the cost of the missionaries' ministries is inherent in the statement at the end of Acts 13:3: "They sent them away." The process of *sending* is inextricably connected, in principle, to the process of *sustaining*. While admittedly we are drawing a conclusion with a minimum of concrete evidence, it would be difficult to believe that the Antioch church sent out its missionaries in complete contradiction to the biblical principles Paul enumerated above. They sent them away but not empty-handed.

Missionaries should expect that, through normal channels of biblical stewardship, God is going to meet their needs in ministry and that they will not be required to serve "at [their] own expense." From Jesus' own experience (Luke 8:1–3), we learn that it is not wrong to *receive* financial support. When He sent out the Twelve, He made it clear to them that it is not wrong to *ask for* assistance (Matt. 10:5–11). From Paul's relationships with the churches, it becomes clear that it is not even wrong to *expect* support (Rom. 15:24, 32; 2 Cor. 1:15–16). And since the expectation is for the giver to receive "fruit" as a result of the giving (Phil. 4:17–19), Paul declares that it is not *selfish to receive* support.

Inasmuch as missionaries have legitimate need for and even a claim to financial support, and since sending churches bears the primary responsibility for their ministries, it is reasonable to expect that such churches will take as large a financial role as possible. Some churches, even some smaller ones, accept the full financial burden of caring for the people they send out. Others shoulder a certain percentage (10 percent, 25 percent, 50 percent), expecting others to pick up the balance. There is no rule to follow. Churches must determine their part by prayer and planning.

Sending out missionaries calls for more, however, than just monetary support from the sending church. Laying hands of blessing and authority upon them, even promising them financial underwriting, should not be the sending church's final acts of assistance. Assuming that the church is not able to underwrite the entire amount of the missionaries' support, there are some practical contributions the church can make when the missionaries proceed into pre-field ministry, commonly called "deputation." During the time the missionaries present themselves, their call, and their burden to other congregations and give these other congregations an opportunity to partner with the sending church in the ministry, they will have many needs. Included among the services the church might render are the following:

1. Permit the missionaries to use the church office equipment.
2. Offer secretarial assistance as needed.
3. Prepare and pay for deputation mailings.
4. Fund initial printing of prayer cards and brochures.
5. Purchase, lease, or loan slide or video equipment, displays, and other equipment.
6. Provide a temporary office and use of a long-distance telephone service (for ministry use).
7. Offer child care when children are unable to travel with parents to meetings.
8. Provide and maintain a church-owned "deputation vehicle."
9. Have a clothing shower to outfit the family for pre-field ministry.

There really is no end to the list. A congregation can help greatly in enabling appointees and underwriting the costs of their ministries. The only limit is the congregation's resources and creativity.

In addition, the pastor of the church can do a great deal for the new missionaries. In some cases, he can actually "make or break" their deputation ministry. Among the things that he, specifically, can do are the following:

1. Encourage the church to respond to the needs listed above.
2. Honor the missionaries in public services, allowing frequent updates.
3. Offer vital counsel and advice.
4. Assist in planning and preparation of deputation literature.
5. Write and distribute letters of introduction/recommendation.
6. Help the missionaries to develop mailing lists.
7. Visit area pastors with the missionaries to help in booking meetings.
8. Network for missionaries, taking them to meetings, fellowships, and so on.
9. Assist with presentations, preparation of messages, and arranging of testimonies.

In short, the pastor would do well to allow "his" missionaries the benefit of all his personal and professional influence. Missionaries are going to be representatives of the sending church, and everything they do (or do not do) will reflect upon its testimony. If God blesses the church with its "own" missionaries, it will be worth all the pastor's efforts to create worthy emissaries. Every investment of time, effort, and money is destined to bear dividends as the church "sends [them] away."

Principle #10: The Church Entrusts the Missionary to the Holy Spirit

Acts 13:3 says,"They [the church] sent them away." Verse 4 begins with, "So they, being sent forth by the Holy Ghost . . ." Who, then, sent them? Was it the church or the Holy Spirit? Both. Having initiated the calling through proper ecclesiastical channels, the Holy Spirit continues the process. The church knows that its missionaries are in the best of care.

Because communication was limited, the church likely never saw or heard from its missionaries until they returned from their first journey. Acts 14:26 says, "And thence [they] sailed to Antioch, from whence they had been recommended to the grace of God for the work which they fulfilled." From Antioch of Syria to Antioch of Pisidia and back; with stops in such places as Attalia, Perga, Iconium, Lystra, and Derbe; sometimes accepted (even worshiped) and sometimes rejected (even stoned and left for dead); now winning people to Christ, and later declaring their hearers unworthy of eternal life (Acts 13:46)—the missionaries toiled. The sending church could do nothing but pray and entrust them to the Holy Spirit's care.

Churches who micromanage the affairs of their missionaries do disservice to the Holy Spirit and His ability to meet needs. The verb used in Acts 13:3 for the departure implies that the church released the missionaries, let go of them, loosed its grip.[9] It is the same word used of Pilate in offering Christ to the crowd at His trial: "Ye have a custom, that I should *release* unto you one at the passover: will ye therefore that I *release* unto you the King of the Jews?" (John 18:39, emphasis added). Inherent in the language is the idea of being cut loose or freed from a hold. Such was the action, difficult as it might have been, required of the commissioning church. The anxiety was blunted, though, by their awareness that the missionaries, far from being cut off from compassionate and capable care, were surrounded by omnipotence. What a comfort!

Summary and Conclusion

God brought local churches into existence to carry out the Great Commission. To assist in this great task, the churches created ministry training schools and mission agencies. The schools and agencies were never meant to govern or direct missionary endeavor. They are *metachurch* organizations, designed to work *with* the churches, not *over* them, in the accomplishment of the churches' God-given responsibilities.

It must be admitted that function has not always followed form. Agencies of human origin can run amok and violate good polity with an exaggerated sense of importance. Pastors and churches can likewise err by surrendering their rightful prerogatives. Only when each party occupies its proper place is God glorified. Only then are churches multiplied and chosen servants biblically moved from the pew to the mission field. While there is still time, may God establish effective sending churches— churches that are willing to use all the resources He has provided for effective Great Commission ministry.

Study Questions

1. How can the local church develop a climate in which missionaries and other vocational Christian workers are consistently encouraged?

2. How might a local church implement a program for discovery of spiritual gifts? At what point in a new member's assimilation into the body should the matter of spiritual gifts be addressed?

3. Name ten church activities or ministries in which children and youth could be involved, with a view toward encouraging them to consider a life of vocational ministry.

4. What are some practical ways in which the church could sensitize itself to the presence of God's calling in a member's life? How should the church respond upon learning of that calling?

5. Carefully plan a commissioning service program for a member of the local sending church, indicating the significance of each item in the program.

6. What specific supportive services could your church already provide if God should call one of its members into missionary service?

7. What are the minimum additions you would make to the above list in question 6?

8. Is a mission agency absolutely necessary in the carrying out of the church's missionary mandate? If a mission agency is involved in helping the church with its missionary program, what should be the relationship between the sending church and the mission agency? How should the missionary relate to each?

Chapter Notes

1. See Walter J. Chantry, *Signs of the Apostles* (Carlisle, Pa.: Banner of Truth, 1973); also see Robert L. Thomas, *Understanding Spiritual Gifts* (Grand Rapids: Kregel, 1999); Merrill F. Unger, *The Baptism and Gifts of the Holy Spirit* (Chicago: Moody, 1974); and Rick Yohn, *Discover Your Spiritual Gift and Use It* (Wheaton: Tyndale, 1974).

2. A good source for a pattern for a spiritual gift survey is Tim Blanchard, *A Practical Guide to Finding and Using Your Spiritual Gift* (Wheaton: Tyndale, 1983).

3. William F. Arndt and F. Wilbur Gingrich, *A Greek-English Lexicon of the New Testament and Other Early Christian Literature* (Chicago: University of Chicago Press, 1957), 471–72.

4. Gary L. McIntosh, *The Exodus Principle* (Nashville: Broadman & Holman, 1995), 45.

5. Fritz Rienecker, *A Linguistic Key to the Greek New Testament,* ed. Cleon L. Rogers Jr. (Grand Rapids: Zondervan, 1982), 291.

6. Garry Friesen, *Decision Making and the Will of God* (Portland: Multnomah, 1980).

7. George W. Peters, *A Biblical Theology of Missions* (Chicago: Moody, 1972), 221.

8. James Orr, ed., *The International Standard Bible Encyclopedia,* 5 vols. (Grand Rapids: Eerdmans, 1939), 2:1335.

9. Rienecker, *A Linguistic Key,* 291.

15

ROBERT W. MILLIMAN

THE IMPACT OF MISSIONARIES' CHILDREN ON THEIR FREEDOM TO SERVE

A perusal of scholarly journals published over the last couple of decades indicates that scholars who devote a good part of their energies to training missionaries do not share an equal concern for helping churches decide if these individuals are qualified to serve. These scholars offer churches little guidance as they seek to apply the criteria enunciated in 1 Timothy 3 and Titus 1 to the candidates seeking their support.[1] Is it any wonder, then, that missions committees do not look primarily to the older, mature men of the church with demonstrated character, wisdom, and experience when searching for qualified people to send to the mission field? Rather, education, personality, and professional achievement are frequently the criteria.

This chapter addresses one of the biblical qualifications for missionaries. What is the relationship between the moral/spiritual status of a person's children and his or her fitness to serve as a missionary? This question is addressed through an exegesis of the two most relevant passages on this topic—1 Timothy 3:4–5 and Titus 1:6. Although the subject of these passages is the role of elder, their examination is appropriate since no better statement on the qualifications for Christian leaders can be found in the New Testament than the lists in 1 Timothy 3 and Titus 1. Furthermore, most missionaries, practically speaking, fulfill the role of elder in their ministries.

1 Timothy 3:1-7

These verses form a self-contained paragraph. They have a single subject—qualifications for bishops—bounded by a preceding paragraph directing women not to teach in certain circumstances and a following paragraph on the qualifications for deacons. It is asserted that bishops *must* (δεῖ) possess fifteen qualities. The necessity for these qualifications is *based* (οὖν) on the office of the bishop being a *good work* (καλὸν ἔργον).

The word καλός is liberally employed by Paul in the Pastorals to mean "good," "useful," or more particularly, "excellent." He frequently uses the word with ἔργον—"good deed."[2] One should especially note the implication that good deeds are a necessary consequence of salvation (cf. Titus 2:14; 3:8a, 14) and that they need to be present in the life of a leader for the purpose of modeling a proper life to others (Titus 2:7).[3] These uses seem to indicate that καλοῦ ἔργου in 3:1 says more than the obvious, that the job of the bishop is a good thing or occupation. Certainly this is not excluded by these words, but more than that, the bishop performs the "good work" *par excellence* and must, therefore, give evidence of the qualifications that follow.[4]

The necessity of these qualifications is conveyed by the expression δεῖ οὖν. While it is true that οὖν often is used simply to move a discourse along, merely denoting transition (cf. NIV, NRSV—"Now"), this function is more characteristic of narrative as opposed to didactic literature.[5] In 1 Timothy 3:2, Paul is probably using οὖν to show that what follows ("he must . . .") can be inferred from what precedes (it is a "good work"). This corresponds with his use of οὖν elsewhere in the Pastorals.[6] A translation of "therefore" or "then" (NASB, KJV) is appropriate.[7]

Because the office of bishop is a good work, Paul teaches that a bishop must (δεῖ) possess the characteristics that he lists.[8] The verb δεῖ itself does not denote the authority that imparts this necessary characteristic. More precise significance is given to the term when it is conjoined with this authority. In many cases, however, δεῖ is weakened by everyday use to simply convey necessity, duty, or what is fitting (cf. 2 Tim. 2:6, 24; Rom. 8:26). Yet ethical or religious obligations based on some law or authority may be denoted by δεῖ (cf. Luke 13:14; 22:7). In classical Greek and in Hellenistic use, a neutral deity, Fate, which determines the course of the world, stands behind this term even in its weakened sense. In the Septuagint and New Testament δεῖ does not express the divine necessity of fate but indicates divine destiny, necessity grounded in the will of God (e.g., Rom. 1:27; 1 Cor. 15:53; 2 Cor. 5:10). In 1 Timothy 3:2, as elsewhere in Paul's writings, δεῖ frequently points to the will of God in Paul's message or exhortation.[9]

The qualifications that follow are not simply ideals to which church leaders are to aspire. They are not goals that Paul hopes bishops will reach. They are absolute requirements necessitated by the will of God. They are necessary because the office of the bishop personifies the "good deed" *par excellence*. Virtually all of these qualities are those that Paul would expect of any believer. Failure to meet these qualifications means removal from consideration for the bishopric because the bishop needs to embody qualities that other church members are meant to show.[10] He is to be a model. One of the qualities indispensable for a bishop is an exemplary home.

The Qualification List

It is maintained by some that the qualification lists in 1 Timothy 3:1–7; 8–12; and Titus 1:5–9 (cf. 2 Tim. 2:24–25) reflect a common, generic (i.e., non-Christian) schema. This is the explanation given not only for the lists' similarity to one another but also for their alleged paucity of Christian elements and qualifications specific to bishops and elders.[11] In support of this, appeal is made to the way the Pastorals' lists resemble secular duty lists and virtue lists in both form and language.[12] The best examples of this resemblance are the general list of requirements for a Stoic wise man given in Diogenes Laertius 7.116–26 and for a military general recorded in Onosander, *Strategikos* 1.1–18.[13] The correspondence of the Pastorals' lists to a supposed pervasive Christianization of the world in these epistles is also used to support the generic schema theory. The Pastoral Epistles, in this view, simply reproduce popular ethics and add Christian motives. They describe "the normal, virtuous life of the good citizen"; they betray a Christian bourgeois.[14]

It should be noted first of all that there are significant differences, both in form and language, between Paul's lists and secular duty lists. For example, Diogenes Laertius 7.116–26 is not a list at all but a lengthy narrative description with only a few verbal likenesses to the Pastorals' lists. Onosander's *Strategikos* is a lengthy treatise on military science— on the responsibilities of a general, whose qualifications and characteristics are spelled out in the first two chapters. When the first part of chapter 1 is isolated from the rest of the treatise, especially the first paragraph, there is an apparent resemblance between this portion and the Pastorals' lists. But on close examination little in common is found. Of the forty items in the Pastorals' lists, only three find exact matches in Onosander and two find synonyms. [15] In the end, the primary point of contact with Diogenes Laertius 7.116–26 and Onosander's *Strategikos* is the emphasis on character instead of functional qualifications. This is not evidence for a shared schema but simply a shared regard for the prerequisite of character qualifications for leadership positions (cf. Acts 6:2–3). [16]

To be sure, there are reasons to believe that Paul used preformed material in 1 Timothy 3 and Titus 1. The introductory phrase in 1 Timothy 3:1, πιστὸς ὁ λόγος, is likely a quotation formula, perhaps associated with the teaching of the prophets. [17] Preformed material is also indicated by the ταῦτα formula in 1 Timothy 3:14, which concludes and refers to 3:1b–13. The position of 3:1b–13 between these two phrases makes it somewhat independent of its context, further lending it a traditional character. [18] The similarities between 1 Timothy 3 and Titus 1 further suggest Paul may have used a common source (perhaps one of his own creation), while the differences, at a minimum, point to significant personal modifications, probably made on the basis of unique life-settings. [19] The use of a source, along with the use of some of the language of his popular milieu (e.g., the general terms μὴ ἀνεπίλημπτον, κόσμιον, ἀνεγκλητος) and a form with resemblance to Onosander's *Strategikos,* however, do not prove Paul used a generic schema drawn from his secular society in contradiction to his theological base. [20]

Though Paul's lists are not made up exclusively of specific Christian elements, it is incorrect to say that these elements are lacking. [21] In addition, a specifically Christian element is hardly missing from the rest of these epistles (e.g., 1 Tim. 4:12; 6:11). It is fair to say that a Christian element is assumed of the bishop/elder. Paul does not provide or add to a conformist ethic but repudiates its presuppositions and establishes a Jewish/Christian/Pauline theological framework. [22] He gives an ethic with a theological grounding, evidenced not only in the lists themselves but also in his use of Scripture, classic Christian virtues and emphases, exemplary paradigms (Christ, Paul, Timothy), and in the assumptions behind his rhetorical deductions. [23]

While using language and a form somewhat similar to those employed by secular writers of his day and sharing a similar concern for character qualities for leadership, there is no evidence that Paul used one of their "duty schemata" nor that he based his ethics on their works. Rather, his lists and their relationship to the rest of the Pastoral Epistles indicate that his ethics were grounded in a Jewish-Christian milieu.

1 Timothy 3:4a

τοῦ ἰδίου οἴκου καλῶς προϊστάμενον

The thirteenth qualification for a bishop given by Paul in 1 Timothy 3:1–7 is that he must manage his own household well (v. 4a). This qualification is further defined in verse 4b, and a reason for it is given in verse 5. These three components will now be considered separately. In this first section, the components of "household," "manage," and "well" in 3:4a are taken up.

The word οἶκος is frequently used to denote a dwelling or even a large building. It is used figuratively for the body of all believers—the spiritual temple of God (1 Peter 2:5). As it does elsewhere in the Pastoral Epistles, in 1 Timothy 3:4a it most certainly stands for a family.[24] By extension, the word can refer to a whole clan or tribe descended from a common ancestor (e.g., οἶκος Ἰσραήλ). The picture of the family, rather than that of the building or clan, seems to be the meaning best suited to the metaphor "household of God" in 1 Timothy 3:15. The local church is pictured as a family in 1 Timothy 5:1–2, where Paul exhorts Timothy to treat church members as family members.

Paul writes to Timothy so that he will know how he *must* (δεῖ) behave in God's household, in His family localized in Ephesus (1 Tim. 3:15). Part of these instructions include what a church leader *must* be (δεῖ, 3:2–7). The leader must be a good at leading his own family, because he will manage God's family, the local church. The word variously translated above by "lead" or "manage" is προΐστημι. The word is used eight times in the New Testament, always by Paul. He uses προΐστημι either to denote a function of leaders (1 Tim. 3:4–5, 12; 5:17; Rom. 12:8; 1 Thess. 5:12) or a way of accomplishing good deeds (Titus 3:8, 14). The exact function of leaders denoted by προΐστημι is not clear. The nature of προΐστημι may be inferred from several aspects of Paul's use. For example, its possession is necessary for evidence of the ability to *care for* (ἐπιμελέομαι, see below) the church (1 Tim. 3:5). It may be exercised alongside of admonition, which may indicate that an aspect of guiding or teaching is included in the meaning of the word (1 Thess. 5:12). In 1 Timothy 5:17 it includes or is associated with preaching and teaching.

Προΐστημι is copiously represented in the Greek literature of the New Testament era, always with primarily three nuances.[25] It is used in the manner Paul employed it in Titus, that is, to be occupied with an object in the sense of "to care for" or "to execute" (e.g., Prov. 26:17). It can mean "preside" in the sense of "lead, conduct, or govern" (e.g., 1 Macc. 5:19; *Ep. Aris.* 111; cf. with οἶκος, 2 Kgdms. 13:17; Amos 6:10).

It is also used to convey the idea of standing or going before something in protection—"to assist, care for, help."[26]

Louw and Nida help to clarify the meaning of προΐστημι in 1 Timothy 3:4. They make a distinction between verbs in the semantic subdomain of "lead or guide"—the subdomain in which they place the use of προΐστημι in 1 Timothy 3:4—and those in the semantic subdomain of "rule or govern."[27] The former verbs contain the idea of showing or demonstrating to another how one ought to do something. They also imply a willingness on the part of others to be led and a minimum of control on the part of the one guiding.[28]

One may conclude that προΐστημι, here, primarily means "to lead" or "to guide." Yet the ideas of protection and support should not be excluded.[29] The aspect of care can be seen in the word's association with ἐπιμελέομαι in verse 5.[30] These two aspects of "lead/guide" and "protect" are supported by the contexts of pastoral care in which one finds Paul's other uses of προΐστημι.[31] The nature of the pastoral task—care for souls—highlights this latter aspect of the word (1 Tim. 5:17, cf. 1 Thess. 5:12). With this requirement Paul implies that God desires leaders who lead by caring. One who is fit to lead the church is one who leads, guides, and teaches his children in a protective and supportive manner. In other words, he does not provoke his children to anger but brings them up by means of training and correction that are exercised under the lordship of Christ.[32]

According to Paul, then, those that lead well (καλῶς) are qualified to serve as bishops. Several of the different shades of meaning conveyed by this word would probably apply in 3:4a: "acceptably" (cf. Matt. 12:12), "rightly" or "correctly" (cf. Phil. 4:14), "fitly" or "appropriately" (cf. Gal. 5:7).[33] Its exact meaning must be derived from the context. That is not difficult in this case, for Paul tells the reader in verse 4b what he has in mind when he writes of leading one's family well.

1 Timothy 3:4b

τέκνα ἔχοντα ἐν ὑποταγῇ, μετὰ πάσης σεμνότητος

Paul modifies προϊστάμενον with the participle ἔχοντα to describe how a person must manage his household in order to qualify for the bishopric.[34] A proper understanding of this qualification compels us to consider the meaning of τέκνα, ὑποταγή, and σεμνότης.

At what point in his child's life would a father no longer be responsible for that child's actions? In contrast to the several other words for "child," τέκνον stands for a child in relation to its parents.[35] It is a kinship term most commonly used to designate one's immediate offspring without reference to sex or age.[36] It is the relationship, not the age, that is conveyed by this term. Since one never stops being a child of one's parents, the answer to the question posed above must be decided apart from the word τέκνον itself. It is most likely that τέκνον refers to those children that Paul's first-century audience would have understood as being under their parents' purview, that is, those under the age of majority or who have not yet set up their own homes (Eph. 5:31; cf. Gen. 2:24).[37] But within that group, it is a man's older children that are being referred to. There are several reasons for this conclusion. Mothers, not fathers, were particularly responsible for the rearing of young children.[38] Furthermore, the children in these qualification lists are deemed capable of personal faith (cf. Titus 1:6). In addition, their fathers are called "elders" (Titus 1:5, cf. v. 6), a designation for someone whose children are probably not young. Finally, the actions contemplated in Titus 1:6 are characteristic of older children (but children, nonetheless, and not mature adults).

Those assessing the qualifications of bishops need to observe if the man has his children ἐν ὑποταγῇ. In early Christian literature ὑποταγή is only found in a passive sense and is usually translated "subjection, subordination, or obedience."[39] Paul's three other uses of ὑποταγή all suggest this meaning.[40]

An analysis of the use of the cognate verb ὑποτάσσομαι may shed some light on the meaning of ὑποταγή. When used passively it means "to become subject, subject oneself, be subjected, or obey."[41] For example, women are not permitted to speak in church but are to be in *submission* (1 Cor. 14:34, cf. ὑποταγή in 1 Tim. 2:11). And employing a family metaphor, Hebrews 12:9 asks, in light of our respect for our earthly fathers who disciplined us, "Should we not much more be *subject* to the Father of spirits and live?" The verb usually denotes a sense falling somewhere between voluntary subordination and acquiescence, but it rarely denotes compulsion.[42] Little practical difference between ὑποτάσσομαι and ὑπακούω can be maintained.[43] As in Colossians 3:20 and Ephesians 6:1, where this latter verb is used to designate the child's duty toward his or her parents, the allusion is most likely to the fifth commandment. The potential bishop is to ensure that his children heed that Old Testament injunction.

From Paul's use of σεμνότης elsewhere one can discern that it has positive connotations, but a precise meaning is not clear. In this context, it implies an attitude contrary to what one might possibly expect from a child called upon to be in submission, viz. bitterness, resentment, or the like. In considering the meaning of σεμνότης one should also assess the use of the cognate adjective σεμνός.[45] Σεμνός, with reference to people, means "worthy of respect or honor, dignified, noble, or serious."[46] Σεμνότης, then, is the quality or manner shown by someone who is σεμνος.[47] Accordingly, reverence, dignity, seriousness, respectfulness are words that may be used to convey what is meant by σεμνότης.[48] Once again, an allusion to the fifth commandment to honor one's parents is likely here. The bishop's children are to be those who, out of respect,[49] are in submission to their father.[50] Fee reminds us that "there is a fine line between demanding obedience and gaining it," yet it is the latter style of parenting that Paul maintains qualifies one to "parent" the local church.[51] The bishop is to be one who influences the congregation, not by coercion, but out of a respect rooted in his demonstrated care.

1 Timothy 3:5

εἰ δέτις τοῦ ἰδίου οἴκου προστῆναι οὐκ οἶδεν, πῶς ἐκκλησίας θεοῦ ἐπιμελήσεται

In this verse Paul gives the reason for the preceding qualification. The δέ is not used as a copulative or with adversative force but to introduce an explanatory parenthesis.[52] In stating his reason Paul frames it in the form of a rhetorical question, using a first-class conditional clause: For if anyone does not know how to manage his own household, how can he take care of God's church? The obvious answer is that he cannot.[53]

The meaning of ἐπιμελέομαι is graphically illustrated in the parable of the good Samaritan: "He *took care* of him."[54] This well-attested meaning is also illustrated in Genesis 44:21(Septuagint). Judah quotes Joseph concerning Benjamin, "I will *take care* of him."[55] The word implies more than just leadership, as is commonly thought; it also involves caring concern.

This corresponds to the Pauline pictures of leadership given elsewhere. For example, Paul said to the Ephesian elders that they had been made bishops by the Holy Spirit to "care for (ποιμαίνειν) the church of God" (Acts 20:28 rsv; cf. 1 Peter 5:2–3). The importance of modeling, being a good example, is also stressed by Paul.[57] In fact, the qualification lists in 1 Timothy 3 and Titus 1 give the strong impression that modeling is the main point and hence one of the functions, if not the main function, of a bishop. Grudem writes, "It is not optional that their lives be examples for others to follow; it is a requirement."[58] In order to care for the church and be an appropriate example, the bishop must know how to lead his home.

Paul is drawing upon a universal principle: "Potential skill in a larger sphere can only be indicated by similar skill in a lesser sphere."[59] The concept of drawing conclusions from a person's private life to determine qualification for public office would not be foreign to Paul's readers. They would have been aware of Eli, who was judged and removed from office because of his failure to restrain the behavior of his sons (1 Sam. 2:29–31; 3:13). The pervasiveness of this concept can be seen through its manifestation in sources as diverse as Polycarp and secular Greek parenesis.[60]

The application of a universal principle, however, is not all that is at stake in this passage. In 1 Timothy οἶκος is a pregnant metaphor for the church (3:15; cf. 5:1–2; Eph. 2:19). Since the church is a family, "the man who is a failure at one (family) is thereby disqualified for the other (church)."[61]

Titus 1:5–9

Following his greeting, Paul gives Titus a list of qualifications for elders (1:5–9), whom he also identifies as bishops (v. 7, see n. 61). A new thought is picked up in verse 10, at which point Paul gives the reason (cf. γάρ) for the qualification begun in verse 9.

At verse 5 Paul indicates to Titus that he had left him in Crete to take care of tasks that remained to be done and to appoint elders if any met the criteria that follow. Paul provides three criteria in verse 6 in the protasis of a conditional clause: An elder was to be blameless, "the husband of one wife," and one who had believing children. "Blameless" (ἀνέγκλητος) appears to function as a broad, all-embracing term (cf. ἀνεπίλημπτος in 1 Tim. 3:2). In verse 6 it is explained positively by two important home-related qualities. It is repeated in verse 7 and then further explained by twelve qualities, negatively by five and positively by seven.

In verse 7, Paul explains why (γάρ) the bishop/elder must be (δεῖ) blameless in the sense of verse 6:[62] He functions as God's household steward (οἰκονόμον).[63] An alternative view posits a second list of traditional qualifications starting in verse 7, reflecting a separate office and perhaps composed or inserted into the text, in the second century with the rise of monarchial bishops. The repetition of ἀνέγκλητος, however, and the use of γάρ argue for the former position.[64]

Since the elder functions as God's "householder," he must have his own household in order, if he is to qualify for this office. Paul is essentially making the same point that he makes in 1 Timothy 3:5 (cf. v. 15).[65] First Timothy 3:4 and Titus 1:6 have different vantage points, though. The potential elder's children are viewed positively in 1 Timothy 3:4—the elder must have them in a submission that is characterized by respect. Titus 1:6c views their behavior positively and negatively: The potential elder must have believing (or faithful) children who are not characterized by debauchery or rebellion.

Titus 1:6c

Τέκνα ἔχων πιστά, μὴ ἐν κατηγορίᾳ ἀσωτίας ἢ ἀνυπότακτα

The first issue that confronts us here is whether Paul requires the elder to have children who are believers or ones who are trustworthy and faithful (presumably to their father). Paul's use of πιστός in the Pastorals allows both options. It is used five times each way and five times in the phrase πιστὸς.[66] The matter must be decided on the basis of context if it can be decided at all.[67]

Lock prefers "trustworthy or loyal," as he thinks this meaning fits the following qualifiers and the parallel 1 Timothy 3:4 better.[68] It may be argued in response that the following characteristics of the children could just as easily be understood as negative evidence for belief. Most commentators opt for the sense, "believers."[69] Indeed, this may be the best alternative. Note the similarity of Titus 1:6—τέκνα ἔχων πιστά—to the phrase in 1 Timothy 6:2—οἱ δὲ πιστοὺς ἔχοντες δεσπότας.[70]

In order to be an elder, a man must have children who are not open to an accusation of debauchery or rebelliousness. The existence of either (ἤ) serves to disqualify the father from consideration.

Κατηγορία is used two times elsewhere in the New Testament. Each time it denotes an accusation in some sort of judicial sense.[71] Κατηγορία is derived from κατήγορος, which means "accusing someone." The cognate noun is κατήγωρ—"accuser." Both the adjective and noun are found only in a judicial sense in the New Testament.[72] The cognate verb, κατηγορέω, is used as a technical term to refer to the action of bringing charges in a court.[73] But it is also utilized without legal connotations to mean accuse or "reproach" (e.g., Rom. 2:15).

In light of this evidence, the best meaning of κατηγορία in Titus 1:6 at first may appear to be an accusation in the context of church discipline (cf. 1 Tim. 5:19) or perhaps in secular court.[74] Yet it is possible that Paul is using the term metaphorically for an accusation brought before the court of public opinion. In other words, the potential elder's children must not have a *reputation* of debauchery. This latter alternative seems more sensible on the grounds that actual guilt and not just a charge (which could be unfounded) would be a more likely basis for the disqualification of the father. In support of this interpretation, Fee observes that here is "the first hint of what will become the dominant theme of the letter—good works with exemplary behavior, with a concern for what outsiders think (cf. 2:8, 10; 3:2)."[75]

A reputation of debauchery or rebelliousness are the disqualifying behaviors.[76] The noun ἀσωτία is found two other times in the New Testament. Ephesians 5:18 associates it with drunkenness, and 1 Peter 4:4 describes it by the unseemly qualities listed in the previous verse: licentiousness, passions, drunkenness, reveling, carousing, lawless idolatry (cf. Prov. 28:7). The cognate adverb, ἀσώτως, is used in Luke 15:13 to describe the nature of the prodigal son's spending spree ("He squandered his property in dissolute living," [ζῶν ἀσώτως, author's translation]). The older son describes this activity as living with prostitutes (v. 30).

The association of ἀσωτία with drunkenness and illicit sexual behavior also occurs in Jewish intertestamental literature.[77] Misuse and squandering of property are also frequently linked with the word in secular contexts (cf. Luke 15:13, 10). Werner Foerster concludes that ἀσωτία has retained "essentially the same sense from classical to Byzantine times," namely, self-destruction characterized by wasteful expenditure and intemperate living.[78]

With this use of ἀσωτία, Paul has in mind the squandering of property to support unbridled, indulgent, sinful living. The word's association with abusive, alcoholic, and sexual behavior should also be kept in mind. The force of ἀσωτία is broader than sporadic misconduct or an isolated incident.

Rebelliousness or insubordination is the probable sense of ἀνυπότακτος. Paul uses this term to characterize those who are rebellious to the law (1 Tim. 1:9), rebellious to sound teaching (Titus 1:10), and rebellious to their father (Titus 1:6).[79] While Paul gives the positive requirement of submission in 1 Timothy 3:4, here he provides the converse, behavior that should not be true of an elder's children. In so doing, he appeals, at least indirectly, to the authority of the fifth commandment.

Paul's main point in this verse is that an elder is expected to have Christian children, ones who do not contradict their profession of Christ by their behavior. It is a necessary qualification in order for a man to be God's household steward (v. 7). A man's home life reveals his character and leadership skills, skills that are necessary to fulfill the role of elder. Essentially this is the same point that is made in 1 Timothy 3:4–5.

Conclusion and Implications

The bishop/elder is involved in a noble work, the good deed *par excellence;* he is a model to those he leads. Because of this, and because he is responsible for caring for God's household, he *must* lead and care for his children in a way that reveals his fitness to lead and care for God's children. He is to lead, guide, and teach his children in a protective, caring, and supportive way, not through heavy-handed dominance. Evidence of his effectiveness will be found in the character of the children themselves. They are to be believers (or possibly faithful) and characterized by respectful submissiveness, not debauchery and rebellion. In other words, they must practice the fifth commandment.

Several implications may be drawn from the preceding discussion. First, one should note that the qualification lists in both 1 Timothy 3 and Titus 1 are made up almost entirely of criteria that measure one's character or the conduct that stems from it (cf. 2 Tim. 2:24–26). In both lists an ability to teach is included, but this is only one of the fifteen items given in each (cf. 1 Tim. 3:8–12; Acts 6:3, 5). When it chooses missionaries, the church needs to follow the lead of God, who does not look on the outward appearance as man does, but who looks on the heart (1 Sam. 16:7; cf. 2 Cor. 5:16). It should not surprise us that He requires an exemplary household from one who will model such to His household.

One should also note that several years of development on the part of the potential bishop and a lengthy period of observation by the congregation are implied in these verses (cf. 1 Tim. 3:10; 5:22).[80] This would add up to and correspond to the usual age for matriculation into leadership roles in New Testament times. Jesus was about thirty when he began His ministry (Luke 3:23). Similarly, the Levites entered into full service at thirty (Num. 4:47; cf. vv. 3, 23, 30); Joseph became prime minister of Egypt at thirty (Gen. 41:46); and David became king over Israel at thirty (2 Sam. 5:4; cf. Ezek. 1:1).[81] It seems that "about thirty" was a generally recognized minimum age for the assumption of a leadership position in New Testament culture. In our society, which delays maturity by the youth-oriented cultures of high school, college, and graduate school and then prolongs it further by postponing marriage and child-rearing, one wonders if thirty years is a realistic age to expect the type of maturity *required* by these lists. Furthermore, one may ask if our contemporary practice of supporting missionaries known to a church only through a few hours of observation is not only contrary to the practice assumed in this passage but is responsible for many of the problems that exist in the mission field. One of these problems is what to do with missionaries whose children do not "turn out." This contrasts with the New Testament pattern of selecting elders from the older, spiritually mature men of the local congregation.

Paul's ethical base is not borrowed from nature or the common morality of his day. Rather, it is derived from a Jewish-Christian milieu and reflects divine destiny, the will of God (cf. δεῖ, 1 Tim. 3:2; Titus 1:7). Specifically, it is found in the fifth commandment of the Decalogue. He would undoubtedly, then, consider his instruction to be normative for all times and places.

In addition, it must be asked whether the requirement given by Paul is consistent with his assumption of free moral agency and personal responsibility. That is, is Paul being consistent when he holds a father responsible for the free actions of his children? Two observations may help to relieve the apparent tension here. First, one should not forget the unique role of the bishop/elder. He is to be an *example* of what a Christian is to be like—this example is the good deed *par excellence.* In addition, he is to be the *leader of God's family* localized in a particular congregation. As a result, a demonstrated ability to lead a family is a necessity for Paul. Second, this tension may be partially due to our modern underemphasis on a parent's responsibility in child-rearing and our overemphasis on a child's freedom. All would agree that a parent has *some* impact on how a child turns out. How much impact? How much responsibility? It is impossible to draw a definite line on the spectrum between responsibility and freedom. The "child qualification" may simply be Paul's recognition of the impossibility of this task from a human point of view.

Does the qualification of having exemplary children serve as a criterion for active missionaries as well? Common sense answers this question affirmatively. Few would have problems seeing drunkenness or immorality as grounds for removal from missionary service and both appear in the same lists with the "child qualification" and under the same verb "must." If the apparent New Testament pattern of selecting elders from among the older, spiritually mature men of the congregation, men who would have children approaching marriageable age, were followed in the selection of missionaries today, this question probably would not arise.[82]

May a missionary who is removed for failing to meet this criterion ever be restored? There is no explicit biblical basis for permanent exclusion from missionary service, provided the missionary can correct the deficiency. After a test period that is deemed appropriate by supporting congregations, he may be considered qualified to serve once again. It may be rare, though, for a missionary's effectiveness in ministry to be regained, if it were lost through the negative reputation of his children. The problem is compounded in that the father's best opportunity to influence his children—during their youth—would have passed. On the other hand, one can imagine that the removal of a father from the mission field could well "wake up" a wayward child.

These observations suppose that missionaries assume the primary responsibility for rearing their own children. Even missionaries, however, who employ the services of boarding schools cannot escape the demands of the "children qualification." Better alternatives may be home education or delaying missionary service until children have completed secondary education. Indeed, this latter option seems to correspond best to the biblical pattern.[83]

The most pressing need of any Christian family, whether here or abroad, is direction in developing and maintaining proper family relationships. Common sense dictates that missionaries should have demonstrated success in bringing up their children. The apostle Paul agrees.

Study Questions

1. What is the main question addressed in this chapter, and what are the main passages used to answer the question?
2. Explain the meaning of 1 Timothy 3:1, especially the meaning in this context of "good works."
3. Are the qualifications of 1 Timothy 3 "ideals to which church leaders are to aspire"? Explain and support your answer from the passage.
4. Some claim the lists of qualifications in 1 Timothy 3:1–7 and Titus 1:5–9 are the common, generic, non-Christian virtues of a good citizen. Give the arguments for and against this viewpoint.
5. Explain the teaching of 1 Timothy 3 concerning a Christian leader's relationship with his family and children.
6. Explain what Paul means by the qualifications "blameless" and "husband of one wife" in Titus 1.

Chapter Notes

1. The comprehensive, electronic databases for *Religious Index One* and *Religious and Theological Abstracts,* as well as the indices for *New Testament Abstracts* from 1975 to the present, were consulted in preparation for this article. Only one article dealing in part or in whole with the qualifications of elders appeared during this time (with the exception of treatments of "husband of one wife" (Ed Glasscock, "The Biblical Concept

of Elder," *Bibliotheca Sacra* 144 [1987]: 68–78). In addition, twelve standard systematic theologies were consulted. Only two went beyond citing
1 Timothy 3 and Titus 1 as qualifications for elders (John Gill, *A Complete Body of Doctrinal and Practical Divinity,* new ed. [1839; reprint, Paris,
Ark.: Baptist Standard Bearer, 1987], 864–66; Wayne Grudem, *Systematic
Theology: An Introduction to Biblical Doctrine* [Grand Rapids: Zondervan,
1994], 916–17).

2. 1 Timothy 5:10, 25; 6:18; Titus 2:7, 14; 3:8, 14. Cf. ἀγαθὸν ἔργον—
1 Timothy 5:10; 2 Timothy 2:21; 3:17; Titus 1:16; 3:1.

3. On the use of the phrase *good works* in the Pastorals to portray the life
of faith, see Robert W. Milliman, "Paul's Theology of the Parent-Child
Relationship" (Ph.D. diss., Trinity Evangelical Divinity School, 1997),
262 n. 246.

4. John Calvin, *The Second Epistle of Paul the Apostle to the Corinthians
and the Epistles to Timothy, Titus and Philemon,* trans. T. A. Smail (Grand
Rapids: Eerdmans, 1964), 221, holds that Paul's meaning of *good* and
work can be found in Plato's maxim "that things that are excellent are
also arduous and difficult." Like Calvin, most commentators ignore the
prevalence of *good deed* in the Pastorals and simply seize upon different
ways to convey *good*: "excellent occupation"—Donald Guthrie, *The
Pastoral Epistles,* 2d ed., Tyndale New Testament Commentaries (Grand
Rapids: Eerdmans, 1990), 91; "noble occupation"—H. P. Liddon, *Explanatory Analysis of St. Paul's First Epistle to Timothy* (London:
Longmans, 1897), 23; "worthwhile job"—J. N. D. Kelly, *The Pastoral
Epistles,* Black's New Testament Commentary (1960; reprint, Peabody,
Mass.: Hendrickson, n.d.), 70. Alternatively, and with less contextual support, some take the phrase καλοῦ ἔργου to mean something like "benevo-
lent undertaking." Under this view, pursuit of the office of bishop is being
encouraged through the portrayal of this position as a charitable deed or
benefaction in the same way public office was depicted to the rich in
antiquity. See David C. Verner, *The Household of God: The Social World
of the Pastoral Epistles,* Society of Biblical Literature Dissertation Series
(Chico, Calif.: Scholars, 1983), 151; and Frances Young, *The Theology
of the Pastoral Letters* (Cambridge: University Press, 1994), 101.

5. F. Blass, A. Debrunner, and R. W. Funk, *A Greek Grammar of the New
Testament and Other Early Christian Literature* (Chicago: University of
Chicago Press, 1961), §451(1); Nigel Turner, *Syntax,* vol. 3, *A Grammar
of New Testament Greek,* ed. by James Hope Moulton (Edinburgh: T & T
Clark, 1963), 337; and A. T. Robertson, *A Grammar of the Greek New
Testament in the Light of Historical Research,* 4th ed. (Nashville:

Broadman, 1934), 1191; W. Bauer, W. F. Arndt, F. W. Gingrich, and F. W. Danker, *Greek-English Lexicon of the New Testament* (Chicago: University of Chicago Press, 1979), 593b.

6. 1 Timothy 2:1, 8; 3:2; 5:14; 2 Timothy 2:1, 21.

7. Cf. Kelly, *Pastoral Epistles,* 73; Martin Dibelius and Hans Conzelmann, *The Pastoral Epistles,* trans. Philip Buttolph and Adela Yarbo Collins, Hermeneia (Philadelphia: Fortress, 1972), 52; Gordon D. Fee, *1 and 2 Timothy, Titus,* New International Biblical Commentary (Peabody, Mass.: Hendrickson, 1988), 79–80.

8. See Walter Grundmann, "δεῖ, δέον ἐστί," in *Theological Dictionary of the New Testament,* ed. G. Kittel and G. Friedrich, 2:21–25.

9. Romans 12:3; 1 Thessalonians 4:1; 2 Thessalonians 3:7; 1 Timothy 3:7, 15; Titus 1:7.

10. See Walter Lock, *A Critical and Exegetical Commentary on the Pastoral Epistles,* International Critical Commentary (Edinburgh: T & T Clark, 1924), 35; cf. Calvin, *Second Epistle of Paul the Apostle to the Corinthians and the Epistles to Timothy, Titus and Philemon,* 223; Guthrie, *Pastoral Epistles,* 91, 93.

11. See, e.g., Dibelius and Conzelmann, *Pastoral Epistles,* 51, 131–32; and A. T. Hanson, *The Pastoral Epistles,* New Century Bible (Grand Rapids: Eerdmans, 1982), 79, 173.

12. Concerning similarity in form to duty and virtue lists, see Philip H. Towner, *The Goal of Our Instruction: The Structure of Theology and Ethics in the Pastoral Epistles, Journal for the Study of the New Testament* Supplement Series (Sheffield: JSOT, 1989), 229; concerning similarity in language to that of moralists and inscriptions, see Reggie M. Kidd, *Wealth and Beneficence in the Pastoral Epistles,* Society of Biblical Literature Dissertation Series (Atlanta: Scholars, 1990), 90–91. Duty lists are a sub-genre of vice and virtue lists. On the latter, see Milliman, "Paul's Theology," 22–29.

13. In the latter, a list is given in 1.1. It is repeated in 1.2–18 with explanatory notes given under each required quality. Dibelius, *Pastoral Epistles,* 50–51, cf. 158–60, provides an elaborate historical reconstruction of the development of these duty lists. Onosander, *Strategikos,* is the only list he cites, but he sees further evidence for a general schema in the two general characteristics enjoined upon a physician in Libanius, *Loci communes* 3.7 and in the connection made between professional and general human qualities in a dancer in Lucian, *De Saltatione,* 81.

14. Dibelius, *Pastoral Epistles,* 39. See the excursus, "The Ideal of Good Christian Citizenship," 39–41. Cf. Hanson, *Pastoral Epistles,* 35.

15. Matches: σώφρονα—sensible, ἐγκρατῆ—temperate, ἀφιλάργυρον

—not a lover of money. Synonyms: μὴ αἰσχροκερδεῖς/μὴ αἰσχροκερδῆ—not greedy for gain. There are also the following: three near synonyms —νηφάλιον (bis), μαρτυρίαν καλὴν ἔχειν ἀπὸ τῶν ἔξωθεν; two non—synonymous parallels—μὴ νεόφυτον, διδακτόν. There are thirty items with little or no relationship to Onos. In fact, one of Onosander's requirements, μήτε πρεσβύτερον, seems to be contradicted in the very title, πρεσβύτερος, used in Titus's list.

16. It is further incorrect to say that there is little or nothing in these lists specific to the function of bishops and elders. This presupposes a job description that is nowhere given in the New Testament and could just as well be inferred from these qualifications.

17. See E. Earle Ellis, "Traditions in the Pastoral Epistles," in *Early Jewish and Christian Exegesis,* ed. Craig A. Evans and William F. Stinespring (Atlanta: Scholars, 1987), 239–40; cf. the evidence given in George W. Knight III, *The Pastoral Epistles: A Commentary on the Greek Text,* New International Greek Testament Commentary (Grand Rapids: Eerdmans, 1992), 99. The other three uses of this phrase in the Pastorals (1 Tim. 1:15; 4:9; 2 Tim. 2:11), as well as the proverbial nature of the words that follow it in 3:1, would seem to indicate that it goes with the following paragraph. Cf. Nestlé-Aland *Novum Testamentum Graece,* 25th ed.; UBS[3] (Kurt Aland, et. al., eds., *The Greek New Testament,* 3d ed. [New York: United Bible Societies, 1975]); and all versions and translations cited in UBS[4] (Barbara Aland et al., eds., *The Greek New Testament,* 4th ed. [New York: United Bible Societies, 1993]) except Westcott and Hort, *The New Testament in the Original Greek.* (London: Macmillan, 1895), contra Nestlé-Aland *Novum Testamentum Graece,* 26th and 27th eds., UBS[4]. See Knight, *Pastoral Epistles,* 152–53.

18. Titus 1:7–9 has a similar independence, with rough connections to its context. See Ellis, "Traditions," 244–45. These features, nevertheless, do not signal an interpolation. This hypothesis is addressed and dismantled by Dibelius, *Pastoral Epistles,* 56.

19. See Verner, *Household of God,* 104–6; and Towner, *Goal of Our Instruction,* 225–26, 229, 233. The similarities between the lists in 1 Timothy 3:1–7 and Titus 1:7–9 are overstated by Dibelius, *Pastoral Epistles,* 133. Each has fifteen items, yet only five are identical and only five or six additional items have points of correspondence. Dibelius also ignores the more ordered nature of the Titus list and the good fit of each list with its epistle's life-setting. See Fee, *Timothy, Titus,* 171, 176.

20. The resemblance to Onosander is coincidental. It no more proves the use of a common source than do the correspondences between 1 Thessalonians

2:3–7 and Dio Chrysostomus, *Oration* 32.5–12. These similarities are pointed out by Charles A. Wanamaker, *The Epistles to the Thessalonians: A Commentary on the Greek Text,* New International Greek Testament Commentary (Grand Rapids: Eerdmans, 1990), 94, 97, 98. Paul's specific word choices and the structure of his lists are better explained by the life-setting he was addressing (e.g., the false teachers) and his purpose in constructing them. Instead of a "random listing of popularly recognized qualities" (Towner, *Goal of Our Instruction,* 230), each list seems to reflect the purpose of seeking to establish "the blamelessness of the candidate's reputation" (ibid., 240, developed on 229–37). Note the heading, ἀνεπίλημπτον, at 1 Timothy 3:2, and the focal position of ἀνέγκλητος in 1 Timothy 3:10; Titus 1:7.

21. There are Christian and/or job specific qualifications, for example, husband of one wife (1 Tim. 3:2, 12; Titus 1:6), hospitable (1 Tim. 3:2), apt teacher (1 Tim. 3:2), keeping children submissive and respectful in every way (1 Tim. 3:4 [cf. Titus 1:6], an allusion to the fifth commandment, see below), not a recent convert (1 Tim. 3:6), not double-tongued (1 Tim. 3:8, cf. the Psalms), holding fast to the mystery of faith with a clear conscience (1 Tim. 3:9), having children who are believers (Titus 1:6), firmly grasping the word that is trustworthy in accordance with the teaching (Titus 1:9), and holding qualifications related to purity and holiness, though expressed in general terms (e.g., above reproach [1 Tim. 3:1], blameless [1 Tim. 3:10; Titus 1:6–7], upright [Titus 1:8], devout [Titus 1:8]). There are enunciations of Christian reasons for qualifications (e.g., 1 Tim. 3:5–7; Titus 1:9). There are also Christian motivations given for possessing the qualifications (e.g., 1 Tim. 3:13).

22. This is ably demonstrated by Kidd, *Wealth and Beneficence,* 111–57, see especially 157–58, 200. Kidd carefully examines Dibelius's view alongside of a survey of ancient society and the position of Christians within it. See also Young, *Theology of the Pastoral Letters,* 32–33.

23. See Young, *Theology of the Pastoral Letters,* 31–39, especially 37–38. In an analysis of the forms of argument in the Pastoral Epistles, Lewis R. Donelson shows that paradigms such as Paul and Timothy undergird the logic (100–108) and that assumptions about God and salvation constitute underlying premises of the author's rhetorical deductions (81–90). *Pseudepigraphy and Ethical Arguments in the Pastoral Epistles,* Hermeneutische Untersuchungen zur Theologie (Tübingen: Mohr, 1986). The Pastoral Epistles do not suggest an interpretation of a Christian bourgeois, a desire to conform to the world. Rather, by focusing on the Christ-event and the salvation it produced, they suggest the central theological

theme of "the reality of salvation in the present age" (Towner, *Goal of Our Instruction,* 139; this is substantiated on 47–141; see especially 139–41). This theme coheres with the missionary motive behind the respectable conduct endorsed in the letters (Towner, *Goal of Our Instruction,* 244, 252–54). Cf. Young, *Theology of the Pastoral Letters,* 39–47, especially 46–47.

24. Cf. 1 Timothy 3:5, 12, 15; 5:4; 2 Timothy 1:16; 4:19; Titus 1:11; cf. 1 Corinthians 1:16. While it is true that "household" may include slaves and real property, the meaning of family here is supported by the modification of the term by "children." Compare Titus 1:6, which just says "children" and leaves out "household." See Verner, *Household of God,* 27–63, especially 27–35 and 44–47, on the meaning of "household."

25. Bo Reicke, "προΐστημι," in *Theological Dictionary of the New Testament,* 6:700–1; cf. Bauer, Arndt, Gingrich, and Danker, *Greek-English Lexicon,* 707a; and Johannes Louw and Eugene A. Nida, eds., *Greek-English Lexicon of the New Testament: Based on Semantic Domains,* 2d ed. (New York: United Bible Societies, 1989), §§68.67, 36.1, 35.13.

26. E.g., Josephus, *Antiquities of the Jews* 5.90; 14.96. This thought of care is highlighted in the cognate noun προστάτις. Paul uses it of Phoebe in Romans 16:2. The word can hardly mean ruler here, for the verbal force contained in this noun has Paul as its object. It is better to take the word as meaning "protector" or "patroness" in this case (cf. G. H. R. Horsley, *New Documents Illustrating Early Christianity* [North Ryde, Australia: Macquarie University, 1987], 4:241–44; Bauer, Arndt, Gingrich, and Danker, *Greek-English Lexicon,* 718d; J. H. Moulton and G. Milligan, *The Vocabulary of the Greek Testament, Illustrated from the Papyri and Other Non-Literary Sources* [n.p., 1930; reprint, Grand Rapids: Eerdmans, 1980], 551b). Another cognate noun, προστάτης, likewise conveys this nuance. For example, it is used of Christ with reference to his role as a protector in *I Clement* 36:1; 61:3; cf. Josephus, *Jewish Wars* 1.385.

27. In addition to προΐστημι, Louw and Nida include ἡγέομαι, κατευθύνω, φέρω, and ἄγω in the same subdomain (*Greek-English Lexicon of the New Testament,* §36.1).

28. Ibid., 465, n.i. These findings are supported by the papyri in which there is a wide range of examples with προΐστημι being used for presiding over or leading various groups. But the word is also found in the context of a guardian protecting, one supporting another with money, and also for someone providing general care. Moulton and Milligan, *Vocabulary of the Greek Testament,* 541abc.

29. Providing care for one's own household is inherent to the family context for Paul (cf. 1 Tim. 5:4, 8).

30. Fee, *Timothy, Titus,* 82; Knight, *Pastoral Epistles,* 161. See also below on ἐπιμελέομαι.

31. A blend of nuances, with "lead/guide" dominating, seems to be a better alternative to the absolute choice of meanings advocated by Bauer, Arndt, Gingrich, and Danker, *Greek-English Lexicon,* 707a (yet even Bauer, Arndt, Gingrich, and Danker, *Greek-English Lexicon,* equivocates, putting 1 Thess. 5:12 and Rom. 12:8 in each category). See Reicke, "προΐστημι," 701–2.

32. Ephesians 6:4; cf. Colossians 3:21. See Milliman, "Paul's Theology," 163–76. In a similar manner, Peter states that the shepherd is to tend the flock, not by domineering over it but by being an example (1 Peter 5:2–3). Jesus taught His disciples not to rule like the Gentile kings, but to serve (Luke 22:25–26; cf. Matt. 20:25–27; Mark 10:42–44).

33. See Bauer, Arndt, Gingrich, and Danker, *Greek-English Lexicon,* 401b.

34. It is better to take this participle as indicating one way or the essence of how one leads his household well rather than as a separate, parallel quali- fication, since the following clause in verse 5 explains both clauses in verse 4. One may argue against this conclusion by noting that in 3:12 deacons are to be those who manage their children *and* households well. This interpretation is certainly possible for 3:12, but it still does not change the natural meaning of verses 4 and 5. It is also possible, on the other hand, that Paul continues the household=family motif in 3:12, begun in 3:4–5 and carried out in this epistle, and the καί should be understood as epexegetical (Blass, Debrunner, and Funk, eds., and trans., *A Greek Grammar of the New Testament and Other Early Christian Literature* [Chicago: University of Chicago, 1961] §442[9]; Bauer, Arndt, Gingrich, and Danker, *Greek-English Lexicon,* 393a).

35. Bauer, Arndt, Gingrich, and Danker, *Greek-English Lexicon,* 808b. For example, Matthew 10:21—father against his child, children against their parents. The other words for child follow, with reference to the appropriate treatment in Louw and Nida, *Greek-English Lexicon of the New Testament:* Βρέφος (§9.45)—unborn to infant (Luke 2:12); νήπιος (§9.43)—beyond helpless infant to age 3 or 4 (Matt. 21:16); παῖς (§9.41); and παιδίον (§9.42)—while in certain contexts synonymous with τέκνον (John 4:51; Luke 11:7), these terms can stand for a young person before puberty without distinction of sex (Matt. 21:15; John 6:9).

36. See Louw and Nida, *Greek-English Lexicon of the New Testament,* §10.36; Albrecht Oepke, "παῖς κτλ.," in *Theological Dictionary of the New Tes- tament,* 5:636–54, esp. 38–39; and Moulton and Milligan, *Vocabulary of the Greek Testament,* 628c. For example, The Oxyrhynchus Papyri 2.237[viii.36]—"the right of ownership after their death has settled upon the

children." Because of the contexts in which it is generally used in the New Testament, the referent of τέκνον is usually a young child, but many uses are without reference to age because this does not seem to be inherent in the meaning of the word (e.g., Matt. 10:21). See, Gerhard Delling, "Lexikalisches zu τέκνον: Ein Nachtrag zur Exegese von I. Kor. 7,14," in *Studien zum Neuen Testament und zum hellenistischen Judentum* (Göttingen: Vandenhoeck & Ruprecht, 1970), 270–80.

37. This is implied by the phrase ἐν ὑποταγῇ (cf. the ὑπο- concept in Gal. 4:2) and perhaps by ἔχοντα (cf. ἔχων in Titus 1:6). See Knight, *Pastoral Epistles,* 161, 289; cf. Ceslas Spicq, *Saint Paul: Les Épîtres Pastorales,* 4th ed., (Paris: Gabalda, 1969), 602.

38. See Milliman, "Paul's Theology," 31–53, 164–65.

39. Bauer, Arndt, Gingrich, and Danker, *Greek-English Lexicon,* 847d.

40. 2 Corinthians 9:13; Galatians 2:5; 1 Timothy 2:11. All four New Testament uses come from Paul. Cf. Ignatius *Letter to the Ephesians* 2:2; *1 Clement* 37:5.

41. Bauer, Arndt, Gingrich, and Danker, *Greek-English Lexicon,* 848a.

42. The passive use of ὑποτάσσω in early Christian literature illustrates this idea of subjection or submission: to one another—Ephesians 5:21; wife to husband—Ephesians 5:22; Colossians 3:18; Titus 2:5; 1 Peter 3:1, 5; child to parents—Luke 2:51; slaves to masters—Titus 2:9; 1 Peter 2:18; *Epistle to Barnabas* 19:7; *Didache* 4:11; to secular authorities—Romans 13:1, 5; Titus 3:1; 1 Peter 2:13; *1 Clement* 61:1; to church officials— *1 Clement* 1:3; 57:1; Ignatius *Letter to the Ephesians* 2:2; to the law of God—Romans 8:7; to futility—Romans 8:20. See Gerhard Delling, "ὑποτάσσω," in *Theological Dictionary of the New Testament,* 8:42–45.

43. See Milliman, "Paul's Theology," 148.

44. 1 Timothy 2:2; Titus 2:7. All three New Testament uses come from Paul. Cf. *1 Clement* 41.1; *Shepherd of Hermas, Mandate(s)* 4.1.3.

45. See Werner Foerster, "σεμνος, σεμνότης," in *Theological Dictionary of the New Testament,* 7:191–96; Richard Chenevix Trench, *Synonyms of the New Testament* (1880; reprint, Grand Rapids: Eerdmans, 1953), 346–48.

46. Cf. Bauer, Arndt, Gingrich, and Danker, *Greek-English Lexicon,* 747a. Paul is responsible for the four New Testament uses of this word, all of which occur in lists: Philippians 4:8; Titus 2:2; 1 Timothy 3:8, 11. It is noteworthy that in the last two examples this positive characteristic is followed by a negative one—speech which shows a lack of respect toward others ("not double-tongued," v. 8; "not slanderers," v. 11).

47. See Foerster, "σεμνος, σεμνότης," 191.

48. See Ceslas Spicq, *Theological Lexicon of the New Testament,* trans. and ed. James D. Ernest (Peabody, Mass.: Hendrickson, 1994), 3:244–48. Spicq

maintains that the copious occurrence of both the noun and the adjective in Hellenistic writing precludes Paul's derivation of the term from Stoicism (244).

49. "Respectful obedience," Dibelius, *Pastoral Epistles,* 50. "The obedience of children is to be won by authority which commands respect," Foerster, "σεμνος, σεμνότης," 195. Cf. Guthrie, *Pastoral Epistles,* 93. On the other hand, Fee asserts that Paul does not mean that the children are to obey with respect but that they "will be known for their obedience and their generally good behavior" *(Timothy, Titus,* 82). Others take μετά πάσης σεμνότητος to modify προΐστημι instead of ὑποταγῇ (i.e., lead with respect; e.g., Kelly, *Pastoral Epistles,* 78: "He must maintain discipline, but without fuss or resort to violence," with "unruffled dignity."). In support of this view is the use of σεμνός in 1 Timothy 3:8, 11; Titus 2:2. Note especially 3:8 where it heads the list of deacon qualifications following the word ὡσαύτως, a word that refers the reader back to the bishop list (σεμνότης in v. 4?). While grammatically possible, context and word order argue against this option. The idea conveyed by σεμνότης, in the immediate context of the submission of children, fits better with the relationship of child to father than father to child. Furthermore, the subject has switched from the leading of the father to the conduct of the children. It seems more likely that Paul would continue this idea than revert to the former one (cf. Liddon, *Explanatory Analysis of St. Paul's First Epistle to Timothy,* 29; Fee, *Timothy, Titus,* 85). The parallel clause in Titus 1:6, which refers to children exclusively, also favors this position. Finally, the probable allusion to the fifth commandment also argues for this conclusion.

50. It is possible that πάσης indicates that the object of the attitude conveyed by σεμνότης extends beyond the father to the whole family (Lock, *Critical and Exegetical Commentary on the Pastoral Epistles,* 38; cf. Spicq, *Saint Paul,* 435; Knight, *Pastoral Epistles,* 162).

51. Fee, *Timothy, Titus,* 83; cf. Adolf Schlatter, *Die Kirche der Griechen im Urteil des Paulus: Eine Auslegung seiner Briefe an Timotheus und Titus,* 3d ed. (Stuttgart: Calwer, 1983), 102–3.

52. Blass, Debrunner, and Funk, *Greek Grammar,* §447(1); Robertson, *Grammar of the Greek New Testament,* 1184; cf. Acts 12:3; John 3:19; 19:23. This is the position taken by most textual versions and translations: NA[27], UBS[4], WH, Nes, BF[2], AV, RV, ASV, NIV, NASB. Cf. dashes: Bov, Zür, NRSV; no punctuation: TR, RSV, NEB, Jer, Seg.

53. Πῶς with a future in a question supposes a negative response; cf. 1 Corinthians 14:7, 9, 16. See Johannes Bauer, "ΠΩΣ in der griechischen Bibel," *Novum Testamentum* 2 (1958): 81–91.

54. Luke 10:34; also used in his charge to the innkeeper in verse 35. These

three uses are the only ones in the New Testament. From the references in Luke, which concern physical care, Gottfried Holtz infers that 1 Timothy 3:5 may be alluding to such activities as the provision of food for the poor at love feasts (cf. 1 Cor. 11) or the obligation to care for missionaries. *Die Pastoralbriefe,* 2d ed., Theologische Handkommentar zum Neuen Testament (Berlin: Evangelische Verlagsanstalt, 1972), 78.

55. Cf. The Flinders Petrie Papyri 2.2; The Oxyrhynchus Papyri 8.1154[4]. See Bauer, Arndt, Gingrich, and Danker, *Greek-English Lexicon,* 296a; and Moulton and Milligan, *Vocabulary of the Greek Testament,* 242a.

56. Barry C. Davis concludes from his study of ἐπιμελέομαι that it "contains within it the ideas of responsibility and great interest in what one is doing." "The Nature of Authority of Church Offices in the New Testament Church" (Ph.D. seminar paper, Trinity Evangelical Divinity School, 1992), 21. Cf. Josephus, *Antiquities* 1.53; 8.297.

57. Paul uses τύπος several times in this way—Philippians 3:17; 1 Thessalonians 1:7; 2 Thessalonians 3:9; 1 Timothy 4:12; Titus 2:7. The concept of modeling is also clearly taught elsewhere by Paul without τύπος—1 Corinthians 4:6; 11:1; Philippians 4:6 (cf. 2 Tim. 3:10–11).

58. Grudem, *Systematic Theology,* 916; cf. Joachim Jeremias, *Die Briefe an Timotheus und Titus,* Das Neue Testament Deutsch (Göttingen: Vandenhoeck & Ruprecht, 1981), 25.

59. Guthrie, *Pastoral Epistles,* 93; cf. Calvin, *Second Epistle of Paul the Apostle to the Corinthians and the Epistles to Timothy, Titus and Philemon,* 226–27. For example, Matthew 25:14–30; Luke 12:42–45; 16:10–12.

60. Polycarp *Letter to the Philippians* 11:2—"For how may he who cannot attain self-control in these matters enjoin it on another?" Isocrates, *Ad Nicoclem* 19—"Manage (οἴκει) the city as you would your ancestral estate (οἶκον): in the matter of its appointment, splendidly and royally, in the matter of its revenues, strictly, in order that you may possess the good opinion of your people and at the same time have sufficient means." Pseudo-Isocrates, *Ad Demonicum* 35—"Whenever you purpose to consult with anyone about your affairs, first observe how he has managed his own; for he who has shown poor judgment in conducting his own business will never give wise counsel about the business of others." Euphronius *Fragments* 4—"He who cannot manage (οἰκονομῶν κακῶς) his own life, how can he help another person?" Plutarch, *Lycurgus* 19.3—"to one who demanded the establishment of democracy in the city: 'Go,' said he, 'and first establish democracy in your household (οἶκος).'" (Cited in Dibelius, *Pastoral Epistles,* 53 n. 25.) Sophocles, *Antigone* 661–62—"For whoever rules his household worthily, will prove in civic matters no less wise."

61. Fee, *Timothy, Titus,* 82. Kelly points out that the home reflects the life and problems of the church in microcosm. Essentially the same qualities are needed for leadership in both *(Pastoral Epistles,* 78; cf. Calvin, *Second Epistle of Paul the Apostle to the Corinthians and the Epistles to Timothy, Titus and Philemon,* 227; Liddon, *Explanatory Analysis of St. Paul's First Epistle to Timothy,* 29; and Lock, *Critical and Exegetical Commentary on the Pastoral Epistles,* 34). Holtz, *Pastoralbriefe,* 77–78, 207, opines that such a household qualification was particularly significant to the readers because churches at this time were house churches. Cf. Jürgen Roloff, *Der erste Brief an Timotheus,* Evangelisch-katholischer Kommentar zum Neuen Testament (Neukirchen-Vluyn: Neukirchener, 1988), 160.

62. Compare the δεῖ in 1 Timothy 3:1. The same necessity of finding men with exemplary families, which exists in 1 Timothy 3:1, is present in Titus on account of the connection of the δεῖ with verse 6 by γάρ. This necessity is also implied in the phrase εἴ τίς ἔστιν, which heads verse 6. See Fee, *Timothy, Titus,* 173–74; cf. Kelly, *Pastoral Epistles,* 231.

63. Οἰκονόμον literally refers to a household manager in a private position (e.g., Gal. 4:2). Figuratively it is used for the administrator of divine things. Both literal and figurative uses are found in 1 Cor. 4:1–2. See Bauer, Arndt, Gingrich, and Danker, *Greek-English Lexicon,* 560ab. With his use of οἰκονόμον here, Paul appears to be making a reference to the previous household responsibilities.

64. The complete lack of manuscript evidence testifies against an insertion. See Dibelius, *Pastoral Epistles,* 56, 132, for arguments against an interpolation. Those believing this text shows a tendency toward a monepiscopate include Günther Bornkamm, "πρέσβυς κτλ," in *Theological Dictionary of the New Testament,* 6:667–68; and Hanson, *Pastoral Epistles,* 32–34, 173. Young, *Theology of the Pastoral Letters,* 105–11, provides arguments for two separate offices with distinct functions. Possibly the two terms, bishop and elder, overlapped in a way not entirely clear to modern readers. Perhaps bishops formed a subset within the elders. See Towner, *Goal of Our Instruction,* 223–27; Dibelius, *Pastoral Epistles,* 56; and Kelly, *Pastoral Epistles,* 74, 231–32. All things considered, it is probably best to equate the two offices. The main argument for seeing a monarchial bishop or two separate offices is the use of the singular ἐποίσκοπον in verse 7 (cf. ἐποίσκοπον in 1 Tim. 3:1) in contrast to the plural πρεσβυτέρους in verse 5. This, however, is most likely a generic singular (cf. the singular "woman" in 1 Tim. 2:11–12, 15, which becomes a plural "they" in v. 15). The singular in Titus 1:7 arose because of the singular εἴ τις in verse 6 as

the singular in 1 Timothy 3:1 corresponds to a preceding εἴ τις (cf. the same phenomenon in 1 Tim. 5:8; 6:3). In addition, the similarity of 1 Timothy 3:2–5 to Titus 1:5–6 as well as the contents of other passages—1 Timothy 5:17; Acts 20:17, 28; 1 Peter 5:1–2—support the equation of the two offices in Titus 1. *Elder* probably describes the office while *bishop* describes its function. See Pierre Dornier, *Les Épîtres Pastorales,* Sources bibliques (Paris: Gabalda, 1969), 128; J. B. Lightfoot, "Synonymes *[sic]* 'Bishop' and 'Presbyter,'" in *St. Paul's Epistle to the Philippians* (1913; reprint, Grand Rapids: Zondervan, 1953), 95–99; and Fenton John Anthony Hort, *The Christian Ecclesia* (London: Macmillan, 1898), 191.

65. See Fee, *Timothy, Titus,* 173–74; and Calvin, *Second Epistle of Paul the Apostle to the Corinthians and the Epistles to Timothy, Titus and Philemon,* 359.

66. Believer: 1 Timothy 4:3, 10, 12; 5:16; 6:2 (bis). Faithful: 1 Timothy 1:12; 3:11; 2 Timothy 2:2, 13; Titus 1:9. Phrase: 1 Timothy 1:15; 3:1; 4:9; 2 Timothy 2:11; 3:8. His use of πιστός is similarly split in the rest of the Pauline epistles. Believer: 2 Corinthians 6:15; Galatians 3:9; Ephesians 1:1; Colossians 1:2. Faithful: 1 Corinthians 4:2, 17; 7:25; Ephesians 6:21; Colossians 1:7; 4:7, 9. Used to describe God: 1 Corinthians 1:9; 10:13; 2 Corinthians 1:18; 1 Thessalonians 5:24; 2 Thessalonians 3:3.

67. Fee is noncommittal (*Timothy, Titus,* 173).

68. Lock, *Pastoral Epistles,* 103. Knight, *Pastoral Epistles,* 289–90, and Towner, *Goal of Our Instruction,* 233, also hold this view, understanding πιστός as "faithful or obedient." This is, indeed, the word's frequent meaning when used of servants, for example, Matthew 24:45–46; par. Luke 12:42–43; Matthew 25:21, 23; 1 Corinthians 4:2; cf. Horsley, *New Documents,* 2:53, 3:39; Moulton and Milligan, *Vocabulary of the Greek Testament,* 515cd. Additional support is provided by Rudolf Bultmann, "πιστεύω κτλ," in *Theological Dictionary of the New Testament,* 6:175, who cites the definition of πιστός given by the fifth-century B.C. lexicographer, Hesychius: εὐπειθής (obedient).

69. Cf. also Bauer, Arndt, Gingrich, and Danker, *Greek-English Lexicon,* 665a; Gerhard Barth, "πιστός," *Exegetical Dictionary of the New Testament,* ed. H. Balz and G. Schneider, 3:98; Bultmann, "πιστεύω," 215; and Verner, *Household of God,* 133–34; NIV; NASB; RSV; NRSV.

70. See Dibelius, *Pastoral Epistles,* 132. Cf. 2 Corinthians 6:15; Acts 10:45; 16:1. Note the frequent use of πιστός to mean "Christian," documented in Horsley, *New Documents,* 2:94.

71. John 18:29; 1 Timothy 5:19 (re: a "legal" charge in a church; a public

proceeding is implied in vv. 19–20); cf. Luke 6:7 verse 1. It is not found in the LXX. Cf. Bauer, Arndt, Gingrich, and Danker, *Greek-English Lexicon,* 423b.

72. See Friedrich Büchsel, "κατήγορος, κτλ," in *Theological Dictionary of the New Testament,* 3:637. Κατήγορος is found four times in the New Testament, all in Acts, with reference to accusing Paul—23:30, 35; 25:16, 18. Κατήγωρ is used only once in the New Testament, of the Devil—Revelation 12:10.

73. See ibid., 637; Bauer, Arndt, Gingrich, and Danker, *Greek-English Lexicon,* 423b; and Moulton and Milligan, *Vocabulary of the Greek Testament,* 337b. For example, Matthew 12:10 (par. Mark 3:2; Luke 6:7); Luke 23:2; John 8:6; Acts 25:5; Revelation 12:10.

74. Ibid., 637 n.2.

75. Fee, *Timothy, Titus,* 173. Most commentators agree with this conclusion; cf. NIV, RSV, NASB, NRSV, TEV.

76. "Debauchery" (NRSV), as well as the rendering "dissipation" (NASB) or "being profligate" (RSV), on account of their rare use in everyday conversation, are words that usually require an English dictionary for most readers. Various other renderings for ἀσωτία—"being wild" (NIV), "loose living" (Dibelius, *Pastoral Epistles,* 132; and Kelly, *Pastoral Epistles,* 213)—attempt to alleviate the problem but do not do justice to the images conjured up by this word.

77. Drunkenness: *Testament of Judah* 16:1—"Take care to be temperate with wine, my children; for there are in it four evil spirits: desire, heated passion, debauchery (ἀσωτία), and sordid gain." Illicit sex: 2 Maccabees 6:4—"For the temple was filled with debauchery (ἀσωτία) and reveling by the Gentiles, who dallied with harlots and had intercourse with women within the sacred precincts." Compare the use of ἄσωτος in Proverbs 7:11 to describe a prostitute. These associations may also be found in secular literature, for example, Lucian, *Vitarum Auctio* 12.

78. Werner Foerster, "ἄσωτος, ἀσωτία," in *Theological Dictionary of the New Testament,* 1:506–7. Compare the examples from the papyri listed by Moulton and Milligan, *Vocabulary of the Greek Testament,* 89a. See also Trench, *Synonyms of the New Testament,* 53–56. Specialized meanings can be found for ἀσωτία in Greek literature, including gluttony and voluptuousness. This latter use appears to be behind Calvin's rendering, "over-abounding in luxury" (*Second Epistle of Paul the Apostle to the Corinthians and the Epistles to Timothy, Titus and Philemon,* 359; cf. Lock, *Pastoral Epistles,* 130, "wasteful extravagance").

79. Ἀνυπότακτος is probably derived from the passive voice of ὑποτάσσω.

Louw and Nida, *Greek-English Lexicon of the New Testament,* §36.26; and Gerhard Delling, "ἀνυπότακτο," in *Theological Dictionary of the New Testament,* 8:47. In light of the natural sense of the context and the parallel, 1 Timothy 3:4, the father is the most likely object of the child's rebellion. It is less likely, though possible, that the object of rebellion is the church or public officials as Lock, *Pastoral Epistles,* 130, suggests; cf. Jerome D. Quinn, *The Letter to Titus: A New Translation with Notes and Commentary and an Introduction to Titus, I and II Timothy, the Pastoral Epistles,* Anchor Bible (New York: Doubleday, 1990), 88. Compare κατηγορία and the command in 3:1—"remind them to be subject to (ὑποτάσσεσθαι) rulers." Cf. Josephus, *Antiquities* 11.217.

80. See Gill, *Body of Doctrinal and Practical Divinity,* 866–67.

81. The age was later changed to twenty-five (Num. 8:23). The rabbis held that this was the age for entrance into a five-year apprenticeship. Thirty is also the age in 1 Chronicles 23:3. The reason for the inclusion of those twenty and over in the census of Levites conducted by David is unclear (23:24, 27).

82. The current practice of missionary recruitment and selection results in fields occupied with young, untested missionaries with young or no families. The application of this disqualification criterion becomes painful and hence frequently ignored or rationalized away when the missionary children have "gone wrong." Congregations find it extremely difficult to apply this requirement to a much-loved missionary who is probably not trained to earn an equivalent salary at secular employment.

83. This raises the question: Does the "child qualification" require missionaries to have children? While the text presupposes that the elder and his wife will have children, it does not explicitly require them. Without children, however, how would the potential bishop reveal to the congregation whether or not he is qualified to lead and care for God's family of believers? This is *the* test: Does he lead and care for his own children? Here, then, is an additional, indirect argument for bishops (and hence missionaries) being older physically as well as spiritually. If a missionary is able to have children and does not, it may simply be that he is too young to serve as an elder.

16

POLLY STRONG

WORTHY OF RESPECT

Honoring Women
Devoted to Christian Service

In a world of shifting values and disappearing standards, in a society competing for honor and hungering for respect, women of God are often caught in the shuffle. Feminist movements, women's liberation groups, and reactionary male chauvinism have left many Christian women confused about their role in ministry. God's answer to the dilemma is as fundamental as God Himself. Respect for His order, purpose, and design gives harmony to the human race and proper perspective to women in ministry.

Respect and submission are the cohesive elements that bind the whole of creation together (Phil. 2; John 5:19–20). Respect for God's person and plan demands respect for human beings—for who they are, and for what they do. Respect and submission bind together marriages, families, and churches, and they are essential in ministry. Respect is the robe with which a woman clothes herself. Submission is the path she proudly walks.

Respect is gained when respect is given. I learned this truth as a young missionary teacher. I do not remember the exact day or incident. It may have been when the boys spent the morning tie-dying T-shirts in the lavatory sinks with food coloring from the dormitory kitchen. Or perhaps when they locked the teacher out of the classroom. Regardless, it was a getting-out-of-control day at the mission high school, and I wrote on the blackboard: *Respect is gained when respect is given.* The words stared back at me. The realization of their truth influenced me for the rest of my life. (Note: Three of the boys in that class are back on the mission field in fruitful ministries.)

Respect, the root of honor, is the strength of society. Men and women have lived and died for it since the beginning of time. Misconstrued honor creates confusion, devastation, and destruction; it produces a frantic fury, a fury like that of bees chased from the hive, going nowhere, a buzzing with a sting. Honor obscured is the opium of deceit. Misplaced honor is simply pride, the seed of an egotistical society.

Humanism has trampled honor in a system concerned with ethnics more than ethics; human rights more than divine rule; politics, possession, and passion more than purity; competition more than competence. Horror is publicized more than honor, and fantasy instead of fact. Mania has replaced morality and rebellion has replaced respect. Superiority is lauded and submission scorned. People are more concerned with saving face than facing up. Guidelines are erased and goals are difficult to define. Women want to be men and men want to be women. In seeking to gain, women (and men) have lost. They have become both victims and vicious promoters of a process that destroys rather than builds up. They misuse and abuse each other, losing respect. The result is devastating (Rom. 1:18–32).

Respect for a woman in missions is first gained externally. She is worthy of respect simply as a person, as God's creation. It is also earned internally. If respect is her heart's choice, it will be evidenced in her relationships with others. The fruit of this respect will then be seen in her work and ministry.

Respect for the Worth of a Woman—Her Person

God created man and woman in His image, for His glory and pleasure. He blessed them and told them to be fruitful, to multiply, and to rule the earth. He spoke directly to man and He spoke directly to woman, holding each accountable. Man and woman are created with ontological equality and functional differences (Gal. 3:26–28; 1 Cor. 12:11–13; Col. 3:9–11). They are the same in essence but different in form and function. They reflect God—Father, Son, and Holy Spirit—one in essence but manifested in different forms and fulfilling different functions.

Woman's first Eden home was exquisitely beautiful, her companionship and purpose pure and perfect. She walked and talked with divinity, as the crowning glory of man. God delighted in this male/female unit and commanded the two to fill the earth with His reflection. There can be no higher honor. A life of perfect harmony, purity, and divine purpose is what every woman craves in the depths of her soul.

Sin, the disregard for God's laws, stripped woman of her honor. God immediately offered her a means of restoration (Gen. 3) through redemption. But still women suffer. In many cultures they are not considered equal to men. They are often treated as inferior or as property to be used (or abused), bought, and sold. Certain cults and religious systems offer hope to women only through male counterparts (e.g., Mormonism). In other systems women are actually deified. Only God's Word can put them back into their proper God-given position.

Honor is restored in women when they are recreated and changed by God's grace. Lifted from devastation, they reflect the glory of God as vessels of service (2 Cor. 5:17). God places women in missions where their very lives are a vital witness to Him. Recorded testimonies of women missionaries challenge and encourage future generations. The examples cited here are only small vignettes of women in ministry. They inspire further reading and exploration.[1]

> In the heart of Africa, incessant buzzing of insects, oppressive heat and humidity, lack of privacy, prevalence of dirt, disease and privation were incidental. What pricked at the women had to do with honor and respect. It was 1921. The river boat was overcrowded with returning African soldiers and white traders, boasting of their vices and experiences in the "civilized" world. Rowena and Blanche thought of the women who would be sold as wives to these men. Shame and hurt for these acts of exploitation filled them with an eager sense of joyful responsibility to be carrying the light and love of Christ to these women and their families, light that would give them honor and respect.[2]

> In the heart of Brazil a woman, persecuted and disowned by her family because she had found Christ, knelt on the dirt floor under her hammock and prayed for her children and the city of Juazeiro do Norte. Her act of faith and honor brought the light of the gospel not only to her family but also to thousands of Brazilians.[3]

> Pite, a tiny Naga street sweeper in India, chased from her home, refuged at the mission where she had found

the light of Christ. Rocking on her heels she sang out:
"They killed Jesus? . . . yes. They buried Him? . . . yes.
But He rose from the dead!" She threw her head back
and laughed with great joy. Her own people had threatened to crush her earthly vessel by breaking her legs.
But God had respect for her and turned her into a vessel
of honor, carrying the joy of His glory.[4]

These extracts illustrate that nothing can rob woman of her honor
when her life is in the hands of God. His regard for her is infinite and
perfect. He will bring to her life a respect that honors Him.

Women in missions are a dynamic display of this respect. They stand
proudly alongside men in unity of purpose and direction for the glory of
God. This unity in diversity may perplex the modern egocentric mind,
but it is no mystery from God's perspective. Its uniqueness is one of the
most awesome parts of God's creation. As stars are to the sky, pebbles to
the beach, trees to the forest, petals to a flower, feathers to a bird, notes
to a song—women and men are distinct, equal parts, forming complex
unities, and held together by God's boundaries. "Oh, the depth of the riches
both of the wisdom and knowledge of God! How unsearchable are His
judgments and His ways past finding out! . . . For of Him and through Him
and to Him are all things, to whom be glory forever" (Rom. 11:33, 36 NKJV).

Uniqueness blends into unity through submission to God the Creator
and to fellow human beings. Submit yourselves, therefore, to God. Submit
yourselves one to another in the fear of God (James 4:7; Eph. 5:21).
Respect is a two-way street; a respectful woman is, in turn, respected by
men, by other women, and by God. Women worthy of respect are an
essential part of the framework of missions.

Respect Is a Heart Choice

Freedom of choice was woman's right from the beginning. She
abused it by liberating herself from God's protective law. Desire destroyed her respect and enslaved her. Seeking to possess, she lost. But
God's grace, bigger than human failure, and God's love, stronger than
human denial, drew her back to Him. He restored her to honor. Through
her daughters, He proclaims His glory. A woman chooses in her heart
either to live for self and sin or to surrender to God. Respect is a choice,
an attitude of the heart.

1. A respectful heart is a consecrated, committed, trusting heart.

> You shall love the LORD your God with all your heart, with all your soul, and with all your mind. . . . You shall love your neighbor as yourself. (Matthew 22:37–39 NKJV)

Committed hearts are rare in today's plastic-and-paper, throw-away society. People live for today's satisfactions and profits. God deals with eternity. A committed heart is willing to wait. It keeps on when the going is rough, the work tough, the goal obscured, and the road long. A heart committed to God does not concentrate on the surroundings, the successes, or the program. It concentrates on the commander-in-chief. A committed heart is a rejoicing heart, because it is assured of victory. A committed heart is a confident heart, because it knows the goal will be accomplished (2 Tim. 1:12). It is a heart that trusts.

Women in missions learn that the heart has to be committed again and again to the Lord. In Africa, Etiennette experienced that when her first baby was burning with fever.

> "O God, don't let her die! You gave her to me. She's mine! Please let her live." The young missionary mother, alone in a remote village, cried out to God for her dying baby. In her heart struggle she yielded, "No, Lord. She is really yours. You do with her as you desire." The little body went limp. The mother sat on the edge of the bed, feeling a peace and contentment with God that she had not known for days. God restored her baby. The committed mother-heart had given all to God and gained a strength that enabled her to bury four other children on foreign soil without losing faith in God or the joy of her ministry.[5]

A woman guards her heart above all else because out of it pour the issues of life (Prov. 4:23). Her heart is vulnerable. It needs protecting, nurturing, continual renewing and refreshing in the Word of God. A woman, daily committed to the truths of the Word, to studying and applying them, becomes a woman of honor and respect (Prov. 21:21; 4:4–8). Only a heart this committed to God can survive the storms of life. Without heart preparation, missionary work is sterile. Centuries of committed women have reached out to a hurting world. They are respected for acts of goodness, mercy, and love. From their hearts they have poured into the hearts of others the treasures of God's grace (2 Cor. 4:7). Esther, a young missionary completing her medical and language training in France, went through the loss of a stillborn baby. An older missionary, more experienced in continual commitment, upheld her.

> "Why? Why?" the young mother cried, hot tears spilling from swollen eyes. "Esther," the older missionary spoke, with firm, loving words of one experienced in suffering, "It is not ours to ask why. We must only say, 'Thy will be done, Lord.'"[6]

Accepting God's will, nothing more and nothing less, at all times, in all places, at any cost—it is a conscious, deliberate heart choice. Total respect for God keeps Him in a woman's heart before everything else: before marriage, home, family, friends, position, and desires. Respect given to God puts respect of others in a proper perspective. That kind of respect is more than emotion and cannot be measured by numbers or success standards. It is treasured within and expressed in speech and acts of submission and humility. It is Spirit-controlled.

Respect, a point of view of esteem and honor, is built on truth and righteousness. Lack of respect is built on deception, egotistical desires, sin, and self. A disrespectful woman, regardless of talent, fame, and good deeds, tarnishes the glory of God and hinders the work of the Holy Spirit.

2. A respectful heart is a clean heart—"Create in me a clean heart, O God" (Ps. 51:10 NKJV).

God's purity can keep a woman clean even in the midst of the world's filth.

The harmattan winds of Africa were heavy with grit. It caked in her nose, burned her eyes, and tasted on her tongue as it touched dry lips. Dirt! She was sick of it. Insects, open sewers, undiapered babies, spit, heat, unwashed children, fly-covered meat in an open market, sweat, and stench. Respect would accept it, because respect knew the God who brought her here would sustain her. But she would need to use the divine resources available to her to escape its effects.

Contamination and disease shock missionary women. Keeping clean is a daily concern—purifying water, proper food preparation, careful personal cleanliness, nets, screens, and pills to avert parasites and disease. Contamination of the heart is even more devastating. Seed-beds for jealousy and irritation thrive in close living. Frustration, fatigue, stress, misunderstandings, language difficulties, differences of opinion and conviction become fertile grounds for sin. The mission field can bring out the worst in a person, as well as develop the best. Faithful attention to heart cleanliness can turn stumbling stones into building blocks of strength and character, bringing the worker closer to the Lord. A woman's time of "heart washing" in the Word is far more important than her time under the shower or over the sink.

Periodic "spring cleaning" through conferences, retreats, or special times alone with the Word (and perhaps taped sermons) can reveal neglected corners. Sometimes God allows illnesses or difficult circumstances to prompt cleaning. Consistent Scripture memorization provides ready cleaning that can be accomplished even in the wakeful hours of the night. A song, a good book, a chat with a friend, sharing the Word, encouraging thoughts, or a kind act are great cathartic measures.

Immediate scrubbing of heart contamination (hurt feelings, disappointments, harsh words, pricked sensitivities) will avoid stains. Spills of gossip, storms of temper, and breakage by criticism and harsh words demand special, quick attention—mopping up and putting things back in order. A soiled heart needs cleansing before molds of discouragement and infections of bitterness destroy its effectiveness. Cleaning often requires tossing. Depressing thoughts, anger, pride, revenge, negativism, and fear should be thrown out. They clutter and burden the heart. God will help do the job. A woman can walk across a room with a rock in her shoe and a burden on her back, but she cannot run a long race with even the tiniest of pebbles in her boot.

One woman cannot clean another's house, but she can prompt purity by keeping her own life clean and preventing the spread of dirt and disease. Speaking out of a clean heart that is honest, true, faithful, compassionate, and void of offense can help another woman get her house back in order.

3. A respectful heart is a controlled heart.

"Mary kept all these things and pondered them in her heart" (Luke 2:19 NKJV). Mary did not immediately share everything she knew. Respect knows when to open and when to close the heart's door. Respect feels, filters, and locks away what is for God alone. Respect is patient. It waits before expressing. How bitter are the regrets of a hastily exposed heart:

Little word, I carelessly tossed you like a pebble into a
deep pool.
You left concentric rings of pain and hurt that widened,
widened.
Little pebble, how I wish I had you back, in my pocket,
. . . forgotten.

Anonymous

In quietness and confidence shall be your strength.
(Isa. 30:15 NKJV)

A controlled heart is not cold and stony, but warm and willing to
open up, both to give and receive. It shares from its abundance. It acts on
intellect, not only emotion. It stores standards and guides application. A
controlled heart gives the keys to God (Rom. 12:2).

Whoever has no rule over his own spirit is like a city
that is broken down, without walls. (Prov. 25:28 NKJV)

4. A respectful heart is a courageous heart—"Be strong and very courageous" (Josh. 1:7 NKJV).

Trials more precious than gold bring honor and glory. The buffeting
and stretching experiences of missionary life can magnify God's glory
or break the vessel. They can polish and purify or puff up and putrify.
They can bring out humility or sprout roots of bitterness. The choice is
made in the heart (1 Peter 1:7, 13–16, 22).

A courageous heart respects fear, allowing it to protect and propel
into action but not cripple and defeat. A missionary woman will have
fears—of rejection (by nationals and coworkers); of failure; of language
and cultural barriers; of position and its demands; of security (physical
attack, theft, war); of sickness; of change. God can overcome all these
fears. Centuries of courageous women have committed their hearts to
God in times of trauma and walked on triumphantly. Vi was one of those
women.

"Tidal wave! Hurry to the mountain!" The cry went out
through the village. Aleut people streamed out of their
houses. The feeling of fear was so strong it nearly paralyzed the people huddled together, waiting for more
tremors to begin. Vi called on God and busied herself

looking after "her people," trying to allay their fears. . . .
Water rushed in to cover the whole village. Sounds of
crunching, splitting and tearing roared through the cold
night air. . . . The village was gone. Years of love and
work had been torn from her and carried out to sea. But
the Word of God, planted in human hearts would never
die. Vi's heart was quiet.[7]

And ye shall hear of wars and rumors of wars: see that
ye be not troubled. (Matt. 24:6)

Courageous women have planted truth and love in stormy seasons.
In a world full of wars, mission evacuations are on the increase. Today's
women are briefed about theft, attack, armed robbery, hijacking, evacu-
ation procedures, and rape. The nations rage, but God is still in charge
(Ps. 2). A firm confidence in and respect for His control can carry a
woman's heart through any situation.

5. A respectful heart is a contented heart.

A respectful heart is an accepting, peaceful heart. Ministry is fulfilling. Doing God's will brings joy and blessing. It renews a thankful spirit
when excitement dims, when the film of newness vanishes and bare realities are exposed. Missionary women can lose their contentment in
ministry when home contacts dwindle; fatigue sets in; noisy, bossy neighbors irritate; staring eyes, sneering looks, and unkind remarks sting. Inconveniences and lack of physical comforts can become adversaries.
Sickness, loneliness, disputes, and frustrations drain. The heart turns
stale and unthankful, and women may begin to long for home, new companions, and different circumstances. They may lose respect for themselves, for their situation, and for God. But God is greater than our hearts,
and He can bring them back to full contentment and respect. Over and
over, missionary women have proved this. The first pioneers of Baptist
Mid-Missions lived with suffering. Food, money, and supplies were
scarce. But Ina learned God met every need and gave contentment.

Ina stood all she possibly could. Knowing how badly
Fred felt about her having to live this way while expecting her first baby, she hid behind some bushes and cried.
While there, she heard a truck. On that truck was mail
with a check that met their needs. Soon after her baby

was born, her strength depleted, she succumbed to fever. Her life hung in the balance for days. Fred and his co-worker, William Haas, prayed fervently. Then they heard Ina singing, "Praise God from whom all blessings flow." . . . "The Lord is in this house," he said. . . . "Indeed, He is," she replied. Their hearts were restored to contentment.[8]

6. A respectful heart is a healed heart that knows the haven of comfort.

A soldier in combat can expect inconveniences, hurt, and wounds. Suffering is a part of service. A missionary woman may be bruised, crushed, or pierced, but she will also be comforted by the One who suffered for her (2 Cor. 1:4–5). How sweet is that comfort!

The pain of repeated separations, the abrasiveness of cultural adaptations, the struggles with a new language, sickness, delays, interruptions, and irritations increase faith, deepen wisdom, and give the missionary woman a more vital walk with the Lord. She learns to shelter in her Rock, not her home, job, position, and family. She finds more than solace. She is healed. A healed heart can comfort because it has been comforted.

A committed, clean, controlled, courageous, comforted heart is a blessed and honored heart—respected and respecting—ready for service.

Relationships of Respect

God made woman as a companion for man, to build society and complement his desire for fellowship (Gen. 2:18). Interpersonal relationships are the most valuable and vulnerable area of human existence. Through them the heart's attitudes are expressed toward God. Biblical missions are built on interpersonal relationships. Missionary work is a people-process that brings together the two eternal elements—the Word of God and human souls.

When a woman enters missionary life, either single or with a husband and perhaps children, she enters a web of intricate personal relationships that can either support and strengthen or choke and break her. It all depends on her, and what she allows God to do in and through her. Each woman has a particular mind-set, a set of habits, and a value system. She feels secure with people she knows. The changes that missionary life brings challenge that security as new relations develop. Initial contacts may (or may not) be easy, but growing the deep roots of relationships takes time, submission, and respect, a putting aside of self and an esteeming of others. A solid relationship with God stabilizes human relations.

Missionaries, especially on foreign fields, weld together with others of like faith and practice (usually within a mission) to form families that are strong and loyal. People who walk difficult miles together, committed to common goals and living in close proximity, bond. Building workable, happy, productive relationships is one of the most crucial areas of missionary life. Incompatibility is devastating. A missionary woman needs to be prepared to build relationships with an attitude of respect.

1. Family units take on new dimensions.

A missionary wife is also a coworker, teacher, friend, and counselor. She must respect her husband and like to do things for him, always considering his tastes and interests. She must accept her husband's calling and willingly encourage him to obey whatever the Lord has for him, even if it means periods of separation. If she does this their friendship will grow with the years. Her husband will treat her with respect because she is respectful (Prov. 31). Her children, too, will reflect this respect. A wife is God's provision for her husband's deepest needs, a garden enclosed, a fountain sealed, just for him. A strong marriage demands mutual submission (1 Peter 3:1–9; Song 4:12).

Single and widowed women respect the marriage relationship of their friends and find their own needs met in a garden sealed to God. In a unique way they understand the words, "Thy Maker is thine husband" (Isa. 54:5). They often integrate into family units, balancing independence and dependence, giving and receiving, aloneness and togetherness—all through respect and caring. Single coworkers often live together, building relationships of mutual love and support. Whether married or single, women find the joy of relationships brings them fulfillment, a sense of well-being, and rest.

Missionary mothers will agonize when separated from their children. Women without children may agonize for the children they never had. Busy wives may chafe under family demands and envy the "free" woman. Mutual respect allows God to heal personal pain of this sort, and this, in turn, allows women to reach out with understanding to the pain of others. A missionary woman respects and cherishes children—her own and those of others. Respect for God's sovereignty removes envy and builds beautiful bridges where parents and nonparents benefit, and children come out the winners.

A woman of respect uses discretion in social relationships (especially with men). As the bride of Christ, she carefully preserves herself for her husband and for the Lord. Today's liberated society tests a woman's sense of propriety. Godly women learn to depend on the Lord alone for physical, emotional, and spiritual satisfactions and joys.

Missionary women become sisters, aunts, and grandmothers in extended family units, and these roles are to be cherished and cultivated. Differences of background, age, opinions, and ideas stretch missionary relationships. Frequent personnel changes sometimes cause apprehension and insecurity. A permanent relationship with an unchanging God stabilizes and secures.

2. Integration into communities of nationals, churches, and mission councils is built on mutual respect.

Mutual respect brings truth and grace even when differing cultural values are not understood or accepted. It distinguishes between personal, cultural, and biblical convictions. It neither withdraws into self nor pushes ideas and convictions on others.

As a woman interacts with nationals in churches, markets, schools, and homes—her familiarity zone is stretched. She accepts differences with respect, being neither offensive nor offending. Some women make friends easily. Others do not. Respect sees relationships as a means to communicate Christ, not to personal gain or satisfaction.

Women like to feel accepted. No one likes being shunned, left out, slighted, scorned, or mocked. A respectful woman cares about the feelings of others and is willing to make sacrifices. She listens to correction and makes needed adjustments. She accepts and respects friendships between others.

A woman who respects God respects God-given male leadership. She manifests a willing, submissive spirit in church affairs and business matters. Her input is given respectfully, without threatening or challenging. A woman who submits to her husband, a field council, executive committees, or any other authority manifests the beauty of subjection as the bride of Christ. There are cases, and complaints, of women missionaries who have headed up church planting projects, normally mentoring national men who do the preaching and official leading. Without known exception, such women would say to their critics, "Send a man to do this work, and I'll gladly step aside."

Women who face conflicts honestly and openly without defense mechanisms, anger, or self-justification remove the bitterness and stresses of pent-up emotions. Rebellious women and unreasonable men are selfish and thoughtless, without respect for God or their fellowmen.

3. Companions talk, walk, work, and worship together respectfully.

Good communication makes for clear, clean relationships. People who talk, listen, and share regularly build secure relations. Controlled godly conversations build up (Phil. 4:8) while mockery, criticism, cynicism, and gossip breed contempt, alienate people, and tear relationships apart. The tongue is powerful no matter what language is used. Verbal abuse destroys harmony on mission fields (James 3). A respectful tongue is of great value.

Respectful people can be objective, thinking through problems and challenges together. They evaluate opinions and reactions and bring out failures, strengths, and weaknesses. They can discuss possible solutions. Love and respect are the common meeting grounds for problem solving (1 Cor. 13; Eph. 5; 1 Peter 3; 1 John 4). Honesty and frankness tempered with tenderness and sensitivity keep the field open. Respect keeps criticisms "in house," not shared outside.

Companions walk together respectfully, accepting differences without rancor or pressuring each other to change. Missionary women, highly motivated and passionately opinionated, can quickly tear each other apart. They can also build each other up. Women who respect each other can laugh together (at each other and at themselves). They delight in simple, ordinary things. They share books, songs, and experiences. They cultivate courtesy, appreciation, creativity, courage, and fair play. Respect observes the cultural courtesies of table manners, proper greetings, seatings, dress, and decorum.

Respect leaves no room for jealousy, covetousness, or destructive competition. It develops trust and delight. It enjoys others; it recognizes their worth and expresses it. It does not intrude in the lives of others (even mates or children). A respectful woman allows space—physically, mentally, emotionally, and spiritually. At times she may distance herself, but she always comes back! Respect protects by recognizing stress loads, sensitivities, and schedules. Occasionally a woman runs interference for a husband or coworker but never when she should not. She helps without hindering. She shows concern with meals, laundry, babysitting, and so on, but there are limits. An overtired, overzealous, or disrespectful helper becomes resentful and resented.

Respect cultivates qualities of sympathy, perception, and courage to give strength to others (Isa. 50:4). It is not impatient; it looks at today through the lens of eternity. A respectful woman practices the art of fitting in by giving and taking. She accepts different opinions but holds firm to truth and standards of biblical principles.

Companions who respect each other work and worship together. They define goals and move toward them. One leads, others follow. They do not isolate or exclude members. They work as a body. The parts of the body may have differing functions, but all are included in the whole. Societies vary in their lines of inclusion and exclusion, especially between men and women. A woman who respects these lines in dress, speech, mannerisms, position, and participation will, in turn, be respected. A respectful woman keeps a low profile, allowing men to lead, taking over only when it is appropriate (usually with other women). Respectful people enjoy being support people, working together as husband and wife, with family, coworkers, and the national church.

Mutual worship, the highest form of fellowship, gives strength to human relationships. People who pray together stay together. Singing and praying with nationals in a new language brings new depths of joy and praise to personal worship. Out of woman's worship comes the sweetest songs of life (Miriam, Ex. 15; Hannah, 1 Sam. 2:1–10; Mary, Luke 1:46–56).

Respectful relationships start with "me." A woman who builds a vital, growing realationship with God, and secure, loving relationships in her home and with coworkers (both missionaries and nationals), builds security for those around her. She exhibits God's will for women, finding joy for herself, and blessing others.

A Woman's Work—Respected in and for Her Position

Women intricately bound together with men, like a web, make up the fabric of society. Throughout history women have been respected for significant roles they have played in the ministry of propagating the gospel of Christ. Their names are not so readily spoken as those of their male counterparts. Their work is not as well known or publicly dominant, but without women the threads of ministry would unravel and become nothing. Missionary work by women was the pioneer feminist movement in America. "By the year 1900 there were forty-one American women's agencies supporting twelve hundred single women miossionaries."[9] In more recent decades, women (single, married, and widowed) are fully integrated as missionaries among men, but they predominate in numbers.[10]

Mothers, wives, sisters, daughters, aunts, and grandmothers weave the world's love-strands of productivity. They strengthen the fibers that maintain men in their upright, proud positions. They are the encouragers, promoters, teachers, sympathizers, caregivers, and nurturers of society. And they stand in their own right as pillars of truth and service.

Few men have attained, or maintained, positions of eminence without a faithful wife, a diligent secretary, and a score of women teachers and helpers—to say nothing of their nurturing mothers and early mentors. Balancing a woman's role with her own needs and those of the people around her is as intricate as woman herself and can only be achieved with a proper sense of honor and respect.

God honors women for their work (Prov. 31, Dorcas, Lydia, Priscilla). He speaks to them (Eve, Hagar, Hannah, Mary, and Martha), assigns tasks (Samson's mother, Mary, Elizabeth, the woman of Samaria), and demonstrates His miraculous power through them (Sarah, Mary of Magdala). He ministers to women and allows them to minister to Him. Some of the greatest acts of love and mercy were demonstrated through women (Rahab, Ruth, Esther, the birth of Christ).

Historically and biblically, certain offices are reserved for men who were chosen by God. Nowhere in the Scriptures is there any record of a woman patriarch, priest, or apostle. There were no anointed queens (Athaliah usurped authority by her own designs). Deborah was appointed a judge in an office that was local and temporary. God gave certain men authority for the direct distribution and preservation of the purity of His Word. This principle is perpetuated in the church in pastors, bishops, and elders, who are always referred to as men, though there were women disciples. The position of women as teachers and leaders is not clearly defined. Principles and guidelines are determined in local assemblies through submission.

Work was a part of the plan in Eden. Women are identified, motivated, and fulfilled in their jobs. They naturally seek involvement and thrive on doing, helping, contributing, and meeting needs. They function best when busy and, without a task, shrivel into self-indulgence and wither into pity.

Home, a Woman's Primary Work of Honor, Expresses Who She Is

Here she cradles new lives and nurtures and trains them to live for God. At home she prepares herself and those around her to reach out to the world. Home is the point of reference out of which other works grow. A woman's home is always at the core of her life and ministry. A respectful home is essential to effective ministry.

Home takes on a new perspective for the missionary woman. No longer rooted with familiar possessions and people, she faces the challenge of creating and recreating home in many different places. Buildings and locations change, but atmosphere and attitude can remain constant.

Home is the haven to which she and her family can retreat for relaxation to escape the strains of foreignness and to be refreshed and renewed for other ministries. Home building for missionary women combines familiar and foreign elements and involves much creating and adapting. A missionary woman needs to be resourceful and resilient. In the kitchen she might find pounds replaced by kilos and cups by scales; in the bathroom, odd facilities; and strangely shaped pillows on the bed. In the market, a cow is a cow and a carrot is a carrot, but their presentation and how or when to eat them may vary. A woman who is clever in culinary and decorating arts is respected. Comfort, convenience, appeal, and godliness can be created anywhere. With nest-building instincts a woman arranges and garnishes her home. She uses comfortable chairs, good lighting and work spaces, colorful curtains and cushions, flowered towels, a daisy border on a dull wall, pictures, and plants. The decor of a room can encourage, or it can become confusing clutter. A woman who respects spiritual growth and enrichment may place memory verses, mottoes, and prayer cards near the table or by the breakfast bowls, and in convenient places around the rooms. Books, magazines, videos, and music are quality-controlled. Kids' corners delight little ones. Rooms are arranged to promote both privacy and friendliness, with each family member considered.

A woman protects her home and those within. She and her husband are in charge and set standards that show respect for God and others. Angry, defiling words are discouraged. Children are included in conversations and activities but shielded from what they should not hear or observe. Respect is taught by being respectful.

A godly woman shares her home. Being a hostess (or a guest) in a foreign culture can be exciting, frustrating—and sometimes humbling. Missionary women learn to survive domestic crises and come out richer for the experience.

Receiving or not receiving guests is a challenge when living among people unfamiliar with a sense of privacy. A missionary home is often more than a residence. It may be an office, school, clinic, business center, meeting hall, bank, print shop, bookstore, and the place to come with any and every kind of problem or need. Answering the door (or phone) can be a major responsibility. A protective woman respects her husband

and her children when dealing with visitors and learns the fine art of differentiating between needs and nuisances. She runs interference graciously and kindly, respecting service, security, serenity, and sanity.

Missionaries who live in clusters and compounds and those placed beside a student village, school or church, encounter special problems. Some adopt an open-door policy to anybody, anytime, for any reason. Others find that filtering and screening makes for a more effective total ministry. A few have a closed-door policy where home becomes off-limits and almost unapproachable. Mutual respect and understanding are necessary on all sides.

Respect builds bridges into neighbors' lives. A helping hand, a listening ear, a cup of coffee or tea, a meal, a party for the children, cross-cultural exchanges, a holiday celebration, or just visiting over the backyard fence are women's best ways of getting to know people and leading them to Christ. Respectful neighbors can build relationships for eternity.

Missionary women may have long-term, live-in guests (families waiting to relocate, short-termers, stateside staff, tourists, children of other missionaries, and so on). Homes are often exchanged during furlough years. A missionary must respect the sensitivities, rights, preferences, and privacy of others. Like traffic laws, schedules and routines maintain stability and help people move freely without bumping into each other. They make self-employment, home-schooling, and dealing with household help possible. Missionaries unable to develop a disciplined schedule often live in a state of confusion and "lostness," which may cause loss of respect.

Women Are Important and Respected in the Mission Workforce.

Wife, mother, homemaker, educator, nurse, doctor, technician, secretary, bookkeeper, computer operator, translator, author, editor, typist, teacher, public speaker, counselor, hostess, cook, banker, builder, mechanic, service technician, communicator, aviation tracker, fund raiser, seamstress, politician, diplomat, expert in public relations and international affairs, economist—as women pioneer new fields and are active in the development of existing mission works, the scope of their job has become vast and varied. Baptist Mid-Missions now uses a set of twenty ministry descriptions to define the varied roles of its missionaries. One of the most common is MD-02, which designates a church planting associate. This category accommodates those persons who contrubute to the establishing of new churches in any role other than as church planting pastor (MD-01). Many women, whether married or single, adopt the ministry description of church planting associate as their honorable designation. Fully 67 percent of the active career missionaries in 1997 were identified as MD-01 or MD-02 as their primary or secondary role.

Medical Ministries

Highly respected women doctors, nurses, technicians, and mid-wives open doors for missions in developing countries. In earlier years, a nursing diploma was required for single women, and married women were strongly urged to get some medical training.

Missionary women deliver babies, dress ugly sores, diagnose parasites, treat malaria, suture wounds, and sit with the sick and dying, telling them and their families about the Great Physician. They reach Muslims and others closed to the gospel. They order medicine and equipment, train and supervise workers, and go into villages by truck, foot, plane, and riverboat. Working with limited equipment and supplies, they battle disease while offering spiritual truths. Techniques and medicines change, but God's message of love and saving grace remains the same.

Education

Every missionary is a teacher of God's Word, either one-on-one or in classes. Discipleship and Bible studies nurture new converts and train and encourage older Christians, strengthening them in the Word. Women teach in homes, hospitals, schools, and churches.

Women reach women around the world. They swap ideas and talk about children, homes, food, clothes, crafts, prices, pickles, and problems in any language. They cry and laugh, criticize and compliment, complain and rejoice, and grow to love and respect each other in the Lord. Missionary women create interesting activities to draw other women to the Word of God. Differences in standards and values present challenges but are to be respected.

Literacy and post-literacy programs are a major ministry in developing countries. Missionary women who respect illiterate women gain treasured friendships and rich fellowship while contributing one of the most priceless treasures on earth—an open door to the written word and the liberty to read and discern independently.

Jesus loves children and youth. So do missionaries. Children are often the first to respond to the gospel. Teen time and Thursday clubs brought in the children of France. Children's classes in concentration camps opened the door in Germany. Gap meetings in the open areas between settlements produced good contacts in the Windward Islands. A post-war orphanage reached children in China. Happy Time Hour was a part of the opening work in New Zealand. Through the children of the world, women have laid firm foundations that make solid churches. A missionary woman involved in village children's classes was asked, "Are you involved in church planting?" The reply was quick and positive, "Yes. I'm making pillars." Thousands of women involved in pillar making are pillars themselves.

Women work in Bible camps, clubs, and classes all over the world. They teach and direct Christian schools. They train teachers and staff. Bible Seekers, Bible Teens, Triple C clubs, JEA, and many other youth program are written and directed by women. Faithful women have led thousands of young people into solid Bible study and Scripture memorization and guided them to Bible school and positions as church leaders. MKs (missionary kids) are an integral part of every missionary's life. Women are responsible for most of the schooling and extracurricular activities of missionary children and youth in foreign countries. They homeschool and teach in mission schools.

Bible schools, institutes, and seminaries offer many opportunities for women in teaching, researching, writing materials, ordering books and supplies, preparing notes, grading papers, and administration. Many mission Bible schools have women's divisions. Women are active in preparatory Bible schools. Some are involved in specialized or advanced training.

Women are respected for technical training in medicine, education, computers, accounting, mechanics, publishing and printing, communications, and other areas. Music is a highly respected ministry for many women. ESL (English as a second language) is a new, fast-developing field in which missionary women are taking an active leadership role.

Literature and Language

Bible translation and literacy are the first steps of church planting. Missionaries in the early 1900s laid solid foundations on which missions continue to build. Women translated, typed, edited, and corrected many Bible manuscripts. They developed literacy programs, wrote concordances, dictionaries, and other helps. Women play a major role in Bible translation. They work on foreign fields and with U.S.-based groups like Bibles International. Post-literacy programs, providing materials for new readers, is a rapidly developing area that interests many women.

Women write, edit, and publish tracts, brochures, books, and teaching materials, especially for people of small language groups who are dependent on missionaries and national leaders for Sunday school materials, hymnals, study books, and Bibles. In this publishing ministry, tasks including writing, correcting, editing, training editors, preparing copy, printing, and marketing consume hours of women missionaries' time.

Women servants of God are honored and respected. Honor is built on humility (Prov. 15:33; 18:12; 29:23). There is honor for a royal servant, concerned with the King's business, in carrying God's glory in woman's hands. She is content with this and seeks nothing more for herself (Ps. 115:1; John 17:22).

Respect in job placement and leadership roles is the practical outworking of the principles of submission and order. Segments of society (family, church, community, mission, field council, school, and so on) function on mutual understanding and respect.

In ministry, job description starts with vision. God speaks to hearts, stirring an interest, desire, and motivation to move in a certain direction. This call is explored, tested, and pursued through prayerful consideration and counsel. "A man's heart deviseth his way: but the LORD directeth his steps" (Prov. 16:9) God opens the way for fulfillment. Respecting this principle is basic.

No man is an island. We work in and as a body. Job placement in the body of Christ is never an individual choice. It is part of an eternal world plan in which God gives each member specific tasks at specific times. Training, gifts, abilities, and desires are only a part of the picture. A woman's job choice will be guided and influenced by numerous people and varying circumstances. Pastors and church leaders, mission administrators, field council officers, station heads, and the people around us all have a part in determining what we do. God will give an effective ministry to the woman who respectfully submits to this total plan. Women who rebel and are disrespectful of leadership and coworkers destroy their own work and harm the body. Leaders who do not respect other workers (especially women) lose respect and effectiveness.

Respect has a servant's heart. It is not self-seeking or promotion oriented. It works conscientiously, not in a spirit of competition or career climbing, but as unto the Lord (Col. 3:16). It makes contracts with God and keeps them. It is neither threatened by others nor threatening. It is not abusive, unfair, or discriminating (of gender, race, or rank). Respect does not take for granted but expresses appreciation. The successes of others do not frustrate it, and menial tasks are accepted with joy. It adjusts to changes willingly. It avoids tunnel vision—"my ministry"— and keeps focused on eternity. Some ministries give instant satisfactions and visible fruits. Others are long-term. Only eternity will reveal their true value. A servant is only required to do her job faithfully.

A woman who respects her contracts—with God, her husband, church, mission, and others—rests assured of the consequences. When God is in control, a woman respects herself, her job, her superiors, her family, and her coworkers. A respectful woman is respected and her work will remain. "Except the Lord build the house, they labor in vain that build it" (Ps. 127:1).

Study Questions

1. Explain why mutual respect among missionaries undergirds all cooperative ministry efforts.
2. How does a woman prepare her heart to give and receive respect in her personal spiritual formation?
3. Describe the nature of biblical submission to authority in relation to the missionary roles of men and women, and of women in a field council of peers.
4. Summarize and prioritize mission field ministries where women have contributed significantly to the advance of the work.
5. Are there any major ministry roles to which women should not aspire? If so, which, and why not?

Chapter Notes

1. Here is a list of suggested mission biographies: R. Pierce Beaver, *American Protestant Women in World Mission* (Grand Rapids: Eerdmans, 1980); Elisabeth Elliot, *Shadow of the Almighty: The Life and Testament of Jim Elliot* (San Francisco: Harper, 1989); idem, *Through Gates of Splendor* (Wheaton, Ill.: Tyndale, 1986); idem, *The Savage My Kinsman* (Ann Arbor, Mich.: Vine, 1981); Ruth Hege, *We Two Alone* (Cleveland, Ohio: Baptist Mid-Missions, 1997); Isobel Kuhn, *By Searching* (Chicago: Moody, 1979); idem, *Green Leaf in Drought* (Littleton, Colo.: OMF Books, 1986); idem, *In the Arena* (Littleton, Colo.: OMF Books, 1988); idem, *Nests Above the Abyss* (Littleton, Colo.: OMF Books, 1983); idem, *Stones of Fire* (Littleton, Colo.: OMF Books, 1984); Jeannie Lockerbie, *By Ones and By Twos* (Pasadena, Calif.: William Carey Library, 1983); and Ruth Tucker, *Guardians of the Great Commission* (Grand Rapids: Zondervan, 1988).

2. Margaret Laird, *They Called Me Mama* (Cleveland, Ohio: Baptist Mid-Missions, 1997).

3. Polly Strong, *Burning Wicks: The Story of Baptist Mid-Missions* (Cleveland: Baptist Mid-Missions, 1984), 62.

4. Ibid., 158.

5. Ibid., 113.

6. Ibid., 130.

7. Ibid., 385.

8. Ibid., 69.

9. David J. Bosch, *Transforming Mission: Paradigm Shifts in the Theology of Mission* (Maryknoll, New York: Orbis Books, 1991), 328.

10. For instance, a statistical study of the nearly nine hundred active career missionaries of Baptist Mid-Missions in 1997 showed that fully 54.6 percent of these were women (married women 44.6 percent, unmarried 8.5 percent, and widows 1.5 percent). If the additional retirees were factored in, the ratio would surge upward several percentage points.

17

CLINTON W. KAUFIELD

A BIBLICAL FRAMEWORK FOR A MULTICULTURAL MINISTRY

How to Assimilate Different Cultures Within a Single Local Church

Within the last half century, God in His infinite wisdom has brought representatives of most of the worlds races, languages, and cultures to our doorstep. The United States has become a land of diverse cultures. Fifty years ago the majority of churches in the United States were monocultural and conducted their ministries without encountering masses of "different" people within their local spheres of ministry. There have always been pockets of peoples of different cultures, but in the past they could be ignored. They had their own churches.

That situation is no longer true, especially in urban areas of America, where four-fifths of America's people live. In any given urban community one might encounter twenty to thirty cultural and racial groups. What an opportunity for evangelism! But therein lies the problem. Many Bible believers do not perform multicultural and/or multiracial ministry very well. Most of our churches suffer from a homogeneity that, at best, ignores other cultures and races and, at worst, practices subtle racism.

The early church was able quickly to get a handle on multicultural issues and to manage them in a biblical manner, even though it was encumbered with more cultural baggage than we have today—namely the cultural barriers between those of Jewish lineage and all other ethnic groups.

John 4	Jesus confronts His disciples with His Samaritan ministry.
Acts 1:8	The commission is given to evangelize the whole world, Jew and Gentile alike.
Acts 2	Jews of many cultural groups are saved at Pentecost.
Acts 6	Deacons are chosen to handle a cultural problem, selecting minority group leaders.
Acts 8	The gospel is preached throughout Samaria.
Acts 10	The gospel reaches the Gentiles.
Acts 13	The first missionaries are appointed for a basically Gentile ministry.
Acts 15	The early church is released from the ceremonial trappings of Judaism and oriented to cultural pluralism, with respect for minority groups.
Galatians 1	Paul defends the gospel from entanglement with Jewish ceremonialism.
Romans 9ff.	Paul, apostle to the Gentiles, outlines God's future plans for Israel.
Revelation 5	People are redeemed "out of every kindred, and tongue, and people, and nation" (v. 9).

The early church so ably assimilated many cultures that Clement, in summing up the lives of the early believers, could say,

> For the Christians are distinguished from other men neither by country, nor language, nor the customs which they observe: For they neither inhabit cities of their own, nor employ a peculiar form of speech, nor lead a life which is marked out by any singularity. . . . But, inhabiting Greek as well as barbarian cities, according as the lot of each of them has determined, and following the customs of the natives in respect to clothing, food, and the rest of their ordinary conduct, they display to us their wonderful and confessedly striking method of life.[1]

Breckenridge elaborates:

> The Day of Pentecost marked a living spiritual experience with all cultures; no identities were lost, no traditions were disvalued. Instead, the gospel simply permeated each cultural situation as encountered. The early church did not attempt any artificial multiculturalism. Instead, the development of house churches preserved as well as affirmed cultural diversity. As the church grew, larger congregations, such as Antioch, assumed a naturally multicultural character. "Though they preserved the ethnic and cultural character of their individual congregations, the Antiochene church demonstrated their unity by working together in a larger body that was multi-ethnic."[2]

Paradigm shifts are difficult and traumatic. Yet they are absolutely necessary within a monocultural church if it is to reach other cultural and racial groups for Christ. What paradigm changes are necessary within an urban church that will allow it to (1) desire to reach out to other cultural groups within its ministry community, (2) make the gospel and the church's ministry relevant and appealing to other cultures, and (3) actually assimilate members of diverse cultural groups within the local church that will enable the members to become truly one body in Christ?

In order to accomplish this task a local church must be, become, and do a number of important things. It must make some vital, even radical changes in its thinking, in its structure of ministry, and in its perception of what constitutes success in ministry.

Spiritually Mature (Eph. 4:1–3)

A church willing to change in this way must be a spiritually mature body of believers with its own house in order, "endeavoring to keep the unity of the Spirit in the bond of peace" (Eph. 4:3). Many churches are feuding, fussing, hotbeds of contention where Christians cannot get along with Christians, let alone abide someone of another culture or race. Many churches have long forgotten what the Christian endeavor is all about. Many are so at ease in Zion that any real effort outside the church walls is considered only worthy of the foreign missionary. There are hurting people all around the average church who need to be ministered to, albeit at great effort and cost, but church members are often content to be ministered to, "to be carried to the skies on flowery beds of ease." Such churches often feel they should not even try to reach out cross-culturally or cross-racially, because they will utterly fail. Better to build a wall around the church and make it "our club" than to disgrace the ministry by failure.

Churches today must heed the advice of Francis Schaeffer, who challenges,

> This is not a day for a sleepy church. The games of yesterday are past. We are in a struggle that the church has never been in before. What then must we do?
>
> 1. Hot Christianity
> 2. Compassionate Christianity
> 3. Open your home for community
> 4. Structure your church for community[3]

Transformed Culture (Eph. 4:13)

Churches must realize that believers, local church members and members of the target group alike, when they become believers move out of their own respective cultures into a transformed culture—a community of those who are conformed to the image of Christ. Ephesians 4:13 reads, "Till we all come in the unity of the faith, and of the knowledge of the Son of God . . . unto the measure of the stature of the fulness of Christ."

We should never be interested in whether or not a target cultural group will become like us. Our goal is to point them to the Scriptures so that new believers from a different background will become like Christ. We ourselves are leaving the likeness of "us" as well, to become conformed to the image of Christ. As we lead a person of another culture to Christ, we and they will follow differing cultural paths toward the likeness of Christ. Others may never love our music, or our form of worship, or our lifestyle. We must, within the bounds of Scripture, allow peoples of other cultural groups to express their faith in a way that may be entirely different from ours. For example, my daughter is lifted to the heavens by the music of Andrae Crouch. I have difficulty bringing myself to worship with her music as a background and prefer the music of Helen Barth and George Beverly Shea. I respect, however, how she chooses to express her faith.

Churches encounter problems if they attempt to reach those of other cultures and races on the assumption that their expression of faith and worship is the only biblical way that faith can be expressed and that any deviation from that holy norm is sinful. This attitude will deal a death blow to any—even well-conceived—ventures into other cultural and racial groups. We must discern between forms of cultural expression that are definitely unbiblical and those that are merely different. Often our own cultural mindset is so established that we find difficulty in distinguishing the two. It is so easy to mistake a personal preference for gospel truth.

Servant/Giving Attitude (Rev. 3:14–22)

Churches must develop a servant/giving attitude rather than a master/receiving attitude (Rev. 3:14–22). The church at Laodicea was "rich, and increased with goods"—so much so that it could not see that it was really "poor, and blind, and naked."

In a day when the church in the rest of the world is facing persecution, deprivation, and death on a scale never before experienced, believers in America enjoy unprecedented wealth, freedom, and leisure. Seldom do we have to put our faith on the line. It is difficult for us to imagine working and suffering for the cause of Christ. We are used to being in a receiving mode, not a giving, serving mode. We are far more interested in getting wealthy, nice people into our churches than we are in ministering to homeless people, inner-city teens, and AIDS patients or addressing the devastating problems of people forced to live in urban ghettos. We have forgotten that the measure of a church's ministry is not the size and cost of its buildings but the degree to which it is willing to impoverish itself to reach people for Christ and to minister to their needs.

We could liken the church in America to a country club. What are the characteristics of a country club?

- It practices an exclusive membership and ministers to its "own kind of people."
- It maintains a certain pride of heritage: "We are not like those others."
- All the services are for the exclusive use of the membership, and they reflect only the culture of the membership.
- The focus is on keeping the rules and not on compassion. "This is how we dress, where we work, and so on."
- Members are selected on the basis of what they can do for the club.

- The club is an oasis for the rich few in a neighborhood of poverty and decay.
- The bottom line is, "This is the way we have always done it."
- Because it is set in its ways, the membership find it hard to admit members who are "not like us," even when they desire to do so.

The average church has its eye on the bottom line and not on the fields white unto harvest. It has a fortress mentality and excuses itself from serving "those sinners out there." During Jesus' lifetime the Pharisees focused on law and tradition—they questioned whether it was lawful to pick corn on the Sabbath, whether it was lawful to heal on the Sabbath, whether it was right to eat with publicans and sinners. Jesus kept His focus on compassion and ministry.

The gospel can reach people at (1) the point of familiarity and at (2) the point of need. At present, almost all church evangelism in America approaches people at the point of familiarity. Most men and women, boys and girls, have accepted Christ because they remember their parents' prayers and lifestyles and have some familiarity with church services. The church finds it much harder to evangelize people at the point of need. Yes, some accept Christ when faced with a crisis or sickness. But how do we confront another culture at the point of need? How do we reach Muslims for Christ? What are their needs? Buddhists? Homosexual AIDS patients? Drug addicts? Very little evangelism takes place at this level. Jesus approached people at both points but more often at the point of need. Witness the Samaritan woman, Bartemaeus, the Syrophoenecian woman. The gospel meets people at the point of their need, but the church prefers to choose the points. The rich man and Lazarus both had needs. Which would the modern growth-hungry church go after? Probably the rich man. He had more to offer.

Very little of a cross-cultural or cross-racial nature will be accomplished, nor will the gospel go forward, until the church changes from a mentality of getting strong and rich, to a mentality of giving until it hurts.

Count the Cost (John 12:24–25)

To "fall into the ground and die" is not the normal cultural expression of the modern American church. People must consider what they are willing to sacrifice to preach the gospel to a target group. It is guaranteed to be an enriching experience. There is nothing more exciting than exposing oneself to the culture and lifestyle of another group, especially as that culture expresses itself in worship and ministry. But it is also a costly experience, and it may mean a lifestyle change or a habitat change.

A local church in my area recently voted to purchase a building and move its congregation into one of the city's most crime- and poverty-ridden neighborhoods in order to minister to that community. Think of the cost of such a venture—families exposing their children to a foul neighborhood for the gospel's sake, an entire congregation running the risk of being vandalized and burned out. Some of the families are actually buying homes in the area in order to be closer to their point of ministry. This is the kind of price the average modern suburban church is not willing to pay. We need to concentrate on giving ourselves away for Jesus' sake.

There will always be a price to pay in pursuing a cross-cultural ministry. It may be subtle—having to give up a familiar style of worship, or it might be more direct—being subjected to expressions of hate and violence from those who do not want your ministry. Many areas of our cities are hostile. It is possible to face culture shock, even in America. The church must make a commitment to reach people where they are, even if it means ministering and living in unpleasant places. The following poem by George MacDonald perhaps best expresses the need:

What Christ Said

I said, "Let me walk in the fields."
He said, "No, walk in the town."
I said, "There are no flowers there."
He said, "No flowers, but a crown."
I said, "But the skies are black.
There is nothing but noise and din."
And He wept as He sent me back,
"There is more," He said, "there is sin."
I said, "But the air is thick,
And fogs are veiling the sun."
He answered, "Yet souls are sick
And souls in the dark undone."
I said, "I will miss the light,
And friends will miss me, they say."
He answered, "Choose to-night,
If I am to miss you, or they."
I pleaded for time to be given.
He said "Is it hard to decide?

It will not seem hard in heaven
To have followed the steps of your guide."
I cast one look at the fields,
Then set my face to the town.
He said, "My child, do you yield?
Will you leave the flowers for the crown?"
Then into his hand went mine,
And into my heart came he.
And I walked in a light divine
The path I had feared to see.[4]

David Claerbaut elaborates on the problems of the city, and the conditions that exacerbate the basic sin problem.[5]

- urban renewal
- property over life
- fire
- epidemics
- bad school systems
- sanitation and health care
- welfare
- unemployment
- police brutality
- justice system inequities
- drugs

Face the Social Issues

The parable of the good Samaritan is a marvel of social interaction and compassion. Among other things, it touches on the areas of personal tragedy, crime, race, and segregation. It also presents the believer with a clear choice. Christ was clear in pointing out that one should count the cost before pursuing a given path. It is important that an individual or a church consider carefully the social, cultural, and racial implications and limitations of a cross-racial/cultural ministry, even within its own community. There will be misunderstandings, attempts to take advantage, some outright hatred, criticism from biblical separatist groups who will perceive your efforts as breaking biblical edicts, criticism from members of your church. There will be a thousand questions from the group you wish to reach. You will make honest mistakes that offend the cultural norms of the target group. And, of course, it will cost time and money. Finally, there will, of necessity, be changes in worship and ministry. Breckenridge elaborates,

> From a multicultural perspective, a beginning for local churches may be in simply adopting a different attitude or posture toward those who come from different cultures. Churches do not have to do away with the *Book of Concord* or the *Westminster Confession of Faith,* nor do they have to radically alter worship services so that they lose the distinctiveness of their traditional moorings. What they do have to do, however, is to increase their sensitivity to other groups in their midst. The local church "language," teaching methods, and even worship must reflect a charity and genuine openness to those who are strangers to "our" history.[6]

Great care must be taken lest we offend others before we have the chance to present them with the gospel. Mayers introduces us to a game—"Instant Rejection."

> The game "Instant Rejection" is a game I developed to let each of us see to what degree we are acceptors or rejecters of others. The rules are quite simple. You select a person as the object of your rejection. Then you proceed to work with all the tools at your disposal to reject that person and communicate the message of rejection to him. The following methods may be used:
>
> You cut him off when he is talking to you.
> You laugh after statements he addresses to you.
> You question his facts.
> You show him lack of trust and confidence.
> You attempt to overprotect him.
> You talk down to him.
> You overreact to something he says or does.
> You avoid his eyes and forget his name.[7]

In order to avoid obvious pitfalls, there are a number of things a church must do.

A Church Must Combat Attitudes of Prejudice and Racism and Promote Justice (Acts 6)

Almost unwittingly, the early church practiced a form of favoritism between Grecian and Judean Jews. It recognized the problem and acted quickly to correct it. Racism in churches is sometimes subtle, sometimes open. Before a church considers a cross-cultural ministry, there must be agreement from the leadership, instruction from the pulpit, and much, much prayer.

A Church Must Be Willing to Empower Members of the Target Group Who Join the Church (Acts 13, 15)

According to Acts 13, the leaders of the Antiochian church were gathered from many cultures, and together they commissioned Paul and Barnabas for missionary service. It is not enough for a church to plan how it will take in members from another cultural group. It must also decide how it will disciple key members and finally empower them by giving them leadership positions in the church. No great dent will be made in reaching the cultural group until such empowering is accomplished.

A Church Must Offer Programs As Varied as the Needs of the Community It Serves

One church in Ohio is growing rapidly. It has over forty different support groups that meet at various times during the week. Some of these groups include prisoners on work release, Weight Watchers, a Hispanic focus group, a learning-disabled children's group, a learning-disabled adults group, a group that ministers to shut-ins, a teen groups, a single mothers' group, plus many others. On Sunday the entire congregation comes together for worship and Bible study.

James and Lillian Breckenridge report, "What we must have is a genuine confrontation with modern culture in which we become determined to reach it on all levels."[8] They quote the words of Gordon Aeschilman, "The urban challenge is also a call back to the lifestyle of *incarnation.*"[9] The challenge facing the local church teacher is often more complex than that faced by missionaries in more remote parts of the world. Rather than dealing with distinct races and cultures, contemporary church educators must communicate with many races and many cultures, all blended in a homogenous social fabric that defies simple analysis or reduction. Urban evangelist John E. Kyle notes,

> There are sixty nations represented in my neighborhood
> in Chicago, sixty nations in the public school where my
> kids went, and the school teaches in eleven languages.
> Thirty-five percent of the neighborhood is black, but
> many black cultures are represented . . . [and] they are
> all different. Twenty-eight percent are Asians, but they
> are all different. There are north, south, east Asians—
> some of them are refugees and poor, but many are
> wealthy. . . .[10]

This complexity demands that our teaching be more than (informing) teaching, and our preaching more than (exhorting) preaching. We must know not only our message but also the lifestyle of those we seek to influence.

A Church Must Never Ignore Its Diversity but Must Acknowledge and Welcome It

We are all creatures of our culture. We act within our culture in ways that are by now automatic. We are hardly aware of this until we face someone from a differing culture. The following are all elements of culture:

- language differences
- symbols
- behavioral nuances
- philosophical outlooks
- taboos
- expressions (opposite of taboos)
- view of time
- view of family
- view of government
- view of community[11]

It is easy for a church to exacerbate the problems of differing cultures without even realizing it. The following example points out the problem:

> Ghanian student Michael Ntow recounts how joyfully
> his people first received the gospel. Having accepted
> Christianity they proceeded to worship this new God in

the ways common to their culture. They loved drums and kept playing them . . . as always, only now they were playing for Christ. Then came the day when a large boat anchored in the harbor and the missionaries unloaded a pipe organ. The Ghanians hated the organ—but they were told that this is what they must play! At this point Christianity became integrated with a type of worship which was alien to their way of life. They still accepted Christianity, but had to adapt to a new cultural artifact.[12]

Churches wishing to reach across cultural barriers might hold a cultural fair or a "Celebration of Culture" and invite members of all community cultural groups to have booths where their music, food, dress, and art are displayed. Such mixing is a healthy way to open the church to the cultures surrounding it.

One of the goals of a multicultural perspective is to understand individuals from cultures different from our own. By doing so, our own lives are enriched as we learn about the values and customs of various groups. Learning about other cultures also enables us to understand and relate more accurately with people who do not share our own socioeconomic and cultural backgrounds. A society as a whole is enriched as it learns to view events and situations from a different perspective.[13]

A Church Must Face Issues Such as Poverty, Homelessness, AIDS, and Dysfunctional Families

We recognize that sin is the real problem, but these concerns exacerbate the problem.

Tony Evans lists the following symptoms of a sick society:

* poverty
* racial and class conflict
* disease
* broken families
* hopeless young people
* abortion
* crime and drugs[14]

If a church wishes to follow Christ into a multicultural ministry, it will need to deal with all of these concerns. These may prove very costly for the church, but nevertheless they must be faced.

John Perkins discusses eight elements that constitute a healthy environment for personal growth. He has titled it "Creating an Environment of Hope."

An expert social worker tries to understand all of the factors that produce a healthy environment for personal development.

1. **Dignity:** We do not confer dignity upon other human beings. God has already given dignity to us when He created us. We can, however, crush in others their understanding of their dignity.

2. **Empowerment:** The urban poor . . . experience powerlessness in the face of the law. In most of their dealings with legal structures they more likely experience the cold, exacting judgment of the legal system in critical times of need.

3. **Education:** Education is not a luxury in modern American society—it is essential for survival. Many of our children are getting a poor education because of the problems of our inner-city public schools.

4. **Employment:** Lack of education, skill development, and opportunity are all qualities of poverty and are direct factors leading to unemployment. One who lives with these circumstances enters a cycle of poverty where poverty leads to unpreparedness, which leads to unemployment, which leads to poverty, and so forth. The other side of the employment dilemma is that a lot of young . . . men choose either to earn quick money through selling drugs or to live off their girlfriends' welfare checks, and ghetto culture has accepted that.

5. **Health:** The poor rarely have the knowledge or resources common to middle-class America for preventive care, such as a healthy diet and simple lifestyle measures that can lead to a healthier body. Cities are also unhealthy places to live.

6. **Security:** When exposés of police brutality erupt on the front pages of our papers, they demonstrate

why the urban poor do not have a good feeling about the police.

7. **Recreation:** We require rest. We need times of rejuvenation and recreation of our spirits. And yet the ghetto environment is not restful. It is rarely quiet and peaceful. The atmosphere is tense, waiting for a conflict of some kind to break out. Safety is always an issue for children playing or adults relaxing outside. Most inner cities are crowded with tall buildings, leaving little or no open space for children to play in or for adults to relax in.

8. **Beauty:** Beauty is increasingly becoming something that only the wealthy have easy access to. Museums, botanical gardens, beautiful buildings, and parks are almost never found in the inner city and frequently cost money to enter, while inner-city neighborhoods are becoming more and more run-down.[15]

Make a Commitment to Bonding (John 15:12–15)

Our text here speaks about love and the test of great love—the willingness to lay down one's life for the one loved. Christ asks no less of us than this kind of love as we seek to reach precious people of other cultures for whom He died. The task is urgent.

It is difficult to reach people for Christ if you hold them at arm's length. People want to see our love for them, our acceptance of them, before they are willing to be introduced to our Christ. I often think of the song, "He looked beyond my faults and saw my needs." We must be willing to look beyond the faults of others, accept where and who they are, hold them close, invite them into our homes, and fellowship with them at all levels. If you are unwilling to get your feet wet in another culture, do not make the attempt.

Exegete a Community to Find Windows of Opportunity for Ministry (John 4)

The disciples would never have considered Samaria as a viable mission field if Jesus had not graphically pointed it out to them. The average church goes merrily on its monocultural way without even considering the "fields white unto harvest" across the street. When a church deliberately takes on the task of identifying community ministry opportunities, it will be amazed at what it finds. There are many hurting people in the city blocks around the average church. I challenge young men who are anxious to get the title *Reverend* in front of their name: Take four square blocks and get acquainted with every person within that area, from the newborn babies to the grandmother rocking on the back porch. Present each person within that four-square-block area with the plan of salvation and for one year keep in touch with those who accept Christ. Then come back and talk about ordination.

As a church, it's important for you to look at various mission fields.

- a given number of blocks around the church
- the immediate neighborhood of each church member who lives in a community away from the church building
- special areas for ministry throughout the city, such as rescue missions, prisons, retirement and nursing homes, hospitals, youth centers, and housing projects
- people with special needs, such as AIDS patients, cancer patients, the elderly, and shut-ins
- opportunities away from the church but within the confines of this country
- the world beyond, with its needs for all types of missionary activity and personnel

Intensively study your community and the group you want to reach for Christ. In order to understand the present situation of the target group, you must understand something of its history. The church may have some traditions that the target group considers ungodly. Though these traditions may not be biblically wrong, the host group may have to give them up for a time to accommodate the sensitivities of the target group. For example, since the Muslim community considers the drinking of coffee sinful, I would abstain from drinking coffee if I were seriously interested in reaching that group for Christ. You must identify and biblically define cultural elements of the target culture and those of your own culture so that both your own people and the people of the culture you are trying to reach are comfortable with the results (Acts 6; 15).

Above all, you must settle the question of intermarriage in your own mind before any attempt is made at reaching another racial group. Feelings and prejudices run high here, most without the slightest biblical justification, or, far worse, because of poor biblical exegesis.

Adopting Some of the Cultural Nuances (1 Cor. 9:19-23)

Be willing to adopt *some* of the nuances of the target culture and appreciate the expression of the rest. In order to become "all things to all men that I might by all means save some," the local church must leave its comfort zone and learn to appreciate the cultural expressions of others, whether it be in regard to food, music, worship styles, or choice of musical instruments. This must go far beyond mere toleration. It must involve appreciation. It must include worshiping within the cultural norms of others.

Instead of feeling threatened by outsiders, Christians should begin to view other cultures as vehicles through which the gospel may be expressed. Consider the attitude of the apostles in the conflict of Acts 15. Their solution was a composite of cultural dietary restrictions to avoid offending the Jews, and the maintenance of theological principles of sexual purity. Multicultural sensitivity was also displayed in the makeup of the church leadership. Thom Hopler notes that the deacons chosen to diffuse the situation were from various cultures, coming as they did from Hellenistic backgrounds. They even included a non-Jew. By sharing the church power structure with a minority, the apostles solved the problem of intercultural relations.[16]

Concentrate on Biblical Reconciliation (2 Cor. 5:17-21; Eph. 2:11-16)

A twofold reconciliation is necessary: reconciliation between God and man through salvation, and reconciliation between man and man through Christian nurture within the local church.

Develop a Discipling Approach to Evangelism (Matt. 28:18-20)

If one-on-one discipleship is needed to nurture people within the church, it is doubly necessary for a ministry that crosses cultural and racial barriers. The intimacy of one-on-one discipleship is vitally needed in such work. New converts from other cultural or racial groups need to sense your acceptance of them as people. They need your care and your love in spite of problems they may have.

Dr. Y. C. Yen's credo for rural reconstruction can be applied to cross-cultural ministry as well:

> Go to the people
> Live among them
> Learn from them
> Plan with them
> Work with them
> Start with what they know
> Build on what they have
> Teach by showing, learn by doing
> Not a showcase, but a pattern
> Not odds and ends, but a system
> Not piecemeal, but an integrated approach
> Not to conform, but to transform
> Not relief but release.[17]

Roger Greenway, in a discussion on how to choose the right evangelistic method, offers the following series of questions for the church wishing to cross cultural barriers:

> *How strong is the extended family of the culture?* If it is very strong, the need for cell groups may diminish, and the family may be our primary vehicle for the spread of the gospel. If not, cell groups and other avenues of evangelism will be more important.

> *What is the people's economic condition?* Among the poor or extremely poor, evangelism may need to be supplemented by programs to help them out of their poverty. If they are wealthy, evaluate how well they will fit into an existing church that is middle-class or poor.

> *Are there linguistic barriers to the spread of the gospel among the people?* If the selected group is one ethnic community it can be assumed that its members all speak the same language. But if they are a social group, they might speak several languages. Even in a single ethnic group there may be an ethnic language and a national language. What then will be the language of worship and instruction?

Are there religious impediments to accepting the gospel? The chosen group may consist of adherents of another faith. They may have been misinformed about Christian teachings. How can this information be corrected? They may be hostile to Christianity. How can the hostility be overcome and the truth communicated? Accurate information regarding non-Christian beliefs, attitudes, and practices is needed to present the gospel gently and persuasively.[18]

Conclusion

We have listed many areas for determining how effective a local church's ministry will be in reaching across cultural barriers and discipling people. Let us constantly pray that we can accomplish, with great effort, what the early church accomplished within one generation. Since red, yellow, black, brown, and white will comprise the rainbow hues of heaven, let us seek the same within our local churches here on earth.

Study Questions

1. What was the early church able to do that the church today has difficulty in doing?
2. In what ways can we compare the mentality of a modern church with a country club?
3. What is the difference between the point of familiarity and the point of need in unsaved people?
4. What are some of the implications of the poem, "What Christ Said"?
5. What are some of the social issues that will be faced in a cross-cultural/racial ministry?
6. According to John Perkins, what are some of the elements of a healthy environment for personal development?
7. How can a church exegete its community?

Chapter Notes

1. Clement, *The Ante-Nicene Fathers* (Grand Rapids: Eerdmans, reprint 1979), 1:11.
2. James and Lillian Breckenridge, *What Color Is Your God?* (Wheaton, Ill.: Scripture Press, 1994), 30–31, including a citation from Gregory Jao,

"Culture in the Flow of Biblical History: A Mandate for Ethnic Identity-Affirming Ministries" (unpublished paper, April 1992), 13.

3. Francis Schaeffer, *The Church at the End of the 20th Century* (Downers Grove, Ill.: InterVarsity, 1970), 103ff.

4. George MacDonald, "What Christ Said" in Thomas Curtis Clark, ed., *Christ in Poetry* (New York: Association Press, 1952), 232.

5. David Claerbaut, *Urban Ministry* (Grand Rapids: Zondervan, 1983), adapted from pp. 94–104.

6. Breckenridge, *What Color Is Your God?,* 37.

7. Marvin Mayers, *Christianity Confronts Culture* (Grand Rapids: Zondervan, 1987), 55–56.

8. Breckenridge, *What Color Is Your God?,* 17.

9. Ibid.

10. Ibid., 17–18.

11. David Claerbaut, *Urban Ministry,* adapted from pp. 163–65.

12. Breckenridge, *What Color Is Your God?* 42.

13. Cited by ibid., 89.

14. Tony Evans, *America's Only Hope* (Chicago: Moody, 1990), chap. 1.

15. John Perkins, *Beyond Charity* (Grand Rapids: Baker, 1993), 90ff.

16. Thom Hopler, *A World of Difference* (Downers Grove, Ill.: InterVarsity Press, 1981), 86, cited by Breckenridge, *What Color Is Your God?,* 73–74.

17. Y. C. Yen, "Credo for Rural Reconstruction," in IIRR eds., *International Institute of Rural Reconstruction: Background, Relevance, and Program* (Silang, Cavite, the Philippines: IIRR, 1983), 73 (current edition of 1962 original "Credo").

18. Timothy M. Monsma, "Research: Matching Goals and Methods to Advance the Gospel," in Roger Greenway, ed., *Discipling the City,* 2d ed. (Grand Rapids: Baker, 1992), 66, emphasis original.